CENSORED EDITION

MY RUDE AWAKENING

An Englishman's Journey - Book One

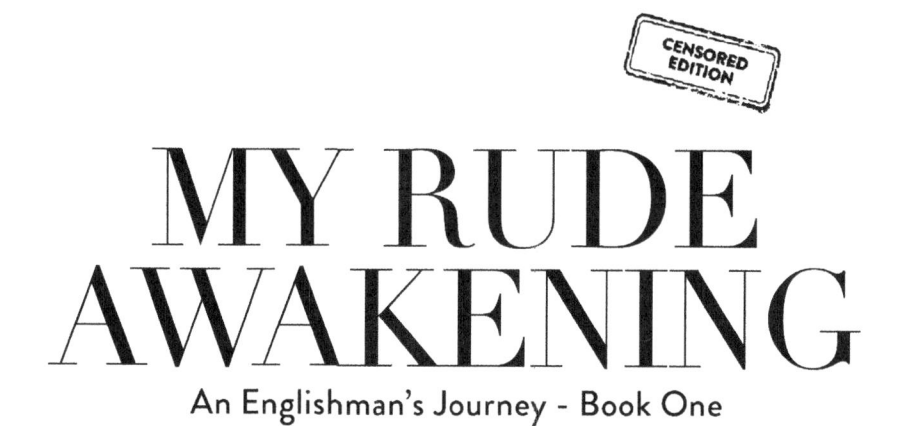

EDWARD CHARLES FEATHERSTONE

My Rude Awakening CENSORED: A Combat Pilot's Memoir of Passion, Peril, and Forbidden Desire (Book 1 of An Englishman's Journey)

Copyright © 2023 by Edward Charles Featherstone, H2Z Foundation Press
For more about this author, please visit https://myrudeawakening.com/

This is a work of creative nonfiction, a genre of writing that uses creative literary styles and techniques while maintaining factually accurate essence and narrative. While some names, characters, businesses, places, events, locales, and incidents have been changed or created, the author has strived to limit creative tinkering so as not to alter the canvas of the profound truth of the story.

All rights reserved. No part of this publication may be reproduced, distributed, or transmitted in any form or by any means, including photocopying, recording, or other electronic or mechanical methods, without the prior written permission of the publisher, except in the case of brief quotations embodied in critical reviews and certain other non-commercial uses permitted by copyright law. Please do not participate in or encourage piracy of copyrighted materials in violation of the author's rights.

No part of this book may be used for the training of artificial systems, including systems based on artificial intelligence (AI), without the copyright owner's prior permission. This prohibition shall be in force even on platforms and systems that claim to have such rights based on an implied contract for hosting the book.

For permission requests, visit https://anenglishmansjourney.com/

Editing by The Pro Book Editor
Interior Design by IAPS.rocks
Cover Design by Spiffing Publishing

Hardcover: 978-1-917111-06-5
Paperback: 978-1-917111-07-2
Ebook: 978-1-917111-08-9
Audible: 978-1-917111-09-6

1. First category—BIOGRAPHY & AUTOBIOGRAPHY / Personal Memoirs
2. Second category—BIOGRAPHY & AUTOBIOGRAPHY / Adventurers & Explorers

CLICK OR SCAN TO SONGS

I often hear people say how important music is to them, as if they are unique in this regard. But of course, it is fair to say that music plays an important role in most people's lives.

So, falling into the same trap, I will say, "Music is especially important to me."

I pointedly remember listening to specific songs at times in my life, and many of them are still my favourites today. There are others I like to avoid because of an incident or a period they'll remind me of, that I would sooner forget. And I am sure like most, when I hear one of "those" songs, the memories come flooding back. The songs referred to in these pages will certainly add depth of understanding to the emotions behind the words of my story, even if the songs are not your typical taste.

To facilitate this aspect, I have included an innovative CLICK OR SCAN TO SONGS feature that invites readers to immerse more fully in my life story by listening to songs as they come up.

In print versions, a 'song junctions' within the pages will offer the choice of QR codes for different streaming platforms so readers can listen to each song on their digital device.

In eBooks, these junctions will display clickable links for each of the three music platform options.

Our feedback has been mixed. Some of the early reviewers loved this feature as it gave them a break from their reading and allowed them to absorb the moments. Others though found it a hindrance and ignored it, not wanting their reading flow to be disrupted. So the jury is out. It would be wonderful if you connected with us on social media and gave us your views.

"My Rude Awakening" Complete Playlist

YouTube　　　　　　　Spotify　　　　　　　Apple

DEAR READER

What can only be described as very unusual circumstances is what led to me writing my autobiography in the style of the autofiction genre, using a pseudonym and some creative licence. The author has strived to limit creative tinkering so as not to alter the canvas of the profound truth of the story. Whilst this is a true account of the important aspects, the purpose of using this approach was for the following reasons.

Many names and some locations have been changed to obviate the need for military and other clearances and permissions. I have few qualms of my own identity being exposed, but doing so would expose all others. The mostly thinly veiled name changes protect those people involved. For those who want to be identified, they can easily reveal themselves and own their characters. For those who would prefer to distance themselves from the manuscript, they can as easily choose not to pierce the thin veil that protects them. The name I have chosen contains both my and my family's names.

I have conflated aspects of the Royal Air Force (RAF) and British Army, being careful not to disclose classified information, and I also altered some elements of the timeline. To give my memoir more of a novel-like style for readers' enjoyment, I elected to use the Creative Nonfiction genre. This genre, often used in writing memoirs, allowed me to use creative licence on some locations and song choices. So whilst I used old photographs for reference, do I really remember some of the detail from when I was in my twenties, that you will read in the pages of my manuscript? Of course not, is the short answer.

In my adulthood, I went from having an Air Force military career to building a start-up digital electronics business into a global technology corporation that became a publicly listed company. The beginning of my life story, however, was filled with shenanigans between playing polo and game-bird shooting, and I had many extraordinary little adventures along the way.

From an early age, I did many extreme things, or perhaps it was the level I took it to that made them extreme. Twenty minutes with my insurance broker confirmed this when I was only able to get life coverage with multiple exclusions that took into consideration all my activities and pastimes.

Whilst I would never shy away from doing almost anything no matter how dangerous, I was by no means reckless. Quite the opposite, in fact. I took a measured approach to everything I did, and after calculating the risk, I then set forth…fearlessly. There were numerous near misses, but unquestionably, I cheated death on at least two occasions. The first occurs in this book, the second instance is in the sequel. Both had me hospitalised in critical care and could have—should have—ended my life. One of those experiences left me on life support for a while and forever changed me. I may have twice escaped death, but I did not evade the resultant post-traumatic stress disorder (PTSD).

PTSD, that formidable condition that lingers and lurks in the confines of your brain, the convolutions of your mind, sometimes expressing itself for no good reason. And then at other times, it shows itself in a way that confounds you. Very often you are not even aware of what is afflicting you. *I wasn't.* And at the cost of being English, I would never let anyone know there was anything wrong with me.

Then, years later, finding myself alone in a world of never-ending COVID confinement, I suffered a further psychological trauma—my third PTSD event. I was at a desperate all-time low. I hated the thought of therapy, thinking it exposing and showing weakness, but it was better than the only alternative I could see, the consequence of which could not be undone.

If you are lucky, you have someone you can turn to. I was one of the lucky ones.

A prior romantic relationship with a Doctor of Psychology, Sexual

Psychology and Urology, who had always kept contact with me, intuitively recognised my condition and came to my rescue. With the help of our history and her expertise, she quickly worked it out…and then began to 'work it out of me.' The perfect psychotherapist.

"There are tried-and-tested methods to treat your condition," she insisted. "We must speak about the traumas that have struck so deep they caused your psychological disorder, your PTSD, and if necessary, we can include medication." I was not receptive to taking any prescribed drugs, fearing I could become dependent on them. My doctor friend agreed. So with that, whilst in Covid lockdown, we began a series of online therapy sessions.

I found it difficult to open up about things I had worked so hard at hiding, so my doctor and past lover added another dimension. In my own time, she wanted me to write about the traumatic events that had caused my PTSD. There was a problem though. I am dyslexic, with no literary inclination, and I soon discovered that writing about my distresses to unburden myself was easier said than done. Emotions on top of my dyslexia threatened to swamp my therapeutic efforts. The doctor was not going to let me off that easily. "Who cares?" she said. "Get it out of you. Rid yourself of this burden, your closely guarded secrets. Then pen all the wonderful things that have happened in your life, your autobiography," she insisted. "And write about our relationship, our sex, and losing your virginity," she added mischievously. Only you and I need read it, so be brutally honest and be open."

Famous last words are what those turned out to be. One thing led to the next, as they say, and with a comprehensive knowledge of my subject matter, my life, coupled with my learnt attitude that if something is worth doing, it is worth doing properly, I began my endeavour.

Sitting quietly alone, I delved into my past, and knowing I was never going to publish it anyway, I had no problem writing from the heart. Before I knew it, these unusual circumstances and the solitude of never-ending Covid confinement turned out to be the perfect birthplace for my creative non-fiction memoir. And just as the doctor ordered, I balanced it by writing about the uplifting parts, not least of which was the sex. *God, I better hide these bits,* I thought, chuckling to myself.

For two years it tore me apart, often bringing me to tears as the jigsaw pieces that created the picture of my life were taken apart and then slowly put back together again. But this time, all the pieces I had so carefully hidden were retrieved and put in their rightful places to present the complete picture of my being. And as far as the therapy was concerned…well, it worked.

What started in mid-2020 was finished by late 2022, and with both COVID and my PTSD receding into the background, I could live again. I was more than happy to shelve my therapy, but only in the figurative sense because it was not yet a book.

Then as the New Year 2023 dawned, I thought I should change that, remove the sex, edit it, and leave it as a legacy for my children.

That was when I met my editor, Debra L. Hartmann. Once she had agreed to take me on, saying, "Your life story is extraordinary, and I see something in your writing style," I sent her my first manuscript.

"Now leave it to me," she said.

Six weeks later, she returned my memoir, but instead of an edited, sexually sanitised legacy for my children, I received 289 action points.

"I thought you were going to edit it," I protested.

"I have. This is step one—Developmental Editing," she replied.

I realised then that she had other ideas for me, and my literary journey was far from over. Debra wanted me to expand numerous of the existing chapters and write some new ones, on top of addressing the countless action notes. This was where the second part of my literary journey began, which has so far lasted well over a year.

Instead of balking at the task, I embraced it as Debra began to show me her own special talents and her even more special psychology. She knew I was still holding back and demanded more. "I want to know about the other aspects of your life that you have only touched on," she persisted. And slowly but surely, she had me reveal more and more until, eventually, I had a tell-all, multipart chronicle of my being. That was fine. I still wasn't going to publish though. Then because of her skill, those sands began to shift.

"You have to publish this," she said emphatically. "It's one of the most authentic, honest, and extraordinary tales about the privileged life of a British heir that I've ever read."

"Well, maybe, but I'll take out the sex," I replied, contemplating her ardent view.

"Oh no, you can't do that. It's crucial to the story for so many reasons. It shows the honesty of your life and drops the curtain on something the British usually do not talk about," was her retort and the gist of the conversation over a few more months.

As we got closer to making the final publication decisions, Debra could see I was still not convinced on the sexual content topic. She made this revelation, not something she usually did.

"Coming of age memoirs are not unusual. Yours is extraordinary. Unlike anything I have ever read. And what makes this a standout is not only how you included your early sexual development, such an important aspect, but the honest, explicit way you have chronicled it is remarkable. To remove this, your uninhibited feelings and experiences, would be cheating your readers out of the product of your therapy…and one incredible read."

While I was taking this all in, she said. "That it has been written by a conservative Englishman makes it unique." And as I was thinking she didn't know me well enough to realise that point held no sway, she asked. "Are you brave enough to break that mould?"

Turns out Debra did know me well…very well.

Just to drive the point home, another reviewer had this to say, "The book is bigger than what happens between consenting adults, between the sheets."

And then another assured me, "A bit of sex pales in significance against the far more meaningful aspects covered in the books and the people this could help."

This was another convincing argument, even more relevant with the sequel. (See H2Z.org)

Ultimately though, the Uncensored Edition exists because I was eventually convinced by no less than 50 reviewers of the value of being this transparent and open for adult readers.

But to make me feel better, and for those who prefer not to read explicit sexual content, most certainly including my older children, I have published this Censored Edition. Still an adult book, but one I am more comfortable with…for the most part anyway. It makes little difference to the story, alluding to rather than detailing the salacious parts.

In addition, I have also published a Young Adult edition.` The reason being, I have a very young adult son and wanted this book to be for him also. And for other young adults, I hope this book will teach them some life lessons and inspire them in their growing-up years. The story in the young adult book is essentially the same except for the romantic elements. There is romance, but of the 'more appropriate' kind suitable for 12- to 17-year-olds. This aspect is mostly fictional.

I grew up being taught that I could have anything if I just wanted it badly enough. With Debra's help and against the odds of dyslexia, that psyche crept back into me and soon I *badly* wanted to successfully finalise authoring my memoir.

Even though this is the censored edition, you may still find the openness in some of the content a little shocking, but after a life that has involved three PTSD events, I have finally arrived at the juncture where I won't "sweat the small stuff."

For the rest…well, it is fair to say I have lived my life in accordance with a quote from the father of modern-day novels:

> *The proper function of man is to live, not to exist. I shall not waste my days in trying to prolong them. I shall use my time.*
>
> —Jack London (1876–1916)

BEING BRITISH

IN WRITING MY autobiographical memoirs, my American editor asked me what did I think being English meant and what the difference could be compared to our American counterparts?

I was aware most Americans were descendants of British settlers who first arrived from the UK in the seventeenth and eighteenth centuries. These settlers played a significant role in shaping American society and institutions, so it is unsurprising that many American families have a strong connection to their British heritage and family history. The difference is that British families are literally closer to their heritage than their counterparts across the Atlantic. Many British families can trace their origins back centuries and are able to visit cemeteries and see tombstones of relatives from the 1800s or even the 1700s. Who says cemeteries don't have a place in our society?

The early pioneering spirit of our American brothers and sisters, which resulted in them becoming detached from their mother country, could be a fundamental reason for our differences. Americans established a democracy while the British have had and continue to have a monarchy, and the reverence of each is very different between the two countries. While politicians are typically all too eager to talk about themselves and make promises meant to get them elected, a monarch sits regally in example of service to their country and its people and their speeches have nothing to do with being re-elected.

Perhaps it is also this significant cultural difference between British and Americans that is behind why we are very conservative and keep our emotions deep inside, seldom, if ever exposing our vulnerabilities to anyone. The Jocelyn Dashwood quote, "No hugging, dear. I'm British. We only show affection to dogs and horses," which could include emotions, sums us up well.

What then made a particularly conservative Englishman literally open the book of his life, confounding the one or two people who knew what he was doing? Surely it was something immense? Perhaps cheating death twice? I don't mean the "one more yard to the left and I wouldn't be here" variety, but the real deal. The ones that take you within inches of death and leave you on life support and give you two of your three episodes of post-traumatic stress disorder. And is it that once you *luckily* find yourself again, all you previously held near and dear in the sanctuary of your unspoken private life is relegated to the "don't sweat the small stuff" bin?

A LETTER TO MY MOTHER

Dear Mum,

Of all the things I have undertaken or attempted in my life, writing an autobiography undoubtedly takes the cake. That I should even consider authoring a creative multipart chronicle as someone with dyslexia could be nothing short of ridiculous. But then your method of helping me overcome my dyslexia and advance my knowledge of English grammar could also be considered *ridiculous.*

Those boyhood hours spent with you, reading William Shakespeare as you helped me decipher his writing and the true meanings of some of his cryptic messages, will always remain with me. I remember how you would teach me to read between the lines and pick out certain words that were the crux of the message. How you drew my attention to what was *not said* as much as what *was said*. I remember, even in our daily conversations, you would first consider my sentence structure, word choice, and morphology before you would consider whatever I was either asking or saying. I was often frustrated when I had to repeat my question because I did not get an immediate response from you but rather a lesson in English language. Those lessons must have rubbed off on me.

The months of COVID lockdown and a lady—*there is always a woman*—are what encouraged me to finally take this *ridiculous* step. Yes, many people said I should write an autobiography because my life has indeed been extraordinary, but whilst I may have agreed, did I really mean it? Methinks not.

My having completed this though, is entirely thanks to you. I realised early on that you have been my guiding force in authoring these books, as I often mentally checked with you. What adjective would you use, or is my sentence structure correct? In that spirit, I have now spent many hours with you over the past two years and found great solace in your inspiration and influence as day by day, paragraph by paragraph, I have accomplished this endeavour.

I have no doubt you are cringing at some of the subject matter. You often said, though, that nothing I did would ever surprise you. I may have done that now. As always, I know you will just shake your head and forgive me anyway. I can imagine our conversation now.

"I wanted to take out the sex, but they said I couldn't. They said it was crucial to the story, its honesty."

Your voice in reply saying, "Sunbeam, you're justifying, which normally means you're in the wrong."

"Guilty as charged, Mum. Sorry."

In words from Shakespeare's *Hamlet*, "Though this be madness, yet there is method in't."

RIP, Mum

Love,

Charles

If you can meet with Triumph and Disaster
And treat those two impostors just the same;
...
Then yours is the Earth and everything that's in it,
And—which is more—you'll be a Man, my son!

Rudyard Kipling

CHAPTER 1
THE BEGINNING

"NOT GOOD, IS it, Fran?" my father said, reading a thin booklet with the Grayston House School coat of arms on the front cover. My dad didn't get very involved in my early years, but reading my school report was one thing he did do. "He is already six, and his first Year 2 report says it all. There are just no signs of improvement," my father pointed out in a gentle tone.

"Arthur, I hate the idea of him going to boarding school at such a young age, and does it have to be West Buckland, in bloody Devon? That's over three hours away. I can't understand why I have not been able to help him. A lot of use reading English literature has been to me." My mother sounded unusually exasperated.

"Frances, we don't want to make another mistake. It would be wonderful if he could stay at Grayston as a weekly or semi-monthly boarder, but they will only take him in the year he turns ten. Charles going to West Buckland is the right decision. They are known for having a very good remedial department. Let them nip Charles's problem in the bud, and then he can come back to Grayston. You cannot take responsibility for not being able to help him. Things have changed, Fran. They teach differently nowadays. Let Hamilton drive you and Charles to Devon in the Bentley. It will give you some quiet time together."

It was a conversation I had not enjoyed overhearing. All my friends were reading well. I just couldn't. Even at that age, it made me nervous.

Boarding school couldn't be that bad, but over three hours away does not sound good. How often will I get to come home? I thought worryingly.

My mum and I arrived at the imposing, castle-like West Buckland

School in Devon, in the South West of England, two days into the second term.

While we were dropping my clothes at the boarding house, Mr. Argyle, my new housemaster, said, "Sorry, not much choice of bed and clothes locker. You will just have to make do with what is left," not sounding very apologetic at all.

There were five steel double bunks around the perimeter of the dormitory. Of the ten beds, all had been taken except for the least favoured bottom bed in the corner of the room.

"There are two lockers beside each other. Take those," Mr. Argyle pointed out.

My mother opened my suitcase and was about to start unpacking my clothes into the doorless spaces when Mr. Argyle intervened.

"Don't worry about that, Mrs. Featherstone. Charles will do it later." It was an instruction rather than a suggestion.

I didn't give it any thought. There were bigger things on my mind right then, like having to say goodbye to my mother.

We then went over to the administrative section, where my mother stopped to read the foundation stone of the school to me.

> *In humble hope that the Great Architect of the Universe, the Maker of Heaven and Earth, the Giver of all Good, will bless and prosper the work this day commenced, and that the School to be raised will prove, under the Divine blessing, an institution for the promotion of God's glory in the extension of sound and practical education, in the diffusion of useful knowledge, upon the imperishable foundation of Divine truth.*
>
> *Laid by Earl Fortescue KG October 4th, 1860.*

The cold and gloomy winter morning, the cold grey buildings, this cold room, and these cold, cold words sent a shiver down my spine.

Once we had finished the formalities, it was time to say goodbye. I struggled to hold back the tears, not wanting to let go of my mother's hand.

"I'll see you in a month, Sunbeam. I love you." She turned away, not wanting me to see the tears streaming down her cheeks. She knew that I had to be strong, just moments away from meeting strangers who would hopefully become my new friends.

"I can take you up to Miss Meagan, your new teacher," said a Mrs. Hyslop, evidently one of the other Year 2 teachers. I followed her to the classroom, then Mrs. Hyslop tapped lightly on the door, opened it, and announced, "This is Edward Charles Featherstone."

Miss Meagan looked nice, but the feelings could not have been mutual. She gave me a disdainful look and said, "You can go and sit on that chair in the corner, young man."

Am I being punished for arriving late? Bewildered and sad, I took my seat as instructed. A few of the boys turned around to snicker and giggle. *I hate this place,* was my irrepressible first impression.

After a while, I heard the bell ring and correctly guessed it was for first break.

"You can stay right where you are, young man," Miss Meagan told me sternly as she walked out of the door.

I looked around the room, finding it much like any other. First-term school projects on the wall. A sign that said Words of the Week, which made me cringe as I noticed how difficult they were. I thought about the sandwiches in my school bag, not because I was hungry—I wasn't—but because I would normally never waste my mother's lovely sandwiches. I was doing everything within my power to hold back the tears. This was the worst day of my life, and there was nothing I could do about it. I was so scared that I would never be able to read, that I was stupid. I hated being there, but it could have been my only chance. I hoped my dad was right, that they could "nip it in the bud."

What if they can't?

When the bell rang again, signifying the end of break, the first person to walk through the door was Miss Meagan. She came straight over to me and took both my hands as she went down on her haunches to be at my level. "I'm so sorry, Edward, or is it Charles I should call you? I thought you had been sent over from Mrs. Hyslop's class because of bad behaviour. I'm so sorry."

The most unusual introduction to Miss Meagan's class was probably the best thing that happened to me in Year 2 at West Buckland. For the rest of

3

the year, she seemed to be continually trying to make it up to me. She soon became my favourite teacher, and perhaps I was her favourite student too.

The worst part about my Year 2 was quietly crying into my pillow, sometimes nights in a row, because of how homesick I was. I counted the days until I would be going home, and as it got closer to my once-a-month weekend pass out, midterm, or holiday, I began to feel better. My bunk bed, "the worst in the dormitory," turned out to be the best in the dormitory. Partly concealed by the lockers it gave me my own secret place where I could slip into a world of daydreams and fantasising about all the things I could do.

The best news in my Year 2 was being diagnosed as dyslexic. Hardly good news but far better than the alternative. Confirming what my difficulty was, was comforting and meant I'd be getting the right kind of help.

When my mother told me, I immediately asked, "Mummy, does that mean I'm not stupid?"

"You are the furthest thing from stupid," was my mother's vehement reply. "You just have an unusual condition the school will now work on. You are cleverer than a bag of monkeys, Sunbeam."

I didn't exactly buy the message of her endearing expression, but there were two other reasons that had me half believing her. First, I was the best at maths. I saw the patterns in everything to do with arithmetic. The second reason was chess. I may have only been six, but I was already a keen chess player and had made it into the West Buckland under-ten chess team.

It took the better part of two years before I learnt to manage being away from home. I even got to quite like West Buckland, especially the sports. And yes, I became fiercely independent. Was that a good thing? Maybe not.

Then in my third year, just before my ninth birthday, I came home for my monthly weekend pass, and it was one I will never forget. My mum and dad sat me down to speak to me, and I instinctively knew it was to give me the bad news that I would not be going back to Grayston House School. I was still struggling with my reading and spelling, but thankfully, I was improving slowly. Even so, I pretty well knew it was not sufficient for me to move closer to home and be a weekly boarder.

"Sunbeam," my mother began, "you have been doing really well at West Buckland, and I want you to promise your dad and I that you will continue making the same effort."

I knew what was coming and so was only half concentrating as I thought more about running across the field to see the horses.

"And if you do, you can go back to Grayston House after the holidays."

What did I just hear? I looked at my mum, then my dad, back to my mum. *Can I do it?* was my overwhelming thought. Never had so few words meant so much.

My mother clasped both my hands and said very quietly, "I am going to help you sort it out, Sunbeam."

Unbeknown to me, my mother had applied herself wholeheartedly to my severe case of dyslexia, something that in those days had become well known but little was known about how to treat it. That wasn't going to stop my mother, though. She believed she knew best how to deal with it. Once her mind had been made up, my father was no match for her determination.

"I love you, Mummy," was all I could say.

That was the start of her applying her purpose of helping me to read. On the nights I was at home, she had me read aloud with her, but she soon realised that I was often guessing the next words instead of reading them.

"See, Sunbeam, you're far too clever for your own good," she remarked.

Then she quickly devised strategies to help me. The first was to have me read Shakespeare because she knew I would not be able to guess the next words of his unusual turn of phrase. I particularly loved *Hamlet* and even named my first puppy Osric, after one of the characters.

My mother's other ingenious ploy was in how we read the Hardy Boys books together. This American collection of adventure stories featuring two teenage boys solving mysteries was so exciting to a young boy with a vivid imagination. First, my mother would read to me, which I adored.

"Joe squeezed Frank's arm, beckoning him to be quiet. They could hear the footsteps coming towards them in the darkness as—"

Where she stopped, I had to take over, which eventually I did without complaining, eager to find out what happened next. Not even my dyslexia was going to get in the way of me satisfying my curiosity. When the excitement had passed and the story got a bit more mundane again, my mother would take over until the next exciting part.

I loved the Hardy Boys, and in the end, thanks to my mum, I quite liked Shakespeare too. Reading snippets of Shakespeare seemed to exercise my brain and prevent me from running ahead, which was one of the symptoms of my condition.

It was while I was still in junior school at Grayston House that I finally got on top of my dyslexia, even if it was not something that would ever be cured. What my mother had done for me was far more than just help me "overcome" dyslexia. She had helped me restore my pride, my confidence, removing a dark cloud that had hung over me through my early school years. Unquestionably, the hours my mother spent helping me were the greatest gift I have ever received.

Excited to be home, I bounded up the stairs three or four at a time, followed by Osric matching my stride, my two legs competing with his four. Our love had been born the moment I was given this cute six-week-old English springer spaniel ball of fluff. He'd grabbed my heart the moment he licked my face and I smelt his puppy breath. As an only child, home only on weekends from boarding school, I cherished his constant companionship.

I was anxious to change out of my school clothes and head out into the woods to have some fun with Osric. I daydreamed about the day he would be my gundog and decided to do some training that day.

"Sunbeam, read your poem…aloud. I want to hear you," my mother called out to me, interrupting my daydream and my escape.

Ah. That bloody poem? I turned to face the framed verses hanging on my bedroom wall and started to read them out loud, which was not difficult because I knew them off by heart. " 'If—' by Rudyard Kipling," I announced. "If you can keep your head when all about you are losing theirs…"

I loosened the restricting necktie and yanked it over my head, kicking my shoes into the wardrobe at the same time.

"If you can wait and not be tired by waiting, or being lied about…"

I shuffled out of my navy-blue blazer and slid it onto a hanger. Boarding school discipline had taught me to take care of my things myself. Had I not,

I would have incurred my mother's wrath. I threw my shirt and trousers over the chair for laundry and, without missing a beat, began dressing for my afternoon in the woods.

"If you can meet with Triumph and Disaster and treat those two impostors just the same…"

I'd already knotted the laces of my boots by the time I got to the salient concluding line. "And—which is more—you'll be a Man, my son!"

I knew it wouldn't end there, so I waited for her questions, itching to get outside with Osric.

"What does Rudyard Kipling mean with the words, 'If you can dream—and not make dreams your master'?"

This one was easy. "It's fine to dream, but don't let the dreams affect your judgement," I blurted out, anxiously waiting to dash through the kitchen towards the back door. "Can we go now, Mummy?"

"No, not so fast."

"Muuuum!"

"What about, 'If you can trust yourself when all men doubt you, but make allowance for their doubting too'?"

"I must trust myself…and understand that not everyone will agree with me or even like me," I responded.

"And? And?"

"Umm… Well, other people might not see things the same way as I do, and that's okay. And if my choice is wrong, I'll still learn from it. May I go now?"

"One last question, Sunbeam. Why should you treat both triumph and disaster the same, and what is an impostor, and why does he call them that?"

I had to think about that one, a more recent difficult question of my mother's.

"Well," I began a little hesitantly. "An impostor is someone or something that comes in disguise to deceive you. And you should not overreact to triumph as it could soon lead to a downfall or a disaster."

"Good show," my mother replied, voicing her approval.

This poem epitomised a large part of my upbringing. My mother tirelessly instilled in me that the key to achieving and succeeding in all my life's pursuits was to believe in myself. I don't know what it was that caused me to be so fiercely competitive and committed in all the things I did, but I imagine Rudyard Kipling's "If—" undoubtedly played a part.

"Don't be late for dinner, and don't either of you get too muddy and wet," Mother warned as we were already bounding out of the door.

I was now ten years old, and Osric was almost two, in the early stages of becoming my first gundog.

Clearly, there would be a lot of mud. We lived in Berkshire, England, about an hour southwest of London, and the high annual rainfall meant the ground was often muddy. It was especially muddy around our parts, probably because we were in an area of thick green foliage, dense woods, and sun-blocking tree canopies. I didn't mind though, not in the least. As far as I was concerned, there was no better place to live. It was central to all my favourite places of interest. A short half-hour drive to my all-boys boarding school, Grayston House, a trip I had been making every two weeks since having left West Buckland School in Devon three months earlier. I was much happier being closer to home and quite comfortable with the thought that I would probably be doing this trip for another seven years, given that my school went all the way through to A-levels. Many of my school friends, who were also boarders, lived nearby. I was at school from Monday morning, when either my mum or dad would drive me, and it felt like no sooner had I got there that I would be getting picked up for the weekend at home, either every Friday or at least every second Friday afternoon, depending on sporting commitments.

Don't get me wrong, I loved everything about home—my family, my granddad, Osric, and especially the cooking—but when I was at school, I was surrounded by my friends. The general camaraderie, the special bonds with best friends, and the sport, which I couldn't get enough of, was all-consuming. I loved that we were all equal at school. We wore the same clothes, we did the same things, we lived in the same boarding house, and very little attention was paid to life outside of school. Outside of school, I was "Charles, you know, Arthur and Frances Featherstone's boy," or "only child," or, sometimes, "They have Rockwell Manor." I had once heard some boys speaking about me behind my back when one of them said, "That's what you call being born with a silver spoon in your mouth." That was bad enough, but when one of the other boys added, "What do you mean a silver spoon? More like a golden spoon if you ask me," followed by their jeers and laughter.

It made me cringe. In hindsight, it only strengthened my resolve to do something about it, even though right then I had no idea what.

I had great difficulty with this, just wanting to be me. The more I was reminded of who my parents were, where I came from, and what we had, the more determined I became to be recognised for who I was.

My home was central to my other favourite places. It was forty minutes from the Royal Berkshire Shooting School, a leading clay-pigeon shooting establishment that I knew well, having gone there many times when my father wanted to brush up on his shooting before the game-bird shooting season started. But it was when my own shooting instructions started there that I fell in love with the place.

Then there was Guards Polo Club, just twenty minutes from our home, where my family had been members for decades. Even though I was only just getting started and my mum had been in a constant tug of war with my father about the dangers of the game, I knew polo would become my most significant sporting pastime. This had been the case with my father and both my grandfathers, so I guess my eagerness was inevitable. This drove my enthusiasm for playing polo and game-bird shooting, to be fair, which was another sport that was passed on to me.

I smiled, remembering when I shared my thoughts with my mum about our home being so central. With a glint in her eye, she had suggested that what was central for us could be considered in the middle of nowhere for others.

Best of all though, Rockwell Manor was alongside the most wonderful Berkshire forest. *How central is that?*

As we reached the woods, my excitement mounted, as did Osric's, with him wanting to dash off. *Let's see how his whistle commands are coming on,* I thought. I blew four consecutive bursts to steady him, as opposed to a long, firm whistle to have him stop or sit. *Bloody hell, he's getting it,* I thought excitedly. "Ohhh, good boy, Osric. Clever boy!" I said as I patted him and gave him his reward.

My favourite activity as a youth was game-bird shooting. Wing shooting, as it is also known, is taking your shotgun to pheasant, partridge, ducks, or grouse whilst they are in flight.

On occasions when our family hosted formal, "driven game" shoots, our gamekeeper, as appointed "shoot captain," would oversee the day's proceedings. One of his tasks was hiring "beaters" to walk through the woods and fields and drive the birds towards a line of eager "guns," while the "pickers-up," with their retriever dogs, would ensure all the dead quarry were collected.

I loved being part of all the activities but wouldn't be permitted to join the men in the gun lineup until after I turned sixteen. Unquestionably, informal "rough shooting" with my gundog would become my favourite game-bird shooting format, venturing out on my own or with a friend. I dreamt of going into the woods on long adventures and shooting the quarry Osric "flushed out," which we would take home for our chef to prepare for our dinner. I confided all my secrets to this special creature, and he always understood, though he never answered back.

After about two and a half years and with guidance from my father, Osric would hunt and flush within shot range, be steady to flushed game birds, and also retrieve our quarry.

I was part of a large family, including uncles, aunts, and lots of cousins, including on my father's side of the family, but my immediate circle was quite intimate. It consisted of my mother, father, my maternal grandfather, and me.

My dad was a mixture of a London Sloane businessman and a country gentleman. For a middle-aged man, he was in good shape. Daily horse riding and playing competitive polo had kept his medium build in good trim. He had strong features, a mop of thick brown hair, and piercing "Featherstone" blue eyes, and he was evidently a good-looking man, not that a son could judge the looks of a parent. Jovial, smart, and quick-witted, he was fun to be around. He had been quite hands-off in my younger school-going years, leaving that side of parenting to my mum, but as I got older, he became more involved.

"Fran, you can look after the education and growing-up stuff, and I can concentrate on the important things like shooting, polo, and business," he would cheekily say to my mother.

He was typically British. There were few displays of affection, except to horses and dogs, and he was old-fashioned and traditional in his approach.

A curious aspect was that he often attracted the attention of younger women. I wouldn't have noticed if I hadn't seen him getting the occasional pinch from my mother, as if it were his fault that he had attracted this attention.

"What?" he would ask innocently.

"You know very well what," my mother would reply lightheartedly.

Perhaps there was some blame at my father's door after all.

From an early age, I developed an interest in business, always fascinated when my father and grandfather spoke about their businesses or investments. My family had shown me that having good business acumen was a surefire way of becoming fully independent, which chimed with my longing for self-recognition in my teenage years.

After I moved up to senior school, my father began coaching me in financial matters, explaining aspects of his investment portfolio. Over the school holidays, when we had more time, and with the *Financial Times* at hand, we would go through the stock prices, earnings per share, explanations around price-to-earnings ratios (P/E ratios), and so forth, pertaining to the shares in his portfolio. We would discuss how prices had moved and why he felt they'd done well or badly, and he'd ask my opinion. This became another area of common interest, continuing unabated when I later started my university studies and went into the Air Force. I loved learning about all of this, and my dad described me as a sponge for this information. My one day becoming a businessman seemed to be the right natural progression. Undoubtedly, the time spent with my dad later helped me invest in my first business enterprise.

My mother was a gifted sportswoman, and you could describe her medium-height physique as, well, sporty. She had short, dark blonde hair that was always neatly cut, and she was a sensible and practical woman, straightforward and honest with no sugar-coating. As sensible as she was, so was her wardrobe. Elegant casual. Trousers or a slacks suit, normally a silk scarf and a polo shirt with flat JP Tod's shoes. Not one for wearing dresses or skirts, she was a formidable county hockey player, then later a scratch golfer and captain of her club's ladies golf team, as well as an accomplished horsewoman.

I had once asked what horse-riding discipline most interested her and was quite tickled by her response. "Transport," she had replied. "That's how I got to school." She had then gone on to explain that in her day it was not uncommon. They didn't worry about saddles and were quite happy to ride bareback with just a simple bridle, and they would then leave their ponies grazing in a field adjacent to the school until they were ready to go home again. She was also quite academic, having studied English Literature at university and later learning computer programming.

Regardless of her sporting and academic achievements, my mother's primary focus was always on me and my character development.

A great sadness in her life was around her own mother. In the throes of a life-threatening double-breech birth of twins, my dying grandmother's last words, now engraved on an urn containing her ashes, had been:

> "If my life is a whole, it is half spoken for.
>
> The years that I have been with you have
> made worthwhile all the years before.
>
> In my womb are two whole lives. Part of them are me.
>
> Edward, I don't have to tell you who comes first."
>
> For Alexander and Frances

In the absence of modern-day medicine, luck was often what one most relied on. A lot was lost that sad day in the absence of luck. A wife to my grandfather. A mother to a pair of newborn twins, my mum and Uncle Alexander.

As a result, her father, Edward Francis George Apsley, had employed a governess to make sure his children were well cared for and at least had a substitute mother. One of my grandfather's requirements had been that the governess should also be a teacher. My mother's first and only governess was Mrs. Kearns, who not only played her part in bringing up my mother and uncle but later, when she was no longer required in the child-minding department, became the Rockwell Manor house manager. Put differently, one might say she became a permanent fixture in the Apsley household until her retirement after my parents got married.

Mrs. Kearns was a widowed English teacher and fit into the Apsley household perfectly. My mother always addressed her as Mrs. Kearns, and so did I. Mrs. Kearns had been very strict with my mother and uncle, and I was brought up with this same strict discipline. I don't remember much about her, as she retired before I started going to school. Of course, much of my mother's personality stemmed from her upbringing. But she was more than that. My mother was a woman of great dignity, moral standing and integrity. She taught me that respect is earned and sympathy should not be sought in any way. This was her character, some of her genetic inheritance.

As I was an only child, you may have expected my mother to be over protective of me, or even mollycoddle me. She did nothing of the sort. In contrast, she often told me I should keep a "stiff upper lip" and would frequently say, "Chin up, Sunbeam," if I was feeling down about something. Never would she entertain any self-pity. Even so, she was always gentle, always kind, and mothered me in the most positive way imaginable. Nothing was ever too much for her. Such was her commitment to me, as I got older, I began to feel she was very likely overcompensating for not having had a mother herself.

Sometimes she could be quite humorous in the way she reprimanded me, especially for little things. As an example, once when I was in the washing closet and she called out for me, it went something like this.

"I'm on the loo, Mum," I shouted back.

There was no immediate response, but when I emerged, my mother explained there was no need for me to announce to the world—a bit of an exaggeration—that I was "on the loo." She went on to say playfully, "It's fine to just say you are busy, Sunbeam. We will understand. Unless you would prefer to go into raptures and tell us exactly *what* you are doing on the loo, hopefully sparing us the details as to whether it involved any splashes."

It was a private conversation, as outside of that it would be "rude" and "unbecoming of a young gentleman" to speak like that.

"Rude"—a word I was all too familiar with in our household. My mother, especially, was determined that I "should not be rude" and would be quick to scold, "That's rude!" or "Don't be rude," if she deemed my behaviour so. She was a stickler for doing everything in her power to make sure I grew up to be a gentleman.

She was also a stickler for good manners, and it went without saying that I should stand when someone got up from the table, open doors for my elders and especially for ladies, and always say please and thank you. She never stopped reminding me I should be grateful for our privileged way of life and never think of myself as more deserving than someone else.

I will never forget my mother's reminder when I once forgot to thank a waitress in a restaurant and how I felt afterwards.

Very quietly, she said, "Sunbeam, you must always respect someone whose job it is to serve you and be sure to treat them as your equal because in some ways they are 'more than your equal.'"

Just those words made me feel very self-conscious, even if I wasn't too sure what she was getting at.

She continued, "Consider for a moment your circumstances. Your good fortune that allows you to be here, to be served. Then think about what *her* circumstances could be. She may have little choice but to do this job. Perhaps it is to provide for her young child left at home, whom she dearly wishes she could be with now. And then another child, you, doesn't have the decency to at least be polite. Imagine this Sunbeam, because you would be surprised how close that could be to the truth."

I never again made the mistake of forgetting to say please and thank you, especially to anyone serving me.

Perhaps the most important thing she ever taught me was that I could have anything I wanted and that my privilege was not the reason I'd get it. It happened over something quite innocuous that I had said I wanted to achieve. In a very measured tone, she said, "Sunbeam, you can have anything you want. Anything in the world. There is only one requirement. You must want it badly enough."

Surely it couldn't be that simple, just to want it.

My sceptical expression had my mother repeating those words as if to implant them into my brain. "Anything you want, Sunbeam, anything. You just have to want it badly enough."

As I got older, so I came to trust these words more and more. Right or wrong, I now believe anything I didn't or don't achieve is simply because I haven't wanted it badly enough.

CHAPTER 2
GRANDDAD

I HAD ONE GRANDPARENT. Edward Francis George Apsley, my mum's dad. I never knew my grandparents on my father's side of the family. Sadly, they were both casualties of the Second World War. I carry names of each of my grandfathers—Edward from Edward Francis George Apsley and Charles from Robert Charles Featherstone. It was not difficult to imagine how my parents met, as both my grandfathers had been keen polo players and often played against each other. Polo was a popular game in rural England, especially among landowners. Both grandfathers also enjoyed game-bird shooting.

Born in 1889, Granddad was the proverbial English gentleman. Standing appreciably over six feet tall with broad shoulders, he had a strong jawline, a thick mop of brown hair, and vibrant blue eyes. His open face often wore a broad smile, the mischievous glint in his eye foretelling his wicked sense of humour, but at times he could have quite a stoic and no-nonsense character. Although I was quite young when he died, I will always remember him as an impeccably dressed man. Monday to Sunday, no matter where he went, he wore a suit as his standard dress. If he was playing polo or cricket or was horse riding, he would change from his suit into his sporting attire and then back into his suit again. I later discovered they were all tailor-made by Chester Barrie—white-collared shirts, tie and family crest tiepin, and cufflinked sleeves. His shoes were Church's, and his hats were made by Lock & Co., who have occupied their premises on St. James's Street in London since 1676, arguably making them one of the oldest shops in the world. This wasn't an attempt to be ostentatious in any way. He was a very private man and kept a low profile, but he liked quality and tradition. He lived by a set of values that he held dear.

There are many wonderful stories about my grandfather, but one that really stands out for me says so much about who he was and the principles he lived by. Excelling in business, he built a successful portfolio of farms, abattoirs, and butcheries, and several large cooperatives, places where farmers could meet to buy and sell produce, probably the forerunners to supermarkets we see today. Behind one of his cooperatives was my grandfather's head office. My mother told me the story of how, one evening when he was about to lock up, two men came into his office, brandishing guns. They demanded he open the safe, threatening to shoot him if he didn't obey. My grandfather calmly refused. The men continued their threats to shoot him if he didn't comply with their demands.

His response was, "Well then, you'll just have to shoot me, because I will not give in to criminals."

They carried out their threat and shot him. He dropped to the floor, and his assailants fled in fright, leaving him for dead. The impact of the shot left him dazed for a few minutes before he recovered his senses. Seriously injured, he assessed the situation and concluded that things couldn't be too bad if he was still conscious and breathing. Given there was a lot of blood, my grandfather decided the best course of action was to patch up the wound as best he could, put on a clean shirt, donned his coat, and then drove himself to hospital.

On the way, he realised he would be going past the police station. Despite being in great pain, he thought it expedient to stop and report the incident. He pulled up and gingerly got out of his car, clutching his coat around him. The duty sergeant watched my grandfather's slow approach, later admitting that he had remarked to his colleagues, "Old man Apsley is certainly getting old." Bent over and shuffling, he made his way into the police station and announced that he'd come to report an attempted robbery and shooting. Even though the staff sergeant had thought old Mr. Apsley was perhaps getting a bit senile, he had not wanted to be disrespectful to someone of my grandfather's standing in the community, so he remarked politely, "Well, at least they missed, sir."

"No," replied my grandfather. "They shot me." He opened his coat, revealing a blood-soaked shirt, as the dressing was soddened with blood from the wound.

Shocked, the sergeant rushed my father to the hospital, where the bullet was removed, having missed his heart by less than an inch.

The next morning, after a night in hospital, he recounted the story to his family. They soon asked the obvious question, which was, why on earth had he risked his life to save the contents of his safe, regardless of how much was in there?

His reply left everyone speechless. "Oh, there was nothing in the safe except my lucky penny. The banking had been done for the day. I wasn't protecting my money. I was protecting my principles."

Hearing this story when I was older had me realise my grandfather was almost certainly subtly reminding his family of the importance of standing by one's principles.

My grandfather's courage was a testament to him being willing to give his life, standing by what he believed in. He certainly left a lasting impression on me, which has persisted all through my life. He often had a different take on things compared to those around him. For example, I once overheard a conversation about someone having made a lot of money.

"Over ten million," the voice had remarked.

I told my grandfather about it and asked, "How much is a lot of money, Granddad, and how much do we have?"

He did not immediately reply, giving it some thought first, but then said, "You will hear a lot of talk like that, my boy. It is unimportant." He then continued with his real message. "A person's wealth should only be measured by what he has given away, nothing else. Because everything else is just egotistical, self-serving, and irrelevant, as it affects just one person or family."

He wasn't finished there.

"There is no reason to ever be proud of how much you have compared to how little another person has."

I hadn't then understood all the words he had chosen, but his expression and emphatic tone made it clear. Words I now fully understand and will never forget.

Another of his lessons that I have never forgotten was when he once said, "You will one day be in business, and you will discover that very often commerce is about creating different focus points, promoting the positives, minimising or even brushing over the negatives. *Marketing* is what they call it. I have another word for it."

"What, Granddad?" I asked enthusiastically.

Because of the way he brought his mouth to my ear, I knew what he was about to tell me was important.

"Bullshit, that's what I call it," he whispered.

My giggle made my tummy wobble. I knew my granddad was being naughty using a word like that with me. And I also knew my mother would object very strongly. But I guess it's just like that. Grandfathers can get away with almost anything.

He smiled and carried on, "It's fine. It's how this modern world works, but always remember this. When you put your head on your pillow before you go to sleep, no matter how you have presented to the world, this is the time to be brutally honest with yourself. Top businessmen never bullshit themselves."

No giggling this time. Granddad was being deadly serious and brutally honest.

Coming home from school usually had me jumping out the back door of my mum's car in excitement, and as always, Osric was the first to greet me. After a quick, impassioned hello and licks aplenty, I most often dropped my school bag outside the front door and excitedly sprinted off to see my granddad who lived in Winston Cottage, 120 yards from the main house. Set amongst some old, established trees on the eastern side of the property, it had two access paths. One was a smooth brown concrete lane, almost dead straight, between two rows of low hedges, my mother's attempt at concealment. It had been put in as an afterthought to accommodate a catering trolley for Granddad's meals when he got a little older and did not feel like going up to the main house. It was only my grandfather, Fabrizio—our chef—and me who used this narrow runway. Everyone else used what I considered the scenic route. It was a combination of stepping stones and old timber railway sleepers, meandering through the treed garden, brush, and indigenous flowerbeds leading down to the front door. Twice the distance to get to the same destination. An inconceivable waste of time to my young mind.

Winston Cottage was a grand garden suite constructed in the same Georgian Palladian style as Rockwell Manor, even though it had only been built sometime after the Second World War. Built for my grandfather when he handed the keys of the main house to my parents, it was undoubtedly my favourite place, alongside the stable block—two areas where I spent many happy hours during my adolescence and beyond. It had large, high ceilings with a reception room and a master suite with ensuite bathroom going out to a large patio, where Granddad loved to sit and look down the rolling lawns and across into the forest. I was always amazed at the deer and the myriad other small game that would come out of the thicket and nibble on the edge of the lawn. It got its name from Sir Winston Churchill, past prime minister of the United Kingdom, a man well known to my grandfather. Theirs was a friendship that Granddad significantly underplayed, preferring to say they were "well acquainted." He told me many wonderful stories about Winston Churchill, some of which have become folklore. The one Granddad knew I found hilarious was from whilst Churchill was a member of Parliament, before becoming Prime Minister. He had gone back to the House of Commons after a boozy lunch. A female member of the house said accusingly, "You are drunk, sir, neither honourable nor gentlemanly," a play on his formal title of The Right Honourable Sir Winston Churchill and his rank as a gentleman.

Churchill replied, "And you, My Right Honourable Lady, are ugly. Tomorrow, I'll be sober."

Granddad had lots of, let's say, *peculiarities*. One of them I discovered in unusual circumstances. It was after school while we were playing a game of chess, something he began coaching me in from the age of four, when our butler arrived for what seemed no particular reason.

"How are they feeling?" Granddad asked Hamilton.

"Perfect, sir. I think they're done," Hamilton replied.

"Good show. Well, let's swap. I have another pair that needs the same treatment. The tan ones," Granddad said.

I listened to this exchange without any idea what they were speaking about, unlike Hamilton, who understood perfectly as he walked over to my grandfather's shoe cabinet.

"These ones, sir?" Hamilton asked, showing my grandfather a pair of Church's shoes, the only brand he wore.

Granddad nodded.

Hamilton took off the black shoes he was wearing and put them into the shoe cabinet. "Not sure what Mrs. Featherstone will say about my black jacket and grey pinstripe trousers with tan shoes, sir," he said, making a valid point as he put on the new pair of shoes.

I still had no idea what was going on! *Is Granddad sharing his shoes with Hamilton?*

Once Hamilton had left the room, Granddad smiled at my enquiring expression. He explained that he did not enjoy "walking in" his new shoes and simply gave them to Hamilton to do it for him. An unusual quirk indeed.

It didn't stop me from looking suspiciously at the sizes of our other staff's feet, comparing them to my father's, and wondering if he had adopted this approach.

I began drinking when I was about nine or ten years old. So as not to give the wrong impression, let me start at the beginning.

It had first taken place on an occasion when my grandfather chose to have dinner in his cottage and I had joined him. Fabrizio, our then thirty-seven-year-old chef, had come down with his catering trolley to serve us. And as always, there was ice cream in the cold compartment for our simple but favourite dessert. Having finished dinner, Granddad and I sat chatting while Fabrizio busied himself preparing our treat. First, he made a chocolate sauce by melting a slab of Lindt milk chocolate before adding chopped hazelnuts with a dollop of fresh cream in a small saucepan, which he placed over his gas plate on the server. While the chocolate was slowly melting, he swiftly prepared two crepes that he served into our bowls, along with a generous scoop of vanilla ice cream. Then, when the chocolate sauce was ready, he poured it over the bowls, me almost drooling as the chocolate and hazelnut sauce hardened on the ice cream.

Granddad sent me over to his liquor cabinet alongside a very old glass cabinet, which had in it the urn containing the ashes of my mother's mother, and had me retrieve the squat black bottle. He then poured some of The King's Ginger liqueur over the top of both our desserts. It pooled over the crepe, and there was a teaspoon or two left in the bottom of my bowl.

From then on while sharing this special treat together, he'd simply say, "Son, go and get *our* bottle," and I knew what was coming…the best part. He always left room for cheese and a cracker, and on this occasion, he prepared two, one for each of us. He carefully cut segments of Camembert cheese and placed them on French-buttered sourdough crackers, and then, using the rounded end of the cheese knife handle, he pressed a little basin into the middle of the cheese on each. With the steady hand of a marksman, he carefully filled the tiny basin to the brim with the same liqueur, and then he took two slices of stem ginger out of its thick, sugary syrup and popped it on the top. In contrast to his careful preparation, he finished it off by dousing his creation with the ginger-and-honey liqueur before passing one of them towards me while he took the other, raised it as if it were a glass, and put it whole into his mouth, indicating for me to do the same.

The alcohol burned and so did the ginger, even if it was also sweet, but the creaminess of the cheese mixed in with these contrasting flavours was the best thing I'd ever tasted. With my eyes watering, I was ready for another.

"That's all, my boy. Too much of a good thing *is never a good thing*," he said, chuckling.

This became a regular occurrence. So regular that it still happens now. Whenever I make this cracker, cheese, ginger preserve, and liqueur snack, fond memories of my grandfather are immediately stirred.

Every now and then, my granddad gave me half a small liqueur glass of The King's Ginger, and instead of "Cheers," he would say, "To the gods of indulgence! Let's indulge."

I later found out that half a glass was actually just a quarter of a glass because of the trumpet shape. I discovered this to my detriment, losing a bet when he took two glasses, each three-quarters-full, and poured one into the other without spilling a drop.

I have never really taken my drinking habits further than that, apart from the odd glass of champagne.

I loved the story of how The King's Ginger came into existence. Granddad even remembered how in 1903, King Edward VII used to take his topless Daimler, something he referred to as his horseless carriage, for joyrides around the English countryside. This was evidently quite a nerve-racking experience because this horseless carriage exposed him to the elements, where he ran the risk of "getting a chill." The royal physician sought to address these concerns by commissioning a London merchant, Berry Bros. & Rudd, to formulate a "warming, fortifying beverage," and hence, the brandy, ginger, honey, and lemon elixir came into being. It soon became very popular, extending beyond royalty and nobility to commoners as well, as a drink for not only when one was driving but also when one went shooting. "A clear case of the British government promoting 'drink driving' in the early years of motoring," Granddad said, chuckling. I could just imagine a panel discussing it, and it making perfect sense to them back then. Luckily though, they eventually did come to their senses and made drink driving illegal in 1925.

A few nights after the shoe exchange in Winston Cottage, Granddad, my mum and dad, and I had been sitting around the table in the family dining room, about to have a light dinner, when Hamilton walked in. He was looking very smart except for his shoes, which did not match his formal attire. On seeing this, I watched in amusement as my mum's mouth opened, about to say something, but then she closed it again, having realised what was going on. She clearly knew Granddad well.

On this occasion, Fabrizio had made his famous tomato soup. Famous only because he had declared it so, as he humorously did with many of his dishes. He was quite happy to stretch the truth on this classification when trying to encourage me to eat more.

At breakfast on a Monday morning before I had to go back to boarding school, he would say something like, "You must have more of my famous scrambled eggs."

Thinking about it, they were *pretty famous*, using his definition. Fabrizio said the secret to good scrambled eggs was double cream. He would cook the egg mixture on low heat, folding it over and over until they slowly turned into the consistency of scrambled eggs. Once they were plated, he added salt and pepper, finely chopped parsley, a little grated parmesan and, splashed artistically on the side, his own tomato sauce made from, of course, Roma tomatoes, his secret herbs (all his herbs were secret), and a little honey. On my dad's encouragement Fabrizio had an adult version of his tomato sauce—it included peperoncino chillies from Tuscany. Hot and sweet. "*Ti morderà*. It will bite you," he often warned me. I quite liked testing myself, and my friends, getting *bitten* by his adult sauce. Alongside would be *roasted* bread—not toasted, an important distinction according to Fabrizio. His tomato soup was also quite exceptional, if not famous. He would fill two large trays of what he insisted had to be Roma tomatoes, *obviously,* preferably from Italy, with red peppers, garlic, and herbs, and then place them in the wood-burning pizza oven. Once roasted, he'd put it all through the food processor before he added clotted cream. He served this with sourdough bread, which, yes, was also roasted in the wood-burning oven.

On this occasion, my mother had been serving the piping-hot soup from the tureen, allowed on the family dining room table but not in the main dining room, into our soup plates when Granddad placed a brown paper packet on the table in front of me.

"A surprise for you, Charles," he said with a twinkle in his eye.

I opened the package and was delighted to discover that my surprise was a large frog.

"Dad! Do we have to do this at the dining table?" was my mother's sharp reaction.

He smiled mischievously, expecting his daughter's rebuke.

She looked on disapprovingly as the frog jumped straight into my bowl of piping-hot soup, only to depart as hurriedly. "Now look what you've done," my mother said, her annoyance with her father having shifted up a gear.

My dad chuckled. My grandfather winced, not having expected that outcome. I loved how he seemingly put his tail between his legs when his daughter tore a strip off him for doing something wrong. I was smiling at this interaction, wondering what Granddad's comeback would be.

"Fran, darling," he began, "I am just giving young Charles here a lesson about life."

This had everyone confused and my dad and me chuckling.

"Charles, did you notice how the moment the frog landed in the hot soup, he leapt straight out again?"

I nodded my head in agreement.

"Well, that was precisely the correct response to the abrupt change to his circumstances." Nobody could deny that. "Now, consider this," my grandfather continued. "Had he been in the pot of soup when it was cold and it had slowly been brought to the boil, it is very likely he would have been cooked into the soup." All eyes were on Granddad as he finished by saying, "So, this lesson is that you shouldn't be lethargic about changing your circumstances just because the changes are happening slowly."

Not bad, Granddad, I thought with a smile.

An unforgettable day in my life was when my grandfather gave me my first shotgun, a Browning 410. I listened and learnt intently as he taught me and then practiced with me the principles of shooting game birds in flight.

"You have to shoot where the bird is going, not where it has been," he continually reminded me. "Start behind, move slowly onto the target and then ahead. Judging the speed, the distance, and how it is moving while keeping a steady hand are the differences between a palooka and a professional."

I smiled. So did my granddad. He had chosen his words purposely, knowing I would do whatever possible not to be a palooka.

One of the exercises he made me do was to balance on a large, rounded boulder at the bottom of the rolling lawns below Winston Cottage, the same rock he liked to sit on and watch some of the wildlife around Rockwell Manor or just enjoy a sunset.

"Always set your feet for where you will shoot your target, lean into the shot, nose over toes, and the rest will follow."

When winter came, he set up a portable clay trap and we would do clay-pigeon shooting. Following his instruction in picking up this three-and-a-half-inch clay disc as it catapulted out of the trap had me hooked in an instant. Slowly but surely, I got to the stage where I was hitting almost as many as I was missing. Watching the pieces breaking off the flying projectile pleased me no end. As I improved further, thereby hitting the targets with the centre of the pellet pattern, the clay discs would disintegrate into a thousand pieces in a cloud of clay dust. No guessing which captured my imagination more. "You smashed it," were words I loved hearing my granddad say.

I will never forget on one occasion when I had foolishly missed a couple of clays and been quite forthright in admonishing myself. My grandfather turned to me and gave me this sage advice. "What's behind you is behind you. Let it go. There is nothing you can do about it. Learn how to do that and it will free you to concentrate fully on the next clay."

This boulder, which he called our "shooting rock," had another use. It is where I often read with my grandfather, my mother giving him instructions about what she wanted him to cover.

On one occasion, we began speaking more broadly about my schoolwork.

"Granddad, Mum says I should concentrate more on the things I am weak at. What do you think?"

I knew his reply was important because of the extra time he took deliberating his answer. Then, in a hushed tone, he said, "I have a different idea to your mum. I think you should concentrate on the things you are good at and only do what is necessary on those subjects that don't interest you."

This contradicted nearly everything I had heard around me. "You need to work on your areas of weakness, young man," is what I was familiar with at school. My mother would say, "Leave the maths and science, Sunbeam. You can do that like falling off a log. Concentrate on your weak subjects like geography, anthropology, and English."

I couldn't get out of my mother's English lessons but almost certainly followed my grandfather's advice on the remainder. Like my mother, he reminded me that success comes more easily on a foundation of success, a simple family philosophy. Do something, no matter how small, and once you have successfully completed it, use it as a foundation and move on.

Edward Charles Featherstone

I enjoyed an incredible life with my granddad until shortly before my thirteenth birthday.

It was a Sunday afternoon, and I went down to Winston Cottage to chat with him, but very unusually, he had been taking an afternoon rest. The next morning, I still remember thinking I should run down to his cottage to say goodbye before leaving for school for the week. I didn't act on those thoughts, a decision that would trouble me for many years to come. I never saw my grandfather again. He had woken up ill on Monday morning and remained in his pyjamas and gown, even agreeing to see a doctor the following morning. He died in his sleep in the early hours of Tuesday morning.

When my mum collected me from school on Friday, she said I should sit in the front seat, and on the way home she told me that Granddad had gone to Heaven on Tuesday morning.

She continued, trying to explain the cycle of life to me, but I didn't want to hear that. None of it made sense to me. I asked "Mummy, does this mean I am never going to see Granddad ever again?" The last few words were barely audible as my tears and remorse enveloped me.

I curled up into the corner of the seat facing the passenger window, and quietly wept all the way home. We drove into our gates up the long, winding driveway, past the spot where I could see Winston Cottage, and I couldn't help the choking sobs that immediately resurfaced. My mother stroked my leg trying to console me, until she stopped the car, and I jumped out and ran up to my room with Osric meekly following. There was none of the typical welcome home we shared and no spring in his step. He understood my feelings. I needed to be alone, to share my sadness with my pillow, something I knew all too well from West Buckland.

Granddad had left clear instructions that he wanted to be cremated. One handful of his ashes was to be sprinkled into the earth at the base of our shooting rock and another at the centre point of the polo field once it had been scarified (mowing the grass to its roots). "Ashes to ashes, dust to dust, darling Fran," he had instructed my mother. The remaining ashes, in their urn, were to always be kept next to the one containing the ashes of his beloved late wife.

I didn't attend the cremation or church service. Not wanting me to experience the austere church ceremony, my parents arranged our own little family send-off that I could be a part of. My father had arranged our groundsman to scarify a one-yard-diameter circle in the centre of the polo field, the bare earth ready to receive a sprinkling of Granddad's ashes.

It was the saddest day as the three of us, hand in hand, walked to the middle of the polo field and sprinkled Granddad's ashes on the exact centre point, then bowed our heads and my dad read.

"From the *Book of Common Prayer*: 'We therefore commit these ashes to the ground, earth to earth, ashes to ashes, dust to dust; in sure and certain hope of the Resurrection to eternal life.' "

We then walked to the rounded boulder below Winston Cottage and repeated the little ceremony. As my dad finished reading the prayer, I looked at the boulder and burst into tears. I no longer had a granddad to learn how to shoot pheasant with. To play chess with. To read with. To drink The King's Ginger with. I could not stop sobbing no matter how my parents tried to comfort me.

We went into the cottage, and I was given the responsibility of putting my grandfather's urn alongside his deceased wife's in the old glass cabinet. I then instinctively realised what I had to do.

Taking the other urn out of the cabinet, I told my parents, "We have to do the same again." I could see they weren't sure what I was getting at, so I put it another way. "Granddad will want Nan's ashes with him, so they can always be together."

They then understood my naive point of view and agreed with it wholeheartedly. With my father holding his wife's mother's ashes, we walked back to the middle of the polo field, sprinkled a handful of her ashes, said our prayer, and then went back to our shooting rock, repeating what we had done before.

This time it was my mum who was sobbing, feeling the loss of never having had a mum and now also losing her only parent, and it was my dad and me trying to console her.

The loss of my grandfather made me think about what he had lost when the mother of his children had died. Seeing them side by side, I realised the only thing I had ever had of my nan was sitting in an urn. I didn't get to call her my nan.

My grandfather was born and died at Rockwell Manor. He knew no other home. My mother was born at Rockwell Manor. Would she die there too? I shuddered at the thought.

I had the most special relationship with my grandfather and have even wondered if he subconsciously made an extra effort with me, attempting to make up for the three grandparents I didn't have. It is quite possible, and certainly the sort of thing he would have done. In many ways it put me in a very fortunate position. Except of course, when I lost him, I lost all four of them and a mentor, and the most patient friend. Perhaps that was just how it is with grandparents. I had come face to face with the realisation that life was not forever. An awful revelation for any young person, I am sure. I became a few years older that day, and from then on I smiled a little less. That's what growing up meant, I guess.

Along with my parents, especially my mother, he taught me many things that guided me all through my life and that I have often used in the course of teaching my own children.

As an adult, I couldn't help reflecting that for all of my grandfather's good intentions in appointing a governess to make sure my mother and uncle had a suitable substitute for a mother, clearly there had still been shortcomings. Mrs. Kearns, having been a schoolteacher, was clearly of the stricter kind. The way we addressed her seemed to confirm it. So, whilst she may have been very caring and a good teacher, I couldn't imagine her having a warm, motherly side. I could understand where my mother got her propensity to teach me from, but what about her softness? Was my mother's gentle, loving nature a looking glass into the character of her own mother's gentle character, the grandmother I never had?

CHAPTER 3
GAME-BIRD SHOOTING

G RAYSTON HOUSE SCHOOL was one of the standout memories of my teenage years.

I loved playing sports, and our school was well known for its many and varied offerings. The moment the bell rang for the end of class or prep, I would dash off to play cricket in the summer, rugby in the winter, and athletics in the spring. If not that, I would be found playing squash, doing gymnastics, or even practising karate. Given my family's sporting background, it was perhaps unsurprising that I did well in all my sports activities.

On the academic side, I had already shown an aptitude that suggested I would achieve distinctions in maths and science, and that I would struggle with almost everything else, especially if it required studying. Also no surprise. What was a surprise, especially for me and clearly thanks to the perseverance of my mother, was that slowly but surely, I started getting better marks in English. I was never to overcome dyslexia, but I was learning how to work with and around it.

It was during my teens that I really advanced my game-bird shooting and polo-playing interests as well, fitting them into my very busy weekends at home. I also learnt to drive, mostly illegally, not that anyone really worried about what took place on our remote country roads.

By the time I was sixteen, Osric and I would go rough shooting at every opportunity. He had become a seasoned gundog, accomplished in the two primary disciplines of flushing and retrieving. At times, I would watch him flush large quarry, even ducks, and I couldn't help but marvel at how steady he was. When a gundog flushes birds from the thicket, there is a great fanfare of wings flapping as they take flight. This can be distracting, but a well-trained dog holds its ground and stands immobile and intense, only breaking when the birds are clear, referred to as "steady to flush." This was Osric.

When we went rough shooting, we never returned home empty-handed. I always aimed to shoot at least a brace of birds. Whenever my mother admonished us for being late, I'd explain that we'd needed one more pheasant or partridge to complete our brace, because one pheasant was not enough to feed our family, including Osric.

An important thing to remember is that one never carries one's game bird quarry by the feet, but rather the neck. This is to keep the blood in the carcass, which adds to the flavour of the meat. I tied some twine between their necks to make a convenient handle.

After several hours, with English weather being what it was, we would arrive home wet and covered in mud. Osric and I were oblivious to this until my mother refused us entry into the boot room, let alone the kitchen. We were required to clean up outside, to make ourselves more presentable before dashing into the scullery. We usually ended up showering together, and being a water dog, Osric absolutely loved it.

While Osric's name came from a minor character in Shakespeare's *Hamlet,* he was by no means a minor character in my early life. He was, for a long time, the main supporting actor. We did everything together. He shared my food, and much to my mother's chagrin, he shared my water bottle, hardly spilling a drop as I held it up to his mouth for a sip. It was when I absentmindedly took a sip myself just after him that my mother would react. At night he slept on my bed, my mother having given up trying to keep him out. She used to tell me how he would mourn my departure on Sunday nights or Monday mornings when I went back to boarding school, and how he only came to life when I arrived home on Friday evenings. When I was at school, I missed Osric almost as much as I missed home.

Like so many pastimes—modern polo, football (soccer), rugby, cricket, tennis, golf, boxing, even baseball and many more—game-bird wing shooting had its origins in Great Britain. Accordingly, it had some interesting British idiosyncrasies, all quite normal to me, although I would discover this was not the case for most foreign visitors.

My Rude Awakening

Once, we had an American, Logan Gates, come and stay because of a polo tournament he was playing with us. He mentioned he enjoyed turkey shooting in Kentucky, USA, so my dad decided we should include him in our own formal shoot.

"Charles, please help Logan get kitted out. Between us, we should have him looking presentable," my dad mused. "And while you are at it, you should explain the proceedings to him. They do things quite differently on the other side of the pond," he said, smiling.

I started by explaining that once we were at the first stand, there would be beaters to get parcels of pheasant to take flight for the first drive of the day. Highly trained retriever dogs would recover anything we shot.

When Logan explained that the turkeys they shot were on the ground, I started chuckling because I was sure he was taking the mickey out of me. Sadly, he was not. My favourite quarry were pheasant and especially grouse because the speed at which they flew made for a great challenge. Shooting a bird that was on the ground—especially a turkey, which I thought of as slow, cumbersome, vulnerable, large, and chicken-like—was a strange concept for an Englishman and brought to mind something I had once read that described perfectly why one should not do this.

> *Damned be the man, so unsporting, that he shall put a bird at the mercy of his shot without giving it the chance of flighted freedom. Let his pot go empty before breaking this unwritten rule.*
>
> —*Anonymous, 1904*

I should add here that years later, when I did go on a turkey hunt in Kentucky, I discovered it was nothing close to what I had imagined. They were crafty little critters, and even using the best decoys to attract them didn't always work. Sorry, Logan, for my judgemental thoughts.

Luckily, he was much the same size as my father, so I didn't expect any difficulty in fitting him out for his first shoot.

"Logan, I'm sure we will find something in my father's wardrobe for you. You seem to be a similar size; what are you, fourteen, fourteen and a half stone?"

Logan looked at me bewildered.

I realised that he had no idea about our stone weight measurement system. "About one ninety or two hundred pounds?"

He nodded his head, still looking confused. "So how much is a stone?" he asked.

"Now it is set at fourteen pounds," I replied.

"What do you mean *now*?" he inquired.

"Oh, don't worry about that. It's just that the system dates back to the fourteenth century when a stone was used in early scales for trading and measuring produce. It's straightforward now, but back in the day, a stone was a different weight depending on the region you were in," I told him, hoping I was making sense.

"Straightforward, you say. And why on earth do you still use such an antiquated system for measuring body weight?"

On reflection, it probably was a bit confusing to a foreigner, especially in a world of the metric system. I supposed it was a case of old habits die hard.

I put together tweed plus fours (much like knickerbockers), a fine wool shirt, a sporting-print tie, a tweed jacket, a woollen cap, leg stockings with bright, ornate woollen garters, and brogue shoes. He would be able to attend our breakfast and luncheon dressed like this, and then just swap the shoes for boots and his tweed jacket for a shooting jacket before heading off for the next drive.

Since ours was a bespoke shoot, we would each need a matched pair of two identical shotguns, so that regardless of which was being shot, they were indistinguishable from each other. I would be taking my early 1900s side-by-side James Purdey & Son matched pair, which had been handed down to me by my grandfather. Logan's guns were a more modern over-and-under identical pair, as they were easier to shoot and more accurate. Experienced shots were more inclined to stick to age-old tradition and not make things easier for themselves with the over-and-under shotgun variety.

I went on to tell him that he would have a loader who would quickly load the one gun while he was firing the other. All he had to do once he had fired his first gun was reach back, and the reloaded twin shotgun would be swapped for his discharged one. This would continue until the quarry had finished flying overhead.

I turned to Logan and asked, "So, what do you think?"

Reeling at the pomp and ceremony, he looked at me incredulously and said, "You must be fucking joking!"

As a teenager who, at worst, only said *bloody*, I'm not sure what shocked me more, his surprise or his language.

The conversation carried on with Logan asking, "Do we stop for tea?"

"We don't, but you shouldn't worry," I said. "Between drives there will always be time for a snack and a sloe gin, or whatever you prefer in your hip flask."

"What is sloe gin? Surely not gin?" he asked.

"It is actually a liqueur made out of gin," I told him.

"You must be kidding me," Logan said in an incredulous tone.

"Why?" I asked innocently.

"Guns are almost outlawed in England. I know it is very difficult to get your licence, but when you finally do, you have no problem mixing alcohol and firearms." Logan looked at me as he finished making his point.

I looked back at him blankly. What he said was true, and I suppose, looking at it from the outside, it was a bit unusual. It was what I'd grown up with, so it seemed completely normal to me. My answer was a shrug of the shoulders, which didn't help Logan much.

As I now write about this, nothing has changed.

Whilst Logan was right about the stringent attitude both the government and society had towards guns, after that little harangue I chose not to mention an even more curious thing about English gun laws. Although guns are regarded as completely unacceptable, handguns even being illegal—not even policemen are armed unless they are in a special unit—sporting guns are more than acceptable, especially shotguns. Even so, when you apply for a sporting-gun licence in England, it is a lengthy process. It starts with a specialist officer coming to your home, forming a firsthand opinion of you, checking your gun safe, getting character references, speaking to your shooting club, and doing whatever else he deems necessary to confirm that you are an upstanding member of society and a genuine sport-shooting enthusiast before recommending you for a licence. The process could take up to a year.

When it comes to children and shotguns, the law is quite bizarre and even surprises most people in England, and that is, there is no minimum age for applying for a shotgun certificate. The law does prohibit children from using the weapons without supervision of an adult though, up until they are fifteen years old. That suited Osric and me just fine, and there were lots of adults around when I needed one.

Pheasant carried by the neck.

I loved game-bird shooting, and we found ourselves cramming in as much as we could during the short season, starting with grouse on the twelfth of August, known as the Glorious Twelfth, and going through to January or early February. We didn't seem to even notice the cold and often gloomy winter days because of shooting, especially when I was rough shooting for pheasant or partridge with Osric.

We often visited Scotland and the Scottish Highlands on the Glorious Twelfth for the start of the season. Cold, gloomy weather set the scene as we walked the Scottish moors with pointer dogs in search of grouse. It always amazed me how the dogs would go "on point," having almost miraculously detected these game birds, with us looking on disbelievingly. Then suddenly, grouse would rise above the heath and beautiful purple Scottish heather, and dart away at high speed. Even with the assistance of our furry friends, grouse would often evade us.

The frenetic shooting season didn't give us enough time to even think about polo, let alone miss it. Come March, we began thinking about spring and summer sports, the first of which was golf.

Game-bird shooting, something of a tradition in our family, would continue to be an important part of my life's journey, and at times it also played a part in my growing up.

CHAPTER 4
GOLF

GOLF WAS ANOTHER sport I carried all through my life. This is not surprising, given that my mother was an exceptional golfer who competed in numerous pro-am tournaments and often won against the professionals. Her having a scratch handicap, I referred to her as being semi-professional.

From when I was about the age of six, my mother coached me on the home polo field. I was able to confidently hit all the clubs in my bag, including the sand wedge, using the horse exercise sandtrack around the perimeter of the field as a bunker. She would place horse water buckets at different places around the expansive 300- by 200-yard polo field and have me select which club to use, then practise until she was happy with the result. I can still hear her words, "Get five balls in a row within ten yards of bucket number one, and we can move to the next. Groove your swing and your distance and you will be halfway there."

"What's the other half?" I once asked, a little perplexed.

"It's the most difficult part, Sunbeam. It's your mind. That is the difference between a good golfer and a top golfer."

It made perfect sense why she was a top golfer.

The best part of my game was undoubtedly my driving. If you knew me, you would understand why. Apart from the satisfaction of watching a good drive sail into the distance, there was another reason.

I was about fourteen or fifteen years old when I asked, "Mum, what distance would be considered a good drive for a man?"

"Around three hundred yards," was my mum's reply.

"Do you think I will one day drive that far?" I asked.

My Rude Awakening

"Of course, but only five percent of male golfers can achieve that distance," she said as a matter of fact.

Coincidently, that was the length of a polo pitch. From there on out, driving the full length of our polo field was a goal that beckoned me every day. I was not going to stop trying until I achieved it.

A story that epitomises my early introduction into golf started with my mother and me speaking about polo and how one practises for it, which is to "stick and ball," something often not understood by people not involved with polo.

"Stick and balling is similar to what one does on a golf driving range, except you are mounted on a horse when hitting your ball," my mother remarked.

I responded, "Yes, but you are cantering, often galloping, using a longer stick, holding it with just one hand because your other one has a fistful of reins, trying to control your leaping horse, *and* it is a moving ball that you are trying to hit." I grinned. "And don't forget, Mum, if you're in a match, you have to try and do all of that while someone is either attempting to obstruct your shot by hooking your stick with his or riding you off with his horse." I said, trying to make the point of how difficult polo was, even though my mother knew very well the intricacies of the sport. "No comparison, Mum," I finished off smugly.

"Oh, all right then, smart aleck. If it is so easy, then I challenge you."

"Okay," I said, still smiling.

By the time of my mother's challenge, I was in my late teens and had achieved my goal of driving the length of the polo field and could comfortably out-drive her, even though we had never actually played against each other.

I was looking forward to our challenge.

Interestingly, I had never played at Wentworth Club and couldn't even remember when we had last been there. It may have been for a lunch when I was much younger, and I was not really paying attention. Given the contest that lay ahead, I was paying full attention now.

The first thing that struck me was the green lawns on each side of the road leading up to the grand entrance. A fitting lead-in to the imposing buildings beyond that looked more like a castle, complete with gun turrets

37

rather than a golf club. As my mother neared the big gates and guardhouse, she slowed down slightly, and when the gatekeeper recognised her, he promptly lifted the boom. She drove through the full car park, and my chest expanded another inch as she turned into a reserved prime parking spot that read:

Ladies Captain

F. D. E. Featherstone

Smiling, I looked at my mother's initials for Frances Dulce and Edwina, the feminine for two of my grandfather's names. *She must've been his favourite.*

We had no sooner parked than a caddy was at the back of the car.

"Hello, Marcin," my mother greeted him. "We will be taking a golf cart today."

"No problem, ma'am," Marcin responded in a thick Polish accent. "It will be a pleasure to take a cart and your golf bags down to the first tee, ma'am."

"Thank you, Marcin," my mother replied smiling happily.

As we went about our preparation, she was greeted by other members who clearly held her in high regard. I'd never really understood my mother's captaincy or scratch handicap status until this moment. I was seeing her in an environment where she reigned supreme. Feelings of admiration and pride permeated through me as I absorbed it all.

Walking down to the first tee of Wentworth's West Course, golf cart with golf bags parked to the side, I was feeling a little less confident about our challenge. *Oh well,* I thought. *If I win my fair share of holes, it will be fine.*

"Take it away, Sunbeam," my mother said with her 3 wood in hand.

I looked at my yardage card, wondering why she was not going for her driver. No question, it was a par four with 420 yards tee to pin, no obstacles for the next 350 yards, and a rough on the right. I confidently took out my driver and addressed the ball. My mother's coaching voice crept into the back of my mind. *"Check setup and direction, relax your shoulders, breathe, don't look up to see your wonderful shot. That's the best way to leave your ball on the tee box."* And then I remembered her last bit of advice before I began my backswing. *"If you're going to force, rather take a 7 iron. It goes farther than a forced driver."*

I was feeling good. My confidence was not unfounded. I executed one of my best drives, coming up short of a water obstacle, probably 110 yards from the pin. I looked at my mother and was surprised she wasn't more impressed.

She hit her 3 wood perfectly, as I'd seen a thousand times before. *A little too far left,* I thought. I remembered one of her little mantras, *"Groove your swing, groove your distances, engage your brain. Your confidence will grow, and that's what makes a great golfer."*

Right then, I was around 60 yards ahead of her ball. If that meant I was in the lead, I would soon discover it would last for just that one ball.

For my second shot, I was faced with a water obstacle between me and the elongated green. It ran from my left to right, where it dropped off aggressively, and behind it lay an arrangement of bunkers. With my next shot, I landed close to the pin, but with so little green to work with, my ball rolled into the bunker.

For my third shot, I nearly knocked myself out. The ball fired back at me after hitting the high lip of the bunker. Rockwell Manor's sand exercise track had nothing like this. Still in the bunker, I knew I had to blast my ball out of the sand and over the raised edge, temporarily forgetting about the water obstacle beyond. No prize for guessing where I ended up.

In contrast, my mother managed the hole beautifully. Having played a little shorter and on the left, her approach to the green was far more strategic. She had the full length of the putting surface to work with. She was on for two, a 5-yard putt lipped out, and then a knock-in for her par.

I very quickly learnt what a bogey was. Pity I had to start with the double variety.

When we finished the first nine holes, I was fourteen shots over par. My short game had let me down enormously. I could hear her voice in my head saying, *"Drive for show, putt for dough."* My mother was two shots under par.

I was so hoping we'd be going home, but I knew my mother. We never ended anything on a note like that.

At the halfway station, a large Cornish pasty with gravy and Worcester sauce, washed down with a Steelworks drink, made me feel slightly better. My mother had a tuna salad and a rock shandy—soda water and bitters.

Between bites she said, "I left you to your own devices for the first nine holes, Sunbeam."

That was obvious and I knew why. I had been precocious, and my first lesson today was to be more humble.

Then with a thoughtful expression, one I knew well and that it usually meant she had something prophetic to say, she continued, "Sunbeam, there was something I noticed that definitely added a few extra strokes to your round."

"What was that, Mum?" I asked, more than happy with any advice to improve my score.

"Well, you need to always remember what's behind you is behind you. Let it go," she said. "Doing so will free you to focus and commit to the next stroke or hole, unburdened by what happened in the past."

My mother did not understand the smile that crept onto my face, so I answered her inquiring look. "That's what granddad used to say to me, Mum."

Now she smiled. "That's because it's the truth, Sunbeam, so practice it." She wasn't finished there. "Master that and it will make the world of difference." She looked at me as I absorbed her words. "And when you have done something silly, don't admonish yourself for more than five seconds. Then work out where you went wrong. Common sense really."

That made me think about something else she would say. *"Common sense is the least common of all sense, so much so it is sometimes mistaken for genius."* I was smiling again.

She carried on. "You can do that for your successes too. A quick mental pat on your back and then analyse what you did right. It is a lesson of life. Learn from your failures and successes, then move on. Always remember, there is nothing gained from dwelling on the past. But I don't mind telling you, I saw enough to know that you could become a really good golfer," she said reassuringly. "If you want it badly enough. Now let's go and have some fun on the second half."

The second nine was very different. My mother started by saying I had remembered most of her coaching, except just one thing. Then, after explaining to me how each hole we arrived at should be played and why, the words that became the mantra for the rest of the afternoon were, "Engage brain, Sunbeam, and manage your mind, your emotions."

Her view was that anyone could hit a golf ball (a bit of an exaggeration), but few people had the mental capacity. Her words were, "Don't overestimate yourself. Don't be too brave. But you can't be too timid."

Crikey, I'm lost.

For the second nine holes, I scored six over par, which included one birdie. That birdie would definitely have me coming back for more. I couldn't help thinking if I had done that for the first nine holes, it could've, should've been a good first round even if I were being coached. A difficult lesson in behaviour, and a wonderful lesson in golf.

Added to that, I got an appreciation for some avian life. I was familiar with partridge, pheasant, and grouse, but now I could add birdies to the list. I saw them on the second, ninth, eleventh, fifteenth (mine on a tough par four), and the last one was on the seventeenth hole, but my highlight of the day was when I saw an eagle, my mother's, on the par five twelfth hole. She said *her* highlights were my halving (drawing) two holes with her on the back nine and beating her with my birdie on the fifteenth.

But my mother refused to show me even one bogie of her own. Yes, she shot five under for the round.

I had been humbled and then coached and uplifted but not humiliated. For my mother, the former were fine, but humiliation was not. I had a feeling that was the reason she had opted not to take golf caddies that day but our own golf cart instead.

I had discovered in no uncertain terms that hitting a golf ball perfectly was not enough to do well at golf. And unlike a perfectly flat polo field, no hurdles to surprise one, a golf course is a very different proposition designed to challenge players in every which way, using all the obstacles in its repertoire and tempting you to do precisely the wrong thing.

It is fair to say I enjoyed my mother teaching me the craft of golf and it did become one of my sports, giving me a lot of pleasure all through my life, especially in my business career. Secretly, I think she had hoped I was going to be a top golfer, but the allure and adrenaline of polo was just too strong. I was never going to put in the time required to reach her level. I did discover later though, that a single-digit golf handicap, which I did achieve, was more than respectable.

    I didn't play often, but when I did, I had no difficulty beating my friends. And no matter that I could out-drive my mum, I had to admit that the next time I beat her would be the first.

CHAPTER 5
POLO

For as long as I can remember, my greatest love has been polo. One of the world's oldest-known team sports, polo had been in our family for generations, so it was only natural that I would also adopt this sport from an early age.

Few sports are as widely recognised but fundamentally misunderstood as polo. Even people who have been around horses their entire lives know little about the sport. Many have suggested there is nothing subtle about the game, describing it as "in-your-face" aggressive horsemanship at its best.

For those of us who love the sport, polo epitomises many things. Power. Balance. Grace. Skill. Coordination. Reflexes. Teamwork. Decision-making. Strategy. Poetry in motion perhaps, and chills and spills aplenty.

Polo looks crazy and intense because it is. It is said that it takes years to learn, decades to master, and a lifetime to perfect. It is truly a horse sport all of its own. I cannot begin to think of anything, in any sport, that is more complicated, challenging, or engrossing.

At a full gallop, shoulder to shoulder, your opponent trying to get the better of you, and you hit a perfect shot—the ball no bigger than one used in cricket—that is an adrenaline rush like no other. The combined athleticism of horse and rider, unavoidably sharing each other's sweat in this dangerous, high-contact sport, is exhilarating.

I embraced it with a fearless passion despite my mother often sternly telling me, "Don't do that, Sunbeam. You will break your neck."

Our family's generational interest in polo started with our home, Rockwell Manor in Berkshire, the middle of polo country in England. It was feted as a rather grand establishment while quite a new estate in

English terms. It was built by my great-grandfather and completed in 1880. Granddad was born there in 1889 and responsible for remodelling part of it after the First World War, around 1926.

It was a vast 36,000 square foot, two-storey Georgian Palladian manor house complete with twelve bedroom suites overlooking its own polo field on extensive grounds bordering a forest.

It was before I was born that my retired grandfather handed over the reins of Rockwell Manor to my dad, perhaps literally and figuratively, and the estate moved from being the Apsley residence to being the Featherstone residence. By then, with the changing times, it was superfluous to have nine guest suites, three of the twelve suites used by our family, but ideal if you were intending to accommodate a polo team and their manager. My father undertook a remodelling and further development of Rockwell Manor that included turning the one wing into polo player and manager accommodations; upgrading the field into a world-class surface and adding a number of sporting elements, including squash, tennis, and beach-volleyball courts; and developing two staff houses for estate grounds and house staff. But the most wonderful element he added was a stable block that housed forty horses.

This was the start of Rockwell Manor becoming a more serious participant in the burgeoning world of professional polo. It then became a Rockwell Manor tradition to invite a team from a foreign country like the USA, Australia, South Africa, or Canada, or an eighteen- to twenty-goal team—always tough competition—from Argentina. Once, there was even a team from Barbados. We would arrange a series of matches against various teams, the highlight being the matches against Rockwell Manor on our home field.

This became ever more exciting as I progressed through my teenage years and was able to enjoy all that the new Rockwell Manor had to offer.

It was when I turned sixteen that I began to realise I was advancing along the Featherstone cycle of life. History had already quite clearly laid out the progression. My parents would eventually move into Winston Cottage, and I would take over the main homestead. Hopefully, my children would have a similar relationship with my parents as I had enjoyed with Granddad. But as they say, only time would tell.

My Rude Awakening

In proving this point, on my sixteenth birthday we were at the dinner table and my mum asked, "How does it feel to be sixteen?" A rhetorical question that had an obvious answer.

I didn't have a chance to even attempt to reply before my dad asked, "How would you like to move into the polo manager's suite in the north wing?"

I was ecstatic and could easily answer my mum's question now. It was *great* being sixteen! Were they allowing me to spread my wings and start the transition into young adulthood? Or perhaps they had heard me masturbating once too often, my long showers a dead giveaway? Actually, the one portends the other, so I shouldn't have been surprised. That's rude, I know. But a reality of life.

Apart from its expansive extent, Rockwell Manor had two enormous upstairs and downstairs patios. We could easily accommodate 200 or more people on game days, overlooking our polo field. Visitors were often amazed at the size of the field at roughly five football pitches. This is necessary, of course, because polo horses can gallop up to forty miles per hour in play, traversing up and down the 300-yard length as the teams attack and then counterattack. Whilst it was mostly used selectively for high-goal matches, on weekends, we often invited friends to use our home field for practises or a bit of stick and ball.

My mother's inclination to be hospitable meant there was always a breakfast buffet set out on one of the expansive patios so visitors could conveniently get something to eat before or just after riding or practising.

For invitation matches at home, special attention was paid to the catering for our guests, with the finest cuisine and vintage French champagne, none of which was of any interest to me. Our guests would typically come for breakfast or brunch beforehand. Fabrizio and his kitchen staff, sometimes with complementing outside catering, would lay out a delicious buffet and be on hand to provide all aspects of the meal.

It was all quite normal, until before a practice match my father came in asking for lobster frittata, complete with beluga caviar, fresh spring onions and chives, and Dom Pérignon champagne to wash it down. That took it to another level. While it would only be late morning, flowing champagne was quite normal for us.

"An effervescent start for a sparkling day," was his toast.

By the time I was seventeen years old, I was already a competitive, rising player. I spent endless weekend hours at the stables when not playing polo. As much as I loved rugby, cricket, and track and field athletics, polo somehow got under my skin like no other sport. A large part of that was the horses, which I was passionate about.

The top polo horses, also referred to as "ponies" in days gone by, are nearly all thoroughbred ex-racehorses of which more than 70 percent are mares, purely because they are nimbler-footed and a lot braver than geldings. My dad would say it was as if geldings, "do not have the balls for the game," the depletion of testosterone production ultimately weighing on the courage and ability of these equine athletes. A literal and figurative statement if ever there was one. On the other hand, stallions cannot be used because they are far too strong and powerful and do not normally succumb to the demands of the rider.

My father and I each had our own string of ten high-goal horses—the most superb equine athletes imaginable—plus twenty other top horses so that we were able to mount a third, and sometimes even a fourth, polo player.

We would seasonally bring in a top player from Argentina with a six- to eight-goal handicap. As I got older and my dad started stepping back, we brought nine- and even ten-goal players to Rockwell Manor. My father was well handicapped as a two-goal player and, as a teen, I was rated at two, going on three. The fourth team member would invariably be our polo manager unless the goal level of the tournament meant we had to find a local player with the right handicap to complete our team.

Speaking of our polo manager, Guy Watkins was a very valued team member, a combined role that was not uncommon in polo. He was playing off a handicap of four, had just turned thirty-two, and was well on his way to attaining at least the six-goal level. Apart from being a top manager and a very solid polo player, his greatest attribute was his expert ability in working with horses, something he did whenever he had completed his other duties. We would regularly see Guy on the polo field either schooling and bringing on a young horse or working on a weakness he had detected on one of the older horses, or just practising to improve his own game. He took great

My Rude Awakening

pride in "his" string of our forty horses and was always watching their every move, whether it was in a match or in training.

"Who are you riding, Guy?" I'd ask.

"It's Noble Wine. Lew played her in the fifth on Saturday. She wasn't stopping and turning to the left as fluidly as I would've liked," he explained. "Just doing some schooling before Grace gives her a bit of physiotherapy."

As I got older, I took an ever-increasing interest in the behind-the-scenes activities of the Rockwell Manor Polo Team. It was probably no coincidence that this was around the same time my father began stepping even further back.

Once when I was around seventeen years old, I sat down in front of him while he was reading his newspaper, wanting to go through all the daily activities around the stables. "Dad," I said a little louder than normal.

He lowered his newspaper to listen to what I had to say.

"Have you ever analysed all the things Guy does during the course of the day?" I asked him pointedly. "Do you know that he is up at about five o'clock, checking on the horses' early-morning preparation, feeding, et cetera? Then he begins the exercise routine on the sand track. After that he goes through the veterinary list with Grace, which, as you know, takes one to two hours every day. Sometimes the farrier is there. Then he moves on to schooling horses. He has amazing skills, especially with the young ones. And it doesn't stop. I think he has his first break at about two in the afternoon, *nine hours* after he started." I stopped rambling for a moment, before deciding to add, "He takes it easy for about two hours and then he's back again to begin the evening preparation." I looked up to see if I was making an impression.

My dad had listened intently to what I'd said, but his short answer surprised me. "Son, you must not lose Guy."

I was a little taken aback. Was this the first sign of him handing over the reins to me? An excited little tremor reverberated through my stomach. It was completely normal that I should continue the tradition and one day take over from my father, as he had done with his father-in-law before that. There would be a difference though. Under my stewardship, I would want Rockwell Manor Polo Team to compete at the very highest level and win, hopefully often.

Then moving on to something else, I had noticed how Guy interacted with our young female vet, Grace Brayers. She didn't work in our yard full time, but with our having such a big string, she spent a lot of time with us. Nobody was complaining, especially Guy, because she was so good at what she did. He had recently given her the responsibility of our horse nutrition programme as well. What with top-grade rolled oats, bran, wheatgerm, full-fat soya, pine nuts, and sunflower seeds, there was no reason to go to the main house for breakfast. *If you're a horse, you can't do any better than ending up at Rockwell Manor,* I thought happily.

"You know, Dad, I wouldn't be surprised if Guy and Grace got married one day."

My father lowered his newspaper and said "Gosh, I have had the same thought! They'd make a good team." And then he got back to his *Financial Times* again.

Clearly, I wasn't the only one who had seen the spark.

I loved it when Guy sent the entire string of forty horses out for their morning exercise. Ten of his grooms, each riding a horse and leading three others, would do a strong trot around the perimeter of the polo field on the custom-built silica sand track, giving each horse a thorough workout on the heavy surface. This routine normally started at around six-thirty in the morning and lasted about twenty-five or thirty minutes, finishing off with the horses being hosed down—weather permitting. Guy would often ride a younger horse on the polo field, just inside this cavalry, conditioning the younger one for when she would begin exercising on the track with the others. At the same time, he would be keeping a beady eye on how each of the main string was responding to the exercise.

Doing well in the sport nearly always boiled down to horsepower, and having so many good horses was one of the reasons for our success in fourteen- to eighteen-goal-level tournaments, the sum of the four players' individual handicaps. This was just slightly below the twenty-two-goal level that we would need to compete in the Queen's Cup, one of my secret goals for the future. My father decided that when I achieved a four-goal handicap, we could start planning our entry into that most prestigious competition. I loved the thought of Rockwell Manor fielding a Queen's Cup or Gold Cup team and playing alongside an Argentinian ten-goaler, the top handicap.

My Rude Awakening

I have said how important the polo horses were and how they contributed to our success; however, I should include a note about Argentina, Argentinian polo players and grooms, and the influence they have had on the modern game.

Polo's origins trace back to 600 BC to AD 100 in central Asia before migrating west to Persia (modern Iran). It was part sport, part war training and later used extensively to prepare army cavalries. Introduced into England in 1834, it only made its way to Argentina just before the 1900s and was played there exclusively by British aristocrats. It was only in 1921, with the formation of their association, that polo became available to Argentinians.

It is fair to say that the rest of the world—wherever polo was played—had a significant head start on the Argentinians. But now here's the rub, which will go some way towards explaining the dominance unparalleled in any other sport, that this country and its players have had on the game of polo. Today, if Argentina were to field six teams, each with four players of Argentinian origin only, the team that came last in that six-team event would beat a "rest-of-the-world-combined" team by such an appreciable margin that it would not be a game worth watching. The first thing one asks is, "Why?" That's both impossible to answer and very easy. It's everything. Firstly, the incredible Argentinian Criollo horses, in recent times crossed with thoroughbreds. Then take their never-ending flat grasslands, especially in the centrally located La Pampa, with rich, fertile soil and an ideal grass species that most often only needs to be mown and you have a polo field. The value of this should not be underestimated, considering each polo field is roughly five football pitches. This amounts to a polo industry probably as big as the rest of the world combined, resulting in an abundance of professional participation. Then add to that the athletic flair of Argentinian men—just think of soccer for a pointer—and it begins to make sense. The moment you have Argentinian influence in your team, you are *in the game*. Importing players from Argentina always gives a team an advantage. I can still hear my father saying excitedly, *"Son, I have found a brilliant young six-goal player, going on eight. I think we should get him."*

It was always a highlight playing against Highgrove Polo Team—the team of the then Prince Charles and very young Princes William and Harry.

Not that it was ever a very competitive game. As much as they may have liked it to be played in the "normal" competitive manner, it never was. Competing teams could not help but approach ride-offs more tenderly and generally give the Highgrove Polo Team the benefit of the doubt in the various phases of the game.

Speaking about the royals makes me think of a story I once overheard my father telling some friends.

He had gone to a luncheon and was listening to a conversation an American gentleman was having with someone sitting across the table from him, about the popularity of polo in England. Evidently, appalled at the costs involved, the visitor said in a pompous, facetious tone that it was clearly only a sport for "kings and cunts." Not wanting to let on that I knew what they were speaking about while he recounted the story, I feigned ignorance, keeping a deadpan face. My father was not going to just sit there quietly and take this indirect abuse, so he tapped the man on the shoulder and told him that he, in fact, played polo. Without any hesitation, the American turned to him and said, "Oh, what country are you the king of?" They both laughed raucously and ended up becoming good friends.

To some, polo's appeal is the exclusivity, the fancy showboating, the champagne, the bling, the fancy cars, the mystique of dashing professional polo players with foreign accents wearing tight white jeans. There is a strong scent of money around this "sport of kings," as it is among the most expensive to play, especially competitively, and it always seems to attract the attention of polo groupies.

It was different for our family. Having been involved in polo from its earliest days in England when it was primarily a military or farmer sport, we were not in polo for the glitz and the glamour. For a time, my father and especially my grandfather would look on in bemusement at where the modern game had gone with its newfound professional elements and, even more so, the trendy socialite tag that was now part of the game.

Whether it was Guards, Cowdray Park, Beaufort, or any of the other clubs around Berkshire, Surrey, and Gloucestershire, they were all familiar to me and I was comfortable at all of them.

I suppose it wasn't all perfect though, and there is a saying that explains some of the frustrations. It goes like this:

My Rude Awakening

> Polo is a gentlemen's game played by hooligans, on the
> far side of the field, on a horse called Fucking Bitch.

A rather rude expression but an accepted one. As long as it is said in an opulent English tone, nobody would bat an eye. My mother wouldn't have agreed. "That's more than just rude," she would've said.

A word often heard around polo is *ridiculous*. Two conversations that had taken place over two consecutive weeks with my good polo-playing friend Malcolm Barwick (Malcs), the captain of the Balthazar polo team, will explain one of the reasons the word *ridiculous* fits so well.

"Good morning, Malcs. Are you up for tennis this morning?" I asked him.

"Absolutely, Charles. The usual, Wentworth tennis courts in an hour." Malcs knew they also played tennis at the famous golf club and that my mother was an honorary life member. "Perhaps afterwards we can have lunch in the clubhouse with whoever is able to join us," he said, making sure the logistics were clear.

"Perfect. I'll bring two tubes of balls," I added, not wanting us to forget anything. We were ready.

Then, the following week I asked him, "Is Balthazar up for a game of polo?"

"Absolutely, Charles," was his same reply. "When would you like to do it?"

In stark contrast to the ease and quickness of arranging the tennis match, we began planning our polo encounter.

"Well, it is a little short notice for tomorrow, so how about Sunday?" I replied, already thinking about the logistics.

"At Rockwell Manor, I assume?" Malcs asked.

"Of course," I affirmed.

"Since we are saving the £5,000 green fee, Balthazar will arrange the two umpires and goal judges and pick up their costs. I think it is about £2,500 for them," Malcs replied. "And I know your mum will do some great catering, to say nothing of your dad. He's always so generous with his champagne stocks. Yes, a good deal for Balthazar."

51

"So how many horses will you be bringing and what vehicles?" I asked, thinking about parking and paddock allocation.

"The normal. For the six chukkas, we will have eight or nine horses for each of our four players, plus two for one umpire we mount. You can mount the other umpire. So, let's say thirty-eight, maybe forty horses for us," Malcs replied.

"And they will all fit into your two pantechnicons?" I asked, needing to confirm these arrangements so I could advise our estate staff and they could make parking arrangements.

"Oh yes, and we will probably manage with six to eight grooms, but I will let our polo manager, Phillip Sergeant, worry about that. Oh, and, Charles, please don't forget our two drivers and co-drivers, just so your gate house has the numbers."

"Okay, got it," I replied, tallying up the head count. "I have fourteen Balthazar support staff, including your manager, and I guess you'll be bringing your vet?" That reminded me to ask Grace Brayers to make a note about the nutrition preparation for Guy, not that he was a forgetful manager but that I was being thorough. "Will you have a safety vehicle ahead?" I asked as an afterthought.

"Yes, I think so. I will let you know and confirm. Oh, and Charles, do you have rolled oats and chopped dry lucerne? It will save Phillip having to organise feed for the horses as well."

"Yes, no problem, and we have all the electrolytes and supplements to replenish them after the match. Maybe get Phillip to check with Guy. Ah, and don't forget your kit, Malcs," I said teasingly, because he once did exactly that and we hadn't let him live it down. "Remember, two helmets, two pairs of gloves, your boots, knee guards, probably twelve polo mallets, four each of fifty-one inch, fifty-two inch, and fifty-three inch, the three common sizes."

Anyone listening to these two friends arranging to play some sport together would concur that for this reason alone, polo was "ridiculous." Perhaps my dad's new American friend had a point about polo only being for "kings and cunts."

So yes, Polo too was another family tradition, perhaps the most noteworthy along with business. Not only did this tradition continue unabated with my generation, but unquestionably the level and competitiveness of our involvement advanced considerably during my adulthood and under my stewardship. To say it played a leading role in many of my adventures would be an understatement.

As much as school taught me discipline, my sports did so too, along with teamwork. I loved the camaraderie with my friends, possibly more so than most, given I was an only child.

CHAPTER 6
EIGHTEEN

MY OTHER OBSESSION was flying. I just had to fly, which was no surprise since my family had flown for generations. With my uncle and great-uncles having served in the Royal Air Force, there was always a sense of inevitability that I would develop an interest in aviation.

Thanks to my father's willingness to traipse me around the country, I never missed an air show. By the time I was fifteen or sixteen, I knew all the aircraft museums and could identify most fixed-wing aircraft and helicopters (or rotary-wing aircraft, as they were also known). Apart from accompanying me to the Farnborough Airshow in England, my parents took me to Le Bourget Airport for the Paris Air Show every alternate year. I really enjoyed this, even if it meant I would also have to take part in a few cultural activities.

"Right, Sunbeam, you can't have planes and helicopters every day. We are in one of the most exciting, artistically rich cities of Europe. Today we are going to take in the Louvre," my mother would say.

As much as I didn't like looking at paintings all day, I knew it was our agreement and so did not say a word. I remember on one occasion I saw an amazing exhibition of Leonardo da Vinci's works. I found his drawings of flying machines particularly astounding because even though he lived in the early 1500s, he seemed to understand rotary-flight aerodynamics.

When I was old enough, my parents would leave me at Le Bourget to consume the world of aviation whilst they went shopping on the Avenue des Champs-Élysées, sending a car to collect me from the prescribed place at the prescribed time. I would get back to the Four Seasons Hotel George

Cinq, having done a fair amount of shopping of my own, which included models of aeroplanes and helicopters that I couldn't wait to build once I got back home and add to the rest of my collection.

I started my private pilot licence (PPL) on a small aeroplane trainer when I was sixteen, having to wait until seventeen to get the licence, but it was helicopters that held a real fascination for me. I remember my first experience of flying in a Bell 47G as if it were yesterday. Mid-flight, the instructor allowed me to take the dual controls of cyclic, collective, and rudder pedals. I already had a good understanding of the flight controls, basic aerodynamic principles, and several technical aspects, and I was driven by an insatiable passion for these machines. I gingerly tried coordinating the opposing forces, a feature of helicopter piloting, and as I relaxed, my tentative approach gave way to my feeling like the aircraft was an extension of me. When I began to control the Bell 47 that day, I knew right then that I would not stop until I became a helicopter pilot.

Whilst I grew up in a family where there was wealth and success, as I progressed through my teenage years it became more and more important for me to find my own identity. Was that my reason for wanting to go into the RAF and become an attack helicopter combat pilot, where success came down to just one thing—one's performance? Very likely.

No amount of money can buy you a career in the RAF. You are judged purely on your ability, your courage, and your appetite for facing danger.

I loved my family and respected and admired the traditions and benefits of our privilege, but I was determined to make my own way in life. It was probably this that drove my ambition, that made me push myself harder than most people.

By the time I was sixteen I yearned for my first car, seeing it as the key to unsupervised independence. Anything would do. Give me a Volkswagen Beetle, anything, but it was still two years away.

Then, on my eighteenth birthday, my mother lectured me even before I knew what my gift was. "If you are not responsible and don't behave like an adult, we will take it back," she said.

With that, my parents gave me the most wonderful gift—a beetle, but not the Volkswagen variety. I was given my father's old Porsche 911 Carrera 4S, with its amazing race pedigree. Even if it was something my mother referred to as, "Dad's midlife crisis"—which my dad downplayed by saying his Bentley and Range Rover were far more to his liking—it was unquestionably the most exciting gift I had ever been given. It was midnight blue, which added to its understated look. It really was very low-key, but it performed like a true race car. With Porsche's newly introduced four-wheel-drive feature, it stuck to the road as if it were on railway tracks. And the feature I enjoyed the most—the extra freedom it gave me.

Looking at the instruments, I figured I had racked up more than half of the low mileage registering on the odometer. It had started with my dad teaching me to drive in it, pretending not to notice my mother scowling at my lessons being done in a Porsche. Thereafter, he allowed me to drive his car on the country back roads, without a licence, mind you. In fairness, it had always been way beyond my father's scope of driving ability.

Oh yes, and I did behave like an adult. An *eighteen*-year-old adult. It is safe to say that I loved driving…fast.

It is also safe to say that my mother hated me driving…fast.

My parents also gave me another very special gift that day, handmade Argentinian Fagliano polo boots made of horsehide. These boots were coveted by every polo player, and now I understood the foot and leg moulding my dad had put me through almost a year earlier.

Another amazing gift was a Breitling Navitimer watch from Aunt Edwina and Uncle Alexander Apsley, my mother's twin who was a pilot in the Royal Air Force during the Second World War. He had always been quite circumspect about telling me "war stories," but he did give me a feel for Air Force life that resonated with me. Because of this, from an early age I imagined that I'd one day go to the Air Force as well. My mother often spoke about her brother and the Air Force with an amount of reverence, which was probably why she ultimately agreed to me going into the RAF, albeit with some reservation. And for his part, Uncle Alexander loved the thought of my "continuing the family tradition" and becoming a pilot.

A Porsche, Faglianos, and a Breitling. What a birthday! Was that cool or what?

Sadly, I felt I fit into the "or what" category. If a girl looked at me, I would immediately blush and look away, sometimes peering over my shoulder to see who she might have been looking at, never believing it could've been me. A symptom of going to an all-boys school, I guess.

One morning, I had been at Royal Berkshire doing a little early-morning clay-pigeon shooting before I was to attend a polo practise at the Guards Polo grounds. Heading over to the club, I chose a route of endless twists and turns. I loved racing my car through the narrow, winding country roads heavily shrubbed on both sides with thick, emerald-green vegetation, sometimes overhead too, which gave the impression of driving through a tunnel of hedges and trees. I was loving the drive when, in my rearview mirror, I noticed the unmistakable sleek, angled lines of a rather gaudy lime-green Lamborghini Countach. I was driving along at some speed, a magnet to its macho driver, complete with his slicked-back hairstyle, muscles bulging from his tight T-shirt, and Barbie-doll lady friend alongside.

Not from these parts, I thought.

It was no surprise that, with a show of his car's impressive straight-line speed, he overtook me. I often attracted these would-be street racers who I typically ignored but not always. This was to be one of the latter occasions. As he drove by, his lady friend stuck her hand out the window and gave me a, "We are better than you, you silly little Porsche," wave. While his car was notably quicker than mine, that was in a straight line and you would be hard-pressed to find even 200 yards of straight line on the country roads of western Berkshire, especially for the next eight to ten miles. And I knew these roads like the back of my hand.

I came up behind him, making as if I were trying to overtake him when, in fact, I was just biding my time while getting his racing spirit going. We were yet to get to the really twisty, winding stretch I knew lay ahead. I grinned, thinking this could be fun. In less than a mile, there would be an ideal place for me to look across an open clearing to check for oncoming traffic. You wouldn't know a road was there unless you saw vehicle rooftops. If the coast was clear, then three bends beyond that, I could nip past him at the start of some treacherous twists and turns.

He was loving that I could seemingly not get past him, with his lady friend glancing over her shoulder as if to really make the point. As I came up alongside the opening, I looked across the field and saw no moving rooftops. *All clear. Brilliant,* I thought. We rounded the next two bends, and he lifted off the gas pedal, wary of oncoming traffic. I pressed hard, knowing it was unlikely, and passed him in a flash. *Too easy.* I didn't immediately draw away from him, making him think he had a chance of regaining his lead. I watched his lady friend egging him on, then tired of watching them, I started ripping through the corners, a tightening in my gut and adrenaline pumping through my veins. With the unmistakable sound of the Porsche flat-six engine singing in my ears and my four-wheel-drive traction responding to my demands, I drew away effortlessly and put more and more distance between us.

I couldn't help thinking about an article I'd read in a motoring magazine in which the journalist reviewed several high-end motor vehicles. What I enjoyed most about this particular reviewer was that he would close by including an all-encompassing throwaway line. I remembered for the Rolls-Royce Phantom, his closing remark was, "Get out of my way, little man," which did seem to describe the character of the vehicle, with its oversized front grille, and perhaps it was a reflection of the owner's character as well. *Probably the reason my father preferred Bentleys,* I thought idly. The funniest one though, was for none other than the Lamborghini Countach. Here, his closing sentence was, "Gentlemen of the adult entertainment industry, your car has arrived."

Touché. I chuckled.

Just outside Calcot, about fifteen miles up the road, I pulled into a petrol station. Once I had finished refuelling my car, I strolled into the quick stop store to get a bottle of water and pay my bill. As I was returning to my vehicle, who should arrive but the unmistakable garish green Lamborghini. I glanced at my watch and smiled, neither consciously intended nor missed by the occupants of the new arrival. As I sped off, I couldn't help very consciously jutting my hand out of the window and giving them a reciprocal wave.

It was no surprise that the moment I had completed my A-levels, I applied to join the RAF. Because I was not yet eighteen, I needed my parents' consent. My father did not hesitate, knowing it was my passion, and that little would stop me anyway. My mother knew this too, and even though the Soviet-Afghan and Iran-Iraq War was escalating conflict in the Middle East, making her very hesitant, she finally agreed.

In the intervening time before basic training started, I enrolled in university to start an undergraduate degree in economics, business science, and management information systems. Although normally an ambitious undertaking—simultaneously starting a bachelor's degree and an Air Force career—I felt confident about it. On all fronts, I would be learning about subjects I enjoyed and found interesting. In just under a month, I would be going to the RAF.

Having received my driving licence and going to the Air Force, I felt that I had now grown up. While this was clearly debatable, there was no question that my learning years lay ahead. The Air Force and university were clear indicators of that. What I didn't realise was that there would be a whole lot more education in store for me.

CHAPTER 7
RAF SHAWBURY

THERE WAS A long way to go before I would get to RAF Shawbury. First up was RAF Halton to begin my basic training shortly after I turned eighteen. Looking back now, the first three months in the military were a blur. It was a tough fourteen weeks of rigorous emotional, mental, and physical stress, with the objective of making sure recruits had the mettle to "cut it" if ever they should end up fulfilling an operational role. For example, we would have to wait for permission to eat or go to the toilet and were woken at all hours of the morning, sleep deprived, and told to prepare for inspection in an hour. A lot of the chaps really struggled with this, but I took it all in my stride because I understood they were merely trying to test us. I thought of the part in "If—" where Rudyard Kipling says, *"And so hold on when there is nothing in you—Except the Will which says to them: 'Hold on!'"*

I would not let them break me.

One of the incidents I remember was on the parade ground, when I mistakenly referred to my rifle as my gun. The corporal taking us for drill instructions seized on this as an opportunity to make an example of me. With my rifle in my left hand, I was required to run around the entire parade ground shouting, "This is my rifle, this is my gun. This is for fighting, this is for fun," and each time I said "rifle" and "fighting," I would raise my rifle, and each time I said "gun" or "fun," I was required to grab my crotch. After thirty-odd minutes of this, I was finally allowed to rejoin the company and continue with the drills. Even though I was exhausted, a smile crept onto my face as I thought about how my friends would laugh

My Rude Awakening

when I told them. I just had to make sure the drill instructor did not see my smile.

Basics over, I went on to do several assessments at every level so I could be put in the running for an RAF pilot career. The entry requirements for pilot school were top A-level results, as well as a myriad of other assessments, including medical, and—most importantly, it seemed—a psychometric assessment. I'm not sure of the statistics, but what I do know is that very, very few candidates were selected. Once I jumped through every imaginable hoop the RAF could dream up, I was finally accepted into the programme.

My years at boarding school—the discipline, the need to be organised and often self-reliant and courageous—held me in good stead. I'd hated being away from home in those early years, always keeping a stiff upper lip. But everything had led up to my taking the Air Force challenges in my stride. Perhaps my biggest challenge was finding an obscure parking spot for my Porsche, not wanting my peers to be aware that it was mine now that I was able to start using my own car.

It is safe to say the RAF continued to develop my character, and later on in life it would be the foundation of my work ethic and determination.

I was enrolled into the officer's course at RAF College Cranwell in Lincolnshire to become a pilot officer, the lowest rank. Initially it seemed to be a continuation of basic training, but later it took a different direction. Referred to as Initial Officer Training (IOT), the course lasted about six months and was designed to develop our leadership and management skills. It included fitness development, military training, and academic study, as well as practical outdoor challenges. We learnt military field skills such as first aid, weapons handling, and protection against chemical weapons. We then went on to specialist training before we were streamed into fast jet, multiengine, or helicopter flight training. My time there flew by, and my nineteenth birthday passed without even a thought of celebration.

It was on the IOT course where I first met James Blackwood. As if singling me out, he walked across the room and extended his hand to greet me. "Hi, I'm Jamie Blackwood," he announced confidently.

"How do you do? Charles Featherstone. Nice to meet you," I replied with unintended inbred haughtiness, immediately kicking myself at my formal response.

Judging by his smile, it didn't go unnoticed. He was a slim, athletic chap, standing a little over six feet tall with a thick mop of black hair sweeping back from his temples; hazel-green eyes, under thick eyebrows; a sharp nose; a broad smile revealing large, straight white teeth behind cherry-red lips; and a cleft chin giving him a roguish grin. Tall, dark, and handsome, and he carried it well. He had an air of confidence, bravado even, in a most endearing way though. Unusually for me, I had felt an immediate connection to him and his natural charm and found myself hoping that we would both make it to 60 Squadron.

As it transpired, a few months later I did indeed receive the amazing news I would be going to 60 Squadron at RAF Shawbury for helicopter flight training. My dream had come true. I soaked up the feeling, barely containing the excitement that threatened to explode inside me. Much to my delight—not that I would say anything—Jamie Blackwood was going there too.

RAF Shawbury is a Royal Air Force Helicopter Flying School near the village of Shawbury, Shropshire, in the West Midlands of England. Founded in 1917, it provided helicopter crew training for the tri-services of the United Kingdom.

Along with the usual en-suite apartment accommodation for airmen, non-commissioned officers, and officers, RAF Shawbury boasted enviable sports facilities. This included a gym, sports pitches and courts, a sports hall, weights bay, cardiovascular fitness suite, two squash courts, three tennis courts, five-a-side indoor football pitch, grass pitches, indoor hockey pitch, and high ropes. There was even a highly rated golf club just six miles away, Hawkstone Park Golf Club. But it was looking over at the airfield and the lineup of different helicopters that captivated me most of all. I was in my element.

By the time we began our *ab initio* pilot training at RAF Shawbury, a solid friendship between Jamie Blackwood and me had begun to develop.

This was the start of a completely different phase of my Air Force career.

My Rude Awakening

I went into a programme where I would learn about flying, engines, airframes and instruments, aerodynamics, navigation, military air law, and a whole lot more. I'd thought my private pilot licence on fixed-wing aircraft would help me a little bit, but I was about to enter a vastly different realm. The very first meeting we went to confirmed this.

We shuffled into the presentation room, Jamie and I taking seats next to each other, and the senior officer walked in.

"Welcome to RAF Shawbury, gentlemen. I am Captain Gallagher. To start with, if any of you have previous flying experience or a PPL, raise your hands."

I hesitantly raised mine, one of three fellows to do so.

"Right. What you have learnt is of no consequence here. In fact, it may even be better if you forgot everything you have learnt. Make this a new beginning."

Far from this having disappointed me, I was thrilled at the thought that I would be learning new things. I was consumed and enthralled by it all.

Our helicopter training was initially on the Aérospatiale AS350, commonly known as a Squirrel, or in French, *Écureuil*. There was a clearly laid out syllabus for each day of the eighteen-month schedule, and the classroom programme was as demanding and relentless as anything we had done previously. Admittedly, the hours and hours spent in lectures did get me down a bit, but I knew we would eventually be flying "until you are sick of it," the lecturer had promised.

The flying was even more intense, with the trainees being expected to make noticeable progress every week or face ejection. We were required to advance at an astounding pace towards mastering our skills on these single-jet-turbine helicopters.

Flying a helicopter is a matter of coordinating three primary controls—the cyclic (or joystick), the collective, and the pedals. Straightforward enough. Before that though, you have to learn how to hover.

For the trainee pilot, hovering the helicopter is arguably the most difficult thing to master. Using all the controls to balance opposing forces is easier said than done. It feels a bit like trying to balance on a large ball whilst patting your head and rubbing your stomach. Much to my delight, I discovered there is a great similarity between flying a helicopter and, would you believe, riding a horse. A good horseman feels his steed in his seat and thereby becomes a part of his equine companion. Flying helicopters is about feel, and a lot of that feel is in the pilot's seat, feeling the movements and then controlling the forces with hands, feet, wrists, and even one's fingers, the helicopter becoming an extension of them. Mind you, I felt a lot of that in my seat behind the wheel of my cherished Porsche too. Seems I may have enjoyed doing things that had me "flying by the seat of my pants," you might say.

Whilst many of the trainee pilots took four or five lessons to conquer just this, I got the knack of it after my very first lesson. With my right arm resting lightly on my thigh, steadying my right hand as it caressed the cyclic control, my left hand on the collective, feeding in small power adjustments, my feet gently controlling the tail rotor, countering the torque effect, I smoothly and gently responded to her every move, as I accomplished the motionless dance against opposing forces, that was the hover.

As I completed the exercise, my instructor remarked, "Humph, we don't see that every day," which had me beaming.

As we progressed, so we began to do more and more complicated flight manoeuvres. Unquestionably, the single most exciting aspect for me was the autorotation—landing without an engine. I understood the mechanics perfectly, having gone over it countless times. There was nothing I had looked more forward to. After a thorough final briefing, we headed off to Ternhill Airfield to do the practical.

When it was my turn, the instructor and I climbed aboard the Squirrel and initiated a well-versed start-up. Then, when we had ascended to 1,500 feet AGL (above ground level), he cut the single engine of the helicopter. I wasted no time lowering the collective, removing all angle of attack on the rotor blades as we purposefully started dropping like a stone. As a result of our high rate of descent, the increased airflow through the rotor blades allowed me to maintain flyable rotor rpm. I had to be quick in establishing a glideslope and 60 knots of airspeed to give me some manoeuvrability to get to the area where I was to land.

"Good show," murmured my instructor.

With the ground fast approaching, I readied myself to flare the helicopter using the cyclic control before pulling the collective for maximum rotor

My Rude Awakening

angle of attack, thereby arresting my fall. I gently slid her on to complete my autorotation.

"Just don't tell me this is the first time you have done that," said Captain Gallagher.

I was beaming again, but I didn't say a word. Autorotations became the exercise that I most enjoyed doing.

After progressing through hovering, basic flying, and autorotations, we stepped it up with tail-rotor and hydraulic failure. Finally, it was time for a decidedly big occasion in every pilot's life—we flew our first solo flights. This was followed by the customary Shawbury ceremony, which involved being unceremoniously dunked into the duck pond and, occasionally, smeared with duck droppings.

I remember phoning home, asking after Osric first and then excitedly telling my parents I had reached this important milestone. My mother, after congratulating me wholeheartedly, asked quite sheepishly if that was not what I had already done when I got my private pilot licence, and why so much fuss was made of a solo flight.

"Mum, flying a helicopter is an entirely different thing, and doing it on your own for the first time is a *big* achievement."

My mother went quiet on the other end of the line.

I wondered if she was feeling apprehension at the thought of her only son flying alone or contemplating the day I would move into a combat role, which was where all of this would hopefully end up. I thought it best to address her fears directly. "What is the matter, Mum?"

"No, nothing's the matter…but isn't that what you are meant to do? You know, fly it on your own?"

I had to smile. I had clearly misread that one. My mother, never one to over emote, thought I should best be getting on with the job at hand and focus on the end goal, not the little steps in between.

The next step was a big transition to the Bell Griffin HT1. Just the complex start-up procedures of this twin-engine helicopter let you know you were progressing. It turned out to be simple for me. I just reduced it to a logical pattern, only needing the long list of steps outlined on the start-up checklist for the first couple of days.

As my knowledge of the helicopter advanced, so my opinion of it increased. It was in many ways, battle ready. It made sense, considering the Huey, its predecessor, had a proud history as a combat helicopter.

The conversion went uneventfully and in no time at all, we were all certified to fly it. We knew this was just the first stage, as we would later be transferred to 60 Squadron (R) for advanced training, still on this twin-jet-engine machine. This would include weapons systems and tactical flying—all aspects we would need once we moved into active service.

We were always under extreme pressure because of the ongoing scrutiny, which resulted in a trainee pilot being dismissed every other week. There was nothing I dreaded more. To top it all, my ongoing university studies took up an appreciable number of hours every week. I was at times really under the whip. Somehow I managed to get through it all, albeit on a lot less sleep, something that would become a feature of my life.

On the subject of losing sleep, one evening while we were in the officers' mess, one of the orderlies handed me a small package. I would often receive letters but not packages, so I was naturally excited and curious to see what it contained. I resisted opening it until I got to my sleeping quarters but was barely through the door when I removed the brown wrapping. Inside was a curious-looking cube made up of numerous haphazardly coloured smaller cubes in red, green, blue, yellow, white, and orange.

My interest was immediately piqued as I read my father's note.

> Hello Son.
>
> I thought this would interest you.
>
> It's called a Rubik's Cube and was invented by a Hungarian professor of architecture who used it to help him teach algebraic group theory to his classes at university.
>
> What it calls for is to mix up all the colours by swivelling the planes around the central axis, and then to return it to a 'single colour per surface area.'
>
> You can see I've got the first part right without any difficulty. Ha ha. I've left the second part to you.

My Rude Awakening

Let me know when you have done it.

Dad

There were no instructions in the box with the Rubik's Cube, just a description that read something like, "Consists of twenty-six cubes that rotate on a central axis; nine coloured cube faces arranged in rows of three by three to form one side of the cube."

I was fascinated.

Fortunately, I had the foresight to complete a university assignment for submission the next morning before I did anything more with this little challenge. Forty-five minutes later, I was ready.

I looked at my bedside clock as I began. 9:02 p.m. I started by understanding the mechanics, twisting the small cube planes in the two possible directions. It took just moments for me to realise that getting a single colour on a surface could not be done sequentially, because as I began solving one dimension, it would undo what I had done elsewhere. I was engrossed. At a glance it looked like I had it half done, only to undo it again when I tried to progress. I had another look at the packaging, making sure there weren't any clues of how I should go about solving this three-dimensional puzzle. Nothing.

I had a sip of water and glanced at the clock. 10:22 p.m. An hour and twenty minutes, and I was nowhere.

I wondered why I kept looking at the clock. I wasn't competing with anyone. Then I remembered—oh yes, I was. I never stopped competing with him. Me.

Going around in circles figuratively but also literally, I continued rotating these groups of little cubes around a mechanism in the centre of the block. *Wonder what it looks like.* No question, I would find out. *It may involve a hammer.* The only thing preventing frustration was that I was beginning to see a pattern.

Another sip of water and a glance at the clock. 11:29 p.m.

Yes, there *was* a pattern. And a formula.

My yelp of excitement in solving the Rubic's Cube happened at 12:12 a.m.

I did the time calculation. *It will be a lot quicker next time,* I thought as I began jumbling it all up. Big mistake.

I finished my second attempt at 1:26 a.m.

Done, and bedtime. But first, a quick note to my dad. Pity I can't attach a photograph. Actually, no problem. I went down to our study centre and photocopied the six sides in colour to include with my little note that said:

Thank you, Dad.

Amazing little challenge. First attempt—3 hours, 10 minutes. Second attempt—1 hour, 14 minutes. I will tick the box once I have figured out how to jumble it up the way you did.

Ha ha.

Charles

Knowing my dad would appreciate my little dig, I mentally ticked the box and happily went to sleep, something that would have been impossible had the box remained unticked.

Two days later I received a letter from my dad—thanks to the Royal Mail being amazingly efficient at times. His flowing longhand on the envelope was something I was very familiar with. The note read:

Hello Son.

Well done. Have a look at this little cutting.

Dad

He'd sent me a newspaper cutting about the Rubik's Cube. Apparently, it was set to take off around the world. The part that had me sitting bolt upright was that there were people doing it in under five minutes. The record was under two minutes. There was also a bit about how best to orient the cube and move the planes with something they called "triggers," which require using your wrists and fingers in a coordinated fashion (as you do on a helicopter's cyclic control) to quickly get through the moves and achieve these unbelievably quick times.

"Jamie, sorry, chum. I have some university work to attend to," I blurted as I hurried to my quarters that night.

So my excuse to Jamie wouldn't be a lie, I did twenty minutes of economics homework before taking the Rubik's Cube in hand.

At a little past midnight, I switched off the light, feeling a little disillusioned. I was still in double digits. Five days later I achieved six minutes and forty-six seconds and ticked the box, disregarding that I had been appreciably slower than the record. I had helicopters to fly.

As our flight training advanced, so the numbers of trainee pilots started stabilising, with fewer and fewer ejections as opposed to what we had seen in the early part of the course. I wondered whether a lot of potentially good pilots had been mistakenly dropped in those first weeks because of the immense stress. The more I thought about it though, the more I realised the approach was most likely by design and little had been left to chance. One of the most important things we would learn in the years to come was how crucial it would be to be able to operate under the most extreme pressure.

We soon realised that the RAF had seen enough skill in our group to continue investing in us. This led to a noticeably positive change in each of the fellows, and I felt we had finally got to the stage where we could start enjoying our time more and certainly with more confidence. As it transpired, those feelings were short lived.

We were introduced to the Grouping System. How it worked was that we would start with a grouping examination that would determine where we were placed on a ranking ladder, strongest to weakest. Not unlike a player ladder you would see at a tennis club. Then each time we completed an important aspect of the flight training course or did a ranking examination, the instructors would adjust the rating board. The top ten were Group A, the next ten Group B, and the remainder were Group C. We never got to see the actual ladder, but from time to time we were told which group we were in. In the early stages, it was an ever-changing table, the primary goal being to stay out of Group C as this was from where ejections from the course were made.

Up until the time we had been introduced to the grouping system, it was us against them, doing our best not to be ejected. The grouping system changed that and overnight we were now competing against each other. It wasn't a big thing initially, but in time we would learn the powers that be were quite happy to up the ante.

I loved RAF Shawbury for many reasons, but none more so than that I was finally flying helicopters. Overall, this training would last just under two years, during which time I would be commissioned as a flight lieutenant, something I had dreamt about since childhood. The only downside was that it was up to a four-hour journey to my home in Berkshire, which would make it nearly impossible for me to get home when I had a military pass for the night or even the weekend. As it transpired, this was not as big a negative as I had imagined.

Just over four months into our training at 60 Squadron, we had the first of five exciting days when we went onto the range and fired the 30mm Browning machine gun, or chain gun as it was also known. At the end of this weapons training introduction, one of the trainee pilots—William Granger, a really decent fellow—emerged as the top shot, setting himself up for becoming a Copilot-Gunner, or CPG, and earning the nickname Great-Shot Granger.

During this time, Jamie and I had become good friends and admitted to each other that we would prefer a Pilot-in-Command role over a Gunner role.

As it turned out, Jamie's home was around thirty minutes from the base, about five minutes outside Shrewsbury—the county town of Shropshire in the West Midlands of England. There he lived with his divorced mother and slightly older sister. It offered me a lovely place to go with Jamie for our nights and weekends off. A lovely place indeed.

CHAPTER 8
SHREWSBURY

I WILL NEVER FORGET the first time I went with Jamie for an overnight pass. He had asked his mother if he could bring a friend, and she had agreed. His sister would also be coming home from the University of Birmingham to see him. We were in Jamie's car, allowing me to take in the surroundings on the short trip to his home. The area around RAF Shawbury was very picturesque, and I'd heard that Shrewsbury was even more special.

As we left the base, dressed in our Number Two's, standard pass out attire consisting of Air Force blue trousers, light blue long-sleeved shirt, tie, and jumper, I began to feel a little pensive. In the Air Force there is very little way of telling the social standing and affluence of the various people you meet, and therefore, I had no idea what lay in store for me. I so wanted our burgeoning friendship to endure, but I knew it would be more difficult if we were from wildly different levels of affluency.

Enjoying the drive between Shawbury and his home in Shrewsbury, nestled amongst the rolling Shropshire hills and just a few miles from the Welsh border, Jamie began to give me a commentary of the surrounding area, which I enjoyed.

"On the left is Attingham Park," Jamie pointed out as we drove past a sprawling wooded area. "And I'm going to take you through the town, just for you to get a feel. We live about five or ten minutes southeast from the centre," Jamie advised.

"What is the population of Shrewsbury?" I asked, trying to get a feel of the town.

"There are around 62,000 Salopians, which is what we are called. You know, inhabitants of Shrewsbury."

Unusual, I thought, *that they should want to give themselves a name. Well, you get Londoners, New Yorkers, why not Salopians?* I had to smile.

As we approached a bridge, he said, "This is the Iron Bridge over the River Severn. It dates back to the late 1700s. The town centre is in the loop of this river." Jamie went on with a twinge of pride in his voice, "You will recognise Shrewsbury's Saxon roots. It has a largely undisturbed medieval street plan with over 600 listed buildings, some possibly going back to the eighth century. Shrewsbury is one of the oldest medieval towns in England."

While he was speaking, we passed rows of half-timbered Tudor homes. We rounded the next bend, and he pointed to a church. "That's St. Chad's Church."

I noted its distinctive round shape and high tower.

"It has a long history with Charles Darwin, who was born in Shrewsbury. This was where he was baptized in 1809. A statue of him stands outside the town library, which was once a school where he was educated," Jamie continued.

"This little town is amazing," I replied, genuinely intrigued.

"And over there is St. Mary's Church, with its well-known stained-glass windows. If you really want to appreciate it though, you need to go inside and look out through them."

Unusually, I found myself wanting to do just that but instead made a mental note that I would do so at some time in the future.

Jamie was not finished there and as we drove a little further, he pointed to a red-bricked medieval structure on the hill. "And that is Shrewsbury Castle, where I must definitely take you. It houses the Shropshire Regimental Museum."

"Bloody hell, Jamie, that is amazing. And it looks really old." I enjoyed learning about the early days of England and the British Empire and appreciated his little guided tour.

"Yeah, AD 1067 old, and it has a whole bunch of military artefacts, old uniforms, and some really old weaponry. You will love it. But if you want to see even older, I can take you to see the Wroxeter ruins."

"I would really like that, Jamie," I said without hesitation.

"Wroxeter is an amazing spot for Roman history. It was founded in around AD 55, and the excavated ruin was once one of the largest towns of Roman England, comparable to the size of Pompeii."

I was astonished at all of these 'early England' little gems and couldn't wait to explore the town and discover more about it. As I watched Jamie, I couldn't help but think there was something so familiar about him. I just couldn't put my finger on it.

We drove a bit further, and I imagined we could only be a few minutes from his home. The mixture of period England attractions and the obvious affluence of the area now made me curious about where Jamie lived, the pensive thoughts having dissipated.

"So, you're about to meet my sister and mother, old chap. I hope you like them. I'm quite certain they will like you." With that, Jamie turned into a pillared entrance and announced, "We're here."

We navigated a two-hundred-yard meandering driveway, and as we rounded the last bend, I took in the typical Tudor-style home fronting a manicured lawn that rolled down to the bottom of the garden. It was a lovely home that suggested the Blackwoods were more than just comfortable. As it transpired, Mrs Blackwoods' family were indeed quite affluent.

What a relief, I thought, now feeling very guilty about my earlier concerns, or even having had them.

As Jamie opened the front door, I was met by a wide passage, a spacious drawing room over on the right-hand side. A mixture of antiques and contemporary furniture pieces. *Just like my mum. Auspicious,* I thought happily.

We wasted no time going inside and dropping our bags in Jamie's room. I followed him out to the back garden where we found the two women on the tennis court, finishing a game. I could not immediately make out which was his mother and which was his sister. All I saw were two extremely attractive, athletic women, clearly proficient tennis players, having a ding-dong rally and neither one immediately able to get the upper hand on the other. It turned out to be Mrs. Blackwood who eventually won the point with a grunted effort.

Seeing us, they walked over to where we were standing and greeted us warmly.

"Hi, I'm Georgina, and this is Charlotte," Mrs. Blackwood made the introductions, both ladies not hesitating to kiss me on both cheeks, making no excuse for being out of breath and quite sweaty.

I was taken aback by how warm and informal they were, something I was quite unused to but rather enjoyed.

I was surprised at how attractive Jamie's mother was, as she removed her cap and undid her ponytail, letting her dark blonde hair fall to her shoulders. She had Jamie's features, or more accurately he had her large hazel-green eyes, high cheekbones, an aquiline nose, and cherry lips. Her curvaceous, hour-glass body and full breasts were certainly more befitting a thirty-something than someone with a nineteen-year-old son. Had I tried to guess her age, she would have had Jamie when she was about twelve years old!

Charlotte was the proverbial "hot blonde with large blue eyes" who surely turned the heads of most men. With straight golden hair, the same cherry lips, and a peaches-and-cream complexion, she had a tall, athletic body with medium to large breasts. It was obvious from where she got both her looks and physique. I guess I was at the age where I noticed these features more.

Most unusual for me, I blurted out, "You and Charlotte look like sisters!"

"Ooh, flattery will get you anything." Mrs. Blackwood chuckled with the cutest little wink. "Yes, I had my children young, just twenty-two when Charlotte was born."

I quickly calculated that Mrs. Blackwood was forty-three, though I could not believe she was that old.

"Come along, let's go to the house and have a fresh lemonade," she invited.

We sat down at the kitchen table with both mother and daughter being ever so friendly and demonstrative with me. I blushed and struggled to string sentences together, my awkwardness due to my rather sheltered upbringing. Going to an all-boys school and never having attended socials or dances—always being far more interested in playing sports, learning to fly, or just rough shooting with Osric—made me very shy around women.

"So, you are a polo player?" Mrs. Blackwood asked.

This was something that came up regularly after meeting anyone new, which immediately seemed to frame me as either having money or being a bit of a "player." Either way, I didn't like it.

"Charlotte and I both had our own horses right up until Charlotte went to university and we decided to sell them. Jamie used to do a lot of riding as well," she continued. "Has he mentioned it to you?"

I vaguely remembered Jamie having told me something about this and now welcomed the common ground I shared with he and his family as we continued chatting about what sort of riding they did and where.

"You don't have any sisters, Charles," Mrs. Blackwood stated rather than asked.

"No, I am an only child. I guess having me changed my parents' minds about having another," I replied in a feeble attempt at being humorous.

My mind was wandering. Did Charlotte have a boyfriend? *God, she could be a* Playboy *Playmate!*

Courtesy of Jamie, I had only recently seen my first *Playboy* magazine, and my interest had been immediate. That was the first time I had been so instantly aroused, and I'd thought there was nothing I would rather do than marry July's Playmate. I did later learn that real beauty is found beneath the skin, as the cliché went, but right then I was face to face with someone who could surely qualify as one of those centrefolds. Looking at Charlotte and having these thoughts made me feel guilty and added to my bashfulness. I was certain she wouldn't have any interest in her younger brother's friend.

Jamie and I made ourselves comfortable in the drawing room while the ladies freshened up. "Let's open some wine and relax a bit. God, it's good to be home," he said, putting his feet up. "So now you've met Charlotte… and my mum. Not sure, but I don't think Charlotte is seeing anyone," he offered even though I hadn't asked.

I looked at him with the proverbial mouthful of teeth and said nothing. I didn't even know where to begin, I was so unused to dealing with matters of the opposite sex.

The ladies returned wearing loose-fitting summer dresses, open sandals, and tousled wet hair they were attempting to dry with hand towels. Jamie poured them each a glass of wine, and we settled in for a lively chat, something not normally easy for me in the company of people I had only just met. It was different with Jamie's mother and sister though. They were animated and demonstrative, and I felt at ease in their presence. Of course, they were anxious to catch up on all Jamie's news, having not seen much of him since he'd joined the RAF, and they also wanted to know about me and my home, which I played down. Jamie had no such sentiment. At the first opportunity, he enthusiastically told his mother and sister that Rockwell Manor was a polo estate, and I had invited him there so he could try polo.

"Ooh, that sounds like wonderful fun," Charlotte enthused. "I would love to come and watch a polo match sometime."

"Yes, yes!" I said, excited at the thought of Charlotte being there too, even though I was sensitive about her seeing my home too soon. I would have preferred her getting to know me first, before meeting my family and seeing our grand homestead. I had this notion about one day meeting *the* girl and wanted to be sure that she was with me for me and did not have her judgement clouded by the Featherstone trappings. Surely I wasn't already thinking, hoping, Charlotte could be *the* girl, or was this just hopefulness because of my insecurities and naivety? I dwelt on this possibility for a long time afterwards, not altogether sure how to reconcile my feelings but still wanting certainty.

We chatted about all the goings-on at the Air Force base, with Jamie touching on some of our training programme. Then Charlotte told us about her days at university. They reminisced about their childhood, Mrs. Blackwood enthusiastically providing context.

Through it all, I consumed every detail about these women: their looks, their mannerisms, every word spoken, their expressions, their little chuckles and ripples of laughter, the scent of their perfume. I was riveted. Not that there was anything unusual about this evening. It was just that I was seldom, if ever, in such intimate company with ladies who weren't members of my family.

The longer we sat, the more enamoured I became with Charlotte and, unexpectedly, Mrs. Blackwood as well. I subconsciously reconciled that this must have meant I was just trying to assess what Charlotte would look like at a later age.

My mother often said everyone has beauty and it is just a matter of seeing where it resides in a person. She also reminded me of the adage, "Beauty is in the eye of the beholder." I looked at Mrs. Blackwood. She was unquestionably beautiful and on top of that, I could see she had "made an effort," as my mother would say. Her real appeal was not as obvious though. Perhaps it was her confident, relaxed attitude that was captivating me. I looked at Charlotte, thinking how one day she would be as beautiful as her mother. They both had the same physical loveliness, but somehow Mrs. Blackwood had matured into hers. "Like a good, young red wine maturing into one that is perfect for drinking," as the cliché goes. I sensed where my thoughts were taking me, so I stopped them abruptly.

Once we finished our predinner drinks, Mrs. Blackwood summoned us to the annex dining area set in a bay window extension of the kitchen, in preference to the larger formal dining room. It was a pleasant, cosy little space with a table for four, and the aroma of their cooking had my stomach grumbling in anticipation. Looking forward to having dinner and sitting between Charlotte and Mrs. Blackwood, I first assisted the ladies with their chairs before taking up my own place.

"Ooh, Berkshire manners! I hope some of that rubs off on Jamie," quipped Mrs. Blackwood.

By this stage, there was a very relaxed and warm atmosphere, no doubt the predinner aperitifs having contributed to everyone's good mood. Sitting in such wonderful company, the occasional demonstrative hand on my arm, even the odd squeeze of my hand as either Charlotte or her mother expressively made a point during conversation, was all quite unfamiliar. I loved the Blackwood ladies' unreserved affections, and it was having a marked effect on me.

Mrs. Blackwood and her housekeeper, Suzie, had made an extra effort with our dinner for Jamie's first visit home. After our starter of pan-seared sea scallops with lemon and chive butter and a little wine, Charlotte turned on the hi-fi as she and her mum went back to the kitchen area. They busied themselves grilling some vegetables to accompany the roast Côte de Boeuf, Yorkshire pudding, and roast potatoes, evidently Jamie's favourite and the source of my stomach's growling. Then I heard the unmistakable voice of Bruce Springsteen singing "Cover Me."

"Cover Me" – Bruce Springsteen & the E Street Band

| YouTube | Spotify | Apple |

I watched as Charlotte and Mrs. Blackwood spontaneously started dancing to the rhythm of this popular song. I was enchanted by their uninhibited, sexy little gyrations. Having never seen anything quite so appealing in my life, I couldn't take my eyes off them!

I had never previously paid attention to the lyrics, but it suddenly hit me. *Surely this is not about what our stallions do to our mares.* Realising the song was unquestionably about that, my mind began to race.

As they danced, they looked over to us, trying to entice us into joining them. They were no doubt oblivious of the effect they were having on me as their hand and body gestures became an element of their dance moves. Then, as the words, "I'm looking for a lover who will come on in and cover me," played, they pointed to themselves and then looked at each other and giggled like schoolgirls. It was not lost on me that mother and daughter were quite comfortable with sharing this personal desire, even if it was done jokingly in a song.

My stomach tightened at the thought of joining them, and I was mesmerised. But this was evidently normal behaviour in the Blackwood household. I was far too shy to do anything except laugh it off as if it were a joke, while Jamie rolled his eyes and ignored their suggestions completely.

This was so different to what I was used to at home. Mrs. Blackwood's trendy, relaxed way of dressing, her music choices, the way she spontaneously danced—her warm and demonstrative charm was simply amazing. Smiling, I wondered if Jamie sometimes thought he had two sisters, not a mother and a sister.

"Excuse their behaviour. They are just trying to compete with Goofy and doing a bloody good job of it," he said, teasing me in a haughty tone.

Goofy to Jamie but tantalising to me. *An example of one man's meat being another man's poison,* I thought wryly.

They finished grilling the vegetables and headed back to the table.

I could feel a "growing" sensation between my legs as I tried to stop thinking about Charlotte lying on a sofa with her legs slightly apart, from one of the vivid images embedded in my mind thanks to *Playboy's* Miss July. I felt that having these thoughts about someone I had just met was immoral, and even more, it was ridiculous of me to be having this physical reaction. I guess these were the symptoms of being a nineteen-year-old virgin still in the early stages of sexual development, without an avenue to vent my burgeoning desires. I thought about one of our sergeant majors in basic training accusing us of being "young, dumb, and full of cum" and suddenly understood what he meant.

Then Jamie's mother asked me with a glint in her eye, "A penny for your thoughts, Charles."

I looked up in mild horror and chuckled nervously. "Uh, n-nothing, Mrs. B-Blackwood."

"Oh no, call me Georgina—or Gigi if you like—but not Mrs. Blackwood. That ship has sailed, or rather sunk," she said, referring light-heartedly to her failed marriage.

"Aah, umm, okay, thank you, Georgina," I replied shyly.

It was the distraction I needed to bring me back to the present, and the thought of trying to conceal an erection had me subsiding quickly. Mrs. Blackwood—Georgina—did have me wondering if what I'd been thinking was that obvious. I also felt quite awkward because in our circles it was unheard of that I should use the Christian name of one of my friend's parents, unless I knew them very well.

Our dinner continued, and with the occasional sip of wine and the enchanting company, I felt incredibly happy. Jamie's mother was the perfect hostess. Courteous and attentive. On more than one occasion, I felt her breast touch my arm as she leant over to give me a little more dessert or a piece of cheese with my port. This aroused me to no end and on one occasion, while I was feigning looking intently at the contents of my dessert bowl, I was instead actually straining my eyes to look in her direction. Her hands were beautifully manicured, her nails quite short and varnished with a dark burgundy red that matched her pedicured toenails on slender, elegant feet. I had never thought of a woman's hands and feet as sexy until then. Her elegant neck and regal look, accentuated by an aquiline nose, were so attractive. *God, she is beautiful,* I couldn't help thinking. The fall of the light allowed me to catch a glimpse of faint dark patches that were her nipples, barely visible through her dress and thin lace brassiere. I was appalled at myself for having sensual thoughts about my friend's mother, yet I was drawn to this mature woman far more than I had ever been to any of the girls around Guards Polo Club. She had a certain poise, a composure, so elegant and so refined, even though our evening was just a casual, light-hearted, and jovial affair.

As the evening drew on, I paid increasing attention to Georgina. By the end of the dinner, I was feeling wonderfully comfortable and sexually alive.

Unfortunately, we eventually had to excuse ourselves from the table, as we were already going to bed far later than we should have, considering the busy programme we had back at Shawbury the next day.

As I stood up, Georgina put her hand on top of mine and asked, "Where did you leave your bag?"

"In Jamie's room."

"No need for that. Let me show you through to the guest suite."

Even though I was more than happy to bunk with my friend, I appreciated this little bit of spoiling. I said good night to Charlotte, waved good night to Jamie, and followed Georgina as she led the way upstairs to the bedrooms. I was very aware of her every touch on my shoulder and arm, or her hand brushing against mine as she chatted about Charlotte and Jamie having grown up in the house, while we continued our way to collect my overnight bag and then on to the guest suite. The tightening of my stomach was palpable. My physical attraction to her was astonishing. I had never been so confused in all my life.

The guest suite was a lovely, spacious room with a king-size bed that had a fluffy goose-down duvet, extra-large pillows, padded headboard, and an ottoman at the foot to complete what were extremely comfortable sleeping arrangements that rivalled Rockwell Manor's. Quite the opposite of what I had become accustomed to in my officers' quarters at RAF Shawbury.

Georgina opened the bed, gave the soft mattress a pat, and said, "I think you will be very comfortable here, Charles." With that, she left the room.

I decided to have a quick shower before going to bed. I was particularly aware of the corrugations of my six-pack as I looked in the mirror before stepping into the shower. While I soaped myself, I was conscious of my toned body. I had always been fit and strong from my very active lifestyle. With my burgeoning maturity, my muscular development was more pronounced than ever. I found it interesting that I was suddenly paying attention to my body. Perhaps I was trying to reassure myself, given my shyness around women and my sexual arousal at dinner.

My Rude Awakening

I finished showering, dried myself off, pulled on boxer shorts, jumped into bed and switched off the light, delighted to finally have a moment to reflect and relive some of the evening's activities. It had all been intoxicating, though not just from the wine and port. I thought again about Charlotte, picturing her in the naked pose I had seen in the *Playboy* magazine. Then I thought about Georgina—the scent of her perfume, the feel of her touch on my arm or hand, her looking into my eyes as she spoke to me. I couldn't help picturing her in that same Miss July pose, naked, more sensual, and tried to imagine her body next to mine, in the flesh.

As a new sensation engulfed me, I reached into my boxer shorts and felt the growing fullness of my manhood quickly becoming erect. It seemed larger, stronger than normal. I pulled the front waistband down and looked. *Ooh yes, much fuller than before.*

As I instinctively clenched my buttocks, raising myself slightly off the bed to remove my boxers, I thought about something I'd once overheard in the barn at the Beaufort Polo Club in the Cotswolds.

Sandra, daughter of Janet and Harold Rawling, Berkshire landowners and friends of my parents, and some of her polo-groupie pals had been in the barn looking around. They had not been aware I was in one of the stalls checking on one of my horses.

"Wow, look at that horse's engine," said Candy Atkinson, one of Sandra's friends.

"That's one of Charles Featherstone's string," said Penelope Grayston, another of the Berkshire locals.

"She's got a backside just like her owner," suggested Candy, comparing my behind to my polo horse's athletic "apple" hindquarters.

"Ooh, I would just love to get my hands around his derrière," Sandra Rawling had remarked.

"I wonder what the rest of him is like, you know?" Candy added with a naughty laugh.

"And having that bum to hold on to, *while he is working it*, will make it all the nicer," said Sandra in a suggestive tone.

Working what? I had thought at the time.

"I will let you know when I have had some of it," Sandra Rawling proffered, all of them now giggling.

At the time I had been a little shocked at this unladylike behaviour. It was far worse than our locker-room banter.

As I thought about it, I couldn't help smiling at how little I understood about female desire and sexuality then. At least I now knew what she meant by "working it."

I grinned, thinking about Sandra Rawling's cheeky comeback as I ran my hand up and down the length, enjoying its hard, arched form. I instinctively began the slow, pleasurable journey of bringing this act to its climactic conclusion. Not in a rush, not wanting to overstimulate myself, but rather wanting the moment to last.

Just then I heard a knock and froze.

Georgina opened the door slightly. "Can I come in?"

I grabbed at the sheet to cover my body. "Aah…um…yes. Yes, of course," I spluttered.

Georgina was already stepping into my room dressed in her night clothes and gown.

My intake of breath was audible. My heart raced. Even in my trepidation, I couldn't help noticing the outline of her stomach, hips, and breasts, and a dark areola showing through her night clothes where her gown had pulled to one side, none of which did anything to ease my now painfully hard erection.

"Everyone's gone to bed, and I feel like a cuppa. Join me?"

Oh, I so wanted to, but how? I couldn't get out of bed with such a full and throbbing erection, and no shorts mind you. So I replied, "N-no, unfortunately we need to make an early start tomorrow. I had better be going to sleep." As I spoke, I felt the deep regret of not being able to accept such an enticing invitation.

"Okay. Good night." She brushed both me and her suggestion aside without another word.

I was crushed and wondered if I would ever be offered a cup of tea like that again.

It was impossible to fall asleep immediately with crazy sexual thoughts about Georgina swirling around in my head. The more I thought about her, the more I knew it was wrong. I decided there and then that I had to bring it to an end. It was ludicrous to be having these salacious thoughts about a woman twenty-odd years my senior, and my best friend's mother to boot.

I decided I should direct my thoughts and energies towards Charlotte instead. After all, she was Georgina's daughter and therefore must have many of the qualities her mother had. I tried to think what her hands and feet looked like and realised I wasn't entirely sure, unlike her mother's, whose I could have described in minute detail. I eventually fell asleep with a pronounced occurrence of lover's balls.

We were up early the next morning for our drive back to RAF Shawbury, and I was disappointed to discover that Charlotte had already left for university. Georgina more than made up for it though, giving us a wonderful breakfast and sending us on our way after planting kisses on our cheeks.

That was so warm and affectionate, I thought, blushing and beaming at the same time.

Back at RAF Shawbury, the frenetic tempo of our training threatened to extinguish my memories of that wonderful first night in Shrewsbury. Amazingly, after a couple of months, a pattern emerged where we were going to Jamie's home every fortnight, even several weekends in a row, and this alternated the ardours of the RAF and the relaxed comfort of Jamie's home perfectly. What a contrast. What a relief. Jamie would let me know when he was getting an overnight or weekend pass, so I could do likewise and accompany him to Shrewsbury. I really appreciated the way he included me. My conscious decision not to go down the very tantalising path his mother had presented to me and the accompanying guilt I would surely have felt made it a lot easier for me to engage with Jamie, and we soon became the best of friends.

CHAPTER 9
OSRIC

THOUGH I WAS not able to visit home very often due to the distance from our base, there was one trip I will never forget. My mother had phoned me on a Wednesday evening and quite unusually almost insisted I come home for the weekend. She ended the call with a seemingly casual, "And Osric is missing you." I put the phone down, thinking my mother was just wanting to see me and included the Osric bit for some added enticement.

I looked at my diary. *Bloody hell.* I had two days left to submit a university paper on IBM marketing strategy analysis that had to be in by Friday. I also had at least an hour of RAF study on turbines and transmissions that was for tomorrow! Just as well I wasn't a big sleeper.

The next day I used the same emphatic approach my mother had used on me and requested a weekend pass from the officer on duty. As it turned out, the officer was Captain Gallagher, who had been pleased with my flying, which probably paved the way to him happily signing me off for the weekend.

Before I knew it, it was Friday afternoon. With more than just a twinge of excitement at the thought of going home I jumped into my car, my pride and joy, and headed off. Three hours and twenty-one minutes later I stepped through our front door. Osric was the first to greet me.

"Osric! Osric! Aw! Come on, boy! There's a good boy."

He lumbered towards me grunting and whining, his rear wiggling with joy as I fondled his head and kissed his soft, wet snout.

"There's my good boy. Ooh, I've missed you." I chortled at his wet, eager licks to my face. "Hellooo? Mum? Dad?"

My Rude Awakening

Osric walked beside me as he always did, guiding me to the study.

"Sunbeam! Welcome home!"

My parents greeted me warmly while Osric, not wanting to be left out of the homecoming welcome, wagged his tail furiously.

That night, over an early dinner in our family dining room, my parents got onto the topic of the RAF, eager to hear how I was getting on.

"Tell us about Shawbury," my father insisted.

"Oh, Dad, I am just loving it. You can't believe how quickly we are progressing. I've already done some autorotations—you know, landing without the engine," I blurted, hardly taking a breath. "But first we had to learn how to hover, which funnily enough, I found quite easy. I basically got it right on the first day. And you will never believe what helped me."

"What, Sunbeam?" my mother chipped in.

"My polo. You have to feel these machines, just like riding a horse," I continued excitedly, not sure I was even making sense.

We carried on speaking for some time about the Air Force, my father interested in the aircraft and my schedule, my mother more interested in my accommodations, the food, and officers' quarters and how my studies were getting on.

Then my mother asked, "And what about your new friend…James, I think you said?"

Only then did I realise I had completely forgotten to tell them about meeting Gigi and Charlotte. "Yes, that's right, James Blackwood. Oh, Mum, how could I forget? I have now met his family, well his mother and sister, and they are so nice."

This was especially interesting to my mother, and she was thrilled to hear that I was able to use my passes to "enjoy some home comforts" as she put it. "Be sure to invite James to Rockwell Manor at the first opportunity," my mother instructed.

"That will be wonderful," I replied. "We have become such good friends."

Having caught up on all the news on both sides, we were ready for bed. As I went up to my room, I couldn't help noticing the effort it took for Osric to get up the stairs. He was getting old. Of course, there was no question where he would sleep.

"Come on, my boy. Up you get!" I helped him onto the bed, and he settled down in his usual spot at my feet. *He really is old.* I shut the thought out as quickly as it had come.

The next morning's plan was a given, a rough shoot starting at one of our favourite spots, Crow's View. There were always pheasant in the thickets above the open ground where I would be at the ready. Once we were done there, we would go down to the brook. We loved this route. Was duck on the menu?

I packed a tasty snack of a few crackers, cheese, sliced ham, cherry tomatoes, fried Cumberland sausages, a peach, and water and placed it all neatly into my haversack. I fetched my Joseph Lang twelve-bore from the gun cabinet, perfect for a relaxed shoot.

"Osric, sausage? Sit! Good boy." And we were off.

Now behaving years younger, Osric bounded out of the door.

We walked almost two miles, around thirty minutes, and arrived at our favourite shooting spot. Osric knew the drill. While I took up my position in a wide, clear area, he went into the woods on the high ground above my position. He flushed a bevy of pheasant. Staying clear of the trees, they flew overhead in clear shot. That first flush yielded six birds, but I missed them all. *Goodness, I'm rusty.* I looked at my gun accusingly anyway.

A short while later, Osric perfectly flushed another parcel before emerging from the hedgerows and looking at me expectantly. This time I got one and he retrieved it and dropped it at my feet. *Perfect shot.*

Encouraged, I decided we would take a break and share a snack. I could see Osric was a little tired.

While we ate, I freely shared my thoughts and felt completely understood by my furry friend. Satiated, we set off again.

Osric headed back into the thicket and flushed four more birds. I missed with my first barrel, hit with the second. This time, Osric was slower to retrieve. Very slow. I tied a piece of twine around the pheasant's necks and hooked it through the loop on my belt. With our brace of pheasant secured, it was time to head down to the brook and try for a wood duck, one of my favourites.

After the creek, it was another forty-minute walk home and Osric had had enough.

I looked down at my faithful companion and asked, "Should we go home, my boy?"

The wag of his tail and the droop of his head said it all.

It was one of our shortest shooting days but in retrospect, the most rewarding. After a few minutes, noticing he was struggling, I picked him up. He licked my face a few times and I chuckled. I carried Osric that way for a while longer, with him snuggling into the crook of my neck. Carrying him was a first.

When I stopped and sat down to hydrate, he turned his nose away, not interested in sharing my water. I put him on my lap, his head resting in the bend of my arm, and stroked him gently.

After some time, he went limp in my arms.

My beautiful, faithful Osric had stopped breathing. His eyes were closed…peaceful.

For a long while, I continued stroking him, holding his head gently and trying to absorb what had happened, the welling of tears in my eyes beginning their gentle stream down my cheeks.

I had lost my best friend.

Eventually, with an aching heart, I organised my gun and haversack and picked him up again. Cradling him in my arms, tears blurring my vision, I trudged home.

I had already decided where his resting place would be and went straight to a spot in the garden that would be in clear view from my north-wing bedroom window.

I laid him down gently and set about burying him. I found a tall rock in an adjacent flower bed and used it as a temporary headstone.

I will get you a proper one later, my boy. I promise.

When I finally came inside, my mother was waiting for me.

"Oh, Sunbeam…Sunbeam…" was all she said and then she just hugged and held me, both of us sobbing gently.

"Thank you, Mum."

She had insisted I come home in the nick of time.

For the first time ever, my dad also hugged me. Hugging was just not our way.

Dinner was sombre. Our little family of three sat very quietly in our family dining room, Granddad's empty seat making our loss feel even greater.

There was no room for anyone else, not in any sense of the word. No one else could understand the grief we were all feeling. There wasn't anything to say. We had all lost a beloved family member.

After picking at my food, I went up to my room. I thought perhaps the best way to distract myself would be to study aspects of helicopter aerodynamics, critical conditions, and height-velocity ratios, also known as "dead man's curve." It didn't work. Every few minutes, I looked up from my desk towards the rock beneath which Osric lay. I couldn't concentrate. That night I tossed and turned, waking every hour or so, desperately hoping to feel his comforting presence at the bottom of my bed.

The next morning, I awakened to a cold, dreary day. Not so much because of the grey weather, but more because it was the first morning after one of the saddest days of my life. I went down to our oversized kitchen where the Aga stove was stoked and generating warmth, and Fabrizio, our Italian chef, had the pizza oven going, baking fresh bread rolls, bacon, sausages, and an egg frittata. Breakfast was especially good when done in a wood-fired oven, and he knew I loved it. Fabrizio was just doing his bit to make me feel better, and this wasn't lost on me.

"Thank you, Fabrizio," I said as I put an arm across his shoulders. Being Italian, he appreciated the physical gesture.

My mum and dad stepped into the kitchen, our favourite eating spot, so that we could all have breakfast together before I left for the Air Force base. I was sipping on a mug of cappuccino—no prizes for guessing who made it—as I watched Fabrizio reach into the oven with the pizza peel. My mother's words, *"It's not a shovel, Sunbeam,"* came to mind. He retrieved about ten crispy bread rolls, dusted them with flour, popped them into a breadbasket, covered them with a napkin, and brought them over to our rustic kitchen dining table. He pushed the French *beurre* towards us and just the thought of the butter melting into the warm bread roll had my stomach grumbling. There was already an assortment of possibilities to accompany the fresh bread rolls on the table, but I ignored them all.

"Prosciutto?" Fabrizio asked, trying to push his Italian wares.

"Nooo, Fabrizio," I said, frowning. "My normal, please," which was a

My Rude Awakening

few rashers of bacon and fried banana with maple syrup. A variation of an English butty roll. I looked up and saw his mischievous expression, realising he was gently teasing me. He then produced his wood-fired-oven breakfast of baked eggs and shredded potatoes, which we had all been smelling since we arrived in the kitchen.

I hated the idea that I was already feeling better. Life shouldn't carry on so close to normal after the horrendous day before.

We had our breakfast, making sure we spoke about anything other than shooting, hunting, the countryside, and the myriad other things that always involved Osric. It did not leave much to talk about, not even polo, because Osric loved that too. My mother held both my hands and, speaking very softly, tried to explain that this was all part of growing up.

God, I didn't like growing up right then.

"You are a man now, Sunbeam…a wonderful man."

I gave her a kiss, shook hands with my dad as he told me, "Take care, son," and then I headed back to RAF Shawbury.

More than ever, I needed the distraction. I understood that an aspect of my life had changed, and it was by far the most difficult. The radio offered no comfort at all as a song came over the airwaves that put Osric straight back on the centre stage of my mind.

"Fire and Rain" – James Taylor

YouTube	Spotify	Apple

Yesterday, Osric hadn't yet gone. I'd come home just in time.

My eyes welled up with tears as each line of the song bored into my soul.

I thought of Osric as a pup, a soft, spotted bundle of cuddles, ears, and thumping tail. Osric in his prime, bounding in the woods alongside me was a vivid picture, now just memories that I knew I would never forget. The thought of never seeing him again sent a tear down my cheeks. I had never considered that Osric wouldn't be around one day, and the sadness of my new reality felt almost unbearable.

"Sweet dreams and flying machines in pieces on the ground…" as the song went.

I had to get my chin up, so I wiped my cheek, blew my nose, and pulled myself together as I continued a very quiet, sad and lonely drive back to RAF Shawbury.

On the passenger seat was a flask and two aluminium-foil-wrapped parcels. It was the work of Fabrizio, and I knew the contents, which made it even more welcome. In around three hours and twenty minutes just before arriving at RAF Shawbury, I would enjoy a hot latte and two bread rolls with Camembert cheese and mixed-berry jam.

Osric would have had a bite of the bread roll and then looked for the bacon.

After a muddy, rough shoot, Osric cleans up good.

I didn't get Osric a headstone because no matter what I had inscribed on it, it wouldn't say enough. Deciding what I should do was simple. The artist did a fine job of transforming a photograph of two pheasant taking flight into a solid brass sculpture.

Well, I'd promised Osric a proper headstone, and now he was lying

My Rude Awakening

under a perfectly flushed brace of pheasant. How could he not be happy with that?

Two pheasant perfectly flushed.

CHAPTER 10
DEFENCELESS

LOSING OSRIC WAS like losing a special friend. He had been my companion all through my childhood, and no longer having him seemed to shut the door on my youth and mark the day I became an adult, if not yet a man. My thoughts had to turn towards continuing my journey into adulthood.

It seemed just the other day that my dad was assisting me with the lengthy application process and then giving consent for me to go into the RAF. None of that now. More than having reached the age of consent, I was in my last teenage year. This transition also reflected in my efforts at RAF Shawbury as I became more determined than ever before to succeed. I *badly wanted* to become a "top pilot," not just "the best pilot I could be," as the less demanding narrative went.

Everything was different after that sad day. Okay, maybe not the driving. Driving at breakneck speed had always been a form of escapism for me and would probably always be.

Another change, perhaps because I was attracted to his quiet and sincere nature, was my making a friend of the other tall, dark, and handsome William (Will) Granger. Over six feet tall with a statuesque broad-shouldered frame, he was a big athletic man. Large, generous hands with well-trimmed nails. His thick black hair, piercing blue eyes, strong jaw, a Grecian nose, full lips, and slightly overlapping front teeth added plenty of character to his charming face. Will smiled easily, which caused his cheeks to dimple. Standing tall on muscular legs and with his "could get any girl" good looks, he was surprisingly reserved—quite the opposite to Jamie who flaunted his attractiveness. And when you looked at the pair of them, you would have sworn that the RAF had recruited for a talent contest. Jamie had an inch on me, and Will had an inch on Jamie. I once remarked that from behind, there was little to tell between them right down to their light olive skin tone. When they were in civvies, they were only distinguishable from each other because Jamie mostly wore white T-shirts while Will preferred navy. We all seemed to wear jeans and flip-flops when we were off duty. I was the odd one out. Blonde and not quite as tall. But while they may have been slightly taller than me, because of polo and riding spirited horses and hours of holding a polo mallet, my torso and upper body were more developed.

Will and Jamie—so similar on the outside, so different on the inside. I loved Will's very sanguine approach to life, truly refreshing. And whereas Jamie could be described as "the life of the party," Will was a lot more like me, preferring to be in the background. I enjoyed our quiet times together. Oh yes, there was another difference. Will was a one-woman man. Jamie wasn't.

I liked them both and ignored that Will was inclined to call me Charlie, which I hated.

Then there was Shrewsbury. Nothing could be compared to our excursions there and how it contrasted life at the air base in every way. The tantalising prospect of seeing Charlotte and Georgina. And Suzie, always making an effort with our delicious dinners, putting the predictable and mundane menu of the officers' mess to shame. One of my favourite meals, which reminded me of home, was the slow-cooked pheasant pie prepared during shooting season. Regardless of the menu, we'd always end with cheese and crackers, including baked Camembert in pastry, served with an assortment of preserves, and accompanied by a vintage Madeira port. It was cosy and comfortable to sit with Jamie's family around their small dining table, though I made sure I was careful not to drink too much wine. The comfortable guest suite with its soft bedding engulfed me, and I was able to easily drift off to sleep. It was such a luxurious comfort compared to the rudimentary rooms and hard beds of the officers' quarters.

The decision to not allow my thoughts and feelings to run rampant about Georgina had worked to some extent, even though I still found her immensely attractive. Instead, I convinced myself it was Charlotte I couldn't wait to see and that in time, I would win her over. But sadly, our visits to Shrewsbury often didn't coincide. Totally inexperienced at relationships, I was blinded by the illusion I'd created about her, enjoying my thoughts of "us" regardless of the reality.

Meanwhile, I had become far more relaxed around Gigi, as Georgina had insisted I call her. Perhaps this was because I had refused to allow myself to have illicit thoughts about her, which had quelled the guilt I felt.

I often found myself thinking about our first meeting, and at times I felt certain she too had strong feelings for me. I even thought we may have arrived at the same juncture at the same time, in not letting ourselves get caught up in our affections for each other. I would invariably chase that idea from my mind, deciding I was just imagining things. Regardless of the reality of those feelings, with every night or weekend pass, we were slowly becoming closer. I found her enormously attractive and loved the feel of her touch as she spontaneously took my arm or placed her hand on top of mine, and I was very conscious of her beautifully manicured nails. In fairness, I sometimes had to catch myself, lest I be caught staring at her, literally drinking in her beauty.

It wasn't unusual for her to knock on my bedroom door shortly after we had all gone to bed, pop her head in and playfully ask "Coffee, tea…me?" I always chuckled politely, but of course declined her alluring charm, quite certain she was just being mischievous anyway. Still, on a few occasions, I was tempted to act on her overtures, just to test that notion, and had to quickly banish the thoughts threatening to invade my mind.

One of the things that did give me food for thought was whenever I visited the Blackwoods, I found a little treat on my pillow or bedside table. This would be anything from Ghirardelli chocolates to Ladurée macarons. One morning I remarked to Jamie how tasty the Rococo Italian pistachio nougat had been, but all I got was a blank look. I realised then that I was the only recipient of these delicacies.

Whenever we left Shrewsbury to go back to the air base, we both received kisses on the cheek. Whereas the first time it happened, I'd been caught by surprise, now I offered my cheek expectantly.

Several months into our training, we received our first long weekend pass. Four nights instead of the usual two. My first thought was to take

My Rude Awakening

Jamie to my home, Rockwell Manor, giving me the opportunity to reciprocate his family's hospitality towards me. By then, broadly speaking, Jamie had a fair idea about my life, polo, shooting, my parents, and the like, even though I had avoided going into too much detail with him. My idea was to balance the few occasions I was able to take Jamie to my home against the regular visits to Shrewsbury by ensuring I crammed interesting and enjoyable activities into our time at Rockwell Manor, especially shooting and polo. He was quite an experienced horseman, and a capable one, and I was quite certain the polo bug would bite, as it often did with new entrants to the game.

"Jamie, are you up for spending the weekend in Berkshire?" I asked him after hearing the news about our pass.

"To your home? Rockwell Manor? Is the pope Catholic?" he asked, a typical quirky reply from Jamie.

A few days later, we stashed our weekend bags in the front of my car and were on our way.

Jamie thought the drive to Berkshire was a good time to catch up on some of the details that I had avoided. Not inclined to do that, I told him a resounding, "Wait and see," preferring him to make up his own mind when we got there.

We carried on chatting amiably, enjoying each other's company, when Jamie asked in a mock-serious tone, "So are there any girls in Berkshire?"

Grinning broadly, I replied, "Who needs girls when you have polo and game-bird shooting?"

"Me." Jamie chuckled.

He was going to have a field day. There were always any number of girls at the polo club, often disparagingly referred to as "polo groupies."

"Don't worry, Jamie. I am sure you will be fine," I assured him.

"Great, so with a bit of luck I should be able to get indecent."

My frowning glance at him was enough for him to carry on.

"Have you ever been *indecent,* Charles, old chap?"

Even though I was quite certain I was being baited, I answered, "What do you mean?"

"Well, when you're in deep, and you're in tight, then you're in…decent."

God, he was incorrigible. I couldn't help laughing though. How were my parents going to deal with this *rude* friend of mine? I simply replied, "Jamie, we're about twenty minutes out. Start getting your bearings because this is our neck of the woods." And I meant our neck of the woods in the literal sense as we drove along the winding country roads of a densely forested Berkshire.

We turned into 1 Polo Drive and soon arrived at the two oversized gate pillars. The signage cut into a large sandstone slab indicated the estate roads to the Manor House, Polo Stables, and Staff Accommodations, which was two large houses, one for the equestrian staff and the other for the housekeeping and ground staff.

I had that old familiar feeling of self-consciousness as I ignored the intercom and touched the remote. The heavy black wrought-iron gates swung open, and we made our way to the homestead entrance. Jamie said nothing as we drove up the mile long tree-lined driveway towards the house with its own entrance and guardhouse. With a little acknowledgement to the guard, I drove the final three hundred yards that ran parallel to the polo field, giving Jamie a clear view at the lush green expanse of grass and the undeniably large homestead. There was no getting away from it, fronted by sandstone pillars Rockwell Manor was an imposing, stately home.

"Jeez, is this grand or what?" was Jamie's drawled response.

Both my parents were on hand to greet us warmly, my mother taking an instant liking to Jamie and what was coming across as his boyish charm, as opposed to the Jamie I was more familiar with. I was secretly pleased. It was important to me that my parents liked my friend. Jamie was given one of the guest suites in the north wing next to me, which became his room from there on out.

My objective for Jamie that first weekend was to get him started on polo and shooting, and much to my relief, he did both admirably. Nothing like his disastrous attempt at playing golf. Having the benefit of our own home polo field, he quickly got the knack of stick and ball. We were similarly able to get him started with clay-pigeon shooting, using the same clay-pigeon launch trap my grandfather had used with me. Very quickly Jamie got the idea of starting behind the flight of the disc, then advancing ahead to establish a lead, then firing so that he was shooting into the space where the clay pigeon was going, as opposed to where it had been. It was quite cumbersome trying to handle the trap and give Jamie instructions, so I made a mental note of organising a trap operator the next time we attempted this.

By the end of his first visit, two things stood out for me. The first, Jamie had almost certainly bedded one of the young ladies at the club. I put it down to him being a ladies' man and wondered, *Was my dad this bad when he was our age?* The second, far from my mother thinking he was a "rude young man" and that she may have to influence him differently, both my parents thought Jamie was the most delightful, charming, respectful, wonderful house guest and well done to me for making such a good friend. The superlatives bordered on my mother gushing about his virtues, something she never did.

By Jamie's third trip to Rockwell Manor, he was already into the swing of things. On polo days he enjoyed playing as much as he enjoyed all the glamorous goings-on. There was no doubt that his contribution to these weekends was his charisma, dashing good looks, and RAF pilot image, which drew a fair amount of attention. My lack of confidence when it came to females made me oblivious of the fact that I too evidently portrayed a similar profile, especially to the polo-groupie set. Jamie had no such insecurities.

As we got closer to the game-bird shooting season, I was eager to prepare Jamie for his first pheasant shoot. Once again, I decided to do this in an opening in the woods alongside Rockwell Manor, but this time I was not going to make the mistake of trying to handle the clay-pigeon trap while also trying to coach Jamie myself. I contacted a local shooting range, and they were happy to give me a couple of names of university students who could do the job.

"Jamie, to help me with the trap I have two contacts. Samuel McGinty or Kelly Peppard. I don't know either of them, so who do you prefer?"

"Kelly's the one," Jamie said without hesitation, as if he knew the girl.

That afternoon, an attractive brunette with perfect, firm breasts arrived to assist us.

I chuckled. *Trust Jamie.*

Kelly was lovely, but I suspected it was her attributes just below her chin that really attracted Jamie. After the shoot, he invited her to join us for a pub dinner.

"Ooh, I would love that!" she gushed.

"I hope you don't mind, Charles?" Jamie asked in a way that showed he was not really concerned whether I did or not.

I had to endure a shamelessly affectionate, excited girl hanging on Jamie's every word all evening. I had to admit that her striking good looks made it somewhat enjoyable. It was clear that *I* was the third wheel encroaching on *their* fun, so I happily bid them good night soon after our meal. "Jamie, well done today. I'm awfully tired, squire! I am going to head off back to Rockwell. I hope you don't mind."

"Oh, okay, chum," Jamie said rather enthusiastically. "I will follow shortly. I also want an early night."

His appearance the next morning, whilst collecting a few things on his breakfast tray from the small patio buffet, suggested his "early night" had not been very restful. "I'll just have this in my room," he said as he scampered off. A convertible Mini Cooper, a perfect young lady car, parked a distance from the house in an attempt for it to not be noticed, was also quite telling.

This made me even more aware of still being a virgin, and that at almost twenty years old, I was in the minority.

A common occurrence back at the air base was some of the chaps telling of their weekend sexual escapades. I wondered if there would be a word from Jamie on this one. I guessed his embarrassment about sneaking a girl back to Rockwell Manor would discourage him from mentioning it.

While I was pretty sure some of the fellows' stories were baseless bravado, I was acutely aware that most of my peers were sexually active and that I was not.

One of the pastimes during our downtime was when one of the chaps saw an attractive lady, he would give her a score between one and ten. He'd then turn to the others to canvas their views. "What do you think?" This was often the start of some debate. I never played along because even though it was done lightheartedly and in good humour, I still felt it was demeaning to women and I had been brought up to celebrate them. Through experience I had discovered from very early on that whilst women were often judged by their looks alone, it was mostly their other attributes that were their greatest qualities. I wasn't going to get into this with anyone at the base though.

With a bunch of fellows of around twenty years of age, I guess one could expect a bit of testosterone jousting. Unsurprisingly, Jamie would add a new dimension.

An attractive civilian lady had come onto the base and was noticed by one of the trainee pilots, who began the process. "Eeeeyes right!" he said, giving a quasi-military command indicating where we should be looking.

"I would give her a six or maybe a seven," the instigator volunteered. After a little bit of the normal debate, he pointedly asked Jamie, as if wanting an expert opinion.

"So, what would you give her, Jamie?" asked the initiator.

Jamie looked at the lady, not rushing his reply, and then answered in a measured tone, "I'd give her one. Yes, I would definitely give her *one*," which drew raucous laughter.

I had hesitated a while longer than the others, not immediately having figured out the joke. *Oh, God,* I thought. *Only Jamie*. I considered countering his arrogance by saying, *She may not want your one, old chap,* but thought better of it.

Interestingly, even though I didn't participate in conversations of my sexual exploits, not that I had any, nobody imagined that I was not sexually active. They simply put me down as being a "dark horse" who preferred not to speak about it.

On one occasion Jamie had been confiding in me, admitting that he sometimes marvelled at how easily he attracted the attention of the opposite sex. He then said to me knowingly, "You're just a blond version of me, aren't you? But you just keep it all to yourself."

Little did he know. We may have had a similar look, a fair versus dark version of each other, but that was where it ended. Shy and introverted around females, I was the furthest thing from a ladies' man. Jamie and I could not have been more different. It made no difference—I liked him anyway. I guess you never really know what it is that draws you to another. A clear case of opposites attract, or was there something else?

It was when Jamie and I were driving back to RAF Shawbury after the Kelly weekend that he voiced his views about us in the ladies' man department. In a forthright manner, he asked "Charles, have you, you know, messed around with any of the girls at the polo club?"

I could literally see the cogs turning in his head, and when I did not immediately answer, he did so for me.

"So, you haven't." Then he continued, "I always thought you and I were similar when it came to girls, but now that I've come to know you better, I realise how different we are."

I said nothing, knowing he had more to say.

"You certainly have the looks and all the trappings...polo, Rockwell Manor, the lot. You could have any of them."

That was the last thing I wanted to hear.

"You are such a gentleman. Surely you aren't going to wait until marriage?"

I was clearly far more circumspect than Jamie, but the gentleman and marriage parts were not what grabbed my attention. It was "having all the trappings" that really did it. Jamie had inadvertently touched on something that was most certainly a contributor to why I was still a virgin. It was in the romance department too that I wanted to be wanted for who I was.

With my self-consciousness about still being a virgin at almost twenty, I gingerly broached the awkward subject with my parents by asking the question in general terms, as in, "When did men generally lose their virginity?" The result, two pieces of conflicting advice.

"When he meets the right girl, Sunbeam," was my mother's simple reassurance, answering me with the same generality.

I could have guessed that would be her response. She was letting me know I shouldn't be concerned that I was still a virgin.

My father had a different take on it. "I think around about now, you know, nineteen or twenty, is a respectable time for a young gentleman to sow his wild oats," he had ventured.

I imagined he had sown his wild oats at a younger age than I was then, and this was a subtle hint that there was no need for me to wait.

I smiled at the thought of them comparing notes later, which they invariably would do. No doubt my dad would get a sharp pinch from my mother. She often teased that my father had been "quite the ladies' man" before they got married, and his response to me would have been consistent with his earlier behaviour, which probably irked her a bit.

One evening, seven or eight of us were sitting around chatting in the

My Rude Awakening

junior officers' recreation room when the topic of women and girlfriends came up. Will announced with great enthusiasm, "I'm in love! I'm in love!"

Not giving him a chance to even begin his story, Jamie chimed in, "I've been in love a few times."

My ears immediately pricked up, wondering if he was going to expand on this unexpected and interesting revelation. I was not the only one interested in what he was about to say, because it seemed to be a contradiction to the "vanquisher of virgins" image he normally portrayed.

Jamie had the floor, his favourite realm. "Do you want to know how I knew I was in love?" he asked his attentive audience.

Everyone nodded their heads in unison, evidently all as interested as I was.

"Well, when you are in the sack, and your chain gun is probing forward in search of its target, and you give a little thrust and then she gasps, 'You're in…love.' And that is how you know."

We all broke into rapturous laughter, including me. I couldn't help it.

Oh, God, he really *is irreformable,* I thought. Jamie being a ladies' man was far too kind of a way to word it. I wouldn't have imagined he would be someone I would end up a close friend of, but damn, I really did enjoy him.

Poor Will. He never did get to expand on his important announcement, Jamie having hijacked the moment entirely.

Another afternoon when I walked into the officers' rec room, Jamie handed me the phone and said, "Charles, my mum would like a word."

The look on my face betrayed my attempt to hide my surprise as I hesitantly took the phone.

"Hello, Charles. I was just telling James that Charlotte will be home tomorrow night. I'm sure she'd love to see you, and it'll be lovely for us all to get together. Be sure to get a pass, all right?"

I was excited. It seemed Mrs. Blackwood—Gigi—was trying to advance things between Charlotte and me? *Fantastic!*

Having to do some work that evening tempered my enthusiasm. I had to go over instrument navigation and vectoring, that was easy; and then for university, economic theory, higher secondary—which would be the bugbear.

The next afternoon we jumped into my car and headed off to

Shrewsbury. We were five or ten minutes into the trip when Jamie turned to me and asked, "So, what do you think of Mum insisting we get together this evening with Charlotte?" It was the "with Charlotte" part of the question Jamie was interested in.

"Umm, not sure," I replied thoughtfully. "What do you think?"

Jamie didn't immediately give me his more carefully considered reply. "Mum may think you and Charlotte are a good match, but I'm not sure about it."

Even if his views were a little guarded, my stomach tightened at the thought. I was imagining things again. I wanted more information.

"What do you mean?" I pressed.

Then after a little more thought, he concluded, "To be honest, I wouldn't want it to change anything between us." He flicked a sideways glance at me.

I couldn't help thinking what my mother would say. *"Oh, so you're not always honest. And are we to assume that if you don't start your sentence with 'to be honest' or something along those lines, there is a good chance that you're not telling us the truth?"* I had long stopped using phrases like that as my mother would not hesitate in pulling me up on it. But I also appreciated Jamie's openness about how he felt about our friendship. I was starting to see a different side to him, and I liked it.

We carried on chatting the rest of the way to his home, Jamie doing most of the talking. I learnt how his mother and father had drifted apart. "I think they stopped loving each other about six or seven years ago," he said. "And then when I was sixteen, they got divorced. Very civil and amicable. Charlotte and I have a good relationship with him, but in truth, he is preoccupied with his work, and since the divorce, he hasn't played a big part in our lives."

Upon our arrival Gigi gave us each a kiss on the cheek, saying, "So lovely that you both came. Charlotte should be here any minute."

We went inside to our respective rooms to quickly change into our normal casual attire—jeans, T-shirt, and flip-flops—and set down our overnight bags. No sooner had I done so than I heard Charlotte's car arriving. I quickly headed outside to greet her. She seemed to have a little more spring in her step, which delighted me no end that she'd be as happy to see me.

I approached her, thinking about giving her a kiss on the cheek, until I caught a glimpse of a fellow coming around the corner.

"Hi, Charles, this is Alex, my boyfriend. I don't think you've met," came the bombshell.

"Er…hi!" I stammered. Alex was probably in his mid-twenties, and I felt very much his junior as he confidently put out his hand and shook mine.

"Hello, Charles. You must be Jamie's pal."

That was all it took to demolish months of endless fantasies. Thoughts of weekends to Rockwell Manor, introducing her to the Berkshire lifestyle, all evaporated in an instant. It was the first time I had felt downright glum at Shrewsbury.

Charlotte was doing everything she could for Jamie and me to engage with Alex, but it was the last thing I wanted, and evidently Jamie was not receptive to him either, judging by his lack of interest in Alex. At the same time, Charlotte was showing a very definite coolness towards me, making sure Alex didn't get the slightest idea of any possibility between the two of us, which I certainly wasn't enjoying.

"Wow, I never expected this," Jamie whispered to me while the others were engaged elsewhere. "Do you think Mum was just trying to give you a heads-up?"

As much as Jamie may have been concerned that Charlotte and me being together could affect our relationship, I was touched by his concern for me learning about Alex.

We squeezed around the little table in the annex dining area, Jamie on my right and Gigi on my left, which put Charlotte and Alex next to each other on the other side. Being seated next to Gigi at dinner improved my mood remarkably. I was acutely aware of her closeness to me, her scent, and especially her touch. Every now and then I felt her leg rest against mine and wondered if she was doing it on purpose. I was careful not to move and disturb the exciting feeling reaching into my stomach.

We started with foie gras, followed by a "bird in a bird," which was a deboned pheasant in a wild, deboned duck covered with a cranberry glaze. Gigi had specially ordered it from the Provenance Butcher in Chelsea, in London, along with a baked cheesecake. This was complemented with a

French red wine from Bordeaux. We finished off with our usual cheese, crackers, and port. Looking across our little table, I realised I'd hardly given Charlotte and Alex a second thought, so preoccupied was I with all the attention and affections of Gigi. I had enjoyed the dinner enormously, which brought into sharp focus where my true affections lay.

With dinner over, the evening seemed to come to a rapid close, everyone appearing to be lost in thought about the day ahead.

I walked into my room and immediately noticed a little parcel sitting on top of my pillow. On closer inspection, I discovered that Gigi had left me a treat from Charbonnel et Walker, the London chocolatier. Opening it, I discovered a pair of lip-shaped chocolates. I was still trying to reconcile my thoughts when Gigi popped her head into my bedroom.

"How were my lips?" she asked pertinently.

"Oh! Umm…are they *your* lips?" I responded mischievously.

"Once you have tried them, perhaps you'd like to try mine?" She winked and closed the door.

What? My mischievousness evaporated in an instant. I could not believe what Gigi had just said to me. Was she inviting me to kiss her? I felt an excited panic and my mind raced.

Of course, it was entirely obvious that Gigi had orchestrated the events of the pass out, wanting me to know that Charlotte and I were not a possibility and ensuring I was aware of where her affections lay.

I had not even given a thought to Charlotte, and of course Alex, being just down the passage in Charlotte's room. And my supposed determination to not have inappropriate thoughts about Jamie's mother had evaporated in an instant.

It was now around five months since I'd first met the Blackwood ladies, and this overt incident marked a notable change in my relationship with Gigi. As much as I enjoyed her new approach, it also had me contemplating the serious aspects of our relationship, not least of which was the effect this could have on Jamie and me.

Over the next couple of months Gigi became far more forthright in what seemed to be her amorous interest in me, and I did nothing to discourage her. I didn't know where this would end up, but I loved our flirtations.

Just before my twentieth birthday, Jamie and I took a weekend pass out and once again headed to Shrewsbury for what Gigi had decided would be my birthday dinner. Charlotte joined us for this celebration without Alex.

"Not sure *I've* ever received this treatment for *my* birthday," Jamie protested.

"Oh, nonsense! It's for all three of my favourite people," Gigi replied.

Jamie and Charlotte seemed happy with that. This interaction was interesting, showing just how accepted I had become into their family.

With no rushing back to base or university the next morning, we were all settling in for a fun, relaxed evening. I was assigned as cocktail waiter and given the task of mixing dry martinis, because that was evidently ideal for the meal that lay ahead. Drinks flowing and music playing, the ladies danced to the rhythm, and the mood immediately replicated what we had enjoyed so many times before. Previously, my eyes would have been darting between mother and daughter, but by now I only had eyes for one person. And it wasn't Charlotte.

With the four of us happy and relaxed, the martinis fuelling our feelings of euphoria, Gigi enthusiastically beckoned us to the candlelit table in her cosy annex dining area. "Come along, darlings! Dinner's ready."

I was acutely aware of Gigi's innocuous little 'darlings' comment, and I liked it. I shot a questioning glance at Gigi, to which she replied with a sexy little smile and a wink. My intake of breath was almost audible.

The sumptuous seafood meal set before us was enticing. The starter was Kumamoto oysters on the half shell—with plenty of lemon, Tabasco sauce, and shallot mignonette with freshly ground black pepper—served on a bed of crushed ice on a large silver platter. Gigi prepared one for me, prying the meat away from the shell, which she brought up to my lips so that I could suck the contents. I was relishing not only the taste, but also the sensation in my mouth as I briefly chewed and swallowed the oyster. Jamie went to get some more ice, and Charlotte got up to change the music.

"I love how you suck those oysters into your mouth, and the way you savour and swallow them," Gigi whispered, smiling.

I sat there with a proverbial mouth full of teeth, at a complete loss for words.

"And I am told they put lead in a man's pencil. Now you just have to find someone to write to," she continued in a most mischievous tone.

God, what is she saying to me? Even though I was reeling at Gigi's provocative behaviour and suggestiveness—along with my self-consciousness about not having anyone to write to—I could still see the funny side and giggled.

The two siblings returned to the table with Gigi abruptly bringing her mischievousness to an end. Decorum resumed.

She was always sure not to let Jamie and Charlotte see any of her flirtations with me. Even so, it was impossible for Jamie and Charlotte not to notice the closeness between Gigi and me. In proof of that, Charlotte remarked, "Ooh, Mum just loves you. Imagine if you were a few years older," she suggested.

I was almost bowled over by this remark, but even more so with Jamie's contribution.

"Oh nonsense, age is just a number," he said with a flick of his wrist emphasising his point.

Gigi and I had gone very quiet. I imagined that Jamie had just used a cliché and surely didn't really feel that way.

Charlotte then turned up the music, which I hadn't even noticed playing in the background. As the romantic lead-in began, Gigi's face lit up.

"Un'altra Te" – Eros Ramazzotti

| YouTube | Spotify | Apple |

Both ladies spontaneously began singing along with the Italian artist. Then Charlotte got to her feet and began to dance as Gigi swayed to the beat, still sitting next to me.

"What's with the Italian music?" I asked.

"Oh, we love Eros," Gigi replied.

"And you understand the words?" I went on.

"I have some Italian and French, mind you. And we sure know *these* words." Gigi smiled.

"Tell me," I said, intrigued.

As the song repeated, making sure Charlotte and Jamie were out of earshot, Gigi translated for me. "Another you." She put an index finger on my chest. "Where do I find it?" She scratched her chin in an animated fashion. "Another one that surprises me."

As she continued her translation of the song, I noticed a hint of bashfulness.

"Another you. A similar trouble." Then she asked in a very suggestive tone, "Are you trouble, Edward Charles?"

I shook my head.

Gigi nodded hers. "I wonder if there is another you." She squeezed me high up on my thigh.

As the song played out, my mind swirling, Suzie luckily provided the distraction. Oblivious of the romantic interlude she was interrupting, she placed a platter of king crab legs on the table and a selection of dipping sauces in front of us.

Seemingly having to physically extract herself from her thoughts, Gigi began to absentmindedly feed me. Jamie and Charlotte seemed utterly unaffected by her familiarity, which would not have been the case had they been aware of what was happening underneath the table. Their mother was rubbing her bare foot against my feet, sending a shiver up my spine. *So naughty and so, so nice…*

Grilled giant tiger prawns came next. Gigi's hands were once again busy deshelling them, dipping the flesh into either the garlic lemon butter or Portuguese peri-peri sauce. Then she surreptitiously brought the flesh to my mouth for me to take a bite before she ate the rest herself, making sure no one would notice. There was something very sexual about the way she was using her hands with our food, and our eating together in this way.

God help me. Without any effort, Gigi was the sexiest woman I had ever met!

She was always careful not to do anything too affectionate or demonstrative with me unless it was behind Jamie and Charlotte's backs. But on occasion, it is fair to say she would do the odd little thing that would have an obvious meaning for us, but not to Jamie and Charlotte. I hoped.

As was often the case, we didn't have dessert but instead, Gigi brought a large cheeseboard to the table, with various crackers, cheeses, and preserves. This would be a perfect way to end the meal, washed down with her favourite Madeira port.

I watched as Jamie took a cheese biscuit, a swipe of butter, and a neatly cut segment of cheese that he placed squarely on the cracker, and then from its jar of thick, sweet syrup, he put a sizeable piece of fig preserve atop his creation. It was when he popped the entire delicacy into his mouth that it hit me. His cheese-and-cracker ritual may have been a coincidence, but the similarity between Jamie and my granddad was unmistakable.

Did this have something to do with why I felt so connected to him? Right then, I felt very close to not only Jamie but also my deceased granddad. Both tall, handsome men. Both with wicked senses of humour. It made me wonder if Granddad had also been a ladies' man. Why not? He wasn't even married. As I played it through my mind, I couldn't help wondering where Mrs. Kearns may have slept, at least from time to time.

Then I wondered if my mother had seen any of her father in Jamie when they first met. It would have explained her instant liking for him.

After everyone went up to bed, I sat down in the kitchen to do my flight folio. Gigi came in, dressed in a sheer chiffon robe with a silk camisole and shorts set underneath. She suggested we have a cuppa before turning in for the night. I was still a little shy around her when we were alone, so I just nodded my head.

"On second thought, you should probably go to bed now. You have such an early start."

She had given me an out, but I couldn't help wondering if there was another reason for her lack of persistence. I sensed she wanted more, as did I, but was holding back. When I stood up to leave, she walked intently up to me. I assumed she was going to give me the usual goodnight kiss on the cheek. As if her resistance weakened for a moment, her carnal instinct overruling her better judgement, she put one hand behind my head, her fingers through my hair, and her other hand on my buttocks. She gently held her body against me as she put her lips firmly on mine in a kiss that lasted much longer than I had previously experienced.

As startled as I was, I did not pull away. I was almost certain one of my hands ended up on her back and held her against me as well. I felt her full breasts against my chest through her scant clothing. She moved back slightly from me, one hand still behind my head as I looked down bashfully. Seeing through her thin top, I had a full view of the darker patches nestled there. Her nipples were hard, their prominence showing through her silk camisole, confirming I was not the only one feeling this intense sexual arousal.

Unsure of what I should do next, I hesitantly said goodnight and went to my room. I switched off the bedside light and lay on my back, and without even thinking about it, my hand found my crotch. Thoughts of my first night at the Blackwoods' came flooding back in an instant. When I realised how aroused I was and that I was well on my way to becoming fully erect, there was no question that the woman having this effect on me was Gigi.

I needed relief. I dashed into the bathroom, my length protruding forward like a rhinoceros horn as I grabbed a facecloth and hair conditioner. I ignored the shampoo, which I had discovered was also a good lubricant but made urination sting like hell. A man only makes that mistake once.

Back in bed, I held my conditioner-lubed erection in my right hand, driving my full length in and out of my clenched fist with the thrusting of my hips, imagining how it would feel being inside Gigi. I quickly reached the point of no return and needed the facecloth.

As I began to subside, I heard someone outside my bedroom door. Knowing it could only be Gigi, I quickly wiped myself and discarded the cloth on the nightstand, then covered myself with the sheet. Just in time I heard the little knock. Without waiting to be invited in, Gigi opened the door and walked quietly over to my bedside. She glanced at the side table where the hair conditioner and crumpled facecloth lay bare what I had been doing. Then she bent over me and slipped a hand behind my head, my hair between her fingers, and kissed me squarely on my mouth. Soft and moist as she slowly parted her lips just slightly. I savoured the feeling, wanting more. Then she clenched her fist, her fingers gently pulling my hair. With her lips more open now, her tongue probed purposefully into my mouth. With a throaty little moan, she pulled my hair again, this time much harder, her kiss more forceful, erotism I was unused to. Then, as if she thought better of letting me experience the full passion of her kiss she pulled away. Still holding the back of my head, she gave me an intense, smouldering look that told me she did not want to stop there. Neither did I. With her other hand she stroked my cheek before putting her fingers on my lips so I could kiss them, taste them. Gigi wiped the wetness across my top lip beneath my nose. That scent, that taste. I wanted more.

Then she pulled back ever so slightly and whispered, "Good night, Darling. Sleep well, my gorgeous."

My eyes followed her exit as if I were in a trance. As my gaze passed over the open tub of conditioner and the facecloth, I wondered what she thought. Surprisingly, I wasn't concerned. Was it her indifference? She did not make me feel uncomfortable. Her own actions told me what I had been doing was natural. What captivated me right then was the intoxicating scent she had left around my mouth and nose. I knew then that in letting me taste and smell her fingers, she wanted me to know she had been touching herself while listening to my masturbating from beyond my closed door.

The feeling that came over me was overwhelming. We had crossed an invisible line, and I knew our relationship had moved into another realm. I wanted this woman, every part of her. I rolled over onto my stomach, savouring Gigi's raw scent, now allowing erotic thoughts of her to overwhelm my brain until I finally fell asleep.

The next day we went into the little town of Shrewsbury to do a little exploring. A croissant and barista coffee in the late morning, and a *very Italian,* Italian restaurant in the afternoon for a late pasta lunch. "Hardly anyone speaks English here," I remarked. It didn't matter. Gigi ordered for us all in what seemed like fluent Italian to me. The time flew by.

Gigi had stepped back from her amorous advances of the previous night, which didn't worry me. There was a new invisible electrical pulse between us that created a connection, a magnetism we both felt and seemingly understood, and I wallowed in the comfort of this new feeling.

That evening there was no repetition of the night before, except a quick passionate kiss and Gigi's words. "I don't think there's another you?" Words from the song the night before.

When the time came for us to leave, Gigi waited for us to have a quiet moment alone. While Jamie helped Charlotte with her overnight bag, Gigi put her mouth on mine moving her full lips slightly, seeking more comfort.

"Goodbye, my gorgeous. I will see you soon." Her whisper was a clear statement of intent.

Heading off to RAF Shawbury, I was feeling happy, excited, alive, sensual, lightheaded. Everything. Or none of the above. Something new perhaps. Yes, a feeling I had never felt before. I drove faster than normal, lost in the lyrics of the loud music.

"What on earth are you so happy about?" Jamie asked.

Turning the sound down, I replied, "It was a lovely dinner and, um, wonderful to be back at Shrewsbury again." Elated, I turned the music up again.

"Hungry Like the Wolf" – Duran Duran

YouTube   Spotify   Apple

As the song got to "do-do-do-do-do" we both joined in, singing loudly over the raspy engine noise as I raced down the road.

I couldn't help but smile at the thought of hunting Gigi down and devouring her, as the lyrics went on about being "hungry like the wolf." I wanted her. I was desperate to feel the drumming heat of her skin. That scent! I was hungrier than the wolf. I wanted to dance in my seat and couldn't wait for another chance to kiss her.

A few days later, I had an early afternoon off and found a note on the message board for me from Gigi that read, "Phone me. Let's do dinner tomorrow night." I was surprised because this was truly short notice and as far as I was aware, Jamie would be at RAF College Cranwell for some lectures over the next few days. With no way of contacting him, I gave Gigi a call, but it was impossible to speak openly. The gist of the conversation was that yes, Jamie was at the college, but he would "almost certainly come home tomorrow evening." The only thing that tempered my enthusiasm slightly was that I still had a university tutorial to get through, which would undoubtedly take me three or four hours.

Oh, well. Another late night. I grimaced at the thought.

The next day the senior officer was more relaxed about giving me a night pass since we were well into the course. Excited about getting back to Shrewsbury, I could not wait to be setting off. Given what had transpired the last time made me a little pensive. Gigi and every delicious moment of that evening had been constantly on my mind. It could have all been so simple, but she was my best friend's mother and her alluring womanly sensuality, against which I had little defence, threatened to envelop me.

CHAPTER 11
LOST IN A STORM

I HEADED OFF TO Shrewsbury on my own, giving me licence to drive even faster than I normally would have done. It was 1610 hours, and I calculated I would get there in just thirty minutes, a good while before Jamie would arrive from Cranwell College, which was at least a two-and-a-half-hour drive to Shrewsbury. This meant that Gigi and I could have a good amount of time together. I wondered how it would turn out. Would she just up-front kiss me again? *What will I do?* I felt a surge of confused emotions about what could happen this evening.

My insecurities returned as I played back some of what had happened the last time we were together. There was no way I could be misreading her actions, but what did it all mean?

And what about the little things she had been saying to me? Had she really been touching herself and wanted me to know it? Thinking about the kiss in the kitchen and about the scent she had left on my top lip only scrambled my thoughts more.

Regardless of what the reality was, my stomach tightened with these thoughts racing through my mind.

I arrived at the Blackwoods' home with overnight bag in hand and walked up the pathway. There, framed in the doorway, stood Gigi. The early evening light subtly washed over her, presenting the most alluring picture. Her hazel-green eyes sparkled boldly, and her tousled honey-blonde hair fell loosely to her shoulders, framing a face that looked particularly beautiful that evening. I took it all in. She was wearing a very plain, loose-fitting, midcalf ivory cotton dress. The fullness of her breasts was accentuated by the way the garment was cinched below them, the low-cut neckline showing her pronounced cleavage. Her large areolae showed faintly through, her nipples more prominent than usual. *Beautifully ripe,* I thought, not wanting to take my eyes off them. I continued, taking in the shape of her waist, hips, and legs, her beautiful feet in flat, tan leather sandals. This was the most tantalising sight I had ever seen, and I could not help the little groan that crept out from the back of my throat.

In complete contrast to what I was feeling, she calmly watched me as I approached, radiating a serenity and quiet confidence that immediately made me feel better. I smiled shyly at her. This beautiful, mature woman, who seemed to know exactly what she wanted, only served to excite me more. Gigi stood there, legs slightly apart, with one hand on her hip, the other hanging down loosely at her side, creating a picture that would stay in my mind forever. In that moment, my insecurities evaporated and I walked towards her as the sound of Celine Dion wafted through from the living room like a greeting. Nothing coincidental about it.

"Think Twice" – Celine Dion

| YouTube | Spotify | Apple |

As the song played, I felt like I was being pulled towards Gigi in slow motion. Our eyes locked. I could see her subtly biting her bottom lip, and I felt a quiver in my groin. I wasn't thinking about anything other than being right there, right then, with this vision before me.

The last thing to go through my mind before I stepped into the frame of that most captivating picture was that I was quite certain neither Jamie nor Charlotte had any idea they were meant to be coming home for the night.

As I entered the doorway, Gigi made no attempt to step back, and I found myself standing right up against her. She looked into my eyes with a piercing intensity, our attraction for each other was breathtakingly electrifying. Holding our gaze, she reached behind me, pushed the door closed, and brought her right hand up to the back of my head, gently taking a handful of my hair in her fist. Our legs slid between each other's, and the inside of her thigh rubbed against me. She leant forward, putting her other hand on my buttocks, and kissed me. Her full lips on mine, mouth open, her tongue not hesitating in being a part of our urgent desire.

Without even realising it, I had reciprocated in every way. My one hand was behind her head, fingers through her hair, the other on the small of her back, holding her against me. My pelvis was pushed hard against her stomach in response to her pubic bone pressing onto my thigh. Our mouths consumed each other's lips as our tongues began to probe, trying to extract every ounce of emotion from our kiss.

Gigi began slowly, rhythmically moving her pelvis against my leg, murmuring her first words since I had arrived. "God, I have waited so long for this."

Then our mouths found each other's again, our bodies still firmly pressed against each other's as our lips and tongues resumed their urgent demands.

I felt a twinge of excited panic. There was no longer any ambiguity. No guilt, nor questioning whether this was right or wrong or what Jamie and Charlotte may think. I had fallen into the passionate embrace of this beautiful woman who I had been dreaming about for months, enveloped by her yearning. It was beyond my wildest dreams that we were there, consuming each other in the most extraordinary way at the entrance of her home. New to all of it, I simply followed her lead. Was it really going to happen tonight?

The urgency subsided for just a short while before I felt Gigi's hand on the back of my head, holding me more forcefully. I did likewise, both of us wanting and demanding more. She became quite rough, pulling my hair noticeably harder as if she wanted to feel more of my presence. I sensed she wanted this from me as well, as my spread fingers slipped through her hair. She gently bit my lips, then teased me with her firm tongue, darting it in and out of my mouth in an overt expression of lust.

A fullness started distorting the front of my trousers, and Gigi's hand reached down onto my crotch. *Oh, God, so forward!* She rubbed me and then unashamedly tried to take a hold of my girth through my trousers. As if it were my cue, without being fully conscious of my actions, I placed my hand on hers, wanting to feel *her* feeling me so fully erect. I'd always loved her hands, which from now on, I would see in a completely different light.

A lot happened between us in those first few moments, the result of months of pent-up desire.

Gigi then broke our embrace. She seemed to collect her thoughts as she held both my hands and smiled broadly up at me. "Well, hello, Charles. Let's go and have a drink. Not that I did not like my greeting."

I couldn't help smiling at how she cheekily lay the blame of our greeting on me.

She took me by the hand and led me into the drawing room. We sat down next to each other, her hand on my knee. I felt a little awkward, as I wasn't sure what I should be doing or what came next.

After a glass of wine, I began to relax, and our conversation took on the joviality and comfort of our usual interactions.

We had an early dinner, sitting close enough so we could touch each other while we chatted and enjoyed our meal. It was no surprise that Suzie was not there that evening, so it was Gigi and me to clear up. Emboldened by our being alone, the sexual energy was unmistakable as we touched each other and held hands for prolonged periods. I could not wait for us to explore each other's bodies, now certain it would happen that night.

As we contemplated our tiramisu dessert, Gigi leant back in her chair. "I have another dessert in mind for you tonight, my love." With a mischievous glint in her eye, she placed one bare foot between my legs and wiggled it, then asked, "Are you ready for me, Charles?"

God, it's really going to happen, was my overwhelming thought. I felt an excited nervousness but could not deny that Gigi's forthright approach again aroused me instantly.

"Ooh, don't do that," I moaned as I held her foot against my crotch.

Gigi got up and seductively led me by the hand to my room, wasting no time in kissing me again. She kicked off her sandals, as I did my shoes, and then she pulled off my socks. She stood on the tops of my bare feet, held me around the neck and kissed me again.

"Clothes off. I want you naked," she demanded as she pulled her dress off in one fluid motion.

The shameless manner of how she exposed her naked body threatened to stupefy me. I found myself trying to work out what to do first. *Shirt, then trousers, or trousers, then shirt?* My brain wasn't functioning properly.

"I didn't realise unbuttoning a shirt was such an arduous task for a helicopter pilot," she teased. "I guess you will have to come back for a few lessons."

Her breasts brushed against my arm and chest as she helped unbutton my shirt.

My insides churned and tightened, to say nothing about what was happening in my groin. My inexperience and overexcitement were taking their toll. I was spring-loaded, waiting to be released. I could only think, *This is going to be embarrassing.* I felt like such a novice, becoming erect with the slightest stimulation.

Gigi made a show of removing my belt, undoing my trouser button, and pulling down my pants and underpants together in one motion.

Even I was surprised by the way he bounced out, already fully erect. "S-sorry," I stammered.

"Ooh, God, yes!" was all I heard.

That simple acknowledgment and appreciation from Gigi had me instantly feeling more relaxed. Her deliberate intention perhaps? She began rubbing her breasts from side to side across my chest and, as her nipples became hard, she leant back and pinched them between her fingers, the sight of which sent a shiver down my spine.

Was her uninhibited sexuality the expression of an emancipated woman taking what she wanted?

There I was—the boy who would turn crimson and hope the ground would swallow him up if a girl even spoke to him—now with this gorgeous woman, her beautiful, sensual hand fondling him in the most erotic way.

As her stroking became more rhythmic, I knew she would have to stop, or I would face the embarrassment of ejaculating right then. Gigi sensed it, as she halted what she was doing and purred, "Okay, my darling, not yet."

I had been stimulated by everything about her. Always aware of her smell: a subtle, fresh summer scent, mixed in with her unmistakeable body aroma, the one I had found so intoxicating the last time I was with her. I discreetly tried to locate it, little sniffs around her neck and behind her ears.

This smell must have to do with her pheromones, I thought, something I had recently heard about.

"Found what you're looking for, Darling?" She chuckled.

Well, perhaps I wasn't *that* discreet. I felt very much the virgin that I was as she gently pushed me onto the bed. Before I knew it, I was lying on my back with Gigi straddling me. I was as surprised as I was intrigued, feeling her wetness against my stomach as she leant forward and started rubbing my chest and shoulders, her eyes seemingly consuming every detail of my body.

Feeling self conscious and wanting to deflect her studying me, I simply said, "God, you are so gorgeous."

She put her hands on my shoulders, leant forward, and gave me a soft kiss on the lips. Then, she pulled slightly back, and even though we were the only ones in the house, she brought her mouth up against my ear and whispered, "Charles Featherstone, there's going to be a storm tonight."

I was quite certain it was not the kind of storm "Think Twice" was about.

Eventually, with us still lying next to each other, her arm across my chest, she said, "My darling, I think you ought to know you passed with flying colours. But there is some bad news. You do have a lot more to learn, and it only gets *harder and harder.*"

I could not help chuckling at the double meaning of her words, and I happily played along. "Well, I am really pleased I have made a good start, but do you think I am going to manage a *big, hard,* syllabus?"

I felt her little giggle as much as I heard it.

"And will it be possible for me to cram? Perhaps I could have another lesson this evening?" I continued.

"That is exactly the response I wanted!" she replied playfully as she reached down to feel between my legs.

Still feeling a little self-conscious, I tried to pull back, but she had already managed to have a little feel. She then raised her cupped hand to her nose. Her "Mmm…nice," was answered with my look of mild horror.

"Two can play *your* game," Gigi said smiling.

Oh yes, I guess so. But I was subtle. Gigi wasn't. But then I was twenty and she wasn't, was how I quickly reconciled it. Even so, it was enough to have me blushing.

Loving this nonchalant banter and the smell of our sex filling the room, I started relaxing sufficiently to be able to join in further with the teasing. "You could have warned me that my cue would be so obvious," I said mischievously. "And I also did not realise that God played such a significant role in this *sex* thing. Does this mean I need to take a few lessons in theology?" Now it was me doing the winking.

We carried on chatting amiably, and then after a while, I asked more seriously. "I've been thinking. What was last week all about, you know, when something was about to happen and then you disappeared?"

"Oh, goodness, Charles. I…I…it didn't feel right, seducing a teenager."

I thought about how she had suddenly pulled back. I understood what she was saying, but really? I had been just days from turning twenty. I would have preferred being nineteen when it happened. Twenty seemed very late to have lost my virginity.

Brushing the conversation aside, Gigi announced she was going to get us something to drink.

"I am not very thirsty," I said, hoping to save her the walk downstairs. "That's fine." She smiled. "But I am hoping that you are going to be." With her body on full display, she confidently walked down to the kitchen.

I loved the view from behind and was fixated on her shapely figure. When she returned, I watched each step as she walked towards the bed, staring at her full, bouncing breasts, her narrowed midriff and the way it widened to form her shapely hips, and her pubic area with its patch of dark blonde tendrils. Taking in the full view as she approached me had me in a state of semi-erectness.

Then standing in front of me, still holding our drinks in each hand, she opened her arms, fully revealing her bosoms in the process, and swayed her hips from side to side, her boobs responding to the motion, teasing me with this tantalising view.

Knowing I would soon be close to another erection and not wanting Gigi to realise how easily I was aroused, I had covered myself with the sheet. I did a little check as I pulled it up further, making sure I was not exposed.

"Uh-uh, no you don't." She placed our Cokes on the side table. "You are definitely not allowed to be covered up while you are looking at my naked body like that," she scolded me playfully. "That is not what an officer and a gentleman does. Remove that sheet right now, Lieutenant," she ordered with a grin.

"Umm, I'm not exactly decent." I laughed shyly, conscious of my seemingly always being in a semierect state.

She gave me a knowing smile and leant forward to remove the covers from across my torso. I instinctively pulled them back up, but she was having none of it and began wrestling with me. I was mesmerised by the way her breasts bounced, and whenever they brushed against me, I pressed against them, wanting more. Then, as our grappling intensified, so our bodies became increasingly entwined with each other's. Gigi was surprisingly strong, and she enjoyed testing her strength against mine. Soon my upper leg was on her groin, and I could feel her slippery wetness. She twisted around and took a firm hold of my arms, pinning me to the bed with all of her upper-body weight. Gigi knelt over me, and the more we wrestled, the more her legs opened and exposed her. I caught glimpses of her vagina. Absorbed by what I saw, I wanted to see more. All the while this play fighting was arousing me no end.

By this stage I had completely forgotten about my self-consciousness, as my full erection was slapping around with gay abandon. We both laughed at what had gone on and were soon quite out of breath.

I caught another glimpse of Gigi's vagina and became embarrassed when she caught me staring. Our wrestling suddenly stopped. Kneeling over me, straddling my upper legs, she looked at me steadily. Then in a very conscious manner, she did something I could only describe as bewildering. Something that would remain with me forever.

When we had finished making love, I rolled Gigi on top of me, feeling the comfort of her full weight on my body, my still surprisingly firm length nestled inside her womanhood. We lay there, not wanting to move as we relished each other's embrace.

Eventually I broke the silence. "So?"

With an exaggerated drawl, she said, "Oh, I don't know. There are lots of areas we are going to have to work on, Lieutenant," she teasingly mocked. "And goodness knows how long it is all going to take."

I didn't know much but certainly enough to realise that all was fine, so I took up the banter. "Oh, really? Could you be more specific?"

With a schoolteacher's tone, Gigi replied. "Well, for starters we need to have a really *hard* discussion about the forcefulness of your efforts. What are you trying to do, kill the poor girl?" She was chuckling now, enjoying this little interaction.

I was quiet for a moment, then voiced my fears. "Gigi, was I very rough and, you know, too, umm, as you said…forceful? Did I hurt you?"

"Of course, you were very rough and forceful. Where were *you*, Lieutenant? Missing in action? And yes, you did hurt me. I am going to feel it for a week, and you had better get yourself back here by then so that you can re-inflict the pleasure," she teased.

I was perplexed and surely wore my confusion on my face, but once again, her laugh suggested there was no problem. To allay my concerns, she added, "I *loved* it rough. A little pain can feel good when I'm in the mood for it."

I made mental notes of exploring this further sometime in the future.

With that, we kissed each other gently, nothing salacious but with an intensity that seemed to reach into my soul. We lay there for a long while. I couldn't believe I was in the arms of the woman I had dreamt about for so long. Eventually I asked her what she was feeling.

She stroked my face and replied, "Same as you, Baby. Same as you."

Snuggled together, we drifted off to sleep in each other's arms.

We woke up the following morning, still cuddling. Before saying a word, we kissed, very gently at first, but it did not take long before our kissing became more passionate.

After a few minutes, Gigi pulled away. "Good morning, Darling. I had the most wonderful dream last night." She made a show of reaching beneath the covers, teasing me as she watched my reaction.

Then she brought her hand out so we could both inspect her two wet fingers. "I guess it wasn't a dream," she said, smiling.

I was almost beside myself. I kept enough decorum to at least try to say something in the spirit of the jovial mood she had created. "Just let me have another look at your fingers," I asked. "I think there's a little skin under your nails, my love. I wonder where that came from?" I feigned ignorance, moving my back slightly.

"Ooh, did I hurt you, Darling?" Gigi pushed my shoulder, beckoning me to roll onto my side so she could inspect me. "Oh, my God, no. I can't believe I did that to you," she said with genuine remorse. "Darling, what happens when you are showering back at the base?"

It was a good question. "I guess I'm just going to become very shy for a while," I suggested.

Our lovemaking that ensued was quite different from the night before. Gigi wanted me to be on top of her, as if she were trying to get every part of our bodies to touch. I was firmly inside the source of last night's wild pleasure but this time, our movements were neither extravagant nor forceful. The small and intense motions of our bodies against each other allowed us to feel every little sensation of our union, which was amplified by the abundant scent of our sex. As our pelvises moved in rhythmic harmony, we held and kissed each other.

Gigi added a level of sensuality in the way she cupped my behind as I gently moved in and out of her. Then she put her hands on the back of my head, sometimes running her fingers through my hair and occasionally closing her fist so that she had a handful and could pull it, which she did very firmly.

We kept this up for a long, long while, enjoying every moment of it. Then Gigi whispered, "Let's cum together now, Darling."

Moments later, we both began the release of the most beautiful, gentle orgasm.

Even though I had barely lost my virginity, I already knew the part of our sex I loved the most. It was the aftermath. Two spent bodies lying limply next to each other, a sheen of sweat glistening on our bodies, chests rising and falling to the sound of our heavy breathing, the carnal scent of our sexual discharge and then, the blissful feeling of contentment as our breathing slowly normalised.

We lay there, our faces close, inhaling each other's breaths until we had fully regained our composure.

I enjoyed feeling Gigi's full weight on me, so I effortlessly rolled her over on top of me.

She pulled back slightly and cupped my head in her hands, looking intently at my face and into my eyes. Then she kissed me, slowly, purposefully, her full lips slightly parted and gently feeling the outline of my lips. Again, she pulled back and looked at me before repeating the process. I wanted to ravish her, but this was Gigi's moment, so I just savoured the touch and softness of her beautiful mouth.

She then rested her head on my chest and let out a gentle sigh. "What am I going to do with you my lovely?" she asked quietly.

I had many ideas but said nothing. Gigi was not looking for an answer to her rhetorical question.

After a short while she lifted herself up, looked at me with a glint in her eyes, mischievousness restored, and spoke.

"Lieutenant Charles Featherstone, I think you ought to know that last night, and again this morning, your performance was very encouraging. All you need to do now is practice, practice, practice" and each time she said the word *practice*, she thrust her pelvis onto mine.

My broad grin was my only reply. Hopefully this was the answer to her question of what she was going to do with me.

I would have preferred to lie with her awhile longer, but unfortunately duty was calling. I had to report back to base at 0730 hours and it was a good thirty-minute drive.

I stepped into the shower, followed by Gigi. I was still feeling just a tad self-conscious, but that worry soon washed away as we lovingly began soaping each other.

Gigi then guided my hands over her lathered body and her most intimate parts before she did likewise with me. "Ooh, I love feeling your semi, Baby," she whispered into my ear.

I had no words as I felt her nipples display a similar firmness.

Eventually, we rinsed ourselves under the warm water and reluctantly got out of the shower. Gigi donned her bathrobe and went down to see to our breakfast, while I got dressed before gathering my things.

We didn't say much as we quietly ate, words replaced by the touch of our hands and the look in our eyes.

Far too soon I found myself standing in the same doorway that just the night before had framed the object of my extreme desire.

How the world had changed for me in the past twelve hours! Our relationship had entered a whole new phase with such a different dynamic.

Without a doubt, there would be all sorts of hurdles, but now was not the time to think about that. I was no longer a virgin and even in my naivety, I suspected I had just experienced the best possible transition into this new world. I felt a myriad of overwhelming emotions towards this woman, who I began to suspect had, over the past months, been advancing my understanding of the opposite sex, with dare I say, a very maternal, sensitive touch. Now that we had made love, was she going to start educating me with her exquisite eroticism that I had been given a taste of? I couldn't wait to find out. And how I loved this new feeling inside me.

Just as I was getting lost in those thoughts, Gigi looked at me and said in a solemn voice.

"Darling, just one thing. Remember last week when Charlotte and Jamie were being quite positive about us being together, the 'age is just a number' comment from Jamie?"

"Yes," was my monosyllable reply.

"Well, I don't think that was necessarily how they feel, so I think we should keep our relationship just between you and me."

Ooh, I didn't like the feeling *that* brought on, as the first pangs of guilt dampened my elation. That aside, I felt exactly the way she did, so I didn't hesitate in nodding my agreement. Reality check or not, Gigi saying we were in a relationship was all I wanted to hear.

"Oh, and one other thing. This is for when you are back at base. Promise?" She put a neatly folded piece of paper into my inside pocket.

As much as I couldn't wait to read it, I said, "I promise."

I drove out of the Blackwoods' main gate a new man. I turned on the radio. A catchy tune from *Saturday Night Fever* had me turning up the volume as I began to sing along.

"More Than a Woman" – Bee Gees

YouTube   Spotify   Apple

My Rude Awakening

My thoughts mirrored the lyrics as I drummed the rhythm out on the steering wheel. Gigi had taken my breath away, and my virginity, so she would be a part of my life forever. Being in each other's arms, our sexual union, was my new paradise.

I thought about her calling me Baby and about how it had nothing to do with our age difference and everything to do with our sexual attraction. Of course she saw me as a man. And right then, I wanted to be *her* man. I was smitten. *Is this love?* Grinning from ear to ear, I continued singing along at the top of my lungs.

I got back to base with about ten minutes to spare and confirmed that Jamie was indeed still at RAF Cranwell College. No difficult questions to sidestep I thought. I then checked the schedule for the day. I was with senior flight instructor Captain Jonathan Swales for a three-hour "desk and flying" session, to review my flight training to that point. My last review had left a lot of room for improvement. I had just not been feeling it then, and it was imperative that you did feel it when flying a helicopter. *Well, too late to worry about it now.* Nothing was going to get me down that day. I just hoped the flight-school training motto—*Imprimis Praecepta* ("Our Teaching is Everlasting")—would hold true.

I progressed through a gruelling morning and finally got to the last part, the flight test.

Things moved along fluidly, and as the examination entered the final, most complicated phase, I was feeling increasingly more relaxed. I seemed to sail through hydraulic failure, tail-rotor failure—loss of tail rotor, and then finally, the autorotation—landing without an engine, my favourite.

As we finished this last exercise, I restarted my engine to reposition the helicopter on the apron. Only then did I look at Captain Swales enquiringly.

"Well, Featherstone, you were on it today. That was great." This was high praise from someone who was typically sparing with his compliments.

I left the airfield feeling on top of the world. I had a sense that my night of passion marked the beginning of a different me. A whole new world had opened up, and I couldn't wait to explore.

All I wanted to do was phone Gigi and tell her how I was feeling. That was when I remembered the letter in my tunic, hanging on the clothes horse.

> My Darling Charles,
>
> It has been seven months and four days since I first met you. I was drawn to you from the start. I'm quite sure you don't remember the song I played the first evening you came to us, or noticed how jubilant I was? Well, the song was "Cover Me" by Bruce Springsteen. Embarrassingly, I had those thoughts about us from that first night. And, by the way, when women are in bed alone, and they have those thoughts, they do what boys do! It seemed so illicit then, but not now. I have lived with a yearning ever since. When Jamie told Charlotte you were still a virgin, she didn't need to tell me. I knew.
>
> What happened last night, I don't treat lightly and never will. It will live with me forever. I hope it will always have a place in your heart.
>
> Love,
>
> Gigi XOXO

In fairness, I'd had no idea what to expect of my first sexual encounter, and I am sure that is true for most virgins. It would almost certainly have been more along the lines of 'beneath the sheets with the lights turned off!' Nothing I had come to know of Gigi had ever given me an inkling of her openness and complete comfort in her lascivious sexuality. And was it rude? Even though her antics were astounding and intoxicating all at the same time, I couldn't accept that Gigi had been rude.

But what I instinctively did know was that the way I'd lost my virginity was unique. An older woman, a younger man, and months and months of a developing relationship, and with it, ever-increasing yearning. And then my being taken along with her in an eruption of pent-up desire that would surely change my world forever. Our relationship had now finally been consummated in the most extraordinary way imaginable.

At this very early stage, it was impossible to know what would come of Gigi and me. What was certain though, was that she had unquestionably become a part of my life.

CHAPTER 12
THE NEXT TIME

THE DAYS THAT followed my stormy night with Gigi were no less frenetic than the weeks before, but somehow, I was different. I seemed to be more in control of my life and, most especially, my flying.

Another big change was that I spoke to Gigi every day. Sometimes it was a quick call between lectures or flight training exercises, but I especially enjoyed our late-night conversations, which went on longer than they should have, keeping me from my university studies. Our dialogue had two themes. First, we amused each other to no end and laughed easily. Then our conversation would become sexual and salacious, where we'd whisper intimate thoughts and naughty details, arousing one another, which spurred us on to make the next arrangement to be together again.

For the first time in my life, I had a woman. Regardless of how different that was for me, it sat comfortably. I just couldn't let Jamie or Charlotte know. On a few occasions, Jamie looked quizzically at me while I was on the phone with Gigi, wondering who I was speaking to. I wish I had fibbed about it being someone other than "my mum" because that excuse was too close to the bone.

One may have thought the distraction of going to Shrewsbury would have a detrimental effect on my demanding flight training and studying towards an undergraduate degree. In fact, it had the opposite effect, except for a few overly long telephone conversations. What may have proven to be a distraction actually enhanced my calmness and concentration, two vital ingredients in dealing with the challenges at RAF Shawbury. Over the next few weeks, we began the most complicated part of our syllabus, yet I was flying with more confidence and competence than I'd ever experienced before.

"You are certainly on it, Lieutenant," complimented one of the instructors, words that had previously been used by Captain Swales.

It seemed there was consensus. Even the other trainees began to hold me in higher regard. That included Jamie, who on one occasion asked me quite pointedly, "What has happened to you, chum?"

"I dunno," was my lax reply, not wanting to get into that conversation.

A few days later, the first time since that unforgettable night with Gigi, Jamie announced, "Get a pass out, Squire. Shrewsbury is on tonight."

My heart jumped and I immediately looked at my watch. 11:58. *Just five hours to go.*

As the afternoon drew on, I couldn't help thinking about how the evening would play out. I knew it would be vastly different to when I'd last been with Gigi, when we were alone. That said, I hoped there'd still be an opportunity for us to have a few moments on our own.

Finally, it was five o'clock, and we were officially on pass. We jumped into my car and sped off. At five thirty-five we drove through Jamie's gates.

As we walked up the pathway, Gigi appeared in the doorway. In an instant, my mind jumped back to the last time I'd seen her standing there. She looked as gorgeous as ever, even if she was not in quite so revealing a dress. Jamie gave his mum a hug and a kiss on the cheek and then she did the same to me, discreetly pinching me on the buttocks. It was so nice to be back in this house.

Charlotte arrived soon after us, alone. In good spirits, she bounded into the drawing room, gave her brother a quick kiss on the cheek and then did likewise to me.

For the entire evening, Charlotte was decidedly friendlier and more demonstrative towards me. Casually touching my arm, squeezing my hand and being far more animated when she spoke to me. I wondered where this warmth was coming from, and then I thought back to the last time I had seen her. Gigi had been very affectionate towards me, and it would have been impossible for Charlotte not to have noticed. Did it have something to do with that evening? If her mother saw something attractive in me, well, maybe there was something, she may have thought. Regardless, unlike previously, I had no interest in her advances. To coin Gigi's expression, that ship had sailed. I was aware that I really ought to maintain my normal demeanour though, or it would be peculiar if I suddenly seemed disinterested. Anyway, it was far nicer than her cooler approach, to which I had now become accustomed.

Just before dinner, Gigi and Charlotte gave Suzie a hand with the meal. Jamie was in the hallway on the phone, so I decided to see what the ladies were up to. Just as I got to the kitchen door, I heard Gigi say to Charlotte "You have been awfully friendly towards Charles this evening. What's up?"

"I like Charles, always have. I think he is cute," came Charlotte's reply.

"Oh, and how does Alex feel about that?" was Gigi's sharp response.

"Oh no, of course he doesn't know," Charlotte said in a hushed tone. "Anyway, I think Alex and I have run our course, Mum."

"Hmm, isn't Charles a bit young for you?" came Gigi's pointed reply.

I couldn't help smiling at her hypocrisy.

"He may be a little young, but he is very mature. I may just have to teach him a thing or two," she said with a giggle.

I was sure Gigi was cringing at that remark, as I quickly retraced my steps back into the drawing room.

Charlotte's newfound interest in me continued unabated through dinner. If anything, it stepped up a gear, as if having told her mother her intentions gave her licence to openly pursue me. Jamie seemed not to notice, which made me think he had known Charlotte and Alex were ending things.

I found myself in somewhat of an interesting situation, comparing mother and daughter, even though I felt very connected to Gigi. It seemed Gigi was feeling the competition. All through our main meal, as affectionate and demonstrative as Charlotte was being, Gigi was decidedly standoffish. I didn't even begin to try and understand it, given how little I knew about the opposite sex. It reminded me of a book I'd heard about, *Everything I Know About Women*. It was a book of entirely blank pages.

By the time we finished our dinner, I had completed my subconscious comparison. It was a simple matter of comparing a green fig to a ripe one. The green fig is very firm and has a great shape, but that is where it ends. The ripe fig is…well, a delectable entity all on its own. It keeps the same shape—with a little bit of softening perhaps—but it is inside the fig where the differences are revealed. The best you can do with a green fig is to leave it to ripen, knowing it will eventually get there. A lovely thought. A ripe fig, on the other hand, is just waiting to be devoured *now*. When you sink your teeth into one, you discover an array of flavours, sophistication, and personality, all acquired through the passage of, aaah…time. You experience something that you will not easily get enough of. I knew I had experienced my ripe fig, albeit in just the smallest sample. And I desperately wanted more.

During a short break before dessert Jamie went to make another phone call, and Charlotte asked if she should help clear the table. Gigi readily accepted her offer, leaving the two of us alone for a few minutes, a good time for me to be forthright in my admiration and desire for her.

I grabbed her hand, brought her fingers up to my lips and kissed them passionately. "No prize for guessing what dessert I would love tonight," I jested, in complete honesty. "Pity you can't curtail Charlotte and tell her I have a delicious, ripe fig. Why would I want a green one?"

It had the desired effect. Gigi looked around, making sure she would not be seen, and boldly leant over and planted a kiss squarely on my lips. She then bounced up from the table and put on the Italian artist, one she listened to often, clearly one of her favourites.

"Cosas de la Vida (Cose della Vita)" – Eros Ramazzotti

| YouTube | Spotify | Apple |

I enjoyed watching her sing along. I loved the song, even though the lyrics were lost on me.

"What is this, still that Italian singer, Eros?" I asked.

Gigi took my hand and looked intently into my eyes. "Yes, but it's one of his Spanish songs, very beautiful. It is a duet with Tina Turner," she said, exposing my complete ignorance.

"What is it about?" I asked, my interest having been piqued.

"Two people unable to stop thinking of each other. He is contemplating matters of life and love and wondering what is happening to him and a girl, and where it could lead," Gigi replied with a quizzical look.

We both went quiet for a moment.

"Have *you* wondered about that, my love?" Gigi asked in a serious tone.

She did not have to spell it out; I knew she was speaking about us.

Like Eros, I too had all these same thoughts, even before that night when I didn't have to *think twice*. Even though the song and the thought had played on my mind, I wasn't sure how to answer Gigi.

I was saved from trying to do so as first Charlotte came back to the table, having finished clearing up, and then Jamie as he too finished his phone call and announced "I'm pooped. Bedtime for me."

"Me too," Charlotte echoed his feelings. That brought the dinner to an end.

Just as I was thinking this would give Gigi and I a chance to have a little alone time together, perhaps speak more about what was happening to us, she too announced she would be going to bed.

"What time do you want to get up tomorrow?" Gigi asked.

Jamie replied, "Oh-six-hundred hours."

"At six a.m.," Gigi confirmed, not used to aviator speak. "I will wake you up," she offered.

"Please wake me at six-thirty, Mum," Charlotte asked.

"Perfect," came Gigi's reply.

After a cursory good night, we headed to our respective bedrooms.

The last thing I wanted to do was sleep, and I got into bed feeling extremely disappointed at not having had even ten minutes of quality time with Gigi. Had it not been for the letter she gave me, my insecurities would've had me thinking the worst.

I switched off my bedside lamp, and just as I resigned myself that I wasn't even going to get the offer of "coffee, tea, me" I heard a soft knock at my door before it opened.

Wearing only a thin silk nightdress clinging to the form of her breasts,

Gigi stepped into my room, alarm clock in hand. She then locked the door, checking it again to make sure it was secured.

She offered a simple explanation for her actions. "If anyone is going to catch us, I would rather wriggle out of them *thinking* the worst than actually *seeing* the worst."

Even in my surprised and excited state, it made sense.

She put the alarm clock down.

9:13 p.m. Still early, I thought excitedly.

Once again, Gigi effortlessly removed her only item of clothing and there she stood, with me unashamedly taking it all in. God, I loved this body, this woman.

Then she literally jumped on top of me and, remembering she had to be quiet, put a finger to her lips as if I had been the one making the noise. She removed my sleeping shorts while I slipped my T-shirt over my head, and very quickly we were lying naked together again.

She started kissing me, one of *our* kisses, and soon we were consuming each other. As before, the eroticism made her kissing me feel like a form of sex. Our mouths very open, tongues probing urgently, savouring each other's lips. All the hallmarks of our urgent desire. She was being very forthright, as if there was no time to waste.

Then she did that *thing*. She reached down, rubbed herself briefly and watched me taking it all in.

Symptoms of our shameless desire soon left us breathless.

"Darling, my baby," she said while looking searchingly at me.

"Yes," I answered.

"Do you want me, you know, down there?" she cooed, gesturing with a glance. "Down there."

Not altogether sure what she was getting at, I replied, "Of course! I want to make love to you again."

"No, not that. I mean, I know you want to make love to me, but do you want me down there, you know…on your face…your mouth?" Gigi was offering her most intimate part to me in the most intimate way possible.

"Yes…I do," I said slowly, absorbing the thought.

What ensued was the most extraordinary expression of our enjoyment of each other and being caught up in the moment, as I unashamedly consumed Gigi in the most sensual way imaginable. Once we began to relax, she put her head in the crook of my neck and, holding one of my cheeks in her hand, she kissed me on the other. It was so endearing. Such a contrast to what had been happening moments earlier.

We lay like that for a while, slowly regaining our composure before she whispered, "Darling, that was beautiful. Beautiful." She then raised herself on one elbow, looked at me and said pointedly, "I will not ask how it was for you because you have already told me…in loads."

Gigi watched me as I looked at the sheets, but there was no evidence of what had just happened.

"Just as well the girl is not on a diet," she said facetiously.

The diet comment ostensibly cleared up any misconceptions I may have had, but I still gave Gigi an enquiring look.

"I'm sure you know, but just to make certain, I will give you a clue," she said. "Do you know what the bird of love is?"

As it turned out, I did know because of Greek mythology stories, so I answered, "Yes, the dove."

"Well done," she replied. "Now, do you know what the bird of lust is?"

I had never heard of that, so I shrugged my shoulders.

"The swallow," was her reply.

"And whoever said that oral sex was a calorie-free meal didn't know what they were talking about." She chuckled.

Okay, now I *really* got it.

As I was dozing off, I glanced at the digital clock and wondered what time Gigi had set the alarm for. The numerals boldly showed 10:38 p.m. We had made love for over an hour, and it had felt like less than half that time.

The alarm went off at five the next morning, and I was surprised at how quickly Gigi reacted. The clock had barely finished its first ring before she switched it off.

We made love again, being especially careful not to make any sound, because everyone would be sleeping much more lightly at that time of the morning, near the end of their sleep cycle.

Gigi slipped out of my room at five forty-five with enough time for a quick shower before going to wake Jamie. She popped her head into my room and whispered, shrugging her shoulders, "James was already awake when I called him."

Oh, God, I thought as I jumped into the shower. Now I had feelings of guilt on top of my concerns.

Once I was finished, I went to the annex dining area feeling no less worried. The ladies were preparing breakfast and, whilst Charlotte was finishing off the eggs, Gigi came through with plain yogurt, berries, pumpkin and chia seeds, and granola. Maple syrup as a sweetener. As she leant over to place it on the table, she whispered, "Nothing to worry about. Jamie had only just woken up."

Once we had all eaten, everyone in good spirits, we gathered our overnight bags and headed for the door. There were kisses all around as we said our goodbyes. Charlotte kissed me fondly, and my uplifted feelings had me reciprocating warmly. Gigi noticed but seemed unconcerned. I was the last one she kissed. Her lips were warm and intent against my cheeks, but it was the sharp little pinch on my waist that I felt the most.

Not totally unconcerned, I thought, smiling.

As we sped off, with Jamie having a go driving my car, the only thing on my mind was how long it would be before we could return to Shrewsbury. I relaxed into my seat, wind blowing in my face as I looked out across the countryside, lost in my thoughts of the previous night and that morning.

The drive was noticeably quiet. I knew why I was not chatting, but I was not too sure about Jamie. Had Gigi been mistaken about him having only just woken up when she went through to him? It made me feel very uncomfortable, nervous about being confronted with a tricky question.

"All good, Jamie?" I asked.

Jamie did not reply immediately, as he was focussed on his new driving experience. "Yeah, absolutely. I never imagined these Porsches handled like this." A mile or two farther down the road, once Jamie had started relaxing, he glanced at me and said, "I must admit, I am quite worried about selection this week."

No looming crisis then, I thought with some relief.

That was the first time I had given any thought to what lay ahead for the day. It was our first grouping examination, a particularly important event as each trainee's all-round competency, theoretical knowledge and practical flying skills were tested. After this, our initial grouping would be determined. Getting into Group A was the minimum requirement for you to choose your streaming and later on, your squadron. Whilst it was not something the trainees would typically speak about, perhaps for fear of not getting into their desired wing, we had a good idea which squadron posting each of us wanted. Jamie and I knew exactly where we wanted to go. Thinking about that it dawned on me that I didn't know what Will's preference was.

There were a few possibilities. Bottom of the list was general transportation. *Please God, no.* There were other equally unexciting noncombat roles such as dignitary transportation, troop carrying or medical evacuation. Medevac was not a bad posting, as you would still be in the fight but just on the outskirts.

We had attended several lectures about flying medevac helicopters and, because spinal cord and head injuries are all too common in polo, this was something that had grabbed my attention. My mother's voice crept into my mind. *"Don't ride like that. You will break your neck,"* and, *"Stop being such an adrenaline junkie."*

Appropriately termed "the Golden Hour," the first sixty minutes after a traumatic accident mostly determined the patient's outcome. What is required in these circumstances is to do everything possible to get the patient into hospital critical care treatment inside the Golden Hour, to counteract the far-reaching consequences of spinal cord or neurological injury, and especially brain swelling.

Flying medevac helicopters—especially the Chinook with its huge twin-rotor blades, also used for troop movement—would always be an important and meaningful role with much appeal. But for Jamie and me, our minds were made up. We both wanted to be at the very sharp end of Joint Helicopter Command (JHC) postings, and that was none other than the Apache attack helicopter squadron.

In the past fortnight, it had become generally accepted that I would get the posting of my choice. Will Granger was also looking pretty good to choose his posting, but it wasn't all that certain for Jamie though.

"Don't worry, you will be fine," I assured him.

"All very well for you to say. We all know *you* will be fine," came Jamie's curt reply.

"I will help you if you like," I offered sincerely.

"Really? Will you?" enquired Jamie.

"No question, chum. Imagine, we may even end up in the same machine together, Pilot-in-Command and Copilot-Gunner," I said.

"Fantastic, let's shake on it."

I knew one person who would not like the idea of her son and lover being in the same attack helicopter in a war zone. It was perhaps a blessing that Jamie, like me, was more comfortable with a Pilot-in-Command role rather than Copilot-Gunner, so it was unlikely to happen. Anyway, it was far too soon to be worrying about that. We still had to get there!

My thoughts drifted off into wondering where we would end up. The Middle East was hot. If the Iran-Iraq War was not enough, Iraq was shaping up for military conflict involving oil with its neighbour, Kuwait. And if it involved oil, it somehow involved us—the USA, NATO, and British Forces. The writing also seemed to be on the wall with Afghanistan's becoming another military conflict zone. In fairness, it was a lot to try to understand, and we didn't spend much time thinking about it. All I understood was that we were needed in a combat zone, and I was up for the task. Correction: I *couldn't wait* for the task.

The mood in the car had changed noticeably. I wondered how much of my offer was because I wanted Jamie and me to be together, well into the future, or whether it was a way of me ensuring that Gigi and I would be together, well into the future. That had my thoughts drifting back to her and how quickly our relationship had advanced from the first time to this time. It was almost unfathomable to me what we had been doing to each other. Yes, of course I had been aware of oral sex, but surely this was at another level.

God, what next? was all I could think.

Then I thought about Jamie and me. He had become a really good friend, and his mother was my first lover. How would he and Charlotte feel about their mother being in a relationship with someone so many years her junior? *More than half her age!* It was a very troubling thought, something

I chased out of my mind right then. I would have to think about it very carefully at some stage though.

Deep down, I knew I would lose one of them. What I did not know was, would it be Gigi or Jamie? It was a dreadful thought that sent a shiver down my spine.

CHAPTER 13
QUALIFIED—NOTHING MORE

NEVER MIND HOW quickly being twenty flew by, my twenty-first birthday was already a distant memory. This important milestone in civilian life was a nonexistent luxury in the middle of flight training in the Air Force. And the next seven or eight months at RAF Shawbury was no different. Soon our eighteen-month initial flight training course seemed to be over no sooner than it had begun.

True to my word, I spent a significant amount of time working with Jamie, coaching him on the practical aspects of flying and our classroom subjects, which was also excellent studying for me that unquestionably improved my flying too. The instructors had become fully aware that we were working together and realised that I was taking a lead role, but they didn't seem to mind.

Even though our programme was demanding and frenzied, we found time to go to Jamie's home at least every fortnight and sometimes several weekends in a row for what became a regular weekend pass.

On the weekends when we stayed at the base, Jamie, Will, and I would often go to the gym, play tennis, and generally keep ourselves busy with the many activities available. It was also the time that I used to catch up on my university work and go over the previous week's Air Force syllabus with Jamie. On one occasion, and I say *one* pointedly because I only ever took Jamie to Hawkstone Park Golf Club once. My mother's assertion that "anybody can hit a golf ball" was proven wrong. No matter how I tried, Jamie *could not* hit a golf ball. Luckily, Will Granger was a solid 12 handicap, having played regularly with his father, William Senior. As a result, he became my golfing partner. We would enjoy spending the best part of a day at the club, nine holes before lunch and then another nine in the afternoon. There was one other person as pleased as me that I had a regular golf partner, and it was Jamie. He was thankful being spared me trying to drum the game of golf into him.

I won't easily forget the first time I played against Will. We had started on the back nine, the term used for the second nine holes. As it transpired, the 10th hole at Hawkstone Park was their longest, a par 5 of over 500 yards. After a short warmup, Will invited, "Take it away, Charlie."

I stepped onto the tee box to start the game. I knew the 10th hole quite well and confidently took out my driver. Not a bad effort as I estimated my ball had gone quite a bit past the 310-yard mark. *Better that,* I subconsciously said to Will. I smiled at his setup routine, which in his case had him moving his feet as if looking for grip, while he wiggled his bum. He looked quite gangly as he unloaded his relaxed swing. I stopped smiling as I watched the flight of his ball before it landed where mine had come to rest. It would roll at least ten to twenty yards past my ball. My mother had told me that only 5 percent of men drove the ball more than 300 yards. I wondered what the statistic was for men who drove the ball over 330 yards! Well, I wasn't going to outdrive him, so my round would have to rely heavily on my short game. Thank goodness my mother was not Will's coach, or I would've been in trouble.

As much as I enjoyed being at the base, it was no comparison to when we went to Shrewsbury, which I loved, and not only because of what had developed between Gigi and me. When we did go to Jamie's home it was most often just the two of us and his mother. But every now and then Charlotte would join us too. Initially, she continued her affectionate overtures towards me, but with no romantic reciprocation, she lost interest for the most part. With that, a steady friendship began to develop between us. That suited me, as Gigi was the only romantic interest I had.

As far as my naivety was concerned, well, this improved steadily but was still prevalent when quite early on Gigi had mentioned she was going on a pill.

"What's wrong, Darling," I had asked, somewhat alarmed, thinking she may have an underlying condition I was not aware of.

"Nothing's wrong, silly. In fact, it is perfectly right, which is the reason for the pill."

Only then had the penny dropped that she had been speaking about contraception.

As it transpired, Gigi and I had not been able to repeat our memorable first night of being alone, but somehow it didn't detract from our enjoyment of our evenings together. And surprisingly, in my opinion it hardly made any difference to our sex, or was this my inexperienced point of view? Little difference except that we had become experts at being quiet. I was a lot better at it than Gigi was, with her emitting sounds of sexual delight and then putting a finger on my lips as if I had been the offender, which always made me smile.

We could not wait to be together again. Gigi often noticeably spurred both Jamie and me off to bed so that she could come to my room, so much so that I was concerned Jamie would notice, if he had not already.

Gigi was becoming very blasé about our evening rendezvous. I remember once when we had all gone to bed early, and she was in my room as soon as the lights were out.

"Surely Jamie hasn't gone to sleep yet? What if he heard you coming into my room?" I whispered.

Not about to be discouraged, she replied "Just be quiet, Darling."

On another occasion we heard Jamie going down to the kitchen and immediately stared at each other, wide-eyed, this time both of us putting a finger to our mouths. We realised we hadn't locked the bedroom door. I was cringing at the thought of him popping his head into my room to ask if I wanted anything. I could only imagine his shock had he done that. He would have found his mother sitting on my midriff, her knees straddling my torso, gloriously naked, breasts positioned over me.

A terrifying thought!

Over the course of the next few months, I often thought back to that instance and other similar occasions and wondered how and why we had never been caught. A feeling of disquiet came over me as I arrived at the only logical explanation; Jamie must have had an idea of what was going on between his mother and me but elected to turn a blind eye.

By then, Gigi and I had our own sexual ritual once we were in the bedroom. We could not hold ourselves back from devouring each other, and oral sex became our regular starting point. Just the smell and taste of her, or even the thought of having her in this way, was enough to cause a reaction in me. And she said I had become "really expert" in the way I teased and satisfied her in this way. It did make me wonder if she was judging me by my progress, which I liked, or comparing me to others, which I abhorred. I would hide my jealousy, nonetheless.

Gigi jokingly once told me about 69 and how it should become our lucky number. She laughed her head off when, in my innocence, I considered it. She explained that *everybody* understood what 69 meant, and there would be no originality in us making it our lucky number. She went on to tell me that she was not a fan of 68, though.

"What is a 68?" I asked innocently.

"Oh, that's where I do you, and you owe me one," she said smiling. Fortunately, my naivety had progressed considerably since those early days.

Over the months, our relationship developed into a comfortable, familiar place that we both thrived on. I didn't allow our goodbyes to get me down but rather thought ahead to when we would be together again. There was no question that sex played a large part in our relationship, consumed by it and consuming each other, both literally and figuratively.

For the most part, it couldn't have been better except for the odd misunderstanding. I remember an incident in the first couple of months of Gigi and me being lovers, when one evening after making love, I decided to broach something with her. She was lying across me with her arm draped over my chest. I held her close, enjoying the comfort of our post-sex cuddle. Once I felt she was fully composed, I initiated what I thought was a delicate subject.

"My darling," I began very tentatively, "I'm not satisfying you."

Gigi didn't immediately say anything, but then, without moving, she asked, "Baby, what do you mean, you're 'not satisfying' me?"

I didn't like that I would have to spell it out, but there was no way of getting around it. "I don't make you cum," I said in a matter-of-fact tone.

Gigi shot up, supporting herself on one elbow, and almost glared at me as she said in disbelief, "You don't make me cum?"

I nodded my reply.

"Baby, are you crazy? I cum so easily with you. Whenever you have a pass out, I cum twice in the evening and at least once the next morning, if not twice again. When you are here for the weekend, we often do that on the Saturday night and Sunday morning as well. How can you say that?"

"Yes, I know that, but *I'm* not making you cum. You have to rub yourself to orgasm. I'm not enough for you," I said, now sounding a little exasperated.

"Oh, my baby, that isn't how it is," Gigi said, sinking back down beside me as she put her arm back across my chest. "Let me explain," she said softly. "It's all you that makes me cum. When I rub my clitoris, it just heightens my pleasure and brings me to an orgasm quicker."

I lay there pondering her words.

She seemed to be thinking about whether she should carry on before continuing, "You know, I recently read that only about 16 percent of women can orgasm without stimulating themselves. Their clitorises." She paused. "Do you know that many women don't orgasm every time they make love? Some women, hardly ever. It was…"

"Tell me, Darling," I said, wanting her to finish the sentence. I had a feeling the rest was about how she had experienced this in her life before. Was that one of the reasons she was now divorced?

Instead, she ended by saying, "I am one of the lucky ones. I no longer have any difficulty orgasming, and it is thanks to you, my baby."

The "no longer" part of her sentence suggested I may have been right.

My expression while thinking about this may have caused Gigi to imagine I had not entirely accepted her explanation. This wasn't the case, as I had experienced how very sensitive she was there, so it made perfect sense.

She carried on. "When I touch my clitoris, all I'm doing is connecting to your cock. From my clitoris to my G-spot, on the upper wall of my vagina."

It was now the attentive look on my face that had Gigi continue.

"From my clitoris to that dimpled place inside me is one continuous erogenous zone, that our lovemaking turns into a bed of sexual ecstasy."

My expression must have now shown my acceptance of her explanation.

"Don't ever think you are not enough for me. The way you fill me. How your sensitive, yet sometimes forceful character is expressed in how you make love to me… You aren't even a dream, as my dreams could never have been so audacious!"

That was Gigi's last word on the matter. Words that made me feel much better, even if it was still a bit confusing. I had so much to learn. Understanding erogenous zones and G-spots would have to wait for another day. For now, I had put to bed a huge concern.

I had just experienced another face of Gigi, and I loved them all.

With my spirits having been lifted no end, Gigi had seemingly seized on this moment of willingness and started masturbating me. If I thought this was going to just be a cursory act, I was mistaken. I would have preferred Gigi not to have done this, yet there was no denying the effect it had on me.

Then, looking up at me with an intense expression, she went on to do the most intimate things to me that stretched the boundaries of my comfort zone.

Later on in my life, I would come to understand that these were expressions of lustfulness, unbridled because of the deep love she felt for me.

The myriad of sensations from earlier had had an enduring effect on me and I was still semirigid.

"Oh, God. May I always be blessed with such a responsive cock," Gigi enthused.

What? I didn't want to hear that. "You can only have *my* cock," I retorted.

She paused for a moment. "And will mine be your only pussy?"

I hated the reality of what Gigi was saying. How was I going to stop myself from falling in love with this woman, or had that already happened?

I dwelt on this possibility for a long time afterwards, not altogether sure how to reconcile the feeling but somehow wanting certainty…wanting more.

On that particular visit to Shrewsbury, Jamie and I had taken our own cars, as I had to first go past Ternhill Airfield, one of our flight training venues. I enjoyed the solitude of driving back to RAF Shawbury on my own, caught up in my thoughts. As I switched on the radio, a familiar song came over the airwaves.

"Is This Love" – Whitesnake

| YouTube | Spotify | Apple |

For the first time, I really felt the meaning of these lyrics. Was this love that I was feeling, wanting? I decided, like the song, that it must be. No one had ever opened that door the way Gigi had. But how could I be sure? We had yet to experience a normal relationship where we were out in the open or were with each other longer than just one or two nights. Was it wrong, or at least wildly premature to be having these thoughts?

Even so, the song became one of my favourites, describing how my feelings grew day by day.

At the end of almost eighteen months of flight training, we finally reached the closing stage of our programme.

It was around this time that Jamie and I started talking about the two-week pass we would get after the wings and commissioning parade. He was intent on going to Rockwell Manor while I was looking for any reason in the world to spend some time in Shrewsbury, desperate for Gigi and me to have some time together during this break. There seemed no way this would happen so I slowly resigned myself to the fact that we would be in Berkshire, at my home, because there was "so much more to do there," as Jamie had insisted. One consolation was that at least my parents would be pleased.

We had just one ground-school class and two practical flight sessions left to do before our final flight tests, and then it would be the Wings Parade and our Flight Lieutenant commissions. All the pilots were feeling quite confident about passing, but less certain about which group they would be in for the next phase, the advanced helicopter training programme. It didn't end there. Our intake was now down to eighteen pilots, and now only the top eight would be in Group A and likely get the posting of their choice. In Groups B and C, the choices became less interesting. There was still a lot of training ahead, during which time we expected to perpetually be moved up or down the ladder and hence the risk of losing one's place in the group. I reminded Jamie there was still plenty of time for him to cement his place in Group A, as he became increasingly nervous about where he would end up.

Both Jamie and I had no problem with the ground-school examination. The time we'd spent together, going through every aspect of every subject, had prepared us perfectly for the first part of the week, and we came out of the exam room giving each other high fives. The big one lay ahead though—next week's flight test.

Jamie and I were scheduled to do ours on the Tuesday. One advantage was that we'd have a chance to watch some of the other pilots and critique their flying, hopefully learning something from it. But I was also worried that the other pilots giving their feedback would make him more anxious about his own test.

I intuitively knew what we should do. I went across to Jamie's room and told him what was on my mind.

"Jamie, let's get a pass for this weekend."

He hesitated for a moment.

"Going home will calm your nerves," I added, justifying my suggestion. Whenever I had been with Gigi, I too was at my best. Jamie made the arrangements and after a little more chit chat, I went back to my room. No sooner had I got there that Will knocked on my door.

"Are you up for a game of golf this Saturday?" he asked.

"Sorry, Will. I'm off to Shrewsbury with Jamie tomorrow for the weekend."

He gave me that knowing look that a game of golf with a good friend was no match for the allure of Jamie's sister. *Imagine if he knew the real attraction,* I thought.

I had considered inviting Will to Rockwell Manor, the only reason I didn't was because I had a feeling that Jamie would have some thoughts around it. Anyone that believed jealousy was only a boyfriend girlfriend thing should think again. It happened between best friends as well. I knew my parents would just love William Granger, and I imagined that he would also fit in very well with many of the Berkshire pastimes, especially golf at Wentworth. I was quite sure that "Great-Shot Granger," as we sometimes teased because of his shooting prowess, would not only enjoy clay-pigeon shooting, but that he would more than likely be a deft hand with a shotgun. As for Guards Polo Club, well, the groupie set would surely begin thinking of me as some sort of Candy Man, bringing them a new treat.

We drove to Shrewsbury separately, which I preferred since I found Jamie's driving too laid-back for my liking. I was five minutes behind him when we left, and five minutes ahead when I got to the Blackwoods'. That would give us enough time for a quick cuddle and kiss after first being berated for driving too fast. *Just as my mother would do!*

Alas, on this occasion, there would be no stolen moment. Gigi was in the kitchen, preparing dinner and speaking to her best friend, Jacqui Courtenay. With her hands busy, she was on speakerphone.

"God, Jacqs, I'll tell you, but you have to keep it to yourself. Promise me," I heard Gigi say.

"Gigi, why so cagey? What did you get yourself into? Is he married?" asked Jacqui.

"Oh no, no, nothing like that. That could not be further from the truth," Gigi replied.

"Okay, so who is he?" Jacqui quizzed. "When did you meet him? Why haven't I met him? What does he do?" was Jacqui's barrage of questions. "Gigi, you've got to tell me! I promise I won't say anything," she said, pleading.

"I met him a while ago, Jacqs, over a year now," Gigi replied, understating it slightly.

"Over a year? Whaaat? And I'm only hearing about this now? Could he possibly be number two?"

Could I be number two? My face dropped, thinking about Gigi getting married again to someone else? *No, that can't happen.*

After some hesitation, Gigi finally relented. "Okay. Okay. His name is Charles. He is in the Air Force…with Jamie."

"One of Jamie's instructors," Jacqui guessed.

Gigi did not immediately say anything. "No…one of the trainee pilots, with Jamie," came her admission.

"Oh, God, no! Jamie's *age*? What are you doing?" Jacqui demanded.

"Yes, he's Jamie's friend. Don't judge me, Jacqs. It hasn't been easy."

"Okay. Tell me about him," Jacqui replied, softening a bit.

"He might be Jamie's age, but he's very mature," Gigi tried to assure her friend.

"Well, I hope so, otherwise I would really start worrying about you, darling," was Jacqui's candid response. "Tell me everything!"

"He's so gorgeous. A mop of blond hair, chiselled jaw, Greek nose and spellbinding blue eyes…oh, and a *great* body," Gigi rattled off enthusiastically, perhaps trying to justify her actions to her friend.

"You and your blue-eyed blonds," Jacqui chipped in. "Of course he's got a great body. What do you expect when you bed a nineteen-year-old?"

"No, he was twenty when that happened," Gigi interjected defensively, as if the one year made a difference.

"Okay, what else?" Jacqui asked, playing into her friend's enthusiasm.

"His mouth is gorgeous, so full and kissable. And I just love his carved bottom."

"You are completely infatuated," Jacqui scolded.

"I am, Jacqs."

"God, I can't believe my best friend is sleeping with a twenty-year-old! What is that even like?" Jacqui chortled at the thought.

"He's amazing…after a slow start," Gigi admitted.

"You've been teaching him? I don't believe what I'm hearing," Jacqui derided. "Oh fuck, you are in total lust, darling. I am so jealous. Tell me more, or does your relationship start and end in the sack?"

"No, never. He has such a gregarious and enthusiastic nature that is so attractive."

"Looks like it worked with you," Jacqui offered.

Gigi continued, "He is friendly and social but very private about himself, never giving too much away. Yes, it has taken me a while to get to know him, but now that I have, I love being with him, Jacqs. He makes me feel so alive."

I couldn't help taking Gigi's words to heart. *God, I love being with her.*

"Jamie has been to his home in Berkshire, and I believe it is quite special. It is a polo estate."

"Oh, God, you've got a polo player! Well, you might start riding again—horses, I mean, not the polo player," Jacqui teased. Then more seriously she warned, "Polo players have bad reputations, I have heard."

"Oh no, Charles is completely different in that department. I'll tell you one day. He has the strange contrast of being sensitive and romantic, yet he loves shooting pheasant and is training to be a combat pilot. How is it that he can be so sensual and gentle, yet so savage? Somehow it is just *sooo* sexy. Oh, God, do not tell anyone I said that. Men and women are so different. I guess that is why we cannot live without them, or them us."

"Oh, Gigi, you're in love, aren't you?" Jacqui submitted, changing her mind about the lust view. "Is there more? I want to know more. Where is he now?"

"Actually, he is on his way here with Jamie. They have a pass out," Gigi replied.

"Wait, what do Jamie and Charlotte say about your Charles?" Jacqui asked, realising she had not even gone there yet.

"That's the thing, Jacqs. They don't know," Gigi confessed.

"God, no. What are you going to do about *that*, darling?" Jacqui asked.

"Nothing…nothing. I am not going to. Not ever, I don't think," Gigi replied in a sombre tone.

Just then, I heard Jamie pull up outside the house and knew Gigi would have heard him too.

"Okay, darling, must go now. They have just driven in," I heard her say. Of course she was unaware we had come separately.

I quickly made my way outside so I would not be discovered as having eavesdropped on such a private conversation.

When I went to Shrewsbury, our lovemaking in the evening had always been drawn out with little regard for sleep as we made up for the time we had been apart. The mornings had typically been a quick and intensely passionate affair because we both knew we would be saying goodbye and weren't certain when we would be together again.

However, because of our programme the next day, we needed an early night. I thought I might have to explain this to Gigi—no protracted sex and our quick and quiet morning approach would be the order of the day. The explanation hadn't been necessary. She was aware of both Jamie's and my main concern that evening and behaved as if our concerns were her priority as well.

Unable to keep our hands off each other, we needed little prompting for us to begin our sex, once again starting in the usual manner. But then, as she quite often did, Gigi surprised me by taking a different slant on the age-old ritual of lovemaking. This time she insisted we watch ourselves in the act.

As I became more used to Gigi's bedroom behaviour, I realised she was not only adding new dimensions to our lovemaking but also purposefully taking me out of my comfort zone, broadening my horizon—probably exactly what a sexually inexperienced young man needed.

I loved it. Her words, "Watch, Darling. Watch your beautiful self going in and out of me, and tell me what you see," will never be forgotten, even though I didn't necessarily agree with her description of my member as "beautiful." But then again, I found her vagina intoxicatingly beautiful as it consumed me. *Beautiful* seemed to be an unlikely word to describe genitals, yet it was the word that naturally came to mind.

Or was this just how two people in love saw each other?

Over my lifetime I came to understand, and indeed, experienced that sex was typically an unimaginative and repetitive act and could in fact become "boring." Even today, it is not lost on me that in all the time Gigi and I were together, our lovemaking was anything but boring.

The more we got to know each other, the more we came to trust each other and the more our bedroom antics developed. One may have thought our behaviour was overly erotic, but on the backdrop of our closeness and with nothing to compare it to, it seemed quite normal. When we were together, we often behaved as if it was going to be the last time, which in a way it was, but only for a week or so.

As our relationship advanced, I often wondered if the pattern of two days and nights together, enveloping each other completely, and then a period of absence, was in fact quite a workable and sustainable existence for couples.

The next morning, before our flight tests, Gigi and I were about to start making love when she said, "Don't hold back now, Darling. Just cum when you are ready."

I did not want that. I got much more enjoyment from feeling us orgasm together. When we climaxed at different times, it took something away from the ecstasy that I normally felt. Perhaps because of what Gigi had said that morning, I made sure our orgasms were perfectly synchronised, not wanting her to deny herself.

From the very first time and all through our relationship, I had an overwhelming feeling of being in a privileged position as Gigi opened her legs for me, the gates to her womanhood, her deeply personal and sacred space. In tune with the rhythm of her emotions, she granted me access *into* her body, inviting me to penetrate her most sensitive and intimate parts, both physically and emotionally. Reaching deep into her, I touched the different vestibules of her soul, her trust allowing me to feel her love, her passion, and her desire. Then, at times when her emotions were so ranged, I would feel her irrepressible lust. From these very early days, I always felt the reverence of our couplings, our bodies becoming one as we became immersed in our lovemaking. In those moments, Gigi was mine.

What I didn't fully comprehend then was that my love life with Gigi had developed in the confines of her home. Her territory, so to speak, and under the same roof as her son, if not both of her children. A practice of constrained, routine sex over many months. Unbeknownst to me, changes lay head—surprisingly perpetrated by both of us.

CHAPTER 14
WINGS—ABOUT TO REALLY FLY

AFTER HAVING ENJOYED A LOVELY breakfast and an affectionate kiss from Gigi on our cheeks, Jamie and I were ready; just a couple hours to go before our flight tests.

As we walked down the pathway, Gigi used her own battle-cry to send us off that morning saying, "Hard and sharp boys. Hard and sharp."

We smiled back at her, both feeling a lot of love for this special woman, albeit vastly different kinds of love.

What Gigi and I had was, of course, not normal, and that extended far beyond just our age difference and my friendship with her children. Only seeing each other sporadically—and being constrained by Jamie's presence in the house with us, sometimes with Charlotte as well—meant it was a relationship that was constrained in so many ways. On top of that, I was training to be an RAF combat pilot. How big a distraction was that for both of us?

I was excited to be heading back to RAF Shawbury. Jamie's flight test was going to be first, and then mine. I couldn't wait, feeling confident that I already had one leg inside an Apache attack helicopter.

I jumped into my car and plugged my Walkman into the stereo. Turning the key gave rise to the raspy sound of my Porsche's engine roaring to life. As I headed down the driveway, I half turned to give Gigi a quick wave before pulling out onto the road that led back to the base. I would take the winding back route, because more than ever I needed to put my foot down and feel the thrill of tearing my car down a snaking road. I selected a song from the Rocky movies, that always got my adrenaline going, and it fit my mood perfectly.

"Eye of the Tiger" – Survivor

| YouTube | Spotify | Apple |

As the intro sounded from my car's stereo, I turned up the volume and banged the steering wheel to the beat of the song. I had never felt so good. *Was I trading my passion for glory?* I wouldn't be *losing my grip on the dreams of the past. Combat missions* had been my dream from when I was just a boy. I was now ready.

God, life was great! Was it *the thrill of the fight,* that had me *rising to the challenge.* I felt so alive. Gigi was such a part of that, which made her words, *"I'm watching your beautiful self, going in and out of me,"* flick across my mind.

I watched Jamie's flight test absorbedly. There were a few areas needing improvement. Once or twice, I saw his helicopter's tail swooping as a gust of wind caught him off guard. It was not the smoothest touchdown when he attempted to land without hydraulics, never an easy thing to do anyway. I would have liked to see a more positive flair, arresting his rapid rate of descent before he slid on after the autorotation. I smiled inwardly. What was I thinking? That I was his instructor or something? I had really taken the role of helping my friend with his flying to heart. It felt good. Overall, as far as I could tell, it was a good test.

Next, it was my turn, and it went more smoothly than I could have hoped. Captain Swales's words, "You have got a lot to look forward to Lieutenant," seemed to confirm it. And once again, I knew that having watched Jamie as closely as I had was very much to my advantage.

We both passed our examination and had finally qualified. I say *finally* not because of the time it had taken, which was less than two years, but because of the constant pressure and ongoing demands of the course and numerous flight tests. Now we'd suddenly reached the pinnacle of the mountain.

My Rude Awakening

It took only a day or two for us to get comfortable with this new accomplishment and very soon we started seeing T-shirts and the like applauding our achievements. A couple of the inscriptions that tickled me were:

> I didn't say I was smarter than you.
>
> I said I was a "helicopter pilot."
>
> It's implied.

In truth, the attack-helicopters squadron was the most difficult RAF squadron to get into.

> 24 months ago, I couldn't even spell heriploctor pliot,
>
> now I are one.

That one was more my style. Not that I had one, but it was certainly how a lot of the trainees felt.

There was certainly a lot of truth in this tongue-in-cheek plaque that Jamie put up in his room:

> The thing is, helicopters are different from airplanes. An airplane by its nature wants to fly and, if not interfered with too strongly by unusual events or a deliberately incompetent pilot, it will fly. A helicopter does not want to fly. It is maintained in the air by a variety of forces and controls working in opposition to each other, and if there is any disturbance in this delicate balance, the helicopter stops flying, immediately and disastrously. There is no such thing as a gliding helicopter. This is why a helicopter pilot is so different a being from an airplane pilot, and why in general airplane pilots are open, clear-eyed, buoyant extroverts, and helicopter pilots are brooders, introspective anticipators of trouble. They know if anything bad has not happened, it is about to.
>
> —Harry Reasoner

Dressed in our Number Ones, pretty much the same as our Number Twos—Air Force blue trousers, light blue long sleeve shirt, Air Force tie, with the addition of our tunic and cap—we all felt very smart and by all accounts looked it too.

It was a multi-squadron special occasion attended by most parents and family members. There was the customary flyover, followed by an aerial display. Then came the actual presentation of wings and officer's commissions to each of the now graduated pilots.

Jamie and I were very pleased with ourselves, having heard that morning that we were both confirmed in Group A. So had Will, which was what I had expected. My excitement was mostly about Jamie's rather than my own success, and our still being together…or was that Jamie, Gigi, and me still being together?

The one thing that could be said at this stage was that I had finally qualified, not only in my RAF flying career but in life too—if that was what you called it when you were no longer a virgin and had a woman and lover in your life. It may have been just the beginning, but even though I was still very inexperienced, it sure felt like *life* to me.

With the proceedings having come to an end, everyone was milling around, trying to team up with family who had come to attend the event. Jamie and I were looking around, seeing where our parents were, and just as I was thinking it would be a difficult task finding them, we saw them, standing just several yards apart in the swilling crowd. Jamie made his way over to his mum and Charlotte and I went over to my parents. After making our way to a quieter spot, we were finally able to formally introduce them to each other.

My parents were looking forward to meeting Gigi and Charlotte, and there was already a familiarity because of the times Jamie had been to Rockwell Manor.

"Oh, how wonderful. You must be Georgina, and you are surely Charlotte. I am Frances," my mother said as she took Gigi's arm and Charlotte's hand. "So lovely to finally meet you both. This is my husband, Arthur. Thank you for taking care of Charles on so many evening and weekend passes."

"Yes, thank you. We appreciate your kindness," my father chipped in.

My Rude Awakening

"Frances, Arthur, lovely meeting you too, and thank you also for having James at your home. He thoroughly enjoys his time with you," said Gigi, reciprocating their greeting.

My father was a naturally charming and gracious man, and women clearly enjoyed his company. His approach certainly never worried my mother, even if it was somewhat flirtatious.

True to form was Charlotte's reaction to my father. She seemed quite struck by him. I wondered if she had one of those father fixations I had heard about. For a moment, I had a vision of my father and Charlotte being together. *Goodness me* I thought as I chased away this ridiculous notion, but not before I did some mental arithmetic, comparing my dad's and Charlotte's age difference to Gigi's and mine, and they had an appreciably bigger difference.

It was customary to give gifts to mark the occasion of pilots' receiving their wings, the most popular one seemed to be none other than the Breitling Navitimer watch, like the one I had received on my eighteenth birthday from my aunt and uncle. I also came to understand that sales of this Breitling model experienced an unusual surge after the release of the popular film *Top Gun* starring Tom Cruise. Was this because there were suddenly more Air Force pilots being trained? *Me thinks not.* Far more likely is that it became a fashionable accessory for wannabe pilots who likely didn't understand half the functions of this timepiece. This alone was almost a good enough reason for me to stop wearing mine.

To mark my wings occasion, my mother gave me a small cushion in RAF navy blue with white trimming and an inscription that said:

You get old pilots,
And you get bold pilots,
But you don't get old, bold pilots.

That summed up my mother and her very controlled emotional disposition to a tee. She was far from starting a profusion of emotional narrative about me being her only son, about how I should be careful and look after myself or, perhaps, about how much she loved me. No, that was not my mother's way. It was not that she was devoid of deep emotions. Not at all, and quite the contrary. She was a very loving and caring mother who played an incredibly special role in my life. In her world though, it was not necessary to put one's feelings on public display. In her mind, it was far more practical and made better sense to give me some sage advice instead.

That cushion has been and remains an important part of my decor. It can always be found in my study, even to this day.

My father gave me his own gift, the latest ASA electronic flight computer, capable of calculating groundspeed, time, fuel and almost any aviation calculation one would need. They are essential to pilots, with nothing fashionable about them.

After a surprisingly good lunch in a marquee set up under the trees, where we had managed to seat the Blackwood and Featherstone families at the same table, it was time to say our goodbyes. I still had mixed feelings about the two-week pass that lay ahead before we were to report back for duty to begin our advanced helicopter training course. I had resigned myself to our going to Rockwell Manor to enjoy his new favourite pastimes, polo, and shooting. Undoubtedly, Jamie would also hope to have some of the polo-groupie "birds" succumb to him. I did need to spend some time at Rockwell Manor because we were playing in an important twenty-goal polo tournament, the Barrett Cup, but that hadn't stopped me from tentatively suggesting to Jamie we also spend a bit of time in Shrewsbury.

"You know, just for you to be fair to your mother and have some time with her," I'd suggested.

Jamie looked at me as if I had lost my mind. "What in God's name could we possibly do in Shrewsbury?" he asked.

I daresay I had a few ideas, but I was not about to share them with Jamie.

When Gigi and I spoke about it, she listened quietly, sullen faced. It was a missed opportunity not being able to see each other over this vacation pass, one of the few occasions when I would be off and not have to worry about getting back to the Air Force base after just a night or two.

Getting ready to say goodbye had put a dampener on what should have been the most wonderful day.

Jamie was heading over to say farewell to his mum and sister before we were to make our way down to Berkshire, when I suddenly had a thought.

Gigi and Charlotte should also come to Rockwell Manor! My mother would be thrilled at reciprocating their hospitality for all the time I had spent at the Blackwoods'. So would my dad. My mind began to race. Nothing like a last-minute change of plan. But I loved the idea. I *needed* to do it, and Gigi and I had both been so disappointed at the thought of not being able to see each other. I wondered what Jamie would think, not that I was going to let it deter me.

Jamie and I had been friends for almost two years. Gigi and I had been lovers for around sixteen months. Jamie had first visited Rockwell Manor over eighteen months ago. It was way overdue for Gigi and Charlotte to come to my home after all the wonderful times I had enjoyed at theirs.

I turned to my mum and dad and, in a lowered tone, said "Don't you think it would be a nice gesture for us to invite Jamie's mum and sister to join us at Rockwell Manor for this extended leave?"

My mother's face lit up. "That is a really wonderful suggestion Sunbeam," she cooed. She clearly loved the idea, as she was not prone to cooing.

My father's grin confirmed he felt likewise.

"Mum, it'll be nice for you to extend the invitation?" Such was my mother's enthusiasm, I thought she should do the selling to Gigi, and I would just sidestep Jamie by making it look like it had all been my mother's doing, not that I thought he would mind. It was better for both he and Charlotte not to think I had been hell bent on getting Gigi to Rockwell Manor.

"Of course, that is entirely appropriate" came her reply.

"Gigi is over there," I pointed out. "Mum, don't take no for an answer."

My mother went over to where Gigi and Charlotte were standing. As expected, Gigi was no match for my mother's persistence or, as it turned out, for Charlotte's, who readily accepted the invitation on behalf of her mother and herself without any hesitation.

When my mother was finished speaking to Gigi, I went over to her and asked, "So what are your plans for the next fortnight or so?"

In a very soft voice, making sure Charlotte didn't hear anything, she quite calmly said, "Oh, nothing much. I'll just be metering out a whole lot of punishment."

I smiled, sensing that a wonderful time was going to be had in Berkshire.

Jamie came over to where we were standing and chatting, and I told him the good news.

"Jamie, my mum has invited your mother and Charlotte to Rockwell Manor."

It was a bit like the night when he had sprung Kelly, the trap loader from clay-pigeon shooting on me.

Jamie gave me a blank look, which made sense because I knew he wouldn't mind as long as we were going to Rockwell Manor.

This sudden change of plan resulted in our two families chatting again, sorting out arrangements, which delayed our departure.

Gigi seemed a little apprehensive though, which was understandable. Being in an unfamiliar environment—with new faces, places, everything—would be a new experience, but almost certainly what gave her and me, the most to think about was how we would be together in the open, in public. I wondered how she would behave outside of her own environment. Time would tell.

I also thought Charlotte coming along would turn out well. It meant that if Jamie and I were playing polo or shooting, Gigi and Charlotte could do some exploring in the area. No doubt my mother would rope our two female guests into all sorts of activities in and around Berkshire.

Having Jamie's and my mother there together did play on my mind. It was just as well they were so different, a good ten-year age difference between them. And in addition, my mum had a vastly different look to Gigi. Whereas Gigi looked like someone in her mid-thirties, often mistaken for being Charlotte's older sister, my mother looked her age. At least that would detract from my thinking of the two of them in a similar light, both being mothers.

I pondered what people would think about our house guests and my connection to Charlotte, never imagining Gigi's and my relationship. It reminded me that I would need to be sensitive to this as we were going around Berkshire and Surrey.

My mother then started chatting to Charlotte. I wondered what the two of them were speaking about, given my mother's sudden keen interest in her. I wondered if she was assessing Charlotte's and my suitability for

My Rude Awakening

each other, possibly wondering, or rather hoping, there was already something between us.

Gigi seemed more relaxed about the idea of staying at Rockwell Manor, and Charlotte seemed rather intrigued to be getting involved in this new world.

"And, son," my dad said, getting my attention, "don't forget you have a big match in the Barrett Cup semi-finals." Then smiling broadly, he said, "Bloody hell, I forgot to tell you. We won our quarterfinal match and are playing against Cambiano."

"Wow, and I believe he's just been rated the best player in the world!" I replied, not able to conceal my excitement.

Jamie listened intently. The moment he heard the word 'polo' his ears always pricked.

My dad carried on. "Our new pro, Nic Aroldin, is fitting in so well. Incredible player, and he couldn't be more match ready. He played a brilliant game in the Coronation Cup and was a key member of the Argentinian team. I'm so pleased they lifted the Barrett Cup to twenty goals this year, out of my league now, but it allows us to contract players like Nic."

It was a pity my dad had started stepping back a bit, but it did pave the way for Rockwell Manor to compete at a higher level.

"I can't wait to meet him" Jamie said spontaneously.

"You will meet him soon Jamie, as my dad has invited him to come and stay." I updated Jamie.

"I think we will change that arrangement until after the Blackwoods have left Rockwell Manor." My mother interjected. "Let's first have a bit of family time," she added.

Does she already have ideals about us? I wondered.

We returned to discussing the logistics of Gigi's and Charlotte's visit to Rockwell Manor. They decided to spend the night in Shrewsbury so as not to rush packing for their trip to Berkshire. They would then leave for the drive to Rockwell Manor the following lunchtime.

With kisses on cheeks all round as we said goodbye to the Blackwood ladies, and after receiving a secretive little squeeze from Gigi and, unsurprisingly as of late, from Charlotte as well—always a little confusing—we went our separate ways. Goodness, I had grown so close to this family.

I'd been so completely absorbed with my flight training and degree, it was as if without warning, I'd graduated from university and received my flying wings. A strange thought given that I had been doing nothing else for an appreciable amount of time. This officially meant I was now a helicopter pilot and would one day be suitably qualified to go into the commercial world with my economics, business science and management information systems degree. But what trumped both of those accomplishments was having received the most unexpected education of the most delectable kind from Gigi.

The Wings ceremony and me having graduated had a special meaning for me. In a way, I had finally become my own man, not just a Featherstone. Somehow though, I didn't feel so bad about being a Featherstone now. Clearly there was no underestimating what a bit of personal success could do for my feelings of self-worth. Was that and Gigi's and my closeness a factor in my spontaneous gesture of having the Blackwoods come to stay at Rockwell Manor? Probably.

CHAPTER 15
ROCKWELL MANOR

I WAS ALREADY FEELING uncomfortable, and the Blackwood ladies hadn't even left Shrewsbury yet. I tried to imagine how my home would look through Gigi's eyes and whether I would be judged for it.

Having her at Rockwell Manor would bring about an array of new emotions. There was still that worry that refused to go away. I had told her very little about my life outside the RAF and especially my home. The reason was simple, stemming from my age-old insecurity about wanting to be wanted for me and not for Rockwell Manor and all that it represented. Jamie and I had got to know each other well before he visited my home, and as a result he too had instinctively said very little to either his mum or his sister, and thankfully they had not seemed very interested. It was for this reason that I so loved the Blackwoods. All of them. They had taken me into their home and their hearts without knowing anything of my background.

But were things about to change? Our relationships had a sincere foundation, but even so, I was still nervous that the overdue trip to Rockwell Manor would shake it somehow.

Turning into 1 Polo Drive, they would soon reach the motorised heavy timber and wrought-iron gates, and that *bloody* sandstone slab signage letting them know they had arrived at Rockwell Manor, with different estate roads to the stables, staff houses and the rest. *Little wonder I'm self-conscious.*

Under the watchful eye of the gatekeeper at the guardhouse, the gate would slowly swing open. They would then pass a row of trees and a gravelled area for guest parking before arriving at the garage forecourt and six garages arranged in an L shape. These of course had been for horse drawn carriages when Rockwell Manor was built in the late 1800s.

The three facing garages housing my mum's and dad's Range Rovers and my beloved Porsche would invariably be left open. The other three were mostly left closed. Behind the first garage door would be my dad's Bentley, which he seldom drove unless he was going to London. Even then, Hamilton would most often do the driving because of the challenges of London parking.

Behind the next door was my mother's ivory-coloured Aston Martin Vantage convertible with a tan canvas top and matching interior. It had been a gift from my father, and when she had thanked him for it, in the same breath she had added with a wink, "Is this because of you buying that ridiculous Porsche? You see, your little midlife crisis has cost you two cars."

My dad had replied that he had visions of his beloved Frances driving with the ragtop down, silk scarf blowing in the wind as she sped around Berkshire. Even I could have told him that was never going to happen, and it didn't.

I was very happy with his "ridiculous" purchase regardless of the reasons. Since my eighteenth birthday when it had been passed on to me, it had been my pride and joy.

In the last garage was a red, late-1950s Ferrari Dino my father had restored to concourse condition. *That* was his pride and joy, and he didn't let anyone drive it, a restriction that seemed to include himself since I had barely ever seen it out of the garage.

Out of view behind the vehicle forecourt was an extensive guest parking area for when we staged big events. Then, looking as if it were an extension of the garages, was another structure. No windows, just vents. People often thought it was an unusual place to have a storeroom and an awfully large one at that. It was only when they descended a steep stairway concealed behind a chest-high wall that they discovered a largely below ground squash court and gym. And there was indeed a sports-equipment storeroom for the myriad of activities that took place at Rockwell Manor. Hamilton, Fabrizio, Ashleigh Houghton our House Manager, and some of the other house and estate staff would make sure that our visitors were well looked after. In addition to arranging rackets, balls, etc. for all the activities, they would also be on hand, offering various refreshments. Rockwell Country Club was what some of my friends jokingly called our home. Hopefully Gigi would be as lighthearted about it as they were.

On the side of the house was a staircase that led up to a separate entrance—the north wing. From there you would have a view of the tennis and beach volleyball courts, some of the horse paddocks, and a silica sand horse exercise track around the polo field. Friends, with our polo manager's consent, would often bring a couple of their own horses in a two-berth horse trailer, and because it was such an expansive area, we wouldn't realise anyone was out there until we actually saw them on the field.

On the other side of the house were two oversized patios, one on top of the other, overlooking the field. Mostly used for watching polo matches, the top patio was also a good vantage point to look down on one of my favourite landscaping features, a twenty-foot obelisk with a fourteen-foot triangular steel section that looked like a protractor. It always confused people until they noticed the twelve large sandstone tiles with Roman numerals I to XII and four very large steel balls. A sundial that showed not only the time but also the seasons.

Alongside the downstairs viewing patio was a much smaller and comfortably decorated terrace, a favourite place for our breakfasts. Concealed behind stainless steel doors was an inbuilt barbecue with a rotisserie. Glancing at it reminded me how much I missed the smell of a ribeye roast and potatoes now that I was in the Air Force.

It also had a very good view of the polo field and beyond that the large stable block. Immediately in front of it was a large all-weather, heated swimming pool with emerald-green tiles so that it blended in with the surrounding garden. My mother's attention to detail of course.

Off the family patio were the "outside rooms," as my mother called them. A changing room, including sauna, steam room and a massage cubicle. A little further along was the bar and game room and my granddad's 120-year-old full-size, green-baize-covered slate billiard or snooker table.

I thought for a moment about a stuffed pheasant in a glass cabinet on the one side of the game room and winced. I wondered if Gigi would have my mother's jaundiced view on that as well. "When it comes to matters of decoration, I think I should get the right of veto," my mother had suggested after my father and I had voted her out of having it removed. Right now, it was a ballot I was sorry we had won. I knew without doubt that Gigi, and Charlotte for that matter, would not have voted with my dad and me. Hopefully they would like the wooden propeller hanging above it that came off a First World War British biplane, a *Sopwith Camel*, even though they were art effects mostly interesting to men.

From the garage forecourt, the entrance to the house was beneath a Georgian-style portico, flanked by a large flower bed on the one side and a long sandstone drinking trough on the other. Drinking from the water gently lapping over the edge was a string of eight, life-size horse heads and necks magnificently sculptured out of sandstone. Because the Blackwood ladies loved horses, I was sure they would like our entrance.

I imagined Gigi stepping through the imposing heavy double doors with the seldom-used brass door knocker, being met by an imposing, cavernous triple volume entrance hall—the gateway to the rest of the house. The most notable feature was the grand staircase sweeping around the right side of the room and up to the accommodations. I can say with confidence I'd never once walked up or down those stairs as an adolescent and seldom even as an adult. I took the stairs three or four at a time. In many ways, it described my character, especially as a young boy.

Looking out through full-height glass panes and double glass doors, opposite the front door was a long, rectangular pond of indigenous fish. My mother's voice saying, *"No koi fish here, please. We are not in Japan,"* came to mind. I smiled, knowing Gigi would agree with her. Looking down the length of the eight-foot-wide, forty-foot-long expanse of water, there was another statue of a horse, again just the neck and head. This one was an early sculpting by Nic Fiddian-Green in bronze, balancing on its nose on a heavy wooden plinth, the familiar pose adopted by this renowned British sculptor.

Underfoot was polished sandstone that swept through the 16,000-square-foot downstairs area of Rockwell Manor, but not the game room and bar area that had teakwood flooring.

Looking up into this enormous space, they would see hanging at mid-height an ancient light fitting of some extravagant proportions that came from a late medieval castle, circa 1460. It was made of hand-forged wrought iron of three concentric circles. On top was the smallest ring with three evenly spaced bulbous globes, the middle ring had five globes and the largest circle at the bottom had eight of these sphere globes.

"Do you know what those circles stand for?" my grandfather had asked me when I was about eleven or twelve years old.

I'd never even imagined they stood for anything, let alone what they were for, so I had just shrugged my shoulders.

"They represent the spread of the English language, once we became civilised," he quipped. Then, more seriously, "From the top to the bottom, the first is the inner circle, then the outer circle, and the last is the expanding circle of our language. There must be something to it, though. Do you know that English is one of the youngest languages in the world but also the most widely spoken, when you take first and second languages into account?"

"The most widely spoken first language must be Chinese?" I had remarked. "Because of the population."

My granddad nodded. "So the size of the circles and the number of lights—squat candles in medieval times—weren't the designer's flair. It was all based on Leonardo Fibonacci's number sequences," he said.

"Who's he, Granddad?" I asked.

"He was an Italian mathematician during the Renaissance who deciphered the patterns or proportions of nature, which reminds me that we were once ruled by Rome." This time, he gave me a wry smile.

That immediately caught my attention. I loved mathematical patterns. I made a mental note to read about Fibonacci. Would I one day learn the proportions of life? *Incredible.*

The significant weight of this light was suspended by irregular-sized links of a thick chain that reached down from a large, rudimentary mechanism used to lower the ancient light fitting to a more manageable working height. Luckily, nowadays, one only had to occasionally change light globes instead of sixteen candles, something that would probably have been done daily back in medieval times.

Because of its history, my granddad and dad loved our "medieval chandelier," as my mother put it.

"Just lift it a bit, Arthur. It really is an eyesore," my mother could be heard saying from time to time.

They were both thrilled she allowed it to stay, and so was I as I loved it. Was it a male thing?

I wondered what Gigi would think, secretly hoping she'd like it too.

An important doorway off the entrance hall was to the guest toilets. *"Water closet,"* I can still hear my mother correcting me. A friend had once teased that our *powder room,* with two other doorways leading to separate Fillies and Colts water closet areas, had clearly been decorated. It was complete with original, now antique, washbasins, brass water faucets, chaise lounges, wingback chairs, artworks, and even a latrine.

"To save us being reprimanded for not lifting the seat," my grandfather had once joked.

Also off the entrance hall was the formal drawing room, my mother's pride and joy. It was decorated in an unusually modern, eclectic style that combined large family heirlooms with a few carefully curated contemporary furnishings. "To add contrast, depth, and character to your home," the interior decorator had said. The walls were adorned with an array of what I understood were important art pieces. The only one that really appealed to me was a large painting with horses and hounds by a well-known English artist, George Stubbs. *Just as well the Blackwoods like horses,* I thought wryly.

To the side of the entrance hall and fitting in with the medieval chandelier was an interesting heavy steel and timber door that opened to a dark, almost mysterious stairway. It descended to a large, contrastingly modern stainless steel and light beechwood finished wine cellar. It did have a long antique table and bench seats in the middle of the room though, for wine and cheese tastings. It was one of only a few parts of the house where my father had any jurisdiction.

From the entrance hall was a wide passageway that led past the expansive kitchen, the formal dining room with its large Victorian dining table and an alcove in one corner that accommodated my mother's favourite musical instrument, a Steinway grand piano. The passageway continued through the spacious informal living area with a significant wood-burning fireplace, complete with a carved sandstone architrave surround. This room had floor-to-ceiling-height glass doors that opened onto the garden at the front. Wide timber railway sleeper steps were set into the lawn, creating a terraced grass walkway.

At the end of the informal living room was the family dining room, a similar idea to Gigi's annex dining area. No prize for guessing which one I preferred. The wonderful intimate dinners I had experienced at the Blackwoods' home were among my favourite memories. Like Gigi's, the family dining room led off the kitchen, which bordered a large courtyard garden of carefully managed vegetables and herbs.

My Rude Awakening

The informal family dining area was a spacious room with a central circular table and a seating area with a burgundy velvet-covered sofa often used for predinner aperitifs when my parents were hosting formal dinners. Hamilton would be on hand to take care of our guests, making sure he had every possible accompaniment to make any cocktail. He would enthusiastically show off his bartending skills, but in fairness, he was really just a very proper English gentleman on the other side of middle-aged and was not about to be mistaken for Tom Cruise in the film *Cocktail*.

The upstairs of the house, where all the accommodations were, matched the footprint of the lower level. This comprised twelve bedrooms with en-suite bathrooms, a master study and several private lounge areas, which in modern times were TV rooms. These were set out in three distinct wings. The west wing was our family accommodation—two junior suites, one of which *had* been mine, and a grand master suite, which had been my grandfather's and was now my parents'. The east wing, where Charlotte would be staying with Jamie, comprised four en-suite bedrooms. These were for family and close friends. I wondered what my parents were thinking. *Are the Blackwoods family or friends?*

When Rockwell Manor was originally built, the north wing was for "other guests," as in *lesser*. Evidence of this distinction from the east and west wings was that they were accessed via the grand staircase off the entrance hall while the north wing had its own separate outside stairway and entrance. Things had changed since then though. In addition to my suite, there were four others for the players of visiting polo teams, each having en-suites with steam showers, and there was a very roomy living area with TVs, stereos, and the like. A clear upgrade from former times and now a very comfortable arrangement, one could say.

That was where Nic Aroldin would be coming to stay for the season, but only after the Blackwoods left, had been the recent change of arrangements.

We may have been a family of just three living in this very large manor house, but it didn't feel that way. To start with, we had a large complement of staff, and we regularly had two or three visitors, and sometimes up to half a dozen or more if there was a visiting polo team. In addition, we predominantly lived in the informal areas when not in our personal suites, my suite in the north wing being separate from my parents, which could prove to be especially convenient now that Gigi was coming to visit.

Having played Gigi's visit over in my mind, I arrived at the conclusion that it was quite normal for people to be interested in their friends' homes, especially if they were as unusual as Rockwell Manor. And there was no reason for Gigi to feel any different, especially since we were far more than just friends. She already knew and cared about me for who I was, and I let that thought dispel my concerns of anything else.

I was now feeling more comfortable with my home and secretly looking forward to Gigi getting to know a little more of my world.

CHAPTER 16
THE ARRIVAL

Jamie and I arrived in separate cars, and my mother was ready to greet us.

"Hi, Fran," Jamie said casually as he gave my mum a peck on each cheek.

"Jamie, you know where your room is," she told him in case he thought he may have been moved because of his mother and sister visiting.

"Mum, I think Gigi will appreciate the comfort and privacy of being in Winston Cottage," I suggested, my stomach in knots at the thought.

The cottage had recently been refurbished and tastefully decorated by my mother. There was a limestone-surround log fireplace in the cosy lounge area, a large L-shaped sofa, beautiful antique tables, an armoire, drinks and display cabinets, and a Persian rug, not to mention all the objets d'art and paintings she'd fittingly placed. The large bedroom housed a king-size four-poster bed made up with a goose-down duvet—or comforter, as it is commonly known in the USA—covered in Frette Italian linen, pillows, and sumptuous cashmere throws and cushions. It led into a spacious bathroom with a towelling-covered chaise longue; a bath, complete with water jets; and a large walk-in steam shower. Two rare instances of my mother allowing technology into her home. I was sure Gigi would enjoy these little comforts, but most of all, I suspected she would appreciate the privacy because of the separation from the main house.

My mother looked at me thoughtfully, and I could literally read her mind. Because of how Gigi had taken care of me in Shrewsbury, she undoubtedly considered the Blackwoods to be *special guests*. Accordingly, she would have preferred her to be in the main house so we could all be together, and she could also make sure Gigi was comfortable.

I was inclined to push my suggestion but thought better of it.

After settling into his room, Jamie accompanied me to the barn to do evening stables.

Guy was already there and greeted us warmly with a broad grin. "You up for a bit of polo this week, Jamie?"

Noticeably excited, Jamie followed Guy through the stable as he pointed out the horses he had selected for him, highlighting some of their characteristics as he went along. Then Guy took me through my string, which was always pretty much the same group of ten horses, unless I had to substitute one or two because of injury.

"They look wonderful, Guy. We are all set for some good polo," I said, now really looking forward to playing in the Barrett Cup.

"Oh yes, and you haven't met Nic yet. Bloody hell, he's good," Guy remarked.

I would've loved to have heard more, but after an exhausting day, all we wanted was an early dinner and to head off to bed.

After a light supper, Jamie and I went to our rooms. I got into bed with excited thoughts of Gigi's arrival the next day. *The sooner I sleep, the sooner I will see her,* was my last thought as I dozed off.

When I called her the next morning, she told me, "Charlotte is just packing up the car. We will be leaving after lunch, Darling."

"It should take you about three and a half hours, my love. Drive safely," I said, barely containing my excitement.

This gave Jamie and me the opportunity to have an early afternoon stick and ball session. We were soon mounted on two energetic steeds and gracefully traversing our perfectly manicured polo field. First, we set about getting our riding legs before going on to practising more complicated polo shots. Then, we slowly increased the tempo until we were close to match pace.

Having just driven the ball up field, I was at a strong gallop to catch up for another shot, when Jamie suddenly rode his horse across the front of me, his horse's hind legs coming dangerously close to my mare's outstretched front hooves.

"Jeez, Jamie," I shouted. "Careful."

The slightest touch could have easily brought both of us down, with bone-jarring, or even limb-breaking consequences for both horse and rider. We stopped our mounts before I continued, needing to remind him of the "right of way" rule.

"Jamie, you must remember, when a player is following the ball on its line of travel, you cannot cross this line if there's any chance of a collision."

I couldn't remember his response, such was my excitement and focus watching out for Gigi, as I checked my watch for the hundredth time that morning.

"Your watch will wear out if you keep looking at it!" Jamie said as I calculated again when Gigi would be arriving.

When I finally caught a glimpse of her car coming down the driveway, I galloped off to meet them. "Come on, Jamie! Your mum and Charlotte have arrived."

Jamie followed me across the field, and when we slowed down, he looked a little disappointed that our stick and ball session had been interrupted just because his family had arrived.

"Only right that I'm there to welcome them, Squire," I said defensively.

Looking back now, I would say this was probably when my relationship with Gigi began interfering with Jamie's and my relationship.

My mother had been pottering around the entrance lobby and was close at hand as Jamie and I arrived to greet the Blackwood ladies. I remembered too late that I had taken my T-shirt off and tucked it into the back of my pants. With my naked torso glistening under a thin sheen of sweat, I dismounted and led my horse up to Gigi's car so I could open her door. Jamie went around to help Charlotte.

She first gave Jamie a quick kiss and then me, as Jamie went to help with the luggage.

"What a beauty," Gigi cooed, as she rubbed my horse on the nose. "And the horse isn't too bad either." She whispered, "I hope you don't welcome all female guests to Rockwell Manor in such a state of undress." Shooting a glance at her son, who was now helping Charlotte at the boot of the car, she ran a finger down my chest, between my pectorals and my six-pack, right down to below my navel. Then she put the tip of her finger in her mouth.

What a start!

I realised Jamie and Charlotte could not have seen anything and hoped the same was also true for my mother.

And as I expected, Gigi seemed unfazed by Rockwell Manor. It made sense. Having come to know her, I wouldn't have expected Gigi to put much importance on anything material. *I must have been overthinking things earlier.*

My mother then approached, enthusiastically welcoming Gigi and Charlotte to our home. "Oh, isn't this just wonderful, having you be *our* guests for a change. Welcome, my dears." My mother kissed them warmly on the cheeks. "I'm sorry Arthur isn't here to meet you," she continued.

I slipped my T-shirt back on as my mum gave a few instructions.

"Jamie, be a dear and show Charlotte to her room in the east wing, next to yours. Sunbeam, you can show Gigi to Winston Cottage."

Perfect, I thought, taking a mental sigh of relief that my mother had agreed to my suggestion.

Jamie and I handed our horses to Pablo, one of our Argentinian grooms, and we helped the ladies with their bags.

Gigi followed as I led the way to the cottage carrying her large, wheeled bag on my shoulder. I wasn't even tempted to use Fabrizio's perfectly concealed catering-trolley path, even if it was ideal for Gigi's case. Not only because my mum preferred guests to use the scenic route, but I too had suddenly developed an appreciation for this picturesque pathway. *Nothing to do with Gigi,* I smiled to myself. I took Gigi down the meandering trail of stepping stones and wooden railway sleepers, carefully arranged to make the hundred-yard walk among the big trees, dense green foliage, and various flower beds an enchanting experience. As we got closer, we reached the part that was lined with peonies in full bloom, as if they were welcoming her. I knew she would notice them, and I was surprised that I did too.

"And here we are," I said, reaching for the door handle. "My favourite place in the world…after Shrewsbury," I quickly added with a wink.

"Very convenient," she remarked as we entered the cottage.

Of all the things she could have said, I was thrilled that convenience was foremost on her mind. I smiled, liking the way she was thinking.

My Rude Awakening

We hardly looked around before we enthusiastically kissed. It was electric.

I grabbed Gigi and pulled her hard against me so that our pelvises were firmly against each other's, locked in this quickly escalating passionate embrace.

I could feel my immediate arousal as she slipped a hand into my jeans.

"Oh, God, my darling, what's going on? You are so hard. I want you so badly," Gigi said, catching her breath.

"I can't wait," I replied.

And how I meant it, but we had to come to our senses quickly or this could go awfully wrong. I gently pulled away, knowing my mum would've expected me to make sure Charlotte was also settled in. But oh, goodness, what a start to what was almost certainly going to be an unforgettable time in Berkshire.

"Why don't you settle yourself in before supper, my love?" I suggested, feeling apprehensive about how Gigi would take to a Rockwell Manor dinner. I was fearing the worst.

"Oh yes, and you will meet Fabrizio," I said, hoping our chef would lighten things up a bit. He often did. "I am very indebted to him," I said jovially. "Thanks to Fabrizio I now know that the best things in the whole world come from Italy. Art, fashion, footwear, cars, but especially their cuisine." Gigi looked at me, making sure I wasn't being serious.

"I may agree with him—Michelangelo, Armani, Prada, Ferrari, and pizza and pasta," she said with a grin.

"Perhaps I will take you for a walk after dinner?" I suggested, smiling. "Anything you need before I go? Coffee, tea…me?" I teased, making light of my having to leave her.

"It's just not right that you give a girl a taste and then leave her hanging," Gigi replied as she straightened her blouse.

I looked back at her before stepping into the early evening air, the expression on my face clearly showing what I would rather be doing.

Nevertheless, I made my way up to Charlotte's room to check on her and see if she was ready to go downstairs.

When I knocked, she immediately opened the door, brushing out her long blonde hair and looking radiant and pretty in a flowing floral dress and leather sandals.

"Oh, Charles, Rockwell Manor is just fabulous. Jamie didn't tell me even the half of it," she gushed. "Just one thing though, can you show me how the steam shower works? Outrageous that I have my own steam shower."

I smiled, even though she was acting more like one of the polo groupies. I pushed the solitary button in the spacious steam and shower room and turned the dial to 42 degrees Celsius. "Keep the door closed when you use it, otherwise you will steam out your entire room," I cautioned.

"Ooh, look at that steam! Dreamy. Any ideas who I could test it with?" she said with a giggle.

I didn't answer, as I didn't really think she was expecting one. I was mistaken.

"Well, don't leave me hanging. Are you going to test the shower with me or not?" she said mischievously.

Sooo like her mother. I was often caught off guard by their similarities.

That was the second time in the past few minutes I had heard the phrase, "Don't leave me hanging." I had to smile.

"Come along, let me take you downstairs," I said, brushing her suggestive request aside.

As we walked down the hallway and past the main dining room, Charlotte hesitated, wanting to stop every few steps to look at a painting, an ornament, or just the room. Of course, she hadn't been to Rockwell Manor before and was taking in the different aspects with some wonderment. *Not now*, I thought. *You can do that with my mum.*

We were at the end of the informal reception room and about to step into the family dining room when she hesitated again.

"Come along, now," I said, eager to hurry her up so I did not get into a guided tour. "If you want to look at anything, my mum can show you around." My preferred guided tours of Rockwell Manor had mostly begun and ended with, "Through that door on the left is the guest cloak." Even from a young boy, I had reckoned that was one part of Rockwell Manor they needed to know about. The stables were a different matter. I could spend ages enthusing about the horses such was my love for them.

When she gave me a disappointed look, I took her by the hand so she would not be sidetracked again, and that's how we arrived, hand in hand, to a mixture of responses. Jamie's face had a look of confusion as he took a gulp of his drink. Both my parents, my dad now back from London, were wearing ear-to-ear smiles, and "our son has a girlfriend" expressions emblazoned across their faces.

I let go of Charlotte's hand, but it made no difference. My actions were merely the result of polite behaviour, not to be holding hands in company.

"Hello, Charlotte. Hello, Sunbeam." My mother cheerfully greeted us as if we hadn't seen each other earlier. She walked up to Charlotte, taking both her hands, and kissed her on both cheeks. "You look beautiful, darling," my mother enthused.

My father, having not yet seen Charlotte, greeted her especially warmly. "Hello, Charlotte, darling, so lovely to have you at Rockwell Manor with us," he enthused.

"Oh, Arthur, so lovely to be here," Charlotte replied, as she did not hesitate and kissed him on each cheek. Their behaviour was typical of people that had known each other for ages, not just one brief prior meeting.

Was this all playing out true to form? My father the ever-charming gentleman, and Charlotte the gusher?

My parents seemed in particularly good form, undoubtedly from what they had just witnessed. I could just imagine the bedroom talk later, enthusiastically thinking of Charlotte as the perfect daughter-in-law.

"Charlotte, darling, what would you like to drink?" my dad offered, affectionately putting his arm across her shoulder as he guided her towards the bar alcove. "Hamilton can suggest some of the Rockwell favourites, just to get you in the swing of things."

On that cue, Hamilton enthusiastically started making recommendations.

She turned to my dad and placed a hand on his arm. "What do you think I should have, Arthur?"

"Well, what about a pink gin or a gimlet—gin, lime juice, caster sugar, and lime zest, if I'm not mistaken?" he said, looking at Hamilton for confirmation.

"Not a good idea if you don't like lime," I tendered.

"Charlotte, dear, why don't you get Kir Royales for you and Charles? It's his favourite" I heard my father say. He really was playing the perfect father-in-law role—laying it on thick.

"Ooh yes, what a good idea, Arthur." Then Charlotte looked across at her brother and my mother sitting on the burgundy bay-window seating, and asked, "And, Fran, what about you and Jamie? Can Hamilton prepare something for you?" She was being the perfect daughter-in-law.

Luckily, what was becoming a rather uncomfortable situation was interrupted by Fabrizio's wanting to make sure he had everyone's dietary requirements.

Just then I heard the heavy brass knocker at the front door, not a familiar sound because ordinarily our guests would be announced by the gatekeeper via intercom way before their arrival at the house. I realised it was Gigi, as no one had yet shown her in. I immediately jumped up to go and greet her, embarrassed that I had not been more attentive. With a quickened stride, I dashed down the long foyer towards the entrance hall as I heard her opening the heavy door and stepping in.

She called out lightheartedly, "Helloooo, is anyone home?"

Arriving hurriedly, I greeted her with, "Hello, Gigi," and then took her hand.

"Hello, Charles," she replied in a measured tone as she took in her surroundings.

Our eyes met; the formality of our greeting not lost on either of us as the corners of our mouths turned up in a discreet, shared smile. How were we going to survive two weeks in the far more formal environment of Rockwell Manor? Gigi looked and smelt beautiful. She wore a summery, relaxed fitting, midcalf cream cotton dress, not dissimilar to the one she'd worn that first stormy night in Shrewsbury. This dress though, was slightly more formal, with the addition of a thin beige patent-leather belt but without cinching beneath her breasts, which I had become used to. And a little unusually for her, she was wearing a brassiere, which didn't do much to conceal her beautiful bosoms. I noticed she was also wearing beige patent-leather strappy sandals matched to her belt, fully exposing her beautifully pedicured toes and feet. Attention to the slightest details, which was just so typical of Gigi. How could I not feel excited?

My Rude Awakening

As we walked from the entrance hall, past the formal dining room with its large crystal chandelier set over the Victorian dining-room table, and then through the informal living area, towards the family dining room, I could see Gigi taking in the wide-open passages, the various pieces of art, the wood panelling, the oversized fireplaces with carved sandstone surrounds, and the antique furniture. That was probably the first time I thought about them having been bought new in the late 1800s and now being over 100 years old. These were probably all the things Charlotte had been looking at just moments earlier.

I became very aware of the exceedingly formal Rockwell Manor decor, which made me miss Shrewsbury and its simpler, more casual homely style even more.

Walking through the family room towards the family dining room, Gigi looked ahead at the double door to the outside area. I wondered again how she would react the next morning at breakfast when she discovered they opened to a view over the polo field, towards the stables on the patio. Something she had probably only caught a glimpse of when driving in.

My parents, still sitting at the bay window of the family dining room with Jamie and Charlotte, got up as Gigi approached. My father also greeted her warmly, seeing her for the first time since she had arrived. *My dad likes the Blackwood ladies,* flicked through my mind.

She sat down next to my mother and immediately remarked, "Oh, Fran, I just love Winston Cottage. I feel very spoiled." She continued with a hand on my mum's arm, "And the meandering pathway up to the house is so, so special. Those big, old trees, the dense foliage and flower beds, and the way you have lit it all up—it's just enchanting."

I loved all the natural affection between my parents and the Blackwoods, and I imagined a large part of their feelings were based on their hoping Gigi was the mother of their potential future daughter-in-law.

Their misguided view was understandable. With all the time I had spent with the Blackwoods for well over a year, it was quite reasonable for them to have thought Charlotte and I had been in a relationship for most of that time.

I cringed at the thought. Not about Charlotte—I really liked her—but about how this was going to turn out. I didn't want to disappoint them, especially my mother.

I couldn't help wondering if something could one day come of Charlotte and me. Was Charlotte in fact my destiny? Having been with Gigi, could I then end up being with her, the green fig? After all, as far as girls went, there wasn't any other I was closer to. My mind was in turmoil.

Jamie got up and went over to Hamilton to get his mother a drink. He smiled as he gave it to her. "Here you are, Mum. I got you a Kir Royale, a Rockwell Manor and Charles's favourite."

I thanked Jamie inwardly. I'd wanted Kir Royale to be mine and Gigi's drink, not Charlotte's and mine.

CHAPTER 17
THE FIRST SUPPER

MY MOTHER WAS soon ushering us into the main dining room, wanting to get dinner started. Rockwell Manor dinners could sometimes be quite drawn out, and she was mindful that Gigi and Charlotte were perhaps a little tired after the trip down to Berkshire.

It was my mother who took charge of all the dinner plans, including the seating and menu, leaving only the wine selection to my father. One of his favourite quips was that he was the head of Rockwell Manor, having received Frances's permission! Yes, the running of the Rockwell Manor household was entirely my mother's domain.

With just six for dinner, the eighteen-seat table had been reduced by removing two leaves, which then left a table that would typically seat twelve people. In addition to the chairs at each head, two chairs were evenly spaced on each side of the table's length. Outstretched arms would still be required to touch hands, but at least it fit better.

We were a traditional family, which was on full display at dinner.

My place was always at my father's right side, and Gigi, as the most senior guest, was at my father's left. Interestingly, this positioned Gigi opposite me, which in English tradition would be appropriate seating had we been partners. *What irony!*

My mother placed Charlotte next to me, certainly to encourage a chance of some intimacy between her and I without compromising English etiquette. Jamie was placed opposite his sister, between his mother and mine, sitting at the other head.

As Charlotte stepped forward, I was a little slow in withdrawing her chair so she could take her seat, caught up in thoughts of my parents accepting Gigi as my partner. This made my mother give me a stern glance, a visual rebuke. I could just hear her words, *"Manners maketh man, Sunbeam. Manners maketh man."* I hurriedly tried to make amends as I helped Charlotte to be seated. A flash of white teeth told my parents she appreciated my gentlemanliness. I suspected it was more that she hadn't been treated like that at university.

My father seated Gigi and gave her a kiss on the hand, such a charmer. I was subconsciously taking it all in. *Why is it not as natural for me?*

I surveyed the scene around me and couldn't help noticing how beautifully dressed Gigi, Charlotte, and my mother were. Unusually, this made me feel self-conscious about having dressed in the first items of clothing I came across when I opened my wardrobe. I had grabbed some white polo jeans, slightly stained from my saddles, which I had over a dozen pairs of, a silk navy-blue shirt that at least had a collar, and some tan slip-on shoes. I had rolled up my sleeves only to the middle of my forearms, since much higher than that was difficult because my arms were quite muscular from spending so much time holding either horse reins or a polo mallet. Not certain I had remembered to brush my hair, I quickly ran my fingers through the thick fringe.

My mother noticed what I was doing and teasingly turned to our guest and said, "Charlotte, you'll have to keep an eye on Charles and remind him to brush his hair."

Oh, goodness, this is getting worse by the minute! I thought.

"I think his messy hair looks sexy," Charlotte replied, smiling as she leant over and put her hand on the back of my head while she looked me up and down.

I heard the soft rumble of my dad's chuckle, but it was my mother's blushing embarrassment that distracted me from thinking how completely wrong she was getting my relationship with Charlotte. But I did smile. *Sexy* was not a common word around Rockwell Manor, and I guess mothers don't think of their sons being described in that way.

Once we were all seated, my dad gave me strict instructions to retrieve two bottles of 1975 Château La Mission Haut-Brion Rouge from his cellar, as he set aside the red wine choices Hamilton had put out. It was not lost on me that my father placed enough importance on this evening that I was to take wine out of his special reserve section in the cellar.

I placed the bottles on the drinks counter so Hamilton could decant the first bottle, allowing it to breathe. There was also a large ice-filled silver bucket with two bottles of Dom Pérignon champagne and two white-wine selections. This looked more like a formal gala banquet than an intimate first dinner with the Blackwoods.

Please take me to Shrewsbury, I thought.

And then there were the place settings. First, the silverware was always set for five courses, which meant there were no fewer than twelve utensils for each of us. Glassware next, we each had four: a water tumbler, a champagne flute, and white and red wine glasses. That was to start with. Cocktail glasses may be required, almost certainly liqueur and port glasses, and brandy balloons could come at the end, especially if there was occasion to bring out the cigar humidor. We also each had our own silver pepper grinder and crystal rock-salt pot, which my mother reminded me was either referred to as a *salt box, salt pig,* or *salt cellar*. It was just as well, because passing these around such a big table would have looked like a baton-passing relay. I was used to this and ordinarily would have thought nothing of it. Right then though, I was cringing. I had never had a formal dinner at the Blackwoods', and so I imagined they didn't care much for them.

And always flowers. There was a tall, elegant centrepiece and then others that were under fourteen inches tall so as not to obstruct anyone's view of someone seated across from them. I used to watch in amusement as the staff took up various places around the table while they were setting up, struggling to find the perfect positions so as not to have any obstructing arrangements. My father also found it quite funny and often remarked teasingly, "Sorry, Fran darling, can't see you. The centrepiece will have to go!" even though said centrepiece stood high and proud so that you could look past the slender vase. Needless to say, the centrepiece always remained.

This evening's centrepiece was thirty or forty very long-stemmed red roses. I didn't think much of it, except that we usually had white lilies. Then Charlotte remarked how beautiful and romantic they were as she leant across the table to take in the scent.

Oh, goodness, Charlotte is on form, I thought. *So is my mum, now that I* think about it. *Red roses!* I glanced around the room and quietly thanked my lucky stars. *At least there isn't a pianist!*

As I surveyed what lay before me, I couldn't help noticing how quiet and reserved Gigi was, the wine having done nothing to lift her spirits. I was certain she was finding it all a bit overwhelming and couldn't stop my thoughts from becoming sarcastic. *Obviously, all this stuff is necessary for us to nourish ourselves.*

I couldn't blame my parents for our rather formal lifestyle. It was just how they had been brought up, and I guess it was now just continuing in that same way with me. I couldn't help but feel the difference between sitting around the cosy table for four in Gigi's annex dining area and what I was looking at now. I would have enjoyed eating in our oversized kitchen, which we only ever did for breakfast and pizza evenings. In fact, among the polo-playing fraternity, pizza evenings at Rockwell Manor were legendary. I made a mental note that we should have one with the Blackwoods and avoid the formal dining room at all costs.

I desperately wanted the dinner to be a success, but realised it was a big ask for it to be comparable to our dinners in Shrewsbury! How could it even begin to compare? Just the formality of the evening, which was so blatantly evident, was the first flaw. I tried to get over my sensitivity and just hoped it would at least be an enjoyable meal. Fabrizio was a top chef, mind you.

Charlotte was as effervescent and happy as ever, way more demonstrative and animated than usual. At least she was thoroughly enjoying the evening and, undoubtedly, the keen interest my parents were taking in her.

As dinner ensued, Hamilton adopted his usual management position over the "out of kitchen" staff, servers, and so on. I loved how he had assumed the kingpin "elder statesman" role amongst Rockwell Manor staff. It was as though, since he had once worn my grandfather's shoes, he now had the right to *be in his shoes.* This had not suited the younger upstart chef, Fabrizio, who eventually got his own way as far as the kitchen being his domain. "Out of kitchen" staff had been something of a compromise between the two of them.

The staff wore formal, black-tie attire and served each person individually from silver platters or bowls. No platters or bowls were allowed to stay on the table, only out of sight in the kitchen, under the warmers. "Only flower arrangements on the table" was what my mother felt was appropriate, but bread baskets emerged when Fabrizio came and told us what he had prepared for our dinner. My mother tried to make sure he did not get carried away using "flowery language," as she put it, when going through the menu. A chef or maître d' who felt the need to say he had drizzled something-or-other over one-thing-or-another would exasperate her. I found it amusing, watching my mother's expression when Fabrizio would emote about the menu in his passionate Italian way.

Fabrizio came in and wasted no time going through our dinner courses. "*Buonasera, miei cari.*" My mother had given up trying to convince Fabrizio it was not entirely appropriate to be calling us and our guests, collectively, "my dears." In his Italian-accented English he continued, "Tonight, we have beautifully fresh-a asparagus spears, a delicate-a butter sauce, and parmigiano shavings. Or, if you prefer you could have-a *foie gras* with ginger *confit*, prepared for you on a thin sourdough cracker. Then, we have an entrée of baked figs with Halloumi, wonderful Italian prosciutto, and basil. Your salad this evening is a fresh *di rucola e pompelmo*, or as you say in English, e-rocket and grapefruit"—he shook his head and rolled his eyes—"peeled segments of *pompelmo*, not grape fruit, and it is served with a Greek yoghurt, *pompelmo*-juice dressing, and my special herbs."

I couldn't help smiling at his exasperation, so I asked, "Fabrizio, is there something you want to explain to us about this *pompelmo* salad?"

With a lot of hand gesticulations, he began, "There are no grapes in the salad. In Italy, we take this grapes, which is a fruit, grape fruit, and we make wine. In England, you ask for grapefruit, you get *pompelmo*. Santo Cielo, *salvami dagli Inglesi*." Fabrizio enjoyed making fun of the idiosyncrasies of the English language.

"*Io sono con te,*" Gigi said, smiling.

Fabrizio's head snapped around in her direction, and he just beamed at her. "*Parla italiana, signora?*" he asked.

"*Solo un po,*" Gigi replied.

My Italian was nonexistent, but from just a little time with Gigi, I understood that Fabrizio wanted to be saved from the English and Gigi had agreed.

183

Fabrizio had a new best friend. He looked around to see if there were any questions, and when there weren't, he carried on. "For your main course, we have two options. Jamie's favourite, Côte de Boeuf with roast potatoes and caramelised shallots. No secrets in this house, Jamie," he said with a wink.

Jamie was definitely a well-accepted member of our extended family, not only because he had been to Rockwell Manor on a number of occasions, but more because of how he gregariously engaged with everyone around him. Everybody loved him, especially my parents.

"For those who are less, ah, how do you say, ah, red-blooded than our pilots and polo players, we have a lightly pan-fried sea bass with lemon butter. The vegetables that will come around are Jersey Royal baby potatoes, broccoli stems, and creamed spinach."

"What about the caramelised shallots?" Charlotte wanted to know.

"*Bella ragazza*, haven't you realised that nothing *you* ask is too much trouble here at Rockwell Manor? Just look at *le belle rose rosse*," he said cheekily, leaning over and putting a hand under one of the deep red blooms as he looked at her.

Everyone chuckled at his perceptiveness, knowing my mother had selected the red roses for their love message aimed at Charlotte and me. And everyone chuckled, except me that is.

Fabrizio smiled broadly, knowing he'd put his finger on it. He probably had. Mercifully, he carried on with the menu. "For dessert we have a chocolate fondant and double-cream vanilla gelato or exotic fruits with mango and lychee sorbet."

"Or both," Jamie interrupted.

Fabrizio shook his finger at him. "No, no, no. Only rucola salad and a leetle piece-a meat for you tonight, Jamie. Guy says you're getting too *grande* for the horses."

More chuckles in the room, especially since a more accurate description of Jamie would have been "athletic Greek god." I was thrilled to see things warming up.

He concluded with, "From the kitchen, you will finish off with a wonderful selection of cheeses, crackers, chutney, glazed kumquats, and fig preserve, which you should pair with French port wine."

My Rude Awakening

I preferred Gigi's serving of Madeira port. I thought of mentioning it to my father, but then decided I would rather keep that in Shrewsbury.

Fabrizio ended with, "And I'm terribly sorry, but at Rockwell Manor, anybody needing balsamic glaze, vinegar, or olive oil will have to do their own dreezzzling."

I couldn't help giggling, and neither could my mum, even if she was having the mickey taken out of her.

"Chefs aren't allowed to use flowery language in this household," I said to Gigi in reply to her smiling but confused look. Thanks to Fabrizio, I saw she was starting to relax.

Just as he was about to leave, he referenced the breadbasket. He had no qualms in leaning over the table between my father and Gigi to pick one up. "*Mi scusi*, make sure to enjoy my bread rolls? They are freshly baked out of the pizza oven. Still warm, and just need a leetle butter, even if it is *Francese*."

I had to admit, looking at the bread rolls—the dusting of flour on the crust, and the thought of the butter melting as you spread it—had me looking forward to eating one. I loved Fabrizio's bread rolls.

On this occasion, I didn't think seven would be enough. I say this pointedly because I knew how many bread rolls were in that basket. Not because I had counted them, but because there were six people having dinner. English etiquette dictated there should always be just one bread roll more than the number of people at the dining table. When as a young boy I had asked my mother why, she had explained it was so that the last person to take a bread roll would not feel embarrassed about taking the last one. It didn't make sense to me because someone may have already taken two bread rolls. "No, Sunbeam. It would be impolite to eat two bread rolls at a prepared dinner. It would be ill-mannered to the chef to fill yourself up on bread when he has gone to such lengths to prepare a nice meal."

What a contrast between my first dinner with the Blackwoods in Shrewsbury and now, their first evening with the Featherstones. There would be no Gigi and Charlotte dancing to Bruce Springsteen's "Cover Me" making me feel so comfortable and relaxed that I would begin playing with myself when I went to bed.

That gave me an idea. "Gigi, would you mind helping me put on some music? We don't have the collection that you have in Shrewsbury, but I'm sure we can connect your Walkman to our stereo. I think my parents will find your choice of music more palatable than mine," I said smiling. "Plus, they won't ask me to switch it off if it's your selection."

Now everyone was smiling.

I stood up, saying, "Gigi and I will dash to get her Walkman. We'll be back before the first course."

She followed me out of the dining room, and the moment we were alone, walking down towards Winston Cottage, I asked her, "Is everything all right, Darling? You seemed so quiet in there."

"Your parents are so delightful, and they have made such an effort for Charlotte and me. I am just trying to take it all in, that's all, Darling. I never realised... Um, Jamie said so little." She thought for a moment, and then trying to reassure me added, "Just give me the night to settle in."

I felt more uncertain than ever, and Gigi could see it.

"Baby, I am very happy to be here with you at your home. And your parents really are so wonderful. There is just so much to absorb."

There's something I am not getting. "Darling, what else? I can't leave it here. Is it something about Rockwell Manor? You said Jamie told you so little. Was it wrong for me to have hidden so much of my life from you?"

"Oh no, it's not that. But had Jamie told me about all of this, I would have run a mile, thinking you were spoiled and had an attitude of being entitled. I wouldn't have even given myself a chance to discover you are nothing like that," Gigi said, smiling.

Just like Gigi to surprise me again. My fear of what might indirectly attract her could have been her biggest deterrent. My heart swelled. This was all I ever wanted. *Gigi likes me despite Rockwell Manor.*

"So, what is it?" I asked insistently.

Gigi took my hands and calmly said, "I have now met the wonderful parents of the man I have been in a relationship with for more than a year. It is a lot for me to absorb, and I'm in the middle of it. What would it take for them to understand it? And, Baby, what are we going to do about them thinking there is something between you and Charlotte, or at least that there is *going* to be something? They have such high hopes for the two of you."

Of course, that's what it was. Gigi was so sensitive about my parents, especially my mother, the mother of a man her son's age. It was so clear now that she had spelt it out.

I felt an unusual gratitude towards Jamie. By saying very little about Rockwell Manor, he may have unwittingly been the reason Gigi and I had ended up in a relationship. She had taken me for me and had not judged me harshly for Rockwell Manor and the Featherstone perspective. There was some merit in our relationship having been conducted almost exclusively in Gigi's home, and not having been coloured by any outside influences. I was just her Charles, her Baby. She had never looked at nor seen anything beyond just me.

"I don't know, my darling. I really don't. We will work it out together." I cringed at the thought, but was pleased she accepted it as our problem, that we were in it together.

Concealed by the darkness, I took Gigi in my arms. She instinctively reached around me, and we kissed, a warm, gentle, loving kiss.

Then, in a quiet whisper, I said, "I have done nothing wrong, Darling, and everything you have done could not have been more right. There is nothing that anyone's loving heart could ever hold against us, especially as loving as my parents' hearts are." I stopped there, wanting Gigi to understand my words before I carried on. "I love Charlotte a bit like a sister, but you and I know that we could never have a romantic relationship. The two pieces just don't fit. My parents will see that soon, at least my mother will, and she will explain it to my father."

"These words, from this man, have me wanting to say so much, but for now, I'll just say thank you." And she sealed it with a kiss.

With Gigi's Walkman in hand, we hotfooted it back to the formal dining room, aware that we had been gone a little longer than it would take to just collect something from Winston Cottage. We need not have worried. The four of them were in animated discussion about goodness knows what, and barely noticed Gigi and me as I went about connecting her Walkman to our stereo system.

It struck me that anyone watching us, giggling and chuckling and teasing each other when deciding what to play, couldn't help seeing the comfortable and affectionate behaviour ingrained between us. Given that our relationship had been established on a foundation of time and depth on so many levels, this behaviour was unsurprising.

I was amused by how nonchalant my parents were acting about Gigi's music. I was used to background classical melodies playing over the entire downstairs sound system, but this was different. The formal dinner that had me cringing earlier was turning into the most wonderful occasion as Eros Ramazzotti and Vaya Con Dios—replacing Richard Clayderman, Chopin, and Rachmaninoff—played in the background.

It could have been worse still, our own pianist. Everybody was chatting in vibrant fashion, the wine was flowing, and a few cocktails were being sampled.

Jamie decided he hated anything made with Guinness stout, the bitterness giving him an excuse to have both desserts. "Black velvet, my arse," he said, and my mother barely noticed as she carried on smiling. I knew I'd better not try it though.

And all seven bread rolls had been eaten. Jamie was the offender, having broken off pieces to dip into the melted baked brie cheese with nuts and glazed figs.

Watching him do this, I had an idea. In a hushed tone I asked Fabrizio to bring me a bottle of The King's Ginger and a round of Camembert cheese.

The momentary flash of his teeth told me he knew exactly what little treat I was going to make, so I did not carry on with the list of ingredients. In no time, he was back with the squat black bottle of The King's Ginger liqueur, a platter carrying six sourdough crackers, a bowl of stem ginger pieces in sweet syrup, and the round of cheese.

I smiled up at Fabrizio as he leant down and whispered, "You are going to introduce your guests to your Nono?"

I was about eight years old when Fabrizio joined our household staff as our chef. He was thirty-five years old then, "unusually young," as my granddad had said. That would have put him at forty-eight by this time. In my mind, I was thinking about his retirement age and how sorry I would be when that day arrived.

I began setting out the crackers, immediately garnering Charlotte's attention.

"What are you making, Charles?" she asked.

"Help me. Please cut six pieces of Camembert cheese, about half an inch thick," I replied, thinking she could help me speed up the process.

This little production attracted Gigi's and Jamie's attention too. My parents knew what was coming next, but the Blackwoods didn't.

While Charlotte cut the cheese, I swiped a little French butter across the crackers before placing the Camembert segments on top. Then I said "Charlotte, please will you also cut six slices of ginger about the same size as the cheese but only half the thickness."

With the rounded back of the cheese knife, I pressed in the soft centre of each piece of cheese to make a basin. Then, just as I had done with my granddad, I filled each tiny basin with The King's Ginger. Steady as you like, I covered each piece of cheese with the ginger pieces. I took one and led the way by placing it on my side plate. Charlotte did likewise before Fabrizio went around the table to serve each guest one of the creations. When everyone had theirs, I held up my cracker of cheese, ginger, and liqueur as if it were a glass.

Everyone replicated my actions, and my dad gave a pointer saying, "Must eat it whole, folks."

I followed with, "To the gods of indulgence. Let's indulge. I miss you, Granddad."

Even though it was quite a mouthful, and I was very busy chewing away, I couldn't help the smile on my face at thinking of Granddad's approvingly welcoming Gigi, because it is quite likely I would have told him about our relationship. Oh, how he would be chuckling at the hole that my mother was digging for me with Charlotte.

It was for that reason I was caught totally off guard as Charlotte grabbed my cheeks with both her hands and gave me an exuberant kiss.

Gigi grinned at my shocked expression after Charlotte's spontaneous gesture. I could tell by the joyous smile on her face that she was feeling the same emotion Charlotte was and, given other circumstances, would have done the same thing. My parents loved it. And without admitting it, I loved it too. Charlotte was very special to me, and ignoring all the expectations, which were my parents' alone, we had become very close.

I loved watching Gigi coming out of her shell, and Fabrizio couldn't do enough for her, especially after he heard her Eros Ramazzotti collection.

Then, breaking tradition, etiquette flew out the window as Fabrizio brought the flambé trolley to the dining room and started making Crepes Suzette for everyone. My father joined in the preparation, having great fun "dreezzzling" Grand Marnier over the pan so that the flame climbed the trickle of alcohol up to the bottle. Fabrizio then made a show of placing them before each of us.

Unquestionably though, my highlight of the evening was when a track titled "What's a Woman" by Vaya Con Dios started playing.

"What's a Woman" – Vaya Con Dios

| YouTube | Spotify | Apple |

As the mellow tubular sound of the saxophone wafted into the room, I watched in amazement as my father got up, threw his napkin onto his place setting, walked the length of the table to my mother, reached out his hand, and simply said, "Fran, dance with me."

My mum, even though she was looking slightly shocked and a little shy, didn't hesitate to take my father's hand.

Was this the start of dancing at Rockwell Manor?

Watching my parents as they began swaying back and forth to the methodical rhythm and eerie vocals of this lovely song was a beautiful sight, even though the lyrics didn't seem to relate to them. The opening line asks, "What's a woman when a man don't stand by her side, when he has secrets to hide and doesn't play by the rules? Will she be weak or have to be strong, struggle hard, or be made to feel like a fool?" *All wrong,* I thought, until I looked at my mother's face. The softness in her eyes, acknowledging my father for being the stalwart he was, secure in the knowledge he would always be by her side, no secrets to hide, always going by the rules. There would be no right turning to wrong there. That little moment showed me how big a part my father played in my mother's power.

I happily looked across the table to see what Gigi was making of it. The wistful look on her face jarred my being. All the things my mother had with my father were absent in Gigi's life. I wanted to be that person, to be at her side, and I wanted it now. It didn't suit me to hide it like this. Caught up in the moment, I was ready to declare my feelings for her.

As if she knew what was going on in my head, Gigi looked at me and subtly shook hers.

With the music and the soothing sound of conversation drifting through the Rockwell hallways, everyone still sipping after-dinner liqueurs and dessert wine, the evening slowly drew to a close. I was feeling a mixture of elation and contentment, not least because unexpectedly, it had been such a lovely evening. But deep down, I couldn't curtail the discontent I was feeling because of mine and Gigi's situation. *How can I be there for her?* I wanted to be for Gigi what my father was to my mother. It would've been so easy had it been Charlotte and I who were immersed in a relationship. An evening like this would be the perfect entrée as our two families came together.

After dinner and all the festivities, Gigi was more than ready for bed. I was hoping to have a little time alone with her and share what I was feeling, even though it didn't seem necessary. I offered to walk her to the cottage.

"I'll come along to see where you are holed up, Mum," Charlotte said jokingly, followed by that familiar little giggle.

Oh well, that settles that, I thought.

The two of us walked Gigi down to the cottage, and I waited patiently for Charlotte to ooh and aah over the place before escorting her back to the hall leading to the east wing and her room.

Disappointed, I headed to the north wing and my own room for some much-needed sleep.

With Gigi having settled into Winston Cottage, an unusual feeling came over me. My lover was now curled up in bed at my home, in my county, surrounded by my family and friends and all of my interests. Following my recent RAF and university qualifications, and now that Gigi had stepped into my world, was this my period of transition? I couldn't wait to take her by the hand, sometimes figuratively, so that she could explore with me the life of the person she had taken as her lover.

CHAPTER 18
THE BARRETT CUP

THE NEXT DAY'S schedule had been finalised. Rockwell Manor Polo were playing against Balthazar in a semifinal match of the twenty-goal Barrett Cup, down to the last four of the top teams and players that had entered the tournament. Jamie was playing in his first mini tournament, a four-goal event over four chukkas. We were all invited to the Guards Polo Club for a dinner dance in the evening, after the match.

I tried to imagine what it would be like, with Gigi and me being out for the first time. The simple truth was, I couldn't imagine it. This was something of a first.

Jamie and I were up early for breakfast, the next most important meal at Rockwell Manor. I didn't expect Gigi to join us that morning, but I still felt disappointed when she did not appear. Jamie and I finished our bowl of bran, berries, chia, and sunflower seeds and then headed out to Guards, less than a twenty-minute drive away.

As we walked out of the door, my father called out that he would follow shortly to watch our game, adding, "I will bring Charlotte and Georgina with me."

I had worried for a moment that he might have forgotten about Gigi, but of course, that would never have happened. It was only me thinking irrationally, caught up in the turmoil of young, romantic—and perhaps lustful—love.

Once Jamie and I arrived at the polo field, it was full focus on the game ahead. Well, that's what was meant to happen. My head was somewhere between where Gigi was and what we'd be doing that evening.

Jamie still had a few minutes before the start of his match, so I took him to our gazebo, complete with our team's colours and emblem, standing

My Rude Awakening

at the end of the field. In addition, there were around a dozen fold-out chairs with Rockwell Manor Polo Team and insignia on the backrest and three tables had been set up with an assortment of snacks, water, energy drinks, and the like. This was where the players and their close connections would be stationed and invariably watch the entire game from. Then, about thirty yards farther back, behind this gazebo, were the full complement of our team's forty-odd horses.

Jamie headed off, excited to be playing in his first tournament, even if it was only at the four-goal level. It was a modest start, but he had to begin somewhere.

The preparation was always the same. Horses were all properly tacked up with specialty saddles, bridles, and especially good leg protection, and their tails are tied up properly. A loose tail could obstruct one's shot. Next, players go about making sure their sticks, or polo mallets, are in good order. Ours were from Villamil, pronounced *Vije Mi-l,* from Argentina. One typically has at least ten in their bag, of generally three lengths—fifty-one, fifty-two, and fifty-three inches—catering for the different heights of the horses. The players need so many mallets because it is common to break a stick or two during play, considering they are made of just a wooden head and a cane shaft. Last, the players put on their knee guards, helmets, riding gloves, and sometimes, eye protection.

I had a quick warm-up, took my first chukka horse for a gentle canter and a little stick and ball, and I was ready for the start of our match at 1100 hours.

I had a quick look around for Gigi but was disappointed that there was no sign of her yet.

Rockwell Manor was fielding a team that had been tried and tested in our mango strip, except for me, having been sidetracked by the Royal Air Force. We were very balanced. Our team captain was Llewellyn "Lew" Tomkinson, who was also the current English polo team captain when he was playing for his country. Our secret Argentinian weapon was Nicolas Aroldin, who was the proverbial seven-goal player going on nine-goals. He was playing for us for the first time and had already given a very good account of himself. And then came Guy Watkins, our polo manager, and a key player in our team. I was on a three-goal handicap—pushing four, people were saying—but perhaps they were just being flattering. There was no question that playing off a four-goal handicap, Guy was punching way above his weight. Hopefully today I would be able to match him, a tall order considering I had not been able to practise as often as I used to. I was secretly hoping that having Gigi there would give me extra motivation, as seemed to have happened with my flying. Rockwell Manor had progressed this far through using our reserve, George "Georgie" Graham, who had been playing exceptionally well. I was acutely aware of the pressure to not let the team down now that I was stepping in.

Our opposing team was good, with their own secret weapon, not that you could call an Argentinian ten-goal player a secret. Alberto "Beto" Cambiano was a consummate professional in his late twenties with mouth-watering skills. He would be playing in the number three position, generally where you would find the best player of the team. Think of him as the quarterback in American football. He was backed up by two solid players, an up-and-coming American teenager, Sebastian "Seb" Brentwood, on four goals and playing in the number two position. At number four, the six-goal Malcolm "Malcs" Barwick, who also played in the back position for England, always recognisable on the field because of his red helmet and square shoulders. And if you saw a ball sailing more than half the length of the field, chances were it came off Malcs's mallet.

The team's sponsor, Jerry Kapper, was a zero-goal player, and he would be wearing the number one on his shirt, indicating he was ostensibly the striker, or primary goal scorer. We didn't need to hold our breath though, as it was unlikely he would influence the game. Not because he was a zero handicap—a young, up-and-coming zero-goal player could be a real handful on the polo field—but because he was an ageing zero-goaler on the way down. Jerry Kapper was the typical "monied sponsor" or *Patrón*, as the Argentinians would say. And he liked to flaunt it, making sure his pilot chose an approach path that took his helicopter in view of the main grandstand on its way to the helicopter landing area. Had he seen himself on the polo field the way others did, he may have been inclined to be a bit more discreet. It just wasn't very English, and he wasn't.

"Monied sponsor, or mounted spectator?" I can hear my young reserve teammate Georgie saying. Cheeky, but accurate.

In truth though, sponsors played an important role in the modern game. Running a top team cost millions of pounds per year with zero return! The thing that irked me was when the sponsor's involvement was more about his image and showboating than the game. Our family were sponsors too, and it is fair to say that every team has an element of sponsorship. For us there was no embarrassment. We had played the game for generations and were significantly involved in thoroughbred horses and breeding, and it was all about the game. Jerry Kapper would have done far better exercising his body, improving his horsemanship and polo skills so that he could make a real contribution to his team, instead of spending two million dollars a year for a top-ten goaler just so he could put silverware in his boardroom. He was their weakness. They were a three-man, twenty-goal team. We were not.

Our simple strategy today was that all four of our players had to be a handful. Four players making an effective contribution meant we should always have an overlap. I hoped these weren't famous last thoughts. Playing against the world's best ten-goal player was never going to be easy. I knew we would have our work cut out for us.

After the customary presentation of the competing teams to the spectators, one of the umpires got the first chukka underway by throwing the ball between the two lines of players.

We got off to a bad start and almost immediately were two goals down, having not even finished the first chukka. Beto, their ten-goaler, had caught us all off guard, weaving his magic and scoring two impressive individual goals. My contribution was nowhere near my three-goal rating, let alone "going on four."

Another duffed backhand by me resulted in a glare from Llewellyn Tomkinson, our captain. "Featherstone, wake up," came his sharp censure.

I may have been the son of our team's sponsor, but on this field I was rightfully treated as the junior. I knew I had to focus, but still I found myself looking to the sidelines for a glimpse of Gigi.

The second chukka was underway, but no sooner had we begun than I heard the shrill blast of the umpire's whistle. Seb had tried to ride-off Nic, but instead of meeting him shoulder to shoulder, he had caught Hurricane, Nic's horse, across the neck, and Seb had come dangerously close to bringing him down.

My concern turned to suppressed rage when I heard Jerry Kapper shouting, "No blood, no foul."

There was no place for this attitude in polo, arguably the most dangerous sport in the world. My anger was no doubt also exacerbated by the fact that we were down by four goals at the end of the chukka.

Chukka three improved only marginally, thanks to the increased contributions of the players around me, resulting in Lew's scoring one, even though he was in the number four back position. Guy was also linking well with Nic, which helped him score a goal.

We were trailing badly. I think the score was six to three. *We can't be beaten by Jerry Kapper,* was my overwhelming thought, even if it all came down to the phenomenal skills of his ten-goaler, Beto Cambiano.

With the end of the third chukka came the Interval, the official halftime that lasted fifteen minutes. While most of the spectators took to the field to tread in the divots, the teams withdrew to their seating areas to discuss tactics, changes in approach, which horses they would be bringing on, and so forth.

Lew had only one thing to say. "I don't know where your head is, Featherstone, but you're missing a good game."

I looked at him ruefully, realising how sorely my game was lacking.

Was my play all down to my being distracted by Gigi, or had my lack of match fitness played a bigger role than I thought? Now that I was in the RAF, would I even get to four-goals? I wondered despondently.

I couldn't make up for the lack of practise just then, but somehow, I had to try to push thoughts of Gigi aside and get my head back in this game.

With just seven minutes of the interval remaining, we started readying ourselves to take to the field for the second part of the match.

Just then I spotted my parents, my Aunt Edwina and Uncle Alexander—who I hadn't realised were coming—and Charlotte, but my eyes were immediately drawn to Gigi. Realising the interval was coming to an end, they hurriedly began making their way across to our gazebo, where we were all sitting.

When they were still thirty or forty yards away, I heard Charlotte say, "Come on, Mum, let's run to them before they go back onto the field."

"Go along," my mother encouraged.

Charlotte and Gigi bent down and removed their shoes.

"Race," I heard Charlotte say.

The sight of them running towards us, barefoot on the soft green grass, hair and dresses billowing as they ran, transfixed me.

My Rude Awakening

They both came straight to me and kissed my rather sweaty cheeks, seemingly oblivious of the other three players whom they had not yet met.

"Ooh la la, *hermosa*," Nic exclaimed.

My Spanish was rubbish, but I knew enough to know *hermosa* meant *gorgeous* or *beautiful*. Nic, the bloody charmer.

Gigi was wearing a very sporty-looking navy-blue-and-white-striped shirt, cinched beneath her breasts, as always, accentuating their fullness. A loose navy-blue skirt reached down to her midcalf, wafting with the occasional gust of wind. Loosely draped over her shoulders was a navy-blue silk shawl. From her wide-brimmed straw hat and Jackie O sunglasses, down to her slip-on JP Tod's shoes, just like my mum—still in her hands, which had me glancing down at her feet—she was perfectly attired for polo.

In contrast, I barely noticed what Charlotte was wearing, other than its being a floral dress, such was my focus on Gigi.

They milled around for only a moment before a groom hurriedly rustled up a few more director's chairs with Rockwell Manor on the backrest. As I watched Gigi settling in to spectate the second half, not from the stands but as a part of our team, I felt an excitement deep in my belly. Suddenly, desperately, I wanted the world to know she was mine.

My mother came across to join them. Unusual for her, but I was pleased, nonetheless. I knew she didn't enjoy watching me play and that it would be followed by her usual "you must be more careful" speech.

As we took to the field for the fourth chukka, the start of the second half of the match, I was feeling a hundred times better.

Lew brought his horse alongside mine and asked, "Have I just seen the reason for your less than wonderful display earlier?"

I knew he was referring to Charlotte, so I allowed myself to smile sheepishly.

As we began to canter to the centre of the pitch for the throw in, a familiar voice called out, "Come on, chum. I haven't come here to watch my best mate lose." Jamie had clearly finished his match and hightailed it across to where we were.

I wouldn't easily admit it, but that was extra motivation too.

Shifting my full focus to the game, I asked "What's the score, Lew?"

For a reply, all I got was, "Oh, God, we both know where your head has been."

We just had to rescue this match. I was not going to have Gigi watch her first game of Rockwell Manor Polo with us losing.

I began playing like a demon, which in turn rubbed off on my teammates, as everyone upped their game. And the second half miraculously improved. Our opposition responded to our increased tempo with no intention of letting their three-goal advantage slip, but I was all over it, playing like a man possessed.

"Now that's more like it," came Lew's encouragement.

We ended the penultimate chukka nine to eight down, but we had the momentum and one more chukka to score two more than them. We could do it!

We got onto our sixth-chukka horses, which normally are your best. Warbird was ready for me, and she was up for it, as always. I had another top horse, Mufti's Dream, in reserve in case I needed to switch her just before the end. Both mares would give me everything.

I had to monitor Warbird carefully, as she gave so much effort that she often drove herself to exhaustion. I loved that about her but was wary she might hurt herself through her unselfish commitment. Once, after she'd finished a chukka with me and I'd removed her saddle and bridle, I started untying her tail, and she threw herself onto the ground. This would normally be an ominous sign for a horse and could portend the start of heart failure. As it transpired, she was just exhausted and that was how she wanted to rest. Most unusual, but extremely endearing. Both Warbird and Mufti's Dream were from the Tom Fool line, a descendant of the notable Buckpasser. They were racehorse thoroughbreds, my favourite. The horses, and especially the mares with this heritage, always have elegant, swanlike necks, dished snouts quite typical in Arabian breeds, bold eyes, and beautiful balance and symmetry in their gait.

We took to the field, everyone ready to fight for the win in this important knockout match. Alberto Cambiano and Malcs Barwick combined well to score the next goal. Pity they were the opposition. The pressure was on, with us being back to two goals down, ten to eight, and with time running out.

Next, I galloped down the left flank of the field and, with a perfectly timed cut shot, hit the ball to centre field, flawlessly placing it for Lew to pick up and score. Now it was ten to nine.

Better. We still need two.

My Rude Awakening

Not wanting to tire Warbird too much in case I needed her for an additional period of play, I waited for the right moment and then shot off the field for a quick swap. I did this because I had a feeling that we could get another goal in this chukka and have to come back for a golden goal and what would then be the final chukka. As was typically done, I rode alongside Mufti's Dream and hopped from one saddle to the next without touching the ground.

Back on the field, I glanced at the big seven-minute countdown clock. Three minutes to go.

Soon, with seconds remaining, we got a well-orchestrated team goal, and I finished off with a perfectly executed neck shot and the equaliser, bringing the score to ten to ten. The clock counted down, and because we were drawn, the chukka would end with the next infringement.

Lew wanted to regroup and didn't want the opposition to sneak in a goal, a big possibility when you had a ten-goaler like Cambiano against you. Lew purposely hit the ball onto the boards. His cool calculation in the heat of the moment was exactly why he was England's captain.

The neck shot needs to be perfectly timed with the gait of the horse so as not to strike their front legs. When holding a polo stick and testing it for whip, there is barely any flex. With the momentum of the mallet head in a full-powered shot, you get a very different result, as captured in this photograph.

The bell rang for the end of the sixth, and because we were drawn, we would play a seventh "golden goal" chukka. The game would end when a team scored the winning goal.

We went off the field to ready ourselves for this last period of play, heads swirling with how to prepare for the crucial sudden-death conclusion of the game.

"Right, chaps, the next goal is ours and then we are through," said Lew pointedly. "Charles, more of the same!" He wasn't one for going into raptures.

Nothing more needed to be said, and no instructions to my seasoned groom were necessary either. Warbird was ready and waiting for me to take her back onto the field. This is customary in high-goal polo, to go back to your best horse for as long as she has something in the tank. I sprang onto her back, immediately feeling the calmness that always came over me when she was under me. My teammates knew I felt this way too.

"If you had nine of those, you would be on six-goals," they would say.

The seventh chukka was relentless, full gallops up and down the field as each team tried to get that golden goal. At three minutes, thirty-five seconds in, still nothing. I knew the horses would soon be starting to noticeably tire. There was no way you could play a whole chukka on your top horse and still expect to have much left for an unexpected extra period of play. I also knew that this was when Warbird was at an advantage because she had, and gave, so much more. The pressure was mounting.

The next moment, Seb was heading down towards our goal. I had to get to him quickly, and using all of Warbird's blistering speed, I caught up. As he was about to strike the ball for goal, I leant fully out of my saddle—perilously close to unseating myself—and straining every sinew of my body, reached under Warbird's neck for the under-neck hook, obstructing Seb's shot at the crucial moment. He could not complete his play as we both now harmlessly galloped over the ball.

Both our best players were free, and it was quite the procession as they galloped into our opponent's half. Lew passed the ball up field to Nic on Chance, the best horse in our yard. Watching him pick up the bouncing ball at a full gallop, bring it under control, and then hit it out of the air to split the wicker goal posts was a thing of beauty. Nic had an unbelievable eye for the ball. *Will I one day be able to do that?* I asked myself.

That was it. We had the golden goal. We were through.

Without dismounting, we rode up alongside our teammates and gave each other big hugs before we circled around to our competitors to shake their hands.

Relieved at having saved face with Gigi, I looked around to find her. There she was, still at our gazebo with Jamie, Charlotte, my parents, and my aunt and uncle, including Georgie—who was beaming from ear to ear for his team's success, even though he hadn't played. I could relax, knowing that I'd redeemed myself by playing well in the second half.

"Thanks to you we won that game, Carlo. That was an incredible hook, right under your horse's neck. Bet Seb did not like it though." Nic grinned broadly.

I smiled at the Italian version of my name, and quite liked the praise too. I thought about that for a moment, and as much as I enjoyed the recognition, he had misattributed a large amount of the commendation.

I had been able to pull off that hook for just one reason alone. Even though I had been hanging out of my saddle at a ridiculous angle, Warbird had maintained perfect balance and position at a full gallop, giving me a stable, reliable platform to confidently put myself out on a limb. Contrary to what most people thought, a horse responds to the rider's legs more than any other aide. The positioning of my legs would have told Warbird to do something completely different to what I needed at that moment. She was seemingly reading the game and what was required of her in that crucial period of play and had remained unswerving and perfectly balanced…*at a full gallop*. Horses are not credited with nearly as much intelligence as they should be.

Still on Warbird's back, I leant forward, my chin resting on the top of her clipped mane, and with both my arms outstretched, I rubbed her sweaty neck. As we walked back to the horse lines, I continued my adulation of her, wiping her face and sweat-frothed sides, letting her know that I knew very well who had really saved the game.

The gazebo was where everyone migrated after a match, so it was always very festive. Horses swilling about in the background. Beaming grooms.

The Featherstone/Blackwood group was joined by a few other well-wishers. Most importantly, Grace, our vet, was there to give our horses a once-over and a vitamin B-12 injection if they needed it, a powerful supplement to aid their recovery.

As we walked over to our waiting entourage, I saw other players leaning back, loosening their horse's tail whilst still sitting in the saddle. Some loosened the girth strap as well so their horse could begin to relax. I often thought of this as being similar to when one leaves a dance ball and immediately removes their bow tie, jacket, and pleated cummerbund.

In the background, I heard their ten goaler, Beto Cambiano, loudly cursing their failure, "*Concha de puta,*" as he hit the ground with his polo mallet. Having played a lot of polo with Argentinians, I had often heard them say this. In fairness, I had also often heard the English equivalent, "son of a bitch," so I thought little of it. At least, not at that moment.

As we got closer, Lew looked towards Charlotte and, picking up from the interval, asked, "So who is the blonde over there?"

"Oh, that's Jamie Blackwood's sister. You know, my Air Force friend," I said.

"Ah, I get it," came his reply. "Now I *really* understand your first three chukkas." He chuckled.

As I approached the horse lines, Mum, Dad, Uncle Alexander, Aunt Edwina, Jamie, Charlotte, and, most importantly, Gigi, met me there. I gave Warbird a final pat and swung off the saddle in a way that was akin to how a gymnast dismounts from a pommel horse, landing effortlessly on my feet. It wasn't entirely necessary, though it was a typical dismount after the adrenaline rush of a game.

Pablo, my Argentinian groom, walked towards me to collect Warbird, and I could see the relieved look on his face.

Acknowledging his feelings, I quite spontaneously repeated what I had just overheard, "*Concha de puta,* we nearly messed that up."

The grin I got from Pablo was so broad I saw for the first time that he was missing an upper molar. While Gigi and Aunt Edwina covered their mouths with their hands in shock, Dad and Uncle Alexander started chuckling. But it was my mother's violent reaction that I was acutely aware of.

"Edward Charles, I beg your pardon!" she almost spat at me.

My mother was begging for nothing, and when she called me Edward Charles, it meant only one thing. I was in trouble.

"Sorry, Mum," I said, looking at her apologetically.

I knew profanities in our home were unacceptable, but surely this was an overreaction for simply saying "son of a bitch" when it was something so often heard. I guessed she had found it disrespectful of women and hadn't expected it to be coming out of my mouth.

Fortunately, everyone brushed it aside and normal order resumed. Festivities immediately began with Guy putting on a mix CD on the portable audio system. An interesting consequence of this was our Argentinian grooms seemingly 'warming' to me. I imagined this little episode somehow made me more approachable.

My inclination was to walk straight over to Gigi, but Charlotte ran up to me instead. This action only confirmed what Lew thought he already knew.

"Ooh, that was so exciting," Charlotte effused as she touched my arm. "Wow, what a brilliant, you know, that *thing* you did to block that goal." Clearly, she had half picked up on what someone else must have said. It was obvious this was not intended to be a conversation opener, as Charlotte looked around, deciding where she should go and socialise.

Charlotte then drifted off to find her mother and I went over to the gazebo to sit down. Others were milling around, chatting happily and we spent the next twenty to thirty minutes reminiscing about the game and going over some of the highlights. Shots made, hooks missed, nearly this or that. You would hear things like, "Jeez, did you see how Abacus turned inside Malcolm Barwick's best horse in the fifth?" or, "What about how Lightning galloped past Jerry Kapper?" Perhaps it was trivial, but we all enjoyed it.

I noticed Jamie listening intently, affected by the post-match excitement, and knew then he was properly bitten.

As exciting as it was, I wanted to go across to where Charlotte and Gigi were chatting.

I was about to walk over to them when Malcs Barwick came up to congratulate me on our win. We spoke for a while before he remarked, "I noticed your mother was really annoyed with you when you came off the field. What was that about?"

"Oh, nothing really," I replied. "They just don't like me using bad language, and when I came off the field, I just said to Pablo, 'Son of a bitch, we nearly messed it up.' I guess it just sounds worse in Spanish."

"Oh, what did you say?" Malcs asked.

"*Concha de puta*," I repeated more quietly, not wanting to be heard again.

With a deadpan face, he replied, "Well, I agree. Your mum's reaction for you saying, '*hijo de puta*'—you know, 'son of a bitch'—would have been a bit over the top. I would say her reaction was far more in line for you saying, 'the cunt of a whore,' which in the context is what you actually said."

I could literally feel the blood draining from my face as Malcs fell into a deep belly laugh. I remembered then that Malcs would have had no difficulty understanding the language. He was fluent in Spanish, having spent a lot of time in Argentina playing polo, but I wondered how my mother knew what it meant. Then I remembered my grandfather had played much of his polo with Argentinians, and I just smiled. I missed him.

With Malcs still enjoying himself at my expense, Nic, having noticed this little interlude, came over to see what was so funny. Malcs recounted the story to him, and he was equally amused.

Once Malcs had left, in a soft, discreet voice out of earshot of everyone else, Nic asked, "Carlo, Charlotte, she's your girlfriend…no?"

I could now hear the Spanish accent but with an overriding American twang. Clearly, he had spent a lot of time there. Almost certainly in Palm Beach, Florida, or possibly the Hamptons, well-known American polo locations.

There was no point in beating around the bush, so I just answered him truthfully. He did not seem surprised by my "no," but I was hoping he would keep it to himself as he gave me a nod and went on to mingle with the others. Right now, Charlotte was a good decoy for where my affections really lay. I was sure Nic had an ulterior motive. After all, Charlotte was strikingly attractive, and he was a very good-looking man with a wicked sense of humour. He and Charlotte could make a great couple.

I was still trying to get over to Gigi when Jamie came up to me. "Tell me about Nic, chum?" he asked candidly, clearly interested in my teammate who'd just departed.

"What do you want to know?" I asked, but then I carried on anyway. "I really don't know him well, but you can see he is an amazing polo player. Really should be an eight or even a nine, but I've heard he may let his love life get in the way of his reaching the top. I hope he doesn't."

"Yes, that's what I want to know about," Jamie replied, getting to the point.

"Well, you can see for yourself what a good-looking chap he is." I looked across the area as if to confirm what I had said. He was pretty tall at around six feet, a good height for Charlotte, and in his late twenties. He had a thick mop of jet-black hair that fell onto his forehead and swept away to the sides; deep, soulful brown eyes with thick eyebrows and long eyelashes; an athletic body; olive-coloured skin. *Yes,* I thought, *if Charlotte knew Nic had the glad eye for her, nature would do the rest.*

"What else can you tell me about him, bud?"

"Well, he has a formidable reputation of the Casanova variety. The girls love him," I said bluntly. Then I teased, "Like someone else I know."

Rather than deny it, Jamie just grinned. "Yes, that's what I have heard, that *he* is a real seducer," he replied, putting a lot of emphasis on *he*.

"Yes, what else?" Jamie pressed.

"Actually, he's a good, fun chap with a naughty sense of humour," I said, trying to figure out Nic's other virtues.

"Georgie tells me he lost one or two professional jobs because of patrons' wives suddenly becoming very interested in their husband's polo," Jamie continued.

"Yes, I've heard that, but not sure if it's true. Sounds like it is right out of the pages of Jilly Cooper's novel, *Polo,*" I replied, tiring of this conversation.

But Jamie still wasn't finished. "Nobody seems to be aware of him having a steady partner."

"Jamie, I think you know him better than I do," I replied with a little chuckle.

"Yeah, a bit of a Brimstone missile, if you ask me," Jamie remarked.

My furrowed forehead showed my confusion, but then I remembered the briefing we'd had on this future weapon. "Oh yes," I said, thinking I understood what he was getting at. "So, you think he's a bit of a fire-and-forget artist?" Brimstone missiles were also known as this because of their lock-on guided capability.

"Yeah, kind of. But probably more like fuck-and-forget, if you ask me." Only Jamie could come up with something like that.

"My dad reckons Nic is heading straight to the top, a certain ten-goaler," I told Jamie. "I hope we get on well with him because he may be around for a while," I continued. "My dad's idea is that we should get him now and let him develop with us."

Having missed the first few games of the Barrett Cup because of my RAF commitments, hence Georgie Graham having stood in for me, I hadn't had the opportunity to get to know Nic. This was a good time to do so, especially considering my dad's view that he may well end up spending a few seasons with us.

Nic has also been a topic of hot conversation around the club and even further afield, not only because of his scintillating polo but also because of his, let's say, other attributes, I thought sardonically.

I had a sense that Jamie would just love to be like Nic Aroldin. He was clearly intrigued by him.

We walked over to where he was sitting, listening to Lew chatting to Guy. "Hi again, Nic," I greeted, beginning the conversation.

"Ciao, Carlo," he answered warmly, wanting to stand up.

I put a hand on his shoulder as I took a seat opposite him.

"Well played today," we said to each other at precisely the same moment, which made us both chuckle.

"No, no, you played really well, especially off a three," he remarked. "You'll be going up soon, no question."

I said a polite thank you but took it from whence it came—a polo professional wanting to be sure of keeping his place in the team. It made me feel good, nonetheless. "Has Guy been looking after you over at Rockwell Manor, and are you happy with the horses?" I asked, even though I knew the answers to both.

Guy was a top polo manager with an easy manner. The question about horses I knew was completely superfluous. With my dad having slowed down a bit and his original string of some of the best horses in England being mostly available, we were able to mount players to the highest standard. The first choice of horses would always be given to the top overseas player of our team, which was now Nic. There would invariably be other of our horses available to bolster the strings of the local players we used. Rockwell Manor's horses were quite simply the best.

"Guy is amazing," Nic replied without hesitation. "And the horses? Well, nowhere in the world am I better mounted. These horses are incredible." He really drew out "incredible" in his American-Spanish accent. "And Chance." He shook his head as if speechless. "She should get Champion Pony for the tournament. One of the best I've ever ridden. Maybe *the* best." He made the ring gesture with fingertip to thumb, showing his appreciation.

I knew what he was saying was true and he wasn't just saying the right things. "So how are you enjoying England?" I asked.

"I love it here. More than anywhere else—Palm Beach, Long Island, Sotogrande. You can call me anytime. I like England the most, after Argentina," he replied.

"What is the big attraction in England?" I genuinely wanted to get a sense of why Argentinians so enjoyed coming to our country.

Nic answered, "Fantastic competitive tournaments. Great level of polo, great countryside, and oh, the women. So many women, so little time."

He said it with such a mischievous face that I had to smile. He may have picked this up as an expression, but I got the impression that it really resonated with him. I thought then that Nic's reputation with women, which had followed him across the Atlantic Ocean, was in all likelihood very well founded.

Jamie had once jokingly referred to his penis as a weapon when speaking about his conquests. Well, if that was an accurate way of describing that notion, then I was afraid Nic's was very likely a weapon of mass destruction.

Deciding to bring our conversation to an end, I asked, "Are you going to the dinner dance this evening, Nic?"

"Of course," he replied in a slow drawl.

"Wonderful, see you there. Ciao, Nic. Very well played today," I said again, before standing and turning on my heels.

As I walked away, leaving Jamie to carry on socialising, I couldn't help thinking he was either going to love Nic or hate him! Nic would be difficult not to like.

After playing any polo match, I always felt more invigorated than normal, especially after a victory when we were competing for a cup, as was the case that day. This was the first time ever that I had someone with whom I was romantically linked watching me play. It gave me feelings of elation I had never experienced before. At that moment, I felt an overwhelming love for her and needed to find her right away.

As I walked towards where Gigi was standing with some of our guests, casually chatting, I looked across to the other side of the gazebo to see where Jamie and Charlotte were. Charlotte and Nic had already found each other. By the looks of things, he was teasing and charming her. And by the looks of things, she was succumbing…quickly.

I felt a pang of jealousy I couldn't explain. I was very fond of Charlotte, even loved her, but our love was that of a slow-grown friendship. One way or another, I saw us being connected somehow, and her being with Nic was not sitting comfortably with me, even if it would ultimately help realign my parents' expectations of Charlotte and me. I also couldn't help thinking she looked very much like a polo groupie. That would change. And would she mature into something like her mother? An interesting thought just as a well-timed old song, "Girl, You'll Be a Woman Soon" by Neil Diamond started playing.

"Girl, You'll be a Woman Soon" – Neil Diamond

YouTube	Spotify	Apple

She was certainly going to be a woman soon, and if she was anything like her mother, it would certainly grab a lot of attention. Would my feelings towards her change once she matured in this way? I wanted to tell her, *Nic, he's not your kind.* I couldn't understand my emotion, as if I wanted to protect her. *Soon, you'll need a man*, as the song went. Was that Nic? Surely not. Or would destiny dictate it was me? Could that happen? Right then, it felt more like brotherly love, but how would I know.

Some hurried steps later and I was standing in front of Gigi, desperately wanting to take her in my arms. Instead, I simply said, "Hello."

"Hello," she echoed. "And very well done for getting into the final. I had better not miss that," she said with a twinkle in her eye. "Not even the first half."

I smiled. She must have overheard the interaction between Lew and me, looked at the scoreboard, and worked it all out. *Nothing lost on her.*

Our greeting was so contrary to how we were feeling, completely belying the heightened energy and passion between us, mine from playing polo and Gigi's from watching it. We both felt it, and it required no explanation from either of us, but we had to constrain ourselves lest our emotions become obvious to others.

Just then, my parents walked up, unaware of the palpable energy between us. Whilst everyone had congratulated me about the daring underneck hook that had saved the day, my mother saw it quite differently.

"Well done, Sunbeam, but I was not happy with that last play of yours." I should have expected this reprimand. And she wasn't finished there. "You know how dangerous that was? If your horse were to lose her footing for one moment, with you leaning out at such a perilous angle, you would certainly have come down with no way of protecting yourself. That's how necks are broken!" she said tersely. "Please, Sunbeam, do not play like that. It is only a game."

After so many years of watching her father—my grandfather—and her uncles playing polo, she understood the game perfectly. She easily recognised all the intricacies, and that what I had done was not unusual. Even if it was a natural part of the game, especially at the high-goal level, my mother did not like my putting myself out on a limb, both literally and figuratively.

My father grimaced slightly and then gave me a little wink. "Well played," he mouthed to me.

There were many more well-wishers, but I couldn't wait to have a moment alone with Gigi. Still standing slightly apart, with people milling all around us, we were not able to hold each other. We had to get out of there.

When we were not in earshot of anybody, I suggested to her, "Darling, would you like to come and look over the horses before we load them up to go back to Rockwell?"

"I would love to," she said without hesitation.

With that, we drifted away to where the horses were being prepared for the trip back home.

Walking close together, we began chatting amiably. It was always like that with us.

"Please explain how players of different levels, like Jamie, as a beginner, are able to play polo together?"

Gigi's question was a good one. How different levels of players were all able to compete against each other was often confusing to the uninitiated. I had to think of a simple way of explaining it.

"You know the handicaps start at zero goals, for absolute beginners, who must still be competent riders and fair strikers of the ball?"

Her nod had me carry on.

"And all the way up to ten goals for the top players. The Pete Sampras of polo."

"Yes," she replied without hesitation.

"And don't be confused by the use of the word *goals* in ten goals or ten-goaler. It doesn't mean he routinely scores ten goals in a match, because that isn't right either. There are ten-goalers who play in the number four, the back position, who may score just one or two goals in a match. Just think handicap when you hear *goal* in that context."

"Okay," Gigi replied thoughtfully, still processing what I had just told her.

"Well, when a player first starts playing, he will be put into low-goal tournaments, like the mini four-goal tournament that Jamie is playing in." I knew I hadn't fully answered the question, so I carried on. "So, what that means is the sum of the handicaps of the four players in the team must not exceed four. You could have two zeros, a one-goaler, and a three-goaler to guide them all. Or a balanced team of four one-goalers."

Gigi nodded her head signifying her understanding as she took my hand and gave it a squeeze.

As we continued our way towards the pantechnicon, I noticed my mother had been watching us. I realised that just because she hadn't broached the topic with me didn't mean she didn't have an inkling what was going on.

My attention was diverted when I overheard one of the tournament directors saying, "Warbird and Chance from Rockwell must be contenders for Champion Pony for the tournament." I loved the sound of that.

Then as we approached the pantechnicon horse rigs, Gigi said. "So that told me a lot about the man I have been sharing my body with."

"What do you mean?" I asked. My hand brushed against hers, which I playfully took a hold of. "Tell me," I demanded, loving the feel of her grasp.

"Well, I don't want to embarrass you, Darling, but you must have been riding those mares of yours for well over an hour. I noticed that your enthusiasm and vigour did not wane in all that time. It explains your performance with another certain mare."

I was enjoying her banter, and recognised there could have been some truth in it.

This time, Gigi chuckled as she spoke. "In fact, what I did work out is that there's a lot more you could do, and for a lot longer."

"*Gigi,*" I said in mock disapproval. How I wanted her *for a lot longer.*

Thirty yards farther on, and finally we were alone. While the grooms were busy booting the horses up with leg protectors for the drive home, Gigi and I sneaked into one of the eighteen birth-horse rigs. Our sexual energy surged back as we put our arms around each other, mouths coming together, uncoordinated passion expressing our pent-up desire. Was it really just the polo having this effect on us?

"I want you tonight," Gigi demanded before changing her stance. "I *need* you tonight. Please, can we get out of the dinner dance at the club?"

I didn't answer, knowing there was no way we could make an excuse not to attend the evening event.

Just in time, I saw the entire team making their way over to the rigs, with my mum and dad, Charlotte, and Jamie in tow. They were all looking

211

forward to the evening ahead, so it hadn't been too difficult dragging them away from the gazebo.

As they got to where Gigi and I were feigning looking at the horses being loaded, my mum came up to me and said, "Well done today, Sunbeam. Granddad would have enjoyed that." This was my mother's way of balancing her earlier reprimand.

With that, Gigi, Charlotte, and my parents left for the car park and the short drive back to Rockwell Manor. Jamie and I followed, and with the early autumn darkness encroaching, we were soon on our way.

Because of the glitz and glamour of polo, an aspect that is not often understood is that it is undoubtedly one of the most dangerous games in the world. Whilst I am unsure of the actual statistics, I understand polo is responsible for more life-changing injuries and deaths per the number of people who play this exclusive sport than any other sport in the world, including motor racing. At the time of writing, years after this chapter I had lost three friends to polo accidents that resulted in spinal cord or neurological injuries. Two of those friends died in the 2000s, soon after being admitted to hospital, which quite naturally seemed the most tragic outcome.

I was closest to the third victim, Nick R, brother to one of my very good friends, JP. Also in the 2000s, Nick suffered a brain stem injury that not only left him quadriplegic—paralysed from the neck down—but also locked-in, which meant he could not speak among other things. He was one of five brothers and from the most incredibly close family whose bond was simply extraordinary.

Watching from the sidelines was devastating for me. I can't even begin to imagine how it was for his young family and JP, all of whom were also there when his accident happened. Nick was the husband to a wonderful wife, father to two lovely daughters. A wife who then dedicated her own life to her injured husband's care. Two daughters who lost forever the hero he was to them.

Nick's injury was the epitome of what is sometimes referred to as a "Hero to Zero" spinal cord or neurological injury. Simply put, once all powerful, more than just capable, at the top of their game, until in the blink of an eye they find themselves fighting death…and winning, only to be rewarded with a life sentence of dependency on others, in a prison of immobility. This then can be nothing other than a tragedy compounded by tragedy. Nick could communicate, but only those closest to him understood what he was saying. One of his wishes was to see his daughters finish school. He got his wish, and then he gave up the fight on 21 December 2016. The end of twelve years of locked-in immobility for Nick and the end of twelve years of loving care for his wife. Nick was a big loss to all of us, but with that loss, there was also relief.

You will never be forgotten, my friend.

CHAPTER 19
GUARDS DINNER AND DANCE

WE ARRIVED AT the club, everyone thrilled to be there except Gigi and me.

The first event of the evening was a little prize giving. Commensurate of it only being the semifinal, we received what would be better described as a token to recognise our participation. The coveted Barrett Cup would only come after the finals.

As I looked across at our opponents, I couldn't help but marvel at the lineup of the eight players from the two teams. The group included handicaps from the lowest, Jerry Kapper on zero, to the highest, Alberto Cambiano, the best player in the world on a ten. The ages ranged from sixteen to sixty. It would've also been possible for a female player to have been in the lineup, as polo was not gender specific. As far as nationalities were concerned, there were three Englishmen, a Scotsman, an American, two Argentinians, and an Australian. A snapshot not dissimilar to most professional polo teams in England.

With the prize giving over, we were able to drift across to our tables.

Looking at the name cards at each of the place settings on our team's round table, I could immediately see my mother's influence. Starting with my father, Gigi was next, then me—*thankfully*—then Charlotte, Nic, Lew and his fiancé Leah, then Guy and his partner for the evening, none other than our vet, Grace Brayers. No surprise that Jamie was next to my mother. *I love how she loves him.* She had managed a boy-girl-boy arrangement that placed everyone who had a partner next to their partner, except my parents who were opposite each other. *Perfect, couldn't be better.* I smiled inwardly, wondering if my mother would regret seating Nic next to Charlotte. She clearly hadn't heard about his reputation.

Looking around the room, I saw in attendance most of the players from all the teams that had been involved in the tournament, including the team we'd be meeting in the finals the following Sunday. One of the things I really enjoyed about polo was no matter how competitive it was, once the game was over, the winners and losers would intersperse quite happily together. I felt then, and still do today, that it should always be that way, in all sports.

The illusion of my being attentive to Charlotte had pleased my parents, but more importantly, it had also unwittingly enhanced Charlotte being a decoy for Gigi's and my relationship. This was now looking like it could at any moment be taking an about turn.

Nic knew Charlotte and I were not romantically connected, and he had wasted no time in making her acquaintance. Our table was already attracting many admiring glances for both Charlotte and Gigi in equal measures. Other men looking at Gigi was also new for me; I wasn't enjoying it, but there was nothing I could do. I was quite certain that now the romantic lines between Charlotte and me had been erased, Nic would meet the challenge of other men paying attention to Charlotte by being even more charming and affectionate. In the face of Nic's offensive, I was certain Charlotte would not resist.

He was already laying on the charm and being such a gentleman with Charlotte. Taking his lead, I decided I should do similarly with Gigi. In being a gentleman, that is.

Dinner progressed smoothly enough, with everybody going to and from the buffet tables, as was always the approach at Guards Polo Club. As a result, nobody paid particular attention to the goings-on between couples. It was quite normal for everyone except Gigi and me. For the first time ever, we were out, in public, *together*. Sitting next to each other. I helped her at the buffet and poured her drink. Lots of friends and acquaintances came over to say hello and have a quick catch-up with us. Our table was very merry, and we all mixed and chatted happily. The more we did these simple things, the more relaxed we became, and the more we enjoyed ourselves.

There were moments when I held Gigi's hand, not thinking, being so caught up in how wonderful it felt to be out in public with her, and at the event itself. Or when she was popping something into my mouth, to see if I liked it before serving it onto my plate. She'd laugh and grab my arm when I pulled a face, showing my distaste for something.

The more we carried on, the more oblivious we became to everyone around us and the more it felt just like the countless dinners Gigi, Jamie, Charlotte, and I had enjoyed in Shrewsbury.

That's when people did begin to notice. Not everyone, and mostly friends' female partners, including Leah and Grace at our table.

"You and Gigi get on so well, Charles," Grace remarked, hoping to learn more.

"Yes, you are all so close," Leah added.

"Well, I guess the Blackwoods have become my second family since going to the RAF and spending so much time in Shrewsbury with them," I suggested, justifying their observations.

With most people having finished their main courses and now onto desserts, the tempo of the music was ratcheted up a few notches. That was enough to draw in the merrymakers. Soon the temperature was rising to the heaving pulse of the party revellers.

Jamie had already left the table and was having a whale of a time chatting and mixing with various groups, and I could see how he was really getting into the swing of the evening. I wasn't the only one who noticed, as Nic and Charlotte got up to go and join him.

The three of them started dancing together, and watching Jamie and Nic moving to the music had me engrossed and mildly jealous. *Bloody hell, that Nic can dance too.* The look on Charlotte's face echoed the same sentiment. I hoped my parents would put the reason I was not there with Charlotte down to my not being a big dancer.

With Jamie and Nic together, it would be fair to expect the worst, or best, depending on where you sat. Two good-looking young men, tall, dark, and handsome and as roguish as each other! *Jilly Cooper, do I have a novel for you.* Had Jamie been a polo player rather than an Air Force pilot, that book idea would have been a definite possibility.

With more and more people moving onto the dance floor, and with Charlotte otherwise engaged, the appropriate thing for me to do was to have a dance with Gigi. Out of politeness, of course, I would wait for the right song and ask her onto the floor.

I was not normally one to spend time dancing, but since Gigi had come into my life, that was slowly changing.

Whitney Houston's "I Have Nothing" started playing, and I knew Gigi would want to dance to this, as Whitney was one of her favourite artists. In contrast to my normal shyness, I stood up without a second thought, turned to Gigi, and proposed, "Gigi, let's dance."

I interpreted my parents' looks as approving of my displaying good manners before they turned back to the people they were speaking to at the next table.

I'm about to dance with Gigi at Guards. The thought caused a tightening in my stomach.

Gigi was slightly taken aback by my unusual confidence but readily agreed to my request and slipped her hand into mine as she rose from her chair.

It had an eerie similarity to my dad's dancing request to my mother at our first dinner together.

"I Have Nothing" – Whitney Houston

| YouTube | Spotify | Apple |

I guided Gigi to the other side of the dance floor, away from our side of the room, to find anonymity among the partying crowd. Not a bad thought but a rather unlikely notion, as I was at a club where my family was well known. Having found the most secluded spot on the dance floor, not too close to the edge, we became hidden in plain sight among bodies all around us, some pushing against us and causing us to be even closer to each other. That we didn't mind was an understatement.

We folded into each other's arms, Gigi's hands on my shoulder and my waist, and my hands around her back. The feeling of her body against mine in this very public space sent a quiver of excitement through me as we gently started moving to the rhythm of the music. Taking in the words of the Whitney Houston song, we held each other a little tighter.

Then Gigi brought her mouth up to my ear to say something, and her warm breath on my neck and her lips brushing my earlobe caused a tension in my stomach that spread down to my groin. She said something that I didn't catch, so I moved my ear closer to her mouth.

Her lips pressed against me as she continued, "Take my love…"

I realised then that Gigi was going along with the words of the song, making them her own, as she repeated them to me.

"I won't ask for too much. Just all that you are. And everything you do."

As we continued to dance closely pushed against each other, her whispering in my ear, our temperatures started rising.

"Stay in my arms if you dare. Do you dare, my baby?" she whispered.

I took Gigi's cheeks between my hands and looked into her eyes before pressing my lips against her ear and, making no effort to spare her the moistness of my mouth, saying, "Darling, I have nothing if I don't have you."

Gigi's arms tightened around my waist as she brought her face closer to mine.

I briefly remembered that we had to be careful not to get completely lost in the moment. Then the moment cleared my mind of all else.

We let the song play out, and this time I made some of the words mine. "You see through to my heart and have broken down my walls with the strength of your love."

Gigi was squeezing me as if she would never let go.

"There's nowhere I want to hide, my darling," I whispered as the song was coming to an end.

Were we ready to open the floodgates of our feelings for each other?

As we were making our way back to the table, Gigi stopped to face me, causing me to stand up against her as she said with fervour in her voice, "Charles Featherstone, you better get me out of this place before everyone discovers our secret."

My Rude Awakening

My response was to put my arm around her waist and pull her towards me, exactly what I should *not* have done, perhaps.

God, I want you, was my overwhelming thought as my own amorous feelings also threatened to expose our closeness.

Luckily, no one was around to notice our demonstrative behaviour as we arrived back to an empty table. Jamie, Charlotte, Nic, Guy, and Grace were on the dance floor, and my parents were sitting at another table away from us with my aunt and uncle and other of their friends.

Gigi got her handbag and shawl as I picked up my jacket, and we looked around to see who we could at least wave goodbye to. She caught Jamie's, then Charlotte's eye, and indicated her tiredness by resting her head against her hand as she gave them a little wave. I did likewise. They all waved back, quite unperturbed by our departure and perhaps relieved they were not the ones who would have to trundle Gigi back to Rockwell Manor. I managed to catch my mother's eye and used Gigi's sleepy gesture, then pointed to Gigi, indicating that she was tired. My mother blew us two kisses. She really was changing.

It had been that simple, and we left.

I couldn't help but wonder what this would mean for our future. Like so many things in life, no matter how carefully you may think things through, the ensuing reality often brings up unexpected results. Did the novelty of our being in public add a new level of excitement to our relationship? And when the novelty wore off, would we want something more?

I couldn't answer that then. I could only imagine I would always want it.

CHAPTER 20
A VERY STORMY NIGHT IN BERKSHIRE

WE CALMLY WALKED out of the clubhouse, appearing very relaxed, which did not at all match how we were feeling. As soon as we were away from the perimeter lighting, I grabbed Gigi's hand, and we ran to my car. I bundled her into the passenger seat and assumed my place behind the wheel, then leant over, desperately wanting to kiss her.

"Later, Babe. Let's get home," Gigi said.

It was the first time she had called me Babe, and I liked it.

The quickest way home was the back roads, endless twists and turns winding through the English countryside. Foxes, rabbits, badgers, and on occasion even deer would pop out of the bushes. These roads had sections through which only one car could pass at a time, the second car needing to drive almost into the thick foliage to allow the other to get by. It was not safe to drive fast, but I put my foot down every now and then to speed up the trip.

Gigi's hand was on my thigh, and when I felt her squeeze me, I realised she was nervous and slowed down.

"Thank you, Darling," she murmured.

We rounded the bend that brought us to Rockwell Manor, the sight of the gates catching Gigi by surprise. Recognising the entrance, she squealed excitedly, "We're home," as she dug her fingers into my thigh.

Gigi did not wait for me to open her car door. She flung it aside and jumped out, shoes in hand. She then half ran, half skipped down the stepping-stone path to the cottage with me in hot pursuit. It was quite a distance, and by the time we got there, we were both out of breath.

My Rude Awakening

She unlocked the door, and as we dashed into the lounge area, she bolted it firmly behind us. "I can't wait to have you," she exclaimed.

Have me in Winston Cottage. My favourite place in the world.

She threw down her shoes, shawl, and handbag on the sofa and then switched on a little side-table lamp as I, too, discarded my jacket and tie.

I looked at the mantle grandfather clock, the small pendulum calmly swinging gracefully back and forth in complete contrast to the chaos of the feelings and expectations pulsing through me. It was only 9:05 p.m., two or even three hours before anyone else would be coming home.

Gigi was in control mode as she led me to the bedroom. We threw our arms around each other, pressing our bodies firmly against each other's and our mouths instantly coming together. We were excited to be alone, but still fully clothed. She pulled slightly away and urgently started undoing my belt.

Her hand plunged into my trousers, and she grabbed my growing bulge. "Ooh yes," she moaned.

We couldn't wait to get rid of our clothes, and she practically ripped my shirt off. We kissed frantically as I tried to get my hand into the top of her dress. Not waiting for me to work it out, she reached down and in a single fluid motion pulled her dress off, over her head, revealing her stark nakedness. My desire intensified as I emulated her action and pulled my trousers and boxers down together.

Gigi roughly grabbed my shaft. "Oh, God, I want him inside me," she blurted.

As eager as we were to vanquish each other, Gigi seemingly came to her senses as she reined back her desire.

"Baby, I had better stop. This is not what I had planned this evening," Gigi blurted.

Planned? My desire for her was surging through my body, and we had already experienced each other in so many ways. *What now?*

She pulled away and leant over to the bedside table to light the wicks of a pillar candle. She looked so beautiful in the soft, flickering candlelight.

I was about to find out in no uncertain terms what Gigi had in mind.

After experiencing something I had never even imagined, I slowly began to recover my decorum. I bashfully glanced at Gigi, and the look on her face was one of pure happiness and contentment, as if she had been the one who had just experienced the climax of her life.

"Darling?" is all I said, lost for words as she embarrassingly wiped the aftermath of our actions from her chin and cleavage.

Then, with a hint of mischievousness, Gigi inquired, "Did you enjoy that, my darling?"

"You drive me crazy." My answer could not have been more truthful.

"I love that I have just given my man a wonderful orgasm and we have experienced that throat thing together," she said gleefully.

Notwithstanding all that had just happened, I couldn't help thinking, *I love Gigi referring to me as her man.*

I leant back on my haunches and took in the wild beauty of this ravishing woman who knew exactly what she wanted and was going to take it all.

It wasn't long and I became slightly more gentlemanly between my legs, and we could both just lie back and savour what was yet again a new experience. We snuggled into each other on the bed and began chatting easily, happily.

"Have you ever heard that in many men's eyes, the definition of the perfect woman is 'A lady on your arm and a whore in your bed'?" Gigi asked.

"I don't think I have. Why, my love?" I answered, a little thrown by this notion.

"Well, I'd like to be your perfect woman."

"You *are* my perfect woman, and the epitome of a lady," I said emphatically. "I don't know about the *whore* bit though," I added.

"In the privacy of our sex, Baby. Just between us in our bed," Gigi explained.

Does Gigi want to behave like that and sometimes have me treat her like that? I knew that thought would be playing on my mind in the days to come. Gigi *was* unquestionably a lady, but I had learnt she was also a woman who was very much in touch with her sexuality. Was this part of that?

She stood up and jokingly pushed her vulva onto my face, giving me a hint of her womanly scent as she announced. "I'm going to get us a refreshment."

I watched her go through to the lounge area to get us a drink from the bar fridge. God, I loved her smell and her sexuality, her body, and her mind. There was so much about her that I loved.

When she returned, Gigi took a sip of her drink and said facetiously, "God, at least I can still swallow."

I couldn't help the embarrassment I felt even if it wasn't entirely my doing. But at least I had the presence of mind to reply to her comment, us always competing to have the last jovial word. "Darling, when you say swallow, is it the same one that is the bird of lust?"

I could see her suppressing a little giggle, so I carried on. "Because if it is, then perhaps it is something you should take up with the person who was in my bed rather than the lady on my arm."

Gigi chuckled, no longer trying to suppress anything as she mouthed the words "fuck off" to me.

As we finished our refreshments, I decided what I was going to do next. *Two can play this game!* My extraordinary orgasm already forgotten, I wanted more. I only needed a few minutes before I would be ready to go again. And Gigi knew it too. Now it was my turn to devour her.

Not knowing I had ideas of my own, she lay back on her love seat as before, instructing me to once again kneel in front of her. "So, can I prepare you for the next round?" she suggested lightheartedly.

I was feigning my obedience as I knelt in front of her. She was about to give me her next directive when I hooked my arms behind her knees and in one motion, pulled her down the bed from her perched position. Seeing the surprise on her face, I looked down at her, and with a throaty little chuckle asked, "Did I misunderstand your instructions?" followed by a drawn out, "*Darling?*"

I couldn't wait to give her a taste of her own medicine and devour her.

Sapped of strength and in the bliss of our sexual aftermath, I rolled onto the bed next to her and she assumed her position in the crook of my shoulder, half on my chest with one leg between mine. We lay like that a while without saying anything.

I thought about her visceral use of the word "fuck" and how the almost vehement, impassioned way she'd made her demand reached down to the depths of my sexual being, fuelling my unconstrained desire for her.

Does Gigi want me to show my desire? Now I understood the "whore in the bedroom" remark. She was the most captivating "whore." The most enchanting "lady." *The perfect woman.*

It was Gigi who first spoke. "I think there is something you should know." Then, catching me completely off guard and in a measured tone, she simply said, "I love you, Edward Charles Featherstone."

There was suddenly so much I wanted to say to her, but I couldn't instantly piece it together, so instead, I simply replied, "I love you, Georgina Blackwood."

It had been building within us both for a long time, and now finally it had been said. We lay quietly, Gigi snuggled into the top of my shoulder and neck. My mind was buzzing as I contemplated this new revelation and my mix of emotions.

She broke the silence and said, "I have a song. It has been my song to you for a long time. Listen to the words. They are what I want to say to you, Darling."

She reached for her Walkman, then gave me a squeeze as I once again heard the unmistakable voice of Whitney Houston.

"Run to You" – Whitney Houston

| YouTube | Spotify | Apple |

I listened to the words as if Gigi were saying them to me, and the message of there being so much I hadn't realised, hadn't seen, bore into me. I couldn't bear the thought that she was scared at times but had to be strong. She could hide her hurt but not her loneliness.

How I wanted Gigi to run to me, so I could hold her safely in my arms. I squeezed her tighter, knowing I would never want to run away. Right then, the only person I wanted to share my dreams with was Gigi. The emotion welled up inside me. Of course she was alone, no one to care for her, but I wanted to be there from now on…and always.

My mind was racing. How could I always be there for Gigi? Was there a way?

I didn't want her to have those tears. I wanted to be there, to kiss away her fears. Overflowing with emotion, I loved her even more than I could ever have imagined.

"You are safe and loved by me now, my darling, and if I could make it forever, I would," I said honestly.

"I know," was Gigi's simple reply.

I turned to look at her, finding her face peaceful and demure, then looked away hoping she would not see my tear-filled eyes.

Sighing, she reached up and wiped away the moistness, saying, "Don't be sad, Baby. I am happy now. Never have I been happier."

"I love you, my darling. I truly love you," I whispered, trying to suppress the emotion in my tone. This time, even though my revelation was no different, this time my words had been carefully considered.

I realised then that Gigi had many emotional needs, and I wanted to fulfil them. I had been so focused on my RAF career, and with only seeing her intermittently, I had not even thought about it. That would have to change now.

I reflected on how she and I seemed to interchange our pet names for each other. When I was not using her first name, I mostly called her *Darling* and sometimes *Baby*, and she did likewise. *Darling* meant the same for both of us, the loving way we addressed each other. *Baby* was different. Gigi was my Baby, and I wanted to give her my protection and support. For Gigi, *Baby* was her expressing her closeness and love. The occasional *Babe,* that was mostly lighthearted.

Am I analyzing this because it is so unfamiliar?

As I lay there with her sleeping in my arms after everything that had just happened, I had so much to think about. Before, I'd only had to worry about how to handle our situation with Jamie and Charlotte. Now, I needed to add my mum and dad to that equation. I just needed some time.

I was in awe of our sexual relationship and how it had progressed and matured. Having only been together in the confines of Gigi's home, with Jamie and sometimes Charlotte just up the hallway, it had been impossible for us to ever be truly open and uninhibited sexually. Gigi's unconstrained use of *the* word and talk of her being my perfect woman as in a "whore in the bedroom" clearly showed that our lovemaking had moved into a new realm, so different from the confines of Shrewsbury. Because of my naivety, I had merely accepted our lovemaking was how it would always be, which captivated me anyway. I never imagined it could possibly be any better. Had I just lost my virginity for the second time to the more demanding, uninhibited, raw, visceral side of Gigi, complete with profanities? A side of her I had previously only caught glimpses of, but had now discovered in Winston Cottage, my favourite place in the world? *Methinks so.*

It would mark a whole new beginning, and I loved it.

Lost in these thoughts and starting to drift off to sleep, I was wondering if I should go back to my suite when I heard a car. This would surely be my parents arriving home.

There would be no one coming down to Winston Cottage, and no house staff in my suite until midmorning. I decided to stay the night with Gigi. How could I leave her after all we had shared that evening?

I'll get to my room early in the morning to ruffle my bed, was my last thought before I fell asleep.

There was a remarkable change in our relationship from both mine and Gigi's perspectives, which was also reflected in our sex. One may have thought it was because of the excitement of dealing with it in the open, even though it was still very much under wraps. But it was more than that. I was in my world, my domain, and had now qualified! I was an RAF pilot, and with my degree, I was now ready for business, even if that was not entirely true. And with our relationship having arrived at this new juncture, had I gone through the final transition? Was I now a man?

It may have happened over just a few weeks, but that period marked a very distinct changeover in my life. Since arriving in Berkshire, at my home, more and more our relationship was moving to the beat of my drum as I instinctively began to take control. And then when it came to the bedroom, no one except Gigi and me under the Winston Cottage roof, no wonder things had stepped up a salacious gear or two.

CHAPTER 21
TWO WORLDS COLLIDE

I WOKE UP VERY early, the dawn only just beginning to grace the day.

Gigi was spooned against my body, and my arm was around her waist.

I'd loved her for so long, and now we had said it. *I love you.* As I lay there, it was impossible not to think about the sex too. *But that song! Why can't I be there for her?* So much to take in, especially those three simple words.

Gigi slowly awakened, and even before she was fully compos mentis, she said, "Thank you, my baby. Thank you for not leaving me. It was such a special night, and I would've hated waking up alone."

My only response was to pull her closer towards me.

Then I gently rolled onto her as she welcomed me in. With very few words spoken, we very gently and quietly made love for the next twenty minutes. Savouring every scent, every feeling, every moment.

Once we were both sated, I put on my trousers and shirt, and with the first tweet of early-morning bird life, I took the meandering path up to the north wing.

With plenty of time to spare, I had a drawn out, steaming hot, steam shower. *I want to do this with Gigi!* immediately came to mind.

As I lay back on the wooden bench in my expansive shower, enjoying the feeling of running my soapy hands over my toned body, my mind inevitably drifted back to the night before.

The sex was extraordinary—it always was. But it was those three words that dominated my thinking. I knew we both loved each other and had felt that way for a long time, but having told each other somehow made it feel different. Was the only reason we had not previously shared those feelings because our time together in Shrewsbury was comparatively rushed, with us only spending a night or two together? Or was it our circumstances, Jamie being my best friend and mine and Gigi's age difference that had been the reason?

Probably yes for both.

Emotionally it sat very comfortably with me, but practically, the discomfort of how it would play out was torturous. Right then my only remedy was to clear it from my mind.

I eventually got out of the shower and changed into fresh clothes and was soon heading out of the door. Only then did I remember to ruffle my bed. My half-hearted attempt suggested that I was not overly concerned where the house maids thought I had spent the night. Feeling invigorated and with a spring in my step, I went down to meet everyone for breakfast in the family dining room.

Jamie looked worse for wear. Charlotte arrived minutes later, looking no better. Next came my mother and father with Gigi in tow.

My dad seemed to be feeling very jovial as he enquired about our evening. Everyone enthused about how wonderful it had been, including Gigi and me. I was half expecting questions about our early departure, but fortunately no one seemed too interested.

My mother gave Gigi and Charlotte an outline of what she had planned for their day. First, a visit to the organic farm nearby and then to London. Lunch at either The Brasserie or Bibendum before heading off to Harrods. Gigi would probably enjoy the day, being so like my mother. Charlotte, not so much. Judging by all the attention she was getting at the dinner dance, I had a feeling she would have preferred to spend the day hanging out with us, or even just around the polo players, especially Nic, at the local pub or the clubhouse.

After breakfast, Gigi and Charlotte left to prepare themselves for their excursion.

I turned to my friend and suggested, "Jamie, let's go and have a light stick and ball session."

Not needing a second invitation, he headed off to put on a pair of jeans.

"See you at the stables," I called after him before excusing myself to go up and get ready. On the way through the drawing room, I was distracted by the latest edition of *POLO Magazine* on the coffee table and sat down to quickly glance through it.

Thinking they were alone, my mum and dad started discussing Charlotte and me, and then also Gigi. "Now that we have seen Charlotte and Charles together, what are your thoughts?" she asked.

"I think they would make a lovely couple. Just give them time," proffered my father.

My mother, being far more attuned to these things, said she was not so sure. "She doesn't seem to engage him. I guess time will tell. No rush, mind you. They are both so young, but it is nice to see him with female companionship."

"It was a pity he had to bring Gigi home last night. He and Charlotte may have had fun together," my dad suggested.

"Your new pro seemed to be the one having fun with her, I'm afraid," my mother countered.

My father grunted.

"Charles has had such a very sheltered upbringing when it comes to the opposite sex, it is just nice to see him with girls," my mother lamented.

"I think Jamie will be a good influence on him in that department," my dad had suggested playfully. Jamie's ease around girls had not gone unnoticed by my father. Was it a case of birds of a feather?

"Let's hope so," my mother concurred, not rising to my father's mischief. "They have become such good friends. And neither of them look like the military type to me. Arthur, do you honestly believe Charles is cut out to be in the RAF? It doesn't make sense to me now. It won't make sense to either of us when he is deployed into one of those godforsaken places."

My father's silence had me wondering if he too was having second thoughts about my RAF career.

"And what about Georgina?" my mother contemplated, not yet finished.

"What an attractive and youthful mother she is," my father replied, a typical observation for him.

"And she and Charles have such a lovely little connection. It is a pity he doesn't have that with Charlotte. I can't believe that she's on her own," my mother intuitively reflected.

"Yes, she is lovely and would really fit in perfectly in these circles," was my dad's take.

"Let's see if we can introduce her to someone. There are many eligible men around here who would be perfect for her," my mother concluded.

With that, I tiptoed out of the drawing room to avoid being discovered having overheard their conversation. *Bloody hell! My parents hadn't missed much. So much to think about.*

My mother and the Blackwood ladies headed off, Charlotte looking a tad more interested, as Jamie and I got ready to ride.

The rest of the day was quite uneventful, with the only interesting part being a call from a friend, Humphrey Throgmorton. He offered me two pegs for the first shoot of the season at their estate, which meant of the eight-gun lineup of shooters, there were two vacancies for this coming Friday and Saturday. It so transpired that our fortnight leave coincided with the end of the polo season and the Glorious Twelfth, the start of the game-bird shooting season in the United Kingdom. The latter was something I hadn't even thought of when we were planning the trip to Rockwell Manor.

Even though they came at a hefty price—five thousand pounds per day, per gun—I jumped at the opportunity. The cost was not something I paid much attention to. I knew Jamie would love to shoot driven grouse or pheasant, and there were going to be six drives per day over two days. English law prohibited the shooting of game birds—or any quarry, for that matter—on Sundays, which worked perfectly for us, as we would be playing the final of the Barrett Cup then.

Of course, I also had an ulterior motive for accepting Humphrey's offer so readily. The guests would all stay at Bovey Castle, built on the edge of Dartmoor National Park in Devon, a county in the South West of England. It was a very convenient stone's throw from the Throgmorton estate, not very far from West Buckland School. By English standards, it was a new establishment, especially in Devon, which comprised numerous medieval towns. It was built as a lavish Neo-Elizabethan manor home on five thousand acres for William Henry Smith (1825–1891), later to become WH Smith and Viscount Hambleden. He was an English bookseller who expanded his business by selling books and newspapers at railway stations. What I found interesting was that WHSmith was my mother's favourite bookstore, to which she dragged me from time to time. After going through a number of changes and developments, by 1980 Bovey Castle had become well known as a very special five-star destination hotel.

The normal form for this shoot was that there would be dinners arranged for both evenings with the other members of the eight-gun lineup and their partners, plus other invited guests. These were often quite festive affairs. Six drives per day split on either side of a leisurely but sumptuous lunch. Then, after Saturday's afternoon shoot, we would head home in time to do evening stables for the big match the following day.

My mind began to race at the thought of this being an opportunity for Gigi and me to spend two nights together in a country hotel. I needed to work out a way of ensuring Gigi would come with us and book her a room close, or even next to mine. I secretly loved the thought of Gigi discovering more of my world.

My mum, Gigi, and Charlotte arrived home from London late that evening, in particularly good spirits. They had enjoyed a wonderful day, cutting short the trip to the organic farm, having a lovely lunch, and then spending the afternoon at their favourite store, Harrods—frequented by the rich and famous. Which made no difference to me. I found it thoroughly boring.

I helped Gigi take her shopping to the cottage, anxious to speak to her.

"Darling, at dinner I'm going to invite you away this weekend. It may not be your idea of fun, but it really will be. Just say you would love to go, and we can chat about it later."

She was understandably confused, but hearing Charlotte approaching, I couldn't say anything more.

Charlotte walked in and announced, "Dinner is at eight, and your dad asked that we meet in the game room for drinks first."

I could tell Charlotte was settling into Rockwell Manor very comfortably, and I liked it. My fondness for Charlotte had been growing steadily, regardless of some of her antics. Not that I could really see her as a potential future partner. She was much more like my older but little sister, which was not surprising, given my very close relationship with both her mother and brother. How could I not love her in a brotherly way?

I went up to my suite to get ready for dinner. After a quick shower, I arrived at the game room first and was greeted by our butler.

"Hi, Hamilton. Kir Royale, please." French champagne and Crème de Cassis liqueur would slide down nicely.

I saw a reflection of myself and instantly understood why I was ahead of the others. I had thrown on a powder-blue silk shirt, untucked and with several buttons undone, white polo jeans that were at least clean, and tan slip-on driving shoes with no socks.

Just then my mum and dad arrived. My mother spontaneously came over to me and ran her fingers through my hair, shaking her head. "Oh, Sunbeam, you haven't even dried or brushed that mane of yours."

Our attention turned to Gigi, Charlotte, and Jamie as they arrived together.

Gigi looked simply stunning. Her skin had a radiant glow, her hair framing a beautiful, relaxed face—certainly in my eyes. I had a feeling her open-toed leather sandals were for my benefit, so I could see her feet, with her perfectly pedicured toes. I was fixated with them. "I think you have a foot fetish," she had once said to me. I didn't altogether agree. When it came to Gigi, I would go further and say, I had a foot *and* hand fetish. I somehow figured that a woman's hands and feet are what she would touch me with. *Feet…touch me?* Interesting that I should think that.

As Gigi walked past me, she made a remark about my having lost my brush or something. Then she ran her fingers through my head of thick wet hair, literally mimicking what my mother had just done.

I looked at my mum, wondering what she made of this show of affection. Her expression was unchanged, finding it completely normal that Gigi, having become so close to me, was just doing a bit of mothering of her own. Were Gigi's actions the antics of my lover or rather an expression of maternal care?

After our aperitif, it was time for dinner. As we went through to the family dining room, I couldn't help reflecting how unusual it was for us not to have other guests. As we sat down, I remarked. "Just the six of us, Mum?"

"Yes, Sunbeam, just a casual family dinner."

I beamed, shooting a sideways glance at Gigi. As enjoyable as our first supper in the main dining room had turned out to be, I was pleased to be in the informal family dining room.

After hearing about the ladies' trip to London, recounted with a lot of enthusiasm and excitement, I had an opportunity to tell the table, but more specifically Jamie and Gigi, about the game-bird shoot. "Jamie, I have wonderful news."

He looked at me enquiringly.

"I have two places for the Throgmorton driven shoot this weekend. Since my dad is busy, I was wondering if you would like to do that?"

The expression on Jamie's face was priceless. "Would I *like* that? Are you crazy? I would *love* that," he blurted.

Out of the corner of my eye, I saw a look of dread on Gigi's face. Because of what I had said earlier, she was expecting me to invite her to go somewhere, but shooting? That was another story altogether. I knew I would be hard-pressed to convince her.

"So, the plan will be for us to leave on Thursday afternoon. There will be a lovely dinner with the other guests and their partners, and usually some other friends of the Throgmortons. We will shoot on Friday, four drives in the morning, break for lunch, and continue in the afternoon with another two drives. Another dinner on Friday night, a bit more relaxed, and then a similar programme for Saturday's shoot, but of course, on six different drives. We will come home on Saturday evening in time to check the horses for Sunday."

Jamie looked thrilled, having been sold at just the mention of a game-bird shoot. Gigi's expression told me she was still not convinced.

I continued, "We will stay at Bovey Castle, which has been turned into a lovely destination hotel. Mum, your favourite booksellers' old home," I added.

"While we are on our shoots, the ladies have a few options. A lot of fun can be had truffle hunting. On the other shooting day, spending time at the health and beauty spa and perhaps a hot mineral mud bath, among other things, are good options."

Gigi's face lit up. Realising she was not expected to traipse through the woods while we shot game birds had totally changed her expression. My moment had arrived.

"Gigi, would you like to join us and experience this aspect of country life?" I hadn't even thought to ask Charlotte, thinking she would almost certainly prefer to be around the polo crew.

My mother then chipped in, "Oh, Gigi, you will love it. Just be sure to find some lovely burgundy truffles for us. We can make truffle oil and some truffle shavings for a wonderful tagliolini with taleggio. You'll have such fun." Trust my mother to say the right thing at precisely the right time.

"Yes, umm, that sounds lovely. Thank you," Gigi said.

I felt as pleased as punch with how well I had orchestrated all of this. Two nights of passion with my lover.

No sooner had I finished subconsciously patting myself on the back than Charlotte said, "I'll come too. I'll just share your room, Mum."

"Of course, Charlotte. You shouldn't miss it for the world," my mother enthused as my dad nodded his agreement.

My jaw dropped. So much for my mum saying just the right thing at the right time.

We retired to the study and a tired-looking Hamilton did his best to be sprightly, offering us after-dinner ports and liqueurs.

"Hamilton, I've got this," I said. Glancing at my parents and seeing their approving looks, I continued, "I'm sure you've finished your chores for the night, and I will be happy to deputise for you."

"Thank you, sir," Hamilton replied with a genuine smile, and without looking at my parents for approval, which was interesting.

With the thought of Charlotte joining us I did my best to hide my disgruntlement, and I could see Gigi was doing likewise. More out of courtesy than anything else, we each had a glass of French port. Still not as good as what Gigi served, mind you.

When we had finished our nightcap, I duly offered to walk Gigi down to her cottage. There was no need for me to tell her what was on my mind, as she spontaneously took my hand in the darkness and said, "Don't worry, Baby, it is still going to be a wonderful two days. I'm sure we will work out a way to have time together."

An "umph" was the best I could do for a reply as we continued down the meandering pathway, past the beautifully lit foliage, to her front door. Gigi's affectionate kiss goodnight before I made my way to the north wing made me feel better.

After last night's Guards dinner dance, followed by our 'very stormy night,' sex wasn't even a thought.

The next day, Jamie and I had another stick and ball session that lasted the afternoon. As we were finishing off, Gigi and Charlotte arrived at the stables, identically dressed in white blouses much like men's shirts, blue jeans, and below the knee black riding boots. I was impressed that they had the foresight to have packed them, which would save me trying to sort something out from our tack room if they wanted to go for a ride.

God, they look good, were my testosterone-driven thoughts. Only then did it hit me. *That's not what they were wearing this morning!* "Typical male blindness when it came to female fashion," my mother would have said.

Grinning broadly, realising it was thanks to my testosterone that I had saved myself certain embarrassment had I not realised they had changed, I suggested happily. "Looks like the two of you are up for an out-ride?"

"We would love to," was Charlotte's enthusiastic reply, also answering for her mother.

"Wonderful. I will sort out the horses," I offered.

I knew it had been some time since Gigi had last ridden a horse, but what a great idea. Jamie excused himself from joining us, no doubt feeling there were more interesting things to engage himself with at the polo club.

I had never seen either of the women ride before, and even though they said they had some experience, I quietly instructed the groom on which horses to saddle up for them anyway, wanting to be certain they didn't end up with two of our more highly spirited horses.

"Let's do a forest ride, and I can show you where I spent many happy years rough shooting with Osric." I looked skyward and saw an ominous build-up of cloud. *It had better not storm.*

We started slowly, going along the twisting path through the forest at a trot. Then the landscape ahead of us opened, and we moved up a gear, into a strong canter. Much to my relief, I could see they were both more than competent riders. I could just imagine the fun Gigi and I would be able to have going on rides…unaccompanied.

There was an open field ahead of us, and being in the open air, on beautiful thoroughbred horses, we soon broke into a gallop. When we got to the other side, we gently pulled up our horses as the girls enthused about our exhilarating ride.

Gigi and Charlotte were both red-faced and out of breath, laughing at the excitement and pure enjoyment of the exercise. The two of them looked beautiful, one an older version of the other. I watched as Gigi's chest rose and fell with her heavy breathing, and I had to consciously stop staring.

I rode up alongside her, and she instinctively took hold of my hand and affectionately gave it a squeeze. "Oh, Charles, my darling, that was so, so lovely," she exclaimed.

I immediately looked over at Charlotte, but she showed no sign of thinking there was anything wrong in her mother's behaviour.

Then I felt the raindrops on my face. "Bloody hell, we are about to be rained on." I had been so preoccupied that I had not noticed the further build-up of weather.

As the heavens opened and let loose a deluge of rain, Gigi and Charlotte seemed unperturbed. Just as well, because it would not have been a good idea to race back to the stables, overly exciting the horses. Notwithstanding the rain, they were still thoroughly enjoying themselves, thrilled to be riding again. After a short while, we turned around and headed home at a slow trot.

By the time we returned to the stables, we were soaked. I couldn't help noticing my two riding companions had sodden white cotton shirts and what must have been thin white lace brassieres that offered almost no concealment of their wonderful physical attributes. I already knew Gigi well, but seeing her like this had me captivated. Her wet and bedraggled hair only added to my enticement.

God, I want her.

I had to forcibly stop myself from staring lest Charlotte saw me taking in this sight of her mother. They still hadn't realised how exposed they were with wet blouses clinging to their skin, until Gigi turned to face her daughter. Charlotte immediately blurted out, "Mum, *your boobs.*" She then looked down at her own chest and, seeing herself equally exposed, started giggling as she covered herself with her cupped hands.

My Rude Awakening

Quite unperturbed, Gigi remarked, "Goodness! Nothing like the two of us giving Charles a wet T-shirt competition."

Speechless, and a bit like a gawking teenager standing there dripping wet, I was not sure what to do next. Then, remembering my manners, I went into the changing room to get them each a towel. Still laughing and quite uninhibited, they went about rubbing their breasts as they towel-dried themselves. I couldn't take my eyes off them. But it struck me they were not making a big effort of concealing themselves either. Were mother and daughter secretly enjoying watching my awkwardness, or perhaps my appreciation?

It was now early evening and the rain had subsided, so we walked across the polo field to the house. My mother had arranged a pizza evening and invited our polo team and several of our other polo friends, among others. I was thrilled. *This is what I want Gigi to experience.* Jamie had phoned home to say he would be staying at the club, but when my mother told him the plan, he had promptly changed his and invited a couple of the Balthazar players, Malcs Barwick and Beto Cambiano. I was certain Charlotte would be quite struck by this dark, handsome, and famous Argentinian. It would be amusing to watch her reaction to him. I was pleased Jamie felt so at home at Rockwell Manor that he was comfortable inviting guests. This was how I felt at his home.

I agreed to meet Gigi and Charlotte in the kitchen after a quick shower and freshening up.

Dry and cosy in a tracksuit bottom and long-sleeved T-shirt, I went to have a look at how our pizza evening preparations were going. The wood-burning oven was generating quite a lot of heat. *Ooh, a bit warm in here,* I thought as I walked over to four almost ceiling-to-floor, ten-inch-wide, heavy wooded vertical windows. I turned them through 90 degrees on their centre pivot pins, and the scent of thyme and mint wafted in from the adjacent herb garden. Mixed in with the aroma of the wood-burning oven, the aroma made our kitchen even more homely and inviting. I was starting to become aware of the smallest details, trying to interpret them from Gigi's perspective.

Not long after, I was joined in the kitchen by Gigi and Charlotte, both looking radiant in their casual attire. Charlotte wore designer yoga tights

237

with a loose top and flip-flops, and Gigi was dressed in her typical below-the-knee length skirt, a relaxed half-sleeve navy-blue top, and her leather sandals. The one thing that Gigi was not wearing was a bra.

My testosterone was surging. The expression, *Young, dumb, and full of cum,* came to mind.

My parents came through next, my mum checking on kitchen arrangements while my father attended to bar matters. We all stood around the warm pizza oven, chatting about our day. They were thrilled to hear we had gone out on a ride, and the glance between my parents told me exactly what they were thinking. Hoping things were developing between Charlotte and me, or something of that ilk.

Our pizza evenings were always festive occasions in our oversized kitchen, the traditional wood-burning pizza oven being the focal point.

As our team members began arriving, Nic stopped to chat with Charlotte, standing next to the oven. Lew, Leah, and Georgie joined us too. Then Uncle Alexander and Aunt Edwina arrived with some other friends of my parents. Having walked up from his manager's cottage was Guy and none other than Grace Brayers. My bet was that Guy would soon be recommending Rockwell Manor have a full-time vet and nutritionist, and Grace would undoubtedly be the one.

Fabrizio had prepared a perfect light and airy dough and arranged a dozen or so large bowls of assorted ingredients: ham, salami, olives, artichokes, prawns, anchovies, peppers, chillies, bacon, banana, brie cheese, cranberry jelly, sweet chilli sauce, pesto, and, of course, his special recipe of tomato sauce and mounds of grated mozzarella cheese. Much to his disgruntlement, he also put out a bowl of pineapple pieces for anyone who wanted to make the unmentionable Hawaiian pizza. Fabrizio always reminded everyone that pineapple had no place in an Italian pizza kitchen. Nearly everyone would join in the pizza making, with us all sharing each other's creations. At the end of the evening, the winner of the best pizza would receive a bottle of champagne, whilst anyone responsible for a substandard result had to down shots of grappa.

Jamie then arrived with Beto Cambiano, along with Sandra Rawling and a girlfriend of hers who I had not met. My parents always thought of Sandra as a "genuinely nice young girl," but among the polo players, she was known to be a little "loose," one might say. *Trust Jamie to bring along some "special" company,* I thought.

A short while later, Malcs, having been invited by my mum, walked into the kitchen with a very attractive blonde English rose on his arm. It was familiar territory for him, a regular at Rockwell Manor, having often played on the home polo field. It was after matches that we would regularly have our pizza evenings, so he was more than familiar with these occasions. His impeccable manners had him first seek out my mum and dad to say hello and introduce his English rose.

"Hello, Arthur. Hello, Fran," he greeted them, shaking my father's hand and placing a kiss on my mother's cheek. "This is Alex, my girlfriend."

"How lovely to meet you," enthused my mother, probably thinking she wished I too had a girlfriend.

Whilst I listened to Fabrizio giving Malcs some guidance on making the perfect pizza, I noticed Alex, or Ale as Malcs called her, in animated conversation with Beto, *in fluent Spanish.* It turned out she was in fact Spanish, probably Malc's motivation for having learned the language. I was quietly envious.

There were probably around twenty-eight of us. It was also quite likely that others would drift in during the evening. It promised to be another typical, if not boisterous, night in the Rockwell Manor kitchen. This was what I'd wanted Gigi and Charlotte to experience. The side of Rockwell Manor that I enjoyed the most. The closest thing to their relaxed Shrewsbury home.

Soon the wine was flowing, dough was being rolled, and Eros Ramazzotti was playing over the sound system. The evening was going along wonderfully, drinks at the ready, people vying to make the best pizza, the occasional grappa shot for anyone who produced a substandard pizza— or any other offence, mind you—and the sound of generally animated conversation mixed in with a background of Italian music. Rockwell Manor's kitchen could best be described as "rocking."

I looked across the room and caught a glimpse of Sandra Rawling. She was another one who was very much at home at Rockwell Manor, chatting happily to almost everyone. Not surprising, mind you. She had been coming here from when she was just a little girl. I suppose it was when I was just a little boy. All I could remember was how she used to annoy me. Perhaps that was why I was only too happy to put a "polo groupie" tag on her. Our parents had been friends for as long as I could remember. She seemed to have grown up very quickly in the time that I had been in the Air Force. I secretly admitted to myself that the gawky little girl who used to irritate me perpetually had grown into an attractive, surprisingly curvaceous, full-breasted young woman with a bubbly personality. Ooh, and I did like her strong, shapely legs. *Who has been lying between those?* I wondered drily.

Just as I was thinking this, Gigi touched me on the arm and asked, "What has captured your attention so?" She followed my gaze and somewhat sarcastically said, "Mmm, now I see."

I was surprised at Gigi's little show of jealousy, even though it mirrored what I sometimes felt with her. Was it an expression of her watching over something that she considered *hers*, or was there a deeper meaning, like feeling insecure about our future together?

I had an interesting moment as I stood behind Nic and Charlotte, when he was telling her how wonderful his Rockwell Manor string of mares was. "Magnifico," he said.

Since he was just speaking about our horses, I hadn't felt there was any harm in my having overheard them. That was until Charlotte gave her take on this point.

"Any chance you could include a new filly in your lineup? You could ride her in your playtime?"

He gave her a blank look, Charlotte's salacious innuendo completely lost on him. I was quite certain she would be more than happy to give him a practical demonstration later. I couldn't help but think of how her approach would have been described around the air base. Yes, Charlotte almost certainly had an "itchy squirrel" that she was now inviting Nic to scratch. *Proper Air Force talk.*

Not wanting to be noticed after this exchange, I went over to where Gigi was kneading a ball of dough for the base of her attempt at a perfect pizza. As she began rolling it out in that rhythmical, rocking motion, every time she moved back and forth her breasts swayed and bounced beneath her loose top. I could not keep my eyes off her bosoms no matter that my mind was cautioning me not to get caught staring. She then placed her selection of toppings on the base before sliding it in the oven with the pizza paddle.

Then the unthinkable happened. Without my giving any conscious consideration to what I was about to do, I rubbed my hands on the floury countertop and as Gigi turned around, in a moment of absolute madness, I placed both my palms and outstretched fingers on her breasts.

Gigi shrieked as she looked down at the confirmation of what I had done. Two perfect white handprints showing clearly on her dark top. We now had everyone's attention, and they all broke into rapturous laughter.

Seemingly coming to my senses, I quickly tried to remove the evidence by brushing the flour off of Gigi's breasts with my still-floured hands.

The look on her face was one of utter disbelief, which only made everyone laugh even louder.

"Oh, that's working out well, isn't it? Floured hands trying to remove flour," Gigi remarked with jovial sarcasm as she regained her composure.

Above the commotion of everyone's laughter and chatter, I heard my mother's lighthearted reprimand. "God's truth, Edward Charles, is that what they teach you in the Air Force? I'm so sorry, Georgina."

I wasn't the only one in the room who appreciated Gigi's delectable breasts, and perhaps it was understandable that someone would be tempted to play this prank on her.

By the end of the evening, all the ladies, barring my mother, had flour handprints on their breasts. On Charlotte's insistence, Nic had to do hers several times because they were not very evident on her light-coloured top.

As the evening was coming to an end, my father stood up and commanded everyone's attention, then in a very formal tone, he announced, "And the winner of this evening's competition is Gigi, unquestionably the very *breast* pizza."

My mother gave him a playful slap and, smiling broadly, once again apologised to Gigi. "Sorry, my dear. The Featherstone men have forgotten they are meant to be *gentlemen*."

Gigi blushed shyly, and everyone chuckled at my father having reminded them of something she would have preferred they forget.

With the evening slowing down, my parents and the older guests went through to the drawing room for some port and tranquillity. My father half-heartedly gestured to Gigi, asking if she would like to join them.

My mother interjected, "Come along, Arthur. Gigi is having a good time here."

Even though she was closer to their age group and the mother of two of my friends, it seemed obvious to them where she best fit in. I guess they thought Gigi was just used to being with twenty-something company.

It would be another hour or more before the kitchen emptied. The ambience with the pizza oven exuding its warmth made it one of the most comfortable places at Rockwell Manor. Nic and Charlotte were to one side of the kitchen, doing their best to exercise some restraint and doing a poor job of it. Jamie, Malcs and Beto had the attentions of both Sandra and her friend, and they were all looking very content. Fabrizio was tempting the remaining guests with small dessert pizzas with fillings of Nutella chocolate spread and raspberries added after the oven process. This was also when further grappa or tequila shooters, served with salt and lemon, would make their appearance, or perhaps Disaronno Amaretto or even The King's Ginger, sipped as an after-dinner liqueur, a less damaging approach.

As much as Gigi and I would have liked to have left then, we instead joined Jamie and his group and shared a glass of The King's Ginger.

A short while later, after chatting with some of the remaining guests and the few quizzical looks from Sandra Rawling, I was ready to leave. It was still early, and I felt like a little fresh air.

CHAPTER 22
A DIFFERENT EVENING STABLES

I OFTEN WALKED ACROSS the polo field to the stables to check on the horses, but that evening I had an ulterior motive. Today's ride, followed by a tantalising wet T-shirt competition, and then the pizza evening activities, watching Gigi's breasts bouncing up and down whilst she was rolling out pizza dough, had me "locked and loaded, hair trigger on," as a good friend used to say.

Making sure I was not overheard, and in as nonchalant a tone as I could muster, I turned to Gigi and asked, "Would you like to go and check on the horses with me?"

Gigi looked around, also wanting to be sure no one was listening, she turned to me and asked, "Will I be safe? Because you won't be."

"Three hundred and fifty yards from the house, out of earshot." I held my chin, feigning giving the idea some thought as I teased about how remote it was, then replied. "I'm going to risk it."

"That could be a big mistake," Gigi purred.

I grinned back at her like a Cheshire cat. *She had a way with me!*

We said our goodnights to the last few remaining people, telling them I was going to check on the horses, and we left.

The moment we got onto the field, with the soft, dewy grass underfoot, I bent down and took off Gigi's sandals and my JP Tod slip-ons. I turned to her and in a hushed voice said, "You do realise that by the time we are in the middle of the field, we will be in complete darkness. And after all the teasing you have subjected me to this afternoon and this evening, you are likely to be vanquished on the halfway line. This is your last chance to turn back."

Gigi looked up at me and replied, "Race you to the middle."

She had no way of knowing what a special place the middle of this field was for me.

After sprinting the 150 yards, we reached the centre, out of breath, and immediately embraced each other.

"So, what now? Should I be scared of the dark?" I teased.

Turning on her Sony Walkman, Gigi said, "I think you should listen to what I have been playing."

The voice of Olivia Newton-John singing "Physical" sounded out into the darkness.

"Physical" – Olivia Newton-John

| YouTube | Spotify | Apple |

As the song's opening lines implied, I didn't think there would be much nonhorizontal talking for us. This was a song I knew well, but I had never really listened to the lyrics.

Gigi's body had been talking to me all day. She took my hips and seductively started dancing in front of me. Then she began walking backwards towards the stables, beckoning me to follow and teasingly reaching for my crotch.

Her antics were driving me crazy, making me want her more and more.

I listened and watched her dancing and singing seductively for a while longer, then, unable to contain myself, I scooped her up over my shoulder and carried her the remaining 150 yards to the stables.

Arriving at the arched teak doorway, I put Gigi down and she blurted, "Take me, Babe. I want you badly. Let's go and find somewhere in the stables."

I doubted Olivia Newton-John's song about "getting animal" had anything to do with where we were.

I led Gigi towards the lounge area, complete with leather sofas. *That would be perfect.*

My Rude Awakening

We didn't get that far. She pushed open the first door we got to, and we found ourselves in the feed room, where she determinedly back kicked the door closed with a little more force than was necessary.

With her back against the door, we gave in to our passion, kissing and exploring each other frantically. Gigi hurriedly hooked her thumbs into my track pants and boxers, pulling them down effortlessly.

Being physical and getting animal, as the lyrics of the song went, only scratched the surface in describing what happened next.

After the rampant expression of our lust, her openness in expressing her desire, was in glaring contrast to Gigi now. She was soft, gentle, and loving, her maturity making me feel safe and secure. A sense of overwhelming warmth and love permeated through my being.

When I withdrew myself and gently lowered my arms so that she could put her weight back on her feet, I felt her legs give way and quickly held her up so as not to let her fall. A mixture of the physical effort of what we had just done, and the strength of her prolonged orgasms had made her weak and unstable. I supported her effortlessly, holding her firmly against me, loving the feel of her bosoms pressed against my chest.

Once Gigi's legs were able to support her again, we gingerly began tidying ourselves up and collecting our clothes off the floor.

As she was about to start dressing, she suddenly exclaimed with a chuckle, "Oh, God! Would you like to know what's running down my leg?"

She knew very well that I did not, so I merely rolled my eyes in response. *Gigi can be so rude at times,* I thought, smiling to myself.

We said very little as we walked back across the polo field, Gigi on still shaky legs and me holding her tight around her waist. We avoided the main house and went straight down to Winston Cottage, falling back into each other's arms as soon as we stepped inside. When we had finished kissing, we continued to hold each other and just look into each other's eyes. Words weren't necessary.

Then Gigi looked up at me and said simply, "Stay with me tonight. I don't want to be alone. You can leave early in the morning."

That settled it. I was going nowhere.

We went inside my most favourite place in the world—now for two good reasons.

We had a steam shower together, as I had promised myself. And me

245

using Gigi's toothbrush before going to bed seemed the most natural thing in the world. We climbed into bed, just my second night of sleeping there and already I had "my side."

We didn't speak for long, but Gigi did have two points she wanted to make.

"I'm not going to say anything about our visit to the stables this evening, but I will say this. I love you."

Even though right then I was not sure of the connection, I replied by simply repeating her words, "I love you."

Somehow nothing more needed to be said. I had a sense that this could quite easily become part of our love language, and this realization filled me with contentment. Lying naked in each other's arms, Gigi soon fell asleep while I stayed awake a while longer.

I reminisced about the first time with Gigi in this cottage a few nights ago, the confessions of our love for each other, and now this evening's events. *Is this true love? It feels like it. I may not have known the answer to that question, but what I did know was that I never wanted it to end.* My sense was that having exposed our true feelings for each other had paved the way for the unbridled and uninhibited demonstration of our deep emotions.

With her breathing even deeper, I had a look at her back, worried what I may find. It seemed fine, but of course I did not have the best light. I was quite certain I would be revisiting how rough our sex had been this evening. I needed to know, *Was I too rough?*

Enveloping her body with mine, the age-old spooning position, I was loving the feeling of Gigi against me. Even more than that though, I just loved that we had christened my two favourite places at Rockwell Manor, first Winston Cottage and now the stables. To say nothing of the special song in another special place, in the middle of our polo field, the resting place of my grandfather's ashes.

And the sex? It seemed our licentious behaviour had no boundaries. At least as a once off anyway. I wouldn't easily forget our time in the stable block and would certainly think twice before engaging in something as rough as this evening had been.

Before drifting off to sleep, I concluded that what we had *was* true love *and I would fight to hold onto it.*

CHAPTER 23
THROGMORTON SHOOT

THE NEXT MORNING I was up early, and after a little cuddle and a kiss, I went up to my suite and repeated the ritual of just two days earlier, right down to almost forgetting to mess up my bed…again. Once dressed, I decided to go across to the stables to *actually* check on the horses. On the way there, I found myself thinking about the upcoming Throgmorton shoot, which until then I hadn't given much more thought to, except for having resigned myself to the fact that Charlotte would be joining us. Her staying in her mother's room ruled out any possibility of anything happening between Gigi and me. Gigi had probably had her fill of sex for the next few days anyway.

If we could just have those two nights on the shoot together… My mind was swirling. I wasn't sure if she even wanted to go on the shoot. As I walked through the barn and past the feed room, memories of the previous night flooded back. Feeling a little perturbed by the possibility that I had hurt Gigi with how forceful our sex had been, I wondered what condition she was in this morning. She was very self-contained, and I knew there was a good chance she wouldn't mention it.

Attempting to kill time until breakfast, I painstakingly tended to the horses. We had organised a practise match, our last opportunity to prepare ourselves for the finals on Sunday.

At eight o'clock, I strolled back across the field to the house for breakfast and was surprised to find everyone had already arrived.

"Good morning, Sunbeam," my mother greeted me. "Where have you been, my love?"

"To the horses, Mum."

"Goodness, you can't leave them alone," she replied.

"I couldn't do it properly last night in the darkness, as I didn't want to disturb anyone with all the lights going on." I caught a glimpse of Gigi's smile.

As I served myself bran and berries, Gigi turned to my mother. "I really can't wait for this weekend at the Throgmortons. I haven't had a good spa day in ages, and your suggestions of what we can do with the truffles sound wonderful."

I was so relieved to hear this!

She continued, "And I have good news. I have just called the hotel and managed to get Charlotte her own room."

I was barely able to contain my excitement after that announcement, which was undoubtedly voiced for my benefit.

"Oh, wow, thank you, Mum," Charlotte exclaimed. "That will be much better, because it sounds like we will have quite a busy time and late nights."

What on earth had I been concerned about?

After breakfast, Gigi and I walked out together. "You don't know how much that means to me, you know, the hotel arrangements. Thank you, Darling," I whispered.

"Tomorrow night, Babe. Tomorrow night. That's when you can show me how much you appreciate it," she said seductively.

The day went by in a flash. Jamie and I enjoyed a great practise match, and I felt ready for the upcoming Barrett Cup final. The timing was perfect. We would exercise the horses the next day before we set off for the Throgmortons' in the early afternoon. The grooms would give them light work on Friday and Saturday, and they would be razor sharp for Sunday's big match.

My mother kept Gigi and Charlotte busy all day, taking them shopping and making sure they had all the appropriate attire for the weekend. Then they went over to Wentworth Club, where my mother had once been the ladies captain, as Gigi had expressed an interest in starting to play golf. My telling Gigi what a wonderful coach my mother was, may have been the trigger. Next, they lunched at Guards Polo Club.

I heard later from Gigi that she had "coincidentally" been introduced to a couple of nice men who were unsurprisingly both single.

Obviously noticing the stabs of jealousy that swept through me, she said, "You have nothing to worry about, Darling."

I didn't buy that. She was so gorgeous, and my mother would have been sure to have chosen the most dashing, eligible single men around. I had to stop myself from asking questions. There was nothing I could do. *Bloody hell, I should just come out in the open about us,* I thought, but that wasn't going to happen.

The next day we set off after lunch to Devon and Bovey Castle. With Jamie and I having decided to take both our cars, to give us a second vehicle for our time there, Charlotte jumped in with her brother, leaving Gigi to come with me. We had over a three-hour drive ahead of us, which I was thoroughly looking forward to. Then I joked that the girls should go in one car and Jamie and me in the other, and Gigi shot me a glare.

The first thing she said when we got in the car was, "Don't say things like that. It could so easily backfire."

We settled into the journey, and I patted Gigi's knee. "Darling, can we speak about the other night?"

"Which night, my gorgeous?" was her deadpan reply.

"You know, the feed room."

"Oh, the family dining room, or is it the formal dining room you are referring to?" she continued.

"No, Darling, in the stables. You know perfectly well what I am speaking about." I was a bit flummoxed.

"Stables, feeding room… No, I'm not with you, Babe. What are you trying to say, my love?" Her slightly upturned lips as a smile crept onto her face, betrayed her efforts at feigning ignorance and exposed that she was really just taking the mickey.

"Okay, so you know exactly what I'm speaking about. Don't do this to me, Darling. We really ought to speak about it."

She reached over and took a firm hold of my thigh. "Now, listen to me, Charles Featherstone. Stop worrying about what happened in the feed room. I'm happy to speak about it, but in all honesty, there's only one word I can say. Beautiful. It was beautiful. Yes, it was *very* physical. You think it was violent, forceful, and it was, but you were caring with it. Baby, sometimes it is just what a woman wants," she continued. "Don't worry, you were still a gentleman," she said with a wink.

I couldn't believe that my behaviour had still been that of *a gentleman*, but I wasn't going to get into that now.

"We both wanted the same thing, everything from each other. That's all. It will be a night I will never forget. How bad can that be?" Gigi certainly had a way of making me feel better about myself.

"Not something we will do every day, mind you. I will almost certainly have one or two bruises to show for it," she said lightly.

Oh, goodness, I hated the thought of her having bruises. "No, no, we won't do that again, Darling," I shot back.

"Oh no, I wouldn't like that, Baby. Next time let's just find a slightly softer back support." Gigi chuckled.

I was still dwelling on these consequences when Gigi said something that gave me a jolt.

"Oh yes, one thing I am very pleased about is that I finally understand the meaning of *'fuck your brains out,'*" she said as she rubbed the back of her head.

As lighthearted as Gigi was being, I hated the thought that I may have *actually* hurt her.

We soon slipped into a space of complete comfort. Gigi held my thigh, affectionately squeezing me from time to time as we chatted amiably about all sorts of things. She made our song choices, fed me the occasional snack, and handed me something to drink, and we just talked and laughed.

Then she slipped her shoes off and put her feet on the dashboard. I was immediately distracted, wanting to kiss them. Then she wiggled her toes and laughed. She had been watching me, waiting to see my reaction. I blushed.

"Ooh, my beautiful, gorgeous darling definitely has a foot fetish," Gigi chortled. "Don't worry. I love that you love my feet, but before they distract you and we end up in a ditch, I better remove them from the dashboard." With that, she put them onto my lap.

I was thrilled.

"Now at least you will keep your eyes on the road," she teased.

I fondled them with my free hand, and every now and then Gigi would jiggle them on my crotch.

"Don't do that, my darling, or we will definitely end up in a bitch, I mean ditch," I said, feigning my dyslexia.

I couldn't help remembering one of my granddad's lessons. *"If you're going somewhere special, start by enjoying the journey."* It didn't end there. He had another point on the matter when he asked me, "Which is more important, the journey or the destination?" I shrugged. "It's the company," he said. I was enjoying this journey, looking forward to the destination, and loving the company.

As we drove through the gates and approached the imposing Bovey Castle, grinning broadly, Gigi remarked, "Upstaging the Featherstones, I see." She was happy and relaxed, which was exactly how she made me feel.

Unusually, I was driving some way behind Jamie, just enjoying the trip with Gigi instead of racing ahead to our destination. We arrived in the car park just a few minutes behind them.

Walking into the entrance of the hotel, I watched Gigi taking in her surroundings. The main building was in Jacobean style, and the interior was high quality, with wood-panelled rooms and elaborately carved features. Some of the rooms were in neo-Elizabethan style.

"Mmm, very interesting," she said, which meant she quite liked it.

We checked in at a separate desk with a sign that announced, Throgmorton Estate Shoot. I was very excited to discover Gigi had done one better than just organising a separate room for Charlotte. She had managed to arrange that her room was next door to mine, and Jamie and Charlotte were a considerable distance from where we were, in the other wing.

Once settled in our rooms, I was wondering what to do when my bedside phone rang.

"Charles, are you going to show us around this place?" came Jamie's enthusiastic request.

"Good idea. Let me call Charlotte and Gigi. I'm sure they would also like to stretch their legs," I said, taking responsibility.

We all agreed to meet downstairs for a quick tour before dinner.

The early evening autumn sky was clear, contributing to the air being more than just a little fresh. A brisk walk, with me pointing out some of the features of Bovey Castle would be the perfect entrée to the dinner ahead. It was an exhilarating feeling, taking charge and showing the Blackwoods around the establishment.

Bovey Castle had lots to offer within its 275-acre estate, including gin making, off-road driving, fly fishing, clay-pigeon shooting, archery, an impressive championship golf course, and lovely long walkways in the park and surrounds. It was also home to a luxury spa and its renowned treatments, with its own Gentlemen's Quarter. Gigi wasted no time in arranging massages and manicures for her and Charlotte, even though their hands looked as beautiful as ever to me.

Dinner required gentlemen to wear a jacket, and most would don ties, as I chose to do, not feeling it appropriate to take a casual approach. I wore a dark green Ralph Lauren cashmere jacket, with a very faintly checked cream shirt and a tie that featured flying ducks, over dark khaki chino-type trousers, and brown Oxford shoes.

My mother had made sure I would be presentable for Charlotte and bought me her favourite aftershave and cologne sprays, which she'd slipped into my toiletry bag.

When I'd asked my father if he agreed with my mum's choice, his simple reply had been, "How would I know? Your mother has been buying my fragrances forever."

I applied both but not lavishly, remembering her words, *"Less is more, Sunbeam."*

For the final touch I put my tie-matching silk handkerchief in my breast pocket, with just the right amount showing, and adjusted my shirt cuffs so only about half an inch protruded from my jacket sleeve. Hands and nails looked neat and trim. Frances Featherstone would be happy. All set, I left the room, excited about the evening that lay ahead.

Jamie arrived in the private dining room, wearing a jacket sans a tie and feeling no qualms about his open neck.

He and I stood on the far side of the room at the bar, enjoying an unobstructed view of the area as we watched the other guests arrive, most of whom were more elderly than us. For this reason, I was very pleased when I saw a friend of mine, Edward Dashwood, walk into the banquet hall. He was well named as he certainly cut a 'dashing' figure as he strode through the room. And what made him even more so was that he was the only son of Sir Frances Dashwood, the 11th Baronet of Great Britain, which meant Edward was destined to become the 12th Baronet on his father's passing. Along with his father, they had begun establishing what was almost certainly going to become one of the country's leading shooting estates. This included the continuation of the manufacture of bespoke English guns under the E. J. Churchill brand. I would be sure to spend some time with him over the course of the weekend and hopefully arrange some grouse shooting, his favourite. Right then though, I was more preoccupied looking out for Gigi, of course.

The place settings indicated there would be about forty guests. It was a grand room, with a large chandelier flanked by two smaller ones, centred over the long Georgian dining table. Various paintings, mostly of hunting scenes, were spaced between ornate glass and crystal wall lights. The waiters wore black tie, and the waitresses wore matching attire with a French-maid feel. Light classical music wafted out from concealed speakers. It all presented a salubrious setting, promising another memorable pre-shoot dinner.

Taking it all in, Jamie turned to me and asked, "Should I have worn a tie?"

"Oh, don't worry, Jamie. A few of the men will be open necked," I replied.

When Charlotte and Gigi arrived, they were immediately noticed. Looking like a Renaissance beauty, Gigi wore a midcalf, ruffled, stone-coloured skirt, a cream blouse with puffed sleeves, cuffs with at least eight buttons on each, and brown knee-high boots that laced up to the top. But it was a beige-and-green-piped under bust corset bodice over her blouse that completed her outfit. Coincidentally, the fabric was a similar duck-shooting scene as the one on my tie. The way the corset laced up on her back gave the effect of creating a very pronounced hourglass figure, while the push-up corset accentuated the fullness of her bosom. She had completed the ensemble with a dark green French beret, which she had set to one side of her dark blonde, tousled head of hair. She had draped a mahogany-brown and gold-trimmed silk pashmina loosely over her shoulders. Anyone would have thought we had colour coded our dress that evening. My eyes never left her, though I regretted that I could not have her on my arm. As she got a little closer to us, I could see the result of her interlude at the beauty salon. Her nails were always on the short side, and once again, she had decided on her favourite dark burgundy varnish. I couldn't wait to feel those hands on my body. *God, she's beautiful,* was my irrepressible thought.

Charlotte looked less country chic but equally as beautiful. She wore a blue-and-brown-checked tweed skirt that landed above the knee, with matching short jacket and quite a low-cut peach silk blouse. Her flesh-coloured tights had a faint netting effect, with high-heeled beige shoes that enhanced her long, shapely legs. She seldom wore makeup, but this evening she had eyeliner, mascara, and a little colouring on her lips. I was seeing her in a different light. She looked older, but still a green fig, just a perfect green fig. They really did look like sisters with no more than ten years between them. It was a wonderful sight, especially for the single men in the room.

Jamie and I were joined by Humphrey, the son of our host, Alistair Throgmorton. There was a certain air of intrigue around us, having just earned our RAF wings. Jamie revelled in it. I didn't. It was nothing compared to the attention Charlotte and Gigi were getting.

From the moment they arrived, it seemed that nearly every man in the room wanted to engage with them, and this continued through the entire evening. My mother had clearly managed to get a message to the Throgmortons that one of our guests was the lovely Georgina Blackwood. What really irritated me was that she could hardly finish one drink before there was another eager man offering her another, somehow always needing to touch her arm or hand. I also questioned why Gigi had to be quite so charming in return! I could plainly see she didn't need any help with meeting men from my parents.

I couldn't then accept that this was just my youthful immaturity and jealousy.

We finally sat down to dinner. It was always mixed placings on the first evening, so everyone could get to know each other. I had already seen my name card but had not yet been able to see where Gigi had been seated. I was pleased to see that whilst she was on the other side of the table, it was just four places down, diagonally across from me.

It was a lavish affair. Foie gras and fig preserve with toasted baguettes,

My Rude Awakening

salmon mousse with caviar, or crab legs, still half in their shell with various dips, were the starter options. The main courses were aged rib-eye roast, baked Scottish salmon, or rock lobster, all served with an array of accompaniments. The dessert trolley would come later.

Usually, Gigi preferred not to have a large meal before we were to spend the evening together. I wondered what her thinking was this night.

The dinner progressed at a steady pace. After the starters, Humphrey's dad, Alistair, stood up and welcomed the guests to the shoot, followed by a short, comical speech. He felt it necessary to let everyone know what a shotgun shell cost. He was correct in assuming that most of the guests were a bit hazy on that point. He went on to estimate how many rounds would be fired, especially if you were a bad shot, which he suspected most of the guests were. He did a brief calculation of the cost of staying at Bovey Castle and then, of course, the cost of being on the shoot itself. He did a hilarious little animated exercise of adding it all up, coming up with the total cost per guest. He then estimated how many game birds would be shot, divided the total monetary value by the number of birds, and came up with a cost per bird, which turned out to be just under £1,000 if you were to bag say twenty grouse or pheasant. No one was particularly concerned and broke into further spirited laughter when Mr. Throgmorton suggested to everyone that, at £1,000 per pheasant, we ought not shoot too many birds. Befuddled logic indeed, which made everyone laugh even more.

I noticed that Gigi had gone with all the lighter dishes. Crab legs and baked Scottish salmon. I wasn't sure if they were her preferred choices or in preparation for what she had in mind for later. Already I was imagining.

Dinner finally ended. The normal form was that everyone would continue mingling and chatting. The music was usually changed to something a little more upbeat, encouraging the guests to have a little dance. I had no interest in being drawn into the remainder of the evening.

Much to the disappointment of at least three hopeful men, Gigi announced that she was a little tired and would be going to bed. The first two men were far too affectionate in saying their good nights, which really irked me, but the third downright annoyed me. He was pressing hard for Gigi not to leave, even taking hold of her hand while trying to convince her to stay. She politely took it back, gave him a brush off, and turned on her heels towards the door, waving good night to Jamie, Charlotte, and me as she left the room.

That was my cue. I just had to make sure that no one noticed me leaving so soon after her.

I looked across at Charlotte. She was chatting merrily enough with two men, who were speaking in an animated fashion. But knowing her as I did, I realised she wasn't responding in the way I knew she would've had she been even half interested. I felt sorry for her not having a partner in such lovely surroundings—crisp country air, sumptuous dinners, a little alcohol to relax and entice—so conducive to romance and what follows naturally from there.

I was just about to say good night to Jamie when one of the waitresses, Candy, came over and asked if we would like another drink. Over the past two hours, she had become awfully attentive towards Jamie. I hadn't given it a second thought because he just had that way with women, especially nubile ones like Candy. I thought it would be peculiar if I said no, so we both ordered something.

I could hear Gigi's voice, *"Don't let the alcohol dull the senses."*

There was a little more chitchat, Candy telling us that she was a second or third cousin to Humphrey. "The poor cousin," she pointed out. From what I could tell, not too poor for Jamie. Well, she may have only been a waitress, but she more than made up for it with a bubbly personality, pretty face, and substantial boobs—right down Jamie's alley.

Candy said she was finishing off shortly and, if we liked, she could come and have a goodnight drink with us. Both Jamie and I agreed, for two different reasons. Jamie would be very pleased to engage with her, and she would be the reason for my escape.

Pleased with our responses, she declared. "Wonderful. Let me go and get your order and then I am *all* yours."

That was an invitation Jamie would undoubtedly accept.

With Candy having left to get our drinks, I told Jamie that when she returned, three would certainly be a crowd and I would slip away. His broad grin was unequivocal agreement.

As I finally left the dining room, I looked at my watch and couldn't believe that I had wasted nearly fifteen minutes getting out of there.

My Rude Awakening

I climbed the stairs three at a time and knocked quietly on Gigi's door, but there was no response. I knocked louder, more urgently, but still nothing. The third time I was now banging away even more loudly, but it was my hotel room door that opened.

Gigi stuck her head out and said, "Please don't wake up the whole establishment," followed by a naughty little chuckle.

I stepped into my room, enthralled that we were finally alone.

She locked and bolted the door as I looked her over from head to toe. She had put the time to good use, changing into a long satin nightdress and hotel slippers, her pedicured toes peeping out, beautiful as ever.

I walked up to her, and we both reached to hold each other's faces as we kissed. I put my hands around her waist, our pelvises pushed together, and just gazed into her eyes.

"Darling, before you say anything, I just want to say you looked beautiful, *so beautiful* tonight. The only problem was that I was not the only one in the room who thought this, and it killed me that I had to stand back."

I could see her considering this for a while before saying, "Well, there could be some benefit."

"But I was as jealous as all hell. How could there be *some benefit*?" I shot back.

"Just think about it, my darling, and in the meantime, you can start imagining how you should punish me?" Gigi replied, suggestively biting her bottom lip.

There was something even more exciting about this evening, which I couldn't immediately put my finger on. Was it that the first time Gigi and I had spent the night alone together was in Shrewsbury—her, Jamie's, and Charlotte's home? Then it was at Rockwell Manor—mine and my parents' home. This night, we were on neutral ground—*no one's* home. The first time in over a year since we became lovers!

Gigi had been *so much more* of who she was that evening. Even more confident, more beguiling than usual. Watching me closely, biting her bottom lip, inviting me in, purposefully provocative. Although we were alone with no one to overhear us, she whispered obscenities into my ear of what she wanted of me. With the soft mood lighting washing over her, my eyes drank in the beauty of her nudity, unashamedly settling on her curvaceous, soft breasts. Very soon, those were the only things that were soft.

Gigi looked more lubricious than usual amid this setting of the large suite with its Victorian furnishing, complete with horses, hounds, and pheasant-shooting artwork adorning the dark green walls. I couldn't help but think of Modigliani's *Reclining Nude*. Gigi was my artwork, in the flesh. I couldn't wait to feel her, fondle her, make love to her, until I felt she was all mine.

We then spent time pleasuring each other in all the familiar, comfortable ways we'd learnt to share. And just as familiar, it led to the same outcome, just this time the 'gentleness' of the evening quickly escalated into a crescendo of two people ferociously vanquishing each other.

This neutral territory was having its effect on me as well. Kneeling in front of her, I had subconsciously begun playing with her beautifully pedicured feet. With a sigh of contentment, she placed them on my chest. Without thinking, I began to rub and massage them. It had an unexpected sexual effect on us both, and once again we soon succumbed to our desire for each other.

Even more unexpected was how Gigi's feet became a feature of our sex that evening as I brought one of her feet up to my mouth and ran my tongue along the undersides of her toes, every now and then probing between them. Going back and forth, "loving" each of her feet in turn.

This new and unusual stimulation added an even greater climactic ending to our already extraordinary sexual compatibility.

Once sated, I flopped down on the bed next to her and cuddled her close, shielding her from the cool night air. I listened to her soft breathing. Was this the best sex we'd ever had? Then again, I often felt that way after we had made love. The way I had enjoyed her feet during our sex that evening would be something I would not easily forget. Another feeling I often had with Gigi.

Did I have a foot fetish? Unquestionably I loved Gigi's feet, but it would be more accurate to say I simply loved every part of her.

I was falling more and more in love with this woman.

After a short while, Gigi playfully pushed me over onto my back. She knelt over me, looking down at my prostrate form with a dominatrix demeanour. Then she took hold of me and began slowly and purposefully transforming my flaccid state.

We were openly exploring each other with our eyes, neither of us hiding our unabashed pleasure in looking at each other. I was mesmerised by her antics. But most of all, it was her expression. A piercing, steely look of determination came over her that reached to her lips and mouth and foretold nothing was going to stop her from getting her own way.

Oh, God, this is all too much.

Then Gigi positioned herself over me. There was no "Babe." No "Darling." Just a piercing, smouldering look of intent. Watching this sophisticated, refined lady speaking and behaving like this threatened to drive me over the edge.

After we came out of the trance of our lovemaking, I lifted myself onto one of my elbows to look at her, nightdress still around her torso. Such had been my urgency to enjoy her this evening that I had neglected to remove it. Gigi lay there in a glorious state of near nakedness, a picture of bedraggled contentment, as her hand gingerly reached down to feel herself. I could not help but think that right then, at my hands, she looked like a vanquished woman of the night.

Oh, God, a whore in my bed, was the shockingly wonderful thought that flicked through my mind.

I lifted her torso and in one gentle movement, removed her unkempt garment, her whorish demeanour being replaced by a picture of innocent nakedness. Thinking I could relax again, I lay down next to her as she turned to face me.

"My baby," I began, "did I ambush your plans for this evening by dominating you, when perhaps that is what you wanted to do to me?"

"So, you could tell, could you?" Gigi replied. "Don't worry, I am going to get my own back," she said, smiling.

"What did you have in mind, my gorgeous darling?" I teased.

Gigi gave a little giggle before replying, "Well, there are quite a few options, and this four-poster bed gives me a few ideas."

"Oh, really, Darling? How does a four-poster bed come into it?" I asked.

"Pretty simple, mind you," Gigi replied. "I could tie you to each post and then do what I threatened earlier. Better still, I will give you some of your own medicine."

"Oh, what would that be?"

"You know, what you once did to me. I will just fuck your brains out."

This time I smiled. *Gigi was enjoying that she was never going to let me live that down. I no longer minded.*

We happily lay next to each other, enjoying the comfort and closeness of being in each other's arms.

Gigi whispered, "I want you, Darling. I want *all* of you. Now and always." She wasn't speaking about sex. She wanted far more than that.

There was nothing I wanted more than this full, wholesome, complete, perfect woman, and I think my eyes said it all.

"How can we make this happen?" she asked, more of herself than me.

We both reached back and switched off our bedside lights, then took each other in our arms and began gently touching and holding each other's faces.

As I was drifting off to sleep, it struck me that Gigi had not used any instinctual language even though our sex had been as lascivious as ever. *She didn't say "fuck" once, and it made it no less visceral, I thought.*

I woke early the next morning with Gigi lying naked beside me, only partly covered by a sheet, her bosom exposed. Nuzzled into her neck, I became very aware of the softness of this part of her body as I took in her delicate aroma from behind her earlobe. I was never able to get enough of her.

My thoughts roamed back to last night's sexual athletics and the enjoyment I had experienced from Gigi's feet. I had to concede, I was certainly in love with them…and her hands…and, and…just all of her.

I had a perfect view of her profile, not only of her face but her body as well. I took in the outline of her nose with its subtle bump, down to her lips. Soft, sensual lips that was her gateway to her passionate mouth. My eyes continued their journey downward, taking in the form of her full breasts. I looked at one of Gigi's hands lying across her belly. I could feel my sexual desire welling up as my eyes drifted further down to where I could see the start of her runway…as always, beckoning me.

God, she drives me crazy.

My Rude Awakening

I couldn't resist. I started gently caressing her hand as she began to stir, then I gently fondled her breast.

Gigi opened her eyes and said, "You can't do that, Darling, unless you promise me you will always wake me up this way."

She then reached beneath the sheets, and whilst I did my best to keep a straight face, I watched as hers lit up.

"Oh, God, am I going to have a glorious morning?"

I couldn't help smiling at the way she had twisted that phrase about what often happens to men at the start of each day.

While we were quite happy lying in bed, enjoying each other's company, for no particular reason, I thought about us being in this very public place, in a secret, undisclosed relationship with my best friend's mother in my bedroom! What if Charlotte or Jamie came looking for either of us?

I posed this question to Gigi, who quite nonchalantly brushed it off with a very casual, "Oh, don't worry about that, Darling. I have taken care of it. I told both that I would be going out for an early-morning jog. I invited them to join me, and when they both said they would rather not—unsurprising, given that I had spoken to them in the middle of our festive dinner last night—I told them I'd have to drag you out with me. Neither of them is likely to knock on my door, and if they do, when I don't answer, they will remember I am out for my run. The same goes for you. Just don't make a noise if there is a knock on your door."

"I can see you have it all worked out," I said. "What about getting back to your room?"

With that, Gigi pointed to her sportswear, trainers, and tracksuit, which I had not previously noticed folded neatly on the ottoman. "I will just put that on after my shower. Goodness knows, I will surely deserve that after the workout I have been given," she said, raising her eyebrows. "Now I just have to work out what to do with my hair," she said, looking in the mirror. "On that note, I don't remember teaching you anything about…whatever that was? What do you call it, Darling? Shaggy dog, as in getting properly shagged, doggy style?"

I went puce. Gigi's words made it sound terrible. "Baby, did I hurt you last night?" I asked. "I saw you feeling yourself. Was I too rough?"

"Don't stop because you think you're hurting me. You're not, or you are, but sometimes I like it. Quite often in fact," was Gigi's candid reply.

I was still embarrassed, but not to let her have it all her own way, I reminded her I was only doing what she rightly deserved.

Gigi looked at me quizzically.

"Punishment, Darling. Punishment, or have you forgotten?"

"Oh, remind me what I did again? Just in case I feel the need to be disciplined again," she said, chuckling.

I smiled, determined she should not be the only one with the banter. "Well, I learnt something very important last night," I continued.

"What was that, Darling?" Gigi enquired.

"I now know between which two toes you are the most sensitive."

"Between which two toes I am the most sensitive?" Gigi repeated thoughtfully. "Oh, I don't know. Between my big toe and second toe, or perhaps underneath my toes?"

"Well, I definitely got your biggest response when I was busy between your two big toes," I drawled with a broad grin across my face. I waited for the penny to drop that the only thing between her two big toes was her vagina.

When she got it, she turned around and said, "Clever dick," and hit me with a pillow.

Gigi went into the bathroom to take a shower, and I glanced at my attire for the day's shoot. I would wear Church's Oxford shoes, long woollen stockings, tweed plus fours, a cream woollen shirt with a thin green-and-blue-check, a tie with a shooting theme, a suede waistcoat, a tweed jacket, and my old faithful shooting hat. That would be my dress for breakfast and lunch. Before we went into the woods to take up our positions on the first drive, I would exchange my tweed jacket and shoes for my shooting jacket and boots.

"Darling, your shower is ready," I heard Gigi calling.

I went into the bathroom, expecting her to already be in her tracksuit and trainers. She wasn't. Instead, she was standing in the shower, door open, provocatively leaning against the wall and covered only in soap suds.

Doe-eyed and feigning innocence, she asked, "One last thing, my darling. Could you help me rinse this soap off?"

My Rude Awakening

I could not get into the shower quick enough and immediately went about rubbing her soapy, slippery body as she began soaping me. The new sensation of the warm water and the smooth and slippery feel of the lathered soap on her body added a new dimension to the beauty of the woman I was desperate to call my own.

I wondered if shower sex was in the cards, but Gigi, in a cursory manner had simply stated, "Sex in the shower is overrated. Anyway, I need to save a little for later."

She finished her shower, stepped out, and turned on her Walkman as she dried herself off.

With my ever-increasing confidence, I stood under the shower and simply watched her.

Gigi held my gaze as I watched her dressing in her sports gear. Donning her tracksuit top, she came over and brought her mouth up to my earlobe. She bit it firmly, sending a sharp pain shooting through me as she whispered, "Ooh, and I can see he is already *up* for my next round of punishment."

Is this the game she is playing? I had to admit, I liked it.

As I began to dry myself, she asked, "Oh, Darling, I think I know, but I just want to be sure. Do you dress left or right?"

I knew she was talking about the natural lie of my penis in my trousers. "I dress left, Darling," I replied. I didn't like that Gigi knew so much about men and these finer details. I hated the thought that her intimacy with another man, or perhaps *other men*, was the reason for her understanding of this.

Gigi interrupted my jealous thoughts with, "I can't wait to see you later, Darling. Don't worry about planning anything for tonight. I will be happy with a repeat performance, as unimaginative as you may think that is. What have you done to me, Edward Charles?"

She then kissed me on the lips, and with that, she was gone. She would have to go through to her own room to prepare for the day's truffle hunt.

Shortly thereafter, as I made my own way out, I decided to get a scarf from my car. The only disturbance to the warm thoughts I was having of my morning with Gigi was the crisp air and crunch of gravel underfoot as I walked through the car park. I couldn't describe my feelings, neither did I bother to. I just felt so alive.

As I walked past the parked cars, an Audi caught my eye. Not the car, but rather the bunch of polo mallets in the boot of the vehicle. They immediately piqued my interest. Taking a closer look, I saw some signage on the front doors.

Audi

Sponsors of the Coronation Cup

and

The Argentinian Polo Team

It was pretty obvious what that meant. An Argentinian polo player was staying at Bovey Castle. In Devon? I had more than a sneaking suspicion of who that would be.

Having retrieved my scarf, on the way back into the hotel I walked past the Audi and inspected the polo sticks more carefully. The heads of the mallets, called the "cigars," bore the initials *NA*. Clearly, a three-hour drive was nothing for a red-blooded polo player in need. No guessing required. I knew only one Argentinian polo player with those initials. I took back my earlier thoughts of Charlotte and "maybe next time." Definitely "this time" was now my bet. I smiled, thinking that in the primal needs department, three Blackwoods and one Featherstone were being properly sorted.

I felt a pang of jealousy about Charlotte even though I had Gigi. Is that how it sometimes is with men, or was it just me?

CHAPTER 24
COMING OF AGE

FEELING REVITALISED, I went down to breakfast alone, Gigi and I having decided not to arrive together. My timing could not have been better. I walked in with a very bright and cheerful Charlotte at my side, which made Jamie give me another of his enquiring looks. *He's really wondering about us.* Just when he may have thought there were possibilities between his sister and me, I was seeing an easy way out of the "relationship"—her involvement with another. I just wondered how my parents would take it.

Gigi arrived minutes later, looking radiant in an elegant cobalt-blue and beige tweed jacket teamed with slacks that she had tucked into her Dubarry country boots.

"You look gorgeous and radiant this morning, Mum. As if you've just stepped out of the pages of *Horse & Hound*," Charlotte remarked as Gigi sat down at the breakfast table between her daughter and me. "Did you have a good sleep?" she asked her mother.

"Oh yes, what a heavenly evening," Gigi replied.

I dared not look at her as I struggled not to grin.

The idle chitchat about the previous night continued, with no one inclined to get into the details of what exactly they got up to. I wondered if I was the only one who knew about Nic being at Bovey Castle. I was faced with a small predicament about what I should say to Gigi. I would need to say something, even if Charlotte might have preferred it be kept secret. Dilemma or not, my relationship with her mother meant I could not withhold this information.

Once Gigi and I were alone, I tentatively broached the subject.

"Darling," I said as nonchalantly as possible, "I noticed one of the Argentine team's Audi courtesy cars in the parking lot this morning."

Gigi covered my hand with hers and with a gentle squeeze said, "I know, Baby, but thank you." And then just as quietly she simply said, "Nic spent the night here."

I should have expected Charlotte and her mother to have that closeness.

"Charlotte and I spoke last night, and she really is quite taken by him," Gigi continued. "And Nic has told her that he loves her."

Those words got my attention. What had taken Gigi and me the best part of a year to say to each other had happened within days between Nic and Charlotte. I supposed that was not unusual for two people in what society would call a "normal" relationship.

"So, how do you feel about that?" I asked.

"Well, I think you might relate to what I said to her since I used a bit of your Shakespeare."

"Oh, and what was that?" I asked, genuinely interested.

"I just quoted, 'Be wary the man who doth profess his love, when he wants to make love.' "

I couldn't help smiling, even if it was a serious moment.

Once outside, Jamie and I walked towards the Land Rovers designated for the game-bird shoot party. Charlotte and Gigi went over to where three Range Rovers and a pickup truck waited to transport their group and a handful of dogs to a nearby forest known for burgundy truffles. In the past, it had been traditional to use pigs for seeking out these delicacies, but pigs were difficult to train and would often devour what they unearthed from the shallow roots of the trees. The hounds had a keen sense of smell, were easily trained, and had no interest in eating the truffles. Instead, they were thrilled to be rewarded with a sausage for their efforts. I enjoyed watching the Blackwood ladies enthusiastically preparing for their outing.

As Gigi walked past me, she popped a folded note into my breast pocket. I would have to wait until later to read it.

The Throgmorton weekend was a bespoke shoot, eight guns, all of whom were men on this occasion, dressed in the proper attire and careful to observe shooting etiquette. Because of the abundance of game bird that would be driven overhead, we each had a matched pair of shotguns.

My Rude Awakening

One of my discomforts was that the loaders were often retired gentlemen who loved the outdoors and being involved in country shooting. In addition to loading, they were responsible for carrying your guns, various items of clothing, and your rather weighty cartridge case, and at the end of the day, they cleaned your gun. Having these seniors looking after me in this way did not sit well with me, so I was very quick to share the burden. Giving them a generous gratuity and as many grouse or pheasant as they desired, at the end of the day made me feel better. And I always cleaned my own gun, something I enjoyed.

As arranged, we did four drives between ten in the morning and one in the afternoon, with plenty of time to move from one location to the next, have a snack, and partake of a little sloe gin, the drink of choice on a shoot. I was sure Gigi and Charlotte would also be warming themselves with sloe gin during their truffle hunt.

It was after the first drive that I had an opportunity to read my note. Unfolding it, I found:

IFLY

ILFY

That was all. I looked at it a few times but could not work out Gigi's cryptic message. It seemed to be about flying because of the first line, "IFLY." I resigned myself to having to try and work it out later.

It was wonderful being in the countryside again, working with the retriever dogs, moving from drive-to-drive and experiencing some of the best driven game birds in the country. I couldn't help but notice how Jamie had progressed. The delight on his face was a looking glass into how he was feeling, and he bagged six pheasant on the first drive.

Four drives later, we returned to Bovey Castle, first changing from our shooting gear into lounge attire. We then met our partners for a sumptuous lunch. I was more than tickled by the thought of lunching with Gigi. *My partner.*

As we drifted into the collecting room outside the dining area, I couldn't wait to hear what she had been up to. She enthusiastically told me about her haul of truffles and that they were having a thoroughly good time.

267

After a jovial lunch, we were preparing to go our separate ways again, the partners heading out to resume their truffle hunting and the shooters to do our two afternoon drives, which would go on until around four-thirty.

The day's shoot was an enormous success. Jamie did well, contributing around sixteen pheasant to the day's bag of 165 birds. I did fine, my contribution being about forty pheasant, after having left the easier pickings to the guns on either side of me. The other guns had noticed that I seldom missed my quarry, often getting two in quick succession, one with each barrel. The loaders would sometimes wager with each other on their respective shooters, which often led to the comical situation of a loader trying to win a bet by coaching his shooter in an attempt to improve his yield.

My favourite part of the shoot was the dogs and how they would retrieve the stricken quarry and bring them to your feet. When I saw an English springer spaniel, I couldn't help thinking nostalgically of my beloved Osric.

We got back to the hotel in the early evening, changed back into our jackets and shoes, and went to the quaint bar for drinks. I watched for Gigi, who eventually arrived along with the other ladies, all rosy-cheeked and looking incredibly pleased with themselves. She was holding a medium-sized wicker basket with a linen cloth lining, her and Charlotte's truffle bag of the day.

Gigi walked up to us, gave me a kiss on the lips, and opened the cloth covering the basket to reveal their truffle haul. It was impressive by any standards. I tried to gesture to her with my eyes that she should kiss her son as well. It was lost on her as she began excitedly telling us about her day with Charlotte interjecting every now and then. They clearly loved the outdoors and the lighthearted competitiveness of truffle hunting. It had been special for them to spend that time together.

"Ooh, and I must tell you about the most delightful bitch that I was working with. Daisy," Gigi enthused. "She was an English springer spaniel, just like Osric I imagine, my darling."

I quickly looked at Jamie and Charlotte to see how they reacted to this very forthright term of endearment their mother had just used for me. They didn't bat an eye.

Gigi carried on, unconcerned. "She's only three years old and so beautifully trained. And guess what else, she will one day be a gundog. And,

My Rude Awakening

Darling, for a moment while I was working with Daisy, I got an inkling of you and Osric." She then looked at me very tenderly and said, "You lost a good friend."

I was seeing yet another side of Gigi, and it spurred all sorts of emotions.

"I just love it here. I would love to live in Berkshire, and we—umm, I could get a springer spaniel," she went on, quickly correcting her slip of the tongue.

"So, what is on the cards tomorrow?" I asked. "More truffle hunting?"

"Oh no. Tomorrow, Charlotte and I are going to have a lovely spa and beauty day together," Gigi replied.

I was thrilled they were having such an enjoyable time. It meant I wouldn't have to do any convincing the next time there was a shoot. I didn't check myself, planning into the future.

We went to our rooms to freshen up for dinner. I took a quick shower and while I was soaping myself, my mind drifted to the same place just twelve hours earlier. Gigi and my relationship had moved into a new phase, and I could not help wondering if it would continue to progress in the normal manner, where we would no longer hide it from the rest of the world. It wasn't that easy for me. How would my parents take it? They had such high expectations for me. What about Jamie and Charlotte? Could they come to terms with Gigi and me being together? I loved Gigi and couldn't bear the thought of her not being in my life, but I knew too, all the complications of what that meant. *Would love find a way?*

Reflecting on it now, it was understandable how conflicted I was and how complex it had been for me, given my youthfulness and inexperience.

I dressed in light beige chino trousers, a white shirt, and a navy-blue Ralph Lauren cashmere blazer. Instead of a tie, I donned a light turquoise paisley silk cravat with a colour-matching pocket handkerchief, no pattern. As I was about to walk out, I remembered my aftershave and cologne spray, courtesy of my mother.

Jamie and Charlotte were already in the bar when I got downstairs. "I told Mum we'd meet here," Charlotte said, glowing in an above-the-knee floral dress and kitten heels. The country air agreed with her. Jamie was now wearing a tie and looked a bit smarter than the previous evening.

Gigi arrived, looking gorgeous in a flowing cream long-sleeved dress, with thin tan leather trimming around the hem, cuffs, and neckline. Like several of her other garments, it showed the form of her bosom without being flagrant. She wore sand-coloured leather platform wedges with a peep toe. They were about four inches high and forced her lower leg to be permanently taut, her calf muscles bunching up just slightly, giving her a very sexy appeal. What really highlighted her outfit was a thin tan leather neck choker with a matching strap around her wrists and ankles. It gave her a definite younger, edgier look I thought, as I continued taking in her curves.

Feeling very relaxed, she assumed a place next to me, and I passed her a glass of water. From an outsider's perspective, we were behaving more and more like a couple. I wondered if Jamie and Charlotte could see that too. I guessed they had slowly become accustomed to our drawing closer and had no reason to think there was anything untoward. Or was that just my wishful thinking?

Once in the dining room, we were greeted warmly by the rest of the team, but it was Gigi who everyone made a special effort with. I struggled to suppress my jealousy.

The evening was a lot more relaxed than the previous night. Having all come to know one another a lot better, we shared stories of our day's activities.

Once when speaking to Humphrey Throgmorton, Gigi left to go to the cloak room and Humphrey whispered to me, "Wow, now that's a hot MILF!"

Not knowing exactly what it meant except that it was to do with an attractive older woman, I wholeheartedly agreed with him.

A short while later our maître d' announced that dinner would be served, so we moved in the direction of our long dining table. As was the norm on the second night, there were no place settings. While I wondered what we should do, I felt Gigi's hand on my arm.

She asked me with a doe-eyed, hangdog expression, "Would you mind terribly taking me to my seat…next to yours?"

Gigi and I were revelling in our newfound freedom and loving it. Any reservations we may have had about being out in the open, and whether this would influence our relationship, had been fully dispelled. I purposefully took us to the opposite end of the table from where Jamie and Charlotte were seated, so that the comfort Gigi and I we're feeling would be slightly less obvious if it was from a distance.

We had another lovely dinner, though we had to be mindful to speak to the people around us and not become totally engrossed with just each other.

I asked her what she would like to eat and was certain that I was not the only one to hear her short reply, "You." Every now and then she would reach under the table and take hold of my thigh, give it a squeeze or rub me up and down the inside of my leg.

After dinner, two dessert trolleys were moved slowly around the table. I knew this would be followed by another trolley and a selection of brandies, ports, and cigars. In an effort to accelerate things a bit, I asked Gigi what she'd like for dessert.

Without hesitation, she said, "*Un vagin cremeux.*"

I looked at her blankly, as my French was nonexistent. Then I remembered that there was a French chef and, doing my best to be a gentleman, surreptitiously asked the waiter if he would call him for me. He promptly went off to call said chef, Patrice.

Notwithstanding my best attempt at discretion, Gigi had overheard me and started giggling, which was a little confusing.

Eventually after she had calmed down a bit, I gestured with my shoulders and upturned hands and asked, "What's so funny, Darling?"

She did not trust herself to speak as she put her head down to hide her laughter. I could see Patrice walking towards us as she put an arm around my shoulder. As I was taking a generous swig of my wine, Gigi, through her laughter, whispered into my ear, "Darling, Darling, before you speak to the chef about what I would like for dessert, I think you ought to know that *un vagin cremeux* is 'a creamy vagina,' and I don't need the French chef to help me with that."

I spluttered on my wine and burst out laughing.

Just then, Patrice drew up alongside me with a typically French inquisitorial look. Trying to control my laughter, I motioned foolishly with a combination of thumbs-up and gesticulations towards the dessert trolley. Looking like some sort of confused traffic conductor, I was doing my best to signal to him that his attendance was not required as his dessert tray looked delicious.

Our laughter, of course, attracted the attention of those around us and then some, all wanting to know what was so funny. I could not wait to get out of there.

When dinner finally ended, Gigi told Jamie and Charlotte she was tired, and very soon after, I feigned a headache. I was not going to waste twenty minutes this evening before going up to my room.

I got to my bedroom and, as if to prove she had meant what she said about a repeat of the previous evening, there she was on the king size bed, propped up against the headboard and already in her satin nightdress.

"Can I assume that suitable arrangements have been made to ensure your empty bedroom won't be noticed?" I asked.

"Easy. Simple," Gigi said.

I didn't bother asking what she had done, instead making sure the door was properly locked. "Think the worst, but unconfirmed by seeing nothing," was now our mantra. Somewhere in there was the distinct possibility that at times they could be *hearing* "the worst" as well!

As I undressed, I told Gigi what Humphrey had said about her, enquiring what exactly MILF stood for. When she told me it was an acronym for Mother I'd Like to Fuck, I was more than just a little riled.

Gigi laughed.

"What's so funny?" I asked.

"*You* are what's so funny, Darling," she said, chuckling.

"Aren't you offended?" I shot back.

"No, quite the opposite, really. You should be pleased, my darling. You're doing what he's dreaming about."

Ooh, I don't like that. No rebuke! Gigi enjoying another man having lewd thoughts about her annoyed me. Those words also had me realise she was well aware of her attractiveness to all men and supposedly enjoyed it. My jealousy flared with just that thought, not that she would ever know. But then her next remark suggested my feelings were not as well concealed as I had imagined.

"So, what is it going to be, my gorgeous? A duel at dawn, my courageous, handsome knight defending the honour of his woman?" teased Gigi.

"Mmm, not a bad idea," I replied. "But before I do that, I ought to have a very stern word with one very naughty MILF whom I may have to punish…*again*…for turning on a bunch of innocent young fellows." Was I in some lighthearted fashion putting the blame on her?

With that, Gigi's eyes lit up. Still lying seductively up against the padded headboard, she teasingly pulled her nightdress up above her thighs, slowly higher and higher. Soon fully exposed, she opened her legs wide, suggesting she was ready for her punishment in the most provocative way possible.

Forgetting my limitations for a moment, I grinned like a Cheshire cat. I was down to just my thin cotton boxer shorts, and the alluring sight and thoughts of me "punishing" Gigi had me on my way.

I climbed onto the bed and gave her a lingering kiss. Gigi responded by taking the back of my head and running her fingers through my hair. I loved the feeling of her soft, full lips against mine, embracing the tenderness of our kiss. Leaning on one elbow, I gently took hold of her neck, and we kissed passionately. As our mouths meshed, we began consuming each other. Our lips parted, the first sign of our actions transcending into something more sexual. So much lust and desire.

I was already thinking of the moment when her orgasm-induced convulsing body made me feel she was mine.

Nobody's MILF. Nobody else's to fuck.

My desire-induced breathlessness exposed my sexual yearning. "Georgina Blackwood, I am really going to punish you tonight… remember?"

Then she remarked mischievously, "Aah, so it sounds like you really want to fuck me?"

She had no difficulty reading my mood.

"Tell me, Babe. Tell me you want to *fuck* me," she said more insistently.

I had always thought it disrespectful to swear at all, let alone when talking about being intimate with someone you loved. But somehow this was different. I wanted to tell Gigi what she wanted to hear, and oh, God, I felt such a primal desire for her right then. I *did* want to fuck her until she was mine, all mine. A real conflict.

Desire and passion quickly won that conflict.

Gigi was soon fully sated from my most determined effort of pleasuring her yet, with just my mouth and hands.

I looked down at her as she lay there in blissful contentment. The only evidence of what had just happened were her breasts gently rising and falling with the continuance of her heavy breathing. The thought, *She's all mine*, gave me as much pleasure as she had just experienced.

God, I love this woman. How often have I thought that? I wondered, moving to lie down next to her.

Gigi put her arm across my chest and looked up at me. Do you remember when we first, you know, first made love, and I told you always to remember a simple—"

"Oh, I remember very well, Darling," I interjected. "You told me to always remember 'ladies first.' " I chuckled at what now seemed so naïve and immature.

Gigi smiled at my recollection of what was probably my first lesson. "Exactly, Darling, but you do more than that. Never mind ladies first, I love how at times you make me happy even if you don't finish yourself."

Taking a leaf out of her book, I decided to humour Gigi about the evening's activities with something Will had found in a men's magazine. "Darling, I read something that has helped me understand a few things about tonight. It was an article that explains how God created woman. Should I read it to you?"

She looked at me quizzically as I stretched over to get it from the bedside table. Looking bemused, she said, "Yes, my gorgeous, I'm all ears."

" 'From head to toe, she was perfection. Gorgeous. God clearly took his time when he made the woman. Especially the—aah. The vagina. He knew he had to make it that good. Work overtime if he needed to. It had to be perfection. Beautiful, enticing…and durable. I can just see God now, in heaven, sculpting it out of clay. 'Oh, they are going to love this. This is some of my best work yet.' "

We were both chuckling as I continued.

"I'll put this little nub just here. Easily accessible. Quick relief. It will need some lubrication. Ooh yes, that works. And let me add some scent. Something to bring out his wild, feral side. When he smells it, he will moan. I'll call it *feral moans*.' "

Gigi was chuckling as I struggled to maintain my own composure so that I could carry on reading.

" 'One last thing. Let me make a special spot, and I will put it way back here. They'll never find it. And if they do, she'll say my name. That will be my spot. We will call it the G-spot.' "

I didn't have to ask Gigi what she thought of it. Her laughter said it all. "That's hilarious, and it saves me a lot of tuition," she said, finally getting over her amusement.

I wondered when we would have an opportunity to be alone like this again. Was this the happiest I had ever been? The happiest I would ever be. I felt so complete with Gigi.

With the onset of sleep, I thought about Humphrey referring to her as a hot MILF. It still annoyed me even though she had assured me it was nothing to worry about. I didn't like it. I found it offhanded and demeaning. Yes, it recognised a more mature woman's sexiness, but I wanted her to know that she was obviously far more than just a MILF to me. She was my *everything*. I thought about her comments of me having a duel with Humphrey, and imagined sticking a sword into him, and I immediately felt better. Retribution indeed. Judging how I felt when I learnt what was going through his mind, that Georgina was a hot MILF, I could see how men in days gone by would have ended up duelling each other for the sake of a woman's honour. I smiled, thinking how ridiculous I was being. And what about Gigi's other comment? Was she really *my* woman? *Could* she be *my* woman?

As I began to drift off, I realised she too had been lying awake thinking. "How do we make it happen?" she asked me.

I knew she was referring to us being together always. I wrestled with this question, but there was no ready answer.

I thought also about Gigi asking, "Do you want to fuck me?" My demeanour and protruding erectness justified the question, but did it go deeper than that? Did she want this attitude and behaviour from me? I thought again about the "I have never been fucked like that before" statement and why it touched a nerve. I realised it was because I didn't like the thought of Gigi with another man, but I absolutely hated the thought that she may have previously participated in hot and steamy erotic sex with someone else. I wanted to believe she had only ever done this with me. My jealousy was clearly because of my age. Only youthful naivety would believe there was a chance a mid-forties lover had only participated in salacious sex with him.

I had also discovered it was not unusual for woman to climax over a longer period and more than once in close succession, unlike men, whose release was comparatively quick and sharp.

Birdsong and a ray of sunlight, streaming into the room through a partly open curtain, woke me early the next morning. It wasn't yet six o'clock, so there would be time for us to enjoy each other before the day started.

Gigi was lying on her side next to me, sound asleep, a hand across my belly, almost touching my semi morning glory. I began taking in the details of this gloriously sexual woman. Charlotte's appearance gave me an idea of how Gigi could've looked in her early twenties. No doubt, she had been a stunning young lady then, but I was now looking at the beautifully ripened version of what she had once been. I took in the outline of her nose, her lips and jawline. I looked at her neck. Her beautiful breasts, with large areolae, a result of her ripening process.

I wanted to touch her but resisted. My eyes enjoyed drinking in the form of her while she was still asleep. I loved her hands, and how they touched me. Everywhere and every time, especially my very first time. And so much had happened since those early days in Shrewsbury. I thought about when I had nibbled and sucked her toes—I could do that every day. Her belly had a softness that was difficult for me to resist, leading to my bushy runway. I wanted to put my nose in her crotch and get lost in her unique scent of her womanly sexuality.

But of all Gigi's enticements, the one that appealed to me the most was the one I could not see nor easily describe. It was something to do with her attitude, or was it her confidence? Perhaps it was her composure whilst behaving in the most licentious way possible. And was this just what happens when a woman blossoms into her middle-aged sexuality?

I knew what I wanted, and I wanted it now.

Soon after the last wave of my pleasure just as I felt the ending of Gigi's orgasmic contractions.

Was our harmonised sexual energy proof of us being perfectly compatible?

With her back to me, I spooned her close against my body, savouring the feeling, immersed in her scent, loving the softness of her skin.

After a while, she turned to me and, with a glint in her eye and the hint of a smile curling the ends of her full lips, said, "So you wanted to fuck me this morning, Baby, and I have finally managed to get you there…and even *say* it! And all I had to do was starve you for a night!" She chuckled.

That little giggle told me the mood she was in. Gigi wasn't finished there.

"And you fucked me so good, Babe," she said.

Regardless of her purposeful use of interesting grammar, I loved what I heard. Her choice of words and the manner she'd said it touched that sexual chord deep inside of me.

I couldn't help but think my behaviour had been inappropriate and unbecoming of a gentleman, rude…or was it? Somehow I wasn't embarrassed. How I had changed.

Then Gigi turned away and, in a sombre tone, said, "I never want to be without you. I never want to lose you."

I couldn't contemplate not having Georgina Blackwood in my life. I wanted to be her man. Could I? What about the RAF? What about the family I wanted someday? There was so much to think about.

Eventually, we got out of bed and showered together.

Once Gigi was dressed, she came over and kissed me, saying that she ought to leave ahead of me.

I agreed. "See you downstairs, Darling."

As I donned my jacket, I thought about her naturally salacious approach and how the love and trust I felt for her had brought me to the same juncture.

Gigi and Charlotte's call to have a health and beauty spa day was a wonderful way to end a most enjoyable time in the countryside, allowing the Blackwood ladies a chance to relax while being pampered.

I had heard of a spa where couples were given a little igloo-type room, covered each other with mineral mud, and then waited for it to dry before cleaning it off each other. I loved the thought of that and made a mental note to get the details for Gigi and me to pay them a visit.

The agenda for the guns was more straightforward. We would continue as we had the day before, the only difference being that we would be going to six distinct parts of the estate. Consistent with trying to save the best for last, the drives arranged for the second day were all quite exceptional. Once again, we did four in the morning, then had another particularly good lunch, albeit a little shorter than the day before because everyone was inclined to leave a little earlier.

The two afternoon drives were unparalleled, with the Throgmortons having placed a far greater number of pheasant at those two locations so that the beaters, responsible for flushing the game birds, were able to put up far more quarry, making sure everyone had a good final afternoon. This was no doubt a little marketing ploy to make sure all the participants came back for more the following season. It worked on me. I think I added no fewer than thirty-five birds to the bag and made a mental note to return next year. There was no thought of Gigi *not* being with me.

At the end of a day or weekend shoot, the participants are at liberty to take as many birds as they desire. This most often amounted to just one to three braces, two to six birds. At a good shoot weekend, if everyone did this, the estate owner would still be left with several hundred birds to send to the town's butchers for gratuitous distribution to the townsfolk.

We returned to the main house and with lots of hugs and kisses, said our goodbyes. I thanked Mr. and Mrs. Alistair Throgmorton, who made sure I would pass on their best wishes to my parents. I then said a cool goodbye to Humphrey, with Gigi making up for my off-handedness with a warm farewell embrace. *She really doesn't mind being called a MILF.*

There was no discussion about who would travel with whom for the drive back to Rockwell Manor. It was taken for granted that Gigi and I would once again travel together.

Once we were out of the gates of Bovey Castle, I looked at Gigi and patted my lap.

She knew exactly what I wanted and slipped off her shoes. After making sure she was still securely in her seat belt, she put her bare feet on my lap.

I had selected some music for the drive home, which I put into the CD changer. The first song, "(I've Had) The Time of My Life" from one of our favourite movies, *Dirty Dancing*, aptly described exactly how I felt as we drove along the winding roads. I listened to Gigi half singing and half humming along to the song, with her feet on my lap and a hand on my

My Rude Awakening

thigh. Every now and then, she gave my leg a little rub or a squeeze, but not because I was speeding. I was in no rush to get back to Rockwell Manor.

"(I've Had) The Time of My Life" – Bill Medley, Jennifer Warnes

YouTube   Spotify   Apple

I really hadn't ever felt like this before, and it had unquestionably been *the time of my life*. Consumed by the fantasy of the moment, I ignored the realities of our circumstances. Each verse seemed to describe us perfectly. Did I now have *someone to stand by me*? As the song played out, the one thing I felt certain of was that I would *never get enough of* Georgina Blackwood.

Being at Bovey Castle with Gigi brought with it new experiences, some of which I could have anticipated, and others not. Even though our relationship was very much under wraps, it felt quite normal with us doing what couples do. Dinners, walks and the like. I loved being out and about with her, but the jealousy I sometimes felt surprised me, and I couldn't do anything about it. Ordinarily I would have shown that Gigi was mine with a subtle arm around her shoulder or taking her hand. I didn't enjoy that I couldn't do that, which made matters worse.

The biggest revelation though, had been in the bedroom. If I'd thought being at *my home*, in *my world* in Berkshire had put a different complexion on Gigi's and my sexual relationship, then going to Devon, which was nobody's domain, had added a whole new dimension to our ever-evolving relationship. Far more than just stepping up a salacious gear or two.

I had read that peoples sex drive, in how much sex they wanted, differed quite significantly and that mismatched sex drives, or libidos, were quite often the cause of strain in relationships. It made me think again it may have been the reason for Gigi's failed marriage. I was quite certain she was at the top of the sex drive scale because she never missed an opportunity for us to have sex, it was never rushed, often adventurous and mostly involved us orgasming more than just once. Where did that place me on the sex drive scale, I wondered. We were perfectly aligned in that department. Or was my sex drive based on my age, with that young and dumb expression springing to mind? I also read that woman often reached their sexual peak in their middle-ages, whilst this was when men's sex drive could wane. Years later I was to learn the medical and psychological reasons for this from a Doctor of Psychology, Sexual Psychology and Urology with whom I had a romantic relationship. She had also been my psychotherapist in helping me overcome my PTSD. (See Dear Reader). Evidently, the most common cause of middle-aged men's sexual appetite decline was their natural reduction in testosterone. The reason female sexuality waxed into their middle ages and even beyond was a little more complex. In short, young women in their 20s would very often be more focused on meeting the right boy and creating the right impression rather than enjoying their sexuality. Then came the homemaking years, followed by children. Only once the children no longer needed mothering did the female in question start exploring her sexual parameters, now more confident in herself, not trying to impress anyone, and just enjoying her sexuality. This seemed to describe Gigi perfectly. Were these the reasons we were so perfectly aligned?

I was quite certain that my mother would struggle to reconcile me being in a sexual relationship with a woman that was twice my age, and *rude* would not even describe it. Gigi's and my unquestionably visceral and raw sex however, was another matter. At the very least it would be considered my mother's version of rude and unbecoming of a gentleman. I just couldn't see it that way. Was it really *rude*? And was my enthusiastic participation in some way me rebelling against my "don't be rude" upbringing? Either way, I wondered how I was going to break it to my parents that I was in a relationship with Gigi and how they would take it. Interestingly, as I look back now, I also wondered what my parents' views of Gigi would be if they had an inkling of what went on in the bedroom. A lady on my arm or the other? I had no other frame of reference, didn't know what anyone else was doing. Could they ever even imagine how Gigi was behind closed doors, beneath the sheets? The moment we were in company, she was reserved and correct and could best be described as "prim and proper."

Right then all I knew was that I was with a woman with an amazing, unashamed sexuality and I was the beneficiary! And…I was simply mad about her.

CHAPTER 25
GOODBYE BERKSHIRE

OUR DRIVE BACK home from Bovey Castle was understandably not as enjoyable as our trip there. Not having any idea when we would next have time alone like that again weighed heavily on both of us. Despite that, Gigi and I, enjoying our time together, soon started chatting happily about the past two days. We didn't speak about our sex; we didn't need to. We both understood perfectly well where we stood on that subject, completely in tune with the physical side of our relationship. The only time our conversation slowed was when a good song made Gigi spontaneously sing or hum along.

En route, we stopped at a petrol station, and she ran into the convenience store to get us water and a snack. A few fellows around my age were giving Gigi a second look, making me wonder if they played the same Air Force game we did, scoring girls on a scale of one to ten. No question, Gigi was at least a nine, and a ten for me. Judging by the looks on their faces, I could tell they had a similar view, but I guessed, annoyingly, that one of them would be lecherously thinking he would "give her one." That made me think of Humphrey Throgmorton and his MILF remark, and again I became irritated by it.

Back on the road, we played a game of guessing each other's likes or dislikes, naming something, and guessing if the other would like or dislike it, agree or disagree. Normally a game that one would play early on in their relationship, but in a strange way that is how it was for Gigi and me, with us having been out in the open for the first time.

We discovered we were aligned on most things and even managed to accurately guess things like favourite colour for an evening dress and so forth.

Of course, I couldn't help being mischievous as well, like posing the question to Gigi, "Formal dinner, panties or no panties?"

"That's for me to know and you to find out," she replied haughtily.

"Well, I already know, but I'm always happy to check to be sure," I said playfully.

We got back to Rockwell Manor in the early evening, with it really hitting home that we would no longer be alone. We were greeted warmly by my mum, but my dad was not yet back from his business trip to London. She assured me that he would not miss the Barrett Cup final the following day.

Being reminded of this, I began getting my head into the next day's game. I was anxious to go across to the stables and check that everything was in order with the horses, even though I didn't have to worry about it with Guy.

Gigi volunteered to come with me, not missing an opportunity for us to be alone. We walked across the field, clasping hands in the darkness until we got to the stables. As we got to the feed room, Gigi stopped and cheekily asked, "Hungry?" referring to my sexual appetite, of course, still not letting me forget the night in the stables.

We wandered around the barn as the horses munched and snorted away, and every now and then Gigi gave one a rub of its snout or a scratch under its chin. Making conversation as we walked, I pointed out one or another horse, how good it was, how many times it won Champion Pony, and perhaps where it came from, Australia, South Africa, and Argentina all being popular supply routes.

"I can see why you love coming here," Gigi said, taking my hand.

After spending a good three-quarters of an hour there, we then headed back to the main house, and I walked Gigi down to Winston Cottage. We were both a bit sullen, all too aware our trip was coming to an end.

The next day, we arrived in good time at Guards for our afternoon Barrett Cup final. Gigi and Charlotte also got there with plenty of time to spare. Our team could not have been more ready.

Because it was a cup final, it was played on Smith's Lawn, the Guards Polo Club main field. It was much like any other polo field except for one inimitable feature. A first-time visitor would perhaps be surprised to discover that a wooden structure about the size of a large house of two stories, each level with slightly oversized balconies, was in fact a building of some significant importance and impossible to duplicate. That it had been built overlooking the centre line of the field would potentially give an inkling of its importance. It was none other than the Royal Box. I knew our match was unlikely to attract the attention of any of the well-known royalty, let alone the attention of our queen, Elizabeth II, or our club's president, Prince Philip. That of course did not concern me one iota. As was the tradition, one of the local regiment bands would lead the two teams out onto the field to be introduced to whichever members of the Royal Family were in attendance and other dignitaries in the royal box, and then to the other guests seated in the stands on either side of this structure. There was always a good turnout, the social world loving the opportunity of being able to put their glitz and glamour on full display. Another reason was that it was a bloody good picnic spot in bucolic surroundings.

After nearly losing our semifinal match with my head being in the clouds for half the game, there were no such scares this time. The entire team was in top form, and so were our horses. I played as well as I'd ever done, with a bit of déjà vu from the previous week's second half, when I'd played with great gusto. The difference could only have been Gigi, she was mine, and possibly the sex.

We ran out comfortable winners with a nine-to-five score line.

When we came off the field, my father was the first to shake my hand warmly and congratulate me as if I had won the match all on my own. Even my mother seemed pleased with the result, and I was spared her normal reproach after a match, singling out various incidents over the six chukkas where I had put myself in harm's way. Gigi gave me a big hug and affectionate kisses on the cheeks. My mother and father could not have missed Gigi's warmth towards me but seemed completely unconcerned. Once again, that had me wondering whether they would accept my relationship with her.

Charlotte was hovering around Nic, I think making sure the polo groupies knew she was his girl. Jamie stood dutifully by, waiting for prize giving. Sandra Rawling was there too. Evidently she also had some inside knowledge about Nic and Charlotte, which may have been behind her catching me unawares and giving me a big kiss, knowing Charlotte and me were not an item. But it was right in front of Gigi.

"Wow, well done, Charles. Your team was brilliant. You can give me more of that anytime," she said.

I was not sure what it was she wanted more of. The expression on Gigi's face told me she would prefer Sandra Rawling keep all her desires entirely to herself.

As was customary, the teams lined up alongside each other for the presentation and speeches. Even though I was not the captain of our team, the trophy was handed to me. Once again, I was aware of the deference shown towards me, which always made me uncomfortable. Best pony was won by Chance, something that was becoming a regular occurrence.

With the formalities having been completed, we drifted over to the clubhouse. Sandra was able to irk Gigi once more when she put her hand on my arm and announced, "Can't wait to celebrate with you later," and she gave another peck on my cheek. It was reasonable for me to think that Sandra would never imagine there could be something between Gigi and me. Or was it? I was very aware of female intuition and how men underestimated it.

With the sun disappearing from the autumn sky, we walked into what was usually the club's main dining room and found the winners table. With none of us in a celebratory mood, we had decided to keep the evening brief, just to show our faces and have a drink before we would leave to go home for our last supper together at Rockwell Manor.

As the evening progressed, Gigi did a good job of steering me clear of Sandra Rawling. Sandra seemed to notice and duly kept her distance, until Gigi went to the lady's cloakroom. No sooner had she left than someone came up behind my chair, covered my eyes with their feminine hands, a pair of breasts pushing into the top of my back, and the immediately recognisable voice of Sandra Rawling asking, "Guess who?" With no effort to disguise her voice. This clearly wasn't intended to be a real guessing game.

"How could it be anyone other than darling Sandra?" I asked, meaning for it to sound sarcastic, but somehow it didn't.

No one seemed to notice except my parents, who found it amusing enough, oblivious of anything unusual, given that Sandra and I had practically grown up together. Wary of Gigi once again having to contend with more of Sandra, I was pleased she disengaged from her little flirtation before Gigi returned to our table.

Soon thereafter, we were all ready to leave. Driving in convoy, we arrived at Rockwell Manor together. After a quick shower, we assembled in the family dining room for dinner.

We had come to the end of our Rockwell Manor and Berkshire visit and were trying to enjoy the last night before we would leave after a light lunch the next day. Without exception, everyone was long-faced.

The mood lifted noticeably when Gigi came through to the family dining room with our entrée, which of course just had to be tagliolini and taleggio with truffle shavings. In fact, she'd asked Fabrizio to step aside, and she'd produced the dish entirely on her own.

Everybody was suitably impressed, especially my father, who loved pasta and knew when it was perfectly prepared. He was not afraid to voice his appreciation and, on this occasion, took Gigi's hand and proffered in his best Italian, "*Mille grazie*," and kissed her hand.

What a charmer, I thought.

The final seal of approval came from Fabrizio, who stepped into the dining room just to let everyone know that it was the best tagliolini with taleggio and truffle shavings he had ever tasted. I couldn't help but feel proud.

We finished our dinner, but sadly Gigi and I didn't spend our last night at Rockwell Manor together. It was appropriate for me to spend a quiet evening with my parents.

The next morning, no sooner had I reconciled I would be saying goodbye to Gigi than things changed.

Jamie was in his own car and said he would be heading straight back to RAF Shawbury. I agreed with him that it was a good idea, sounding like his instructor again. Charlotte had wanted to use Gigi's car to go to London to spend the night with a friend, before heading back to Shrewsbury, but had decided against it, not wanting to inconvenience her mother. Gigi had sensed an opportunity for us to be together for a night at her home and convinced her daughter to do the London excursion. I became a bit concerned that what Gigi was angling for would become obvious. There was a certain recklessness in her approach, but Charlotte agreed and the plans were set. Of course, I would just go via Shrewsbury on my way back to Shawbury. I sensed that it was not only me who had a tightening in the belly with the excitement of having stolen a little more time together.

Nobody was enjoying the fact that we were leaving, my mother especially. To say she was feeling pensive was an understatement. She was well aware I would be starting the next phase of my RAF instruction, the advanced-training segment, and then transferring to Joint Helicopter Command and, hopefully, the AH-64 Apache attack helicopter squadron. There was nothing that excited me more and nothing that excited my mother less.

We threw our last bits of luggage into the boots of our respective cars, mine into the tiny space in the front of my car. I took the water and snacks my mother had prepared for us and handed them around, feeling a little like my mother was still treating me as if I were at boarding school. In addition, there was a basket covered with a cloth, holding a few bottles of truffle oil and truffles, the riches from Gigi's hunt. I hoped we would be tasting those again soon, but back in Shrewsbury.

It was now time for the matter of goodbyes. The three Blackwoods seemed to have imagined it would be a drawn-out affair, but not in the Featherstone household. Because my mother was always emotional at these times, in contrast to her normal more stoic manner, our goodbyes were unusually brief, with my father always on hand, ready to put a comforting arm around my mother's shoulders. We bid our brief farewells to my mum and dad, with Gigi and Charlotte promising to return. I opened the car door for Gigi, and we drove off.

In contrast to the trip from Bovey Castle to home just two days before, we were both feeling quite sombre. We would sorely miss the fun times we'd had together this past fortnight, but also the warmth that had grown between the Blackwoods and Featherstones. Even though we had stolen a little more time together, we both knew that this journey was likely the beginning of the end of our being alone for some time.

I reached down and took hold of her hand. "We will work it out, my darling," I said.

"How did you know what I was thinking?" Gigi asked.

My Rude Awakening

"Because I'm feeling the same thing," I replied.

I wondered how we could make this happen. The RAF was a manageable obstacle, but our age difference and Gigi having a family—and my wanting one—were three overwhelming factors.

We were about ten minutes into our journey when, out of nowhere, Gigi asked me, "What does love mean to you, Darling?"

I thought about this for a while and then just said what came into my head. "It is when my heart and my mind are filled with only you all the time. When I cannot wait to see you. The feeling of not being able to get enough of you. When we make love, I want the moment to last forever. That is just the start of what love means to me," I concluded.

Gigi looked at me, and I could tell she liked part of what I said but wanted more. I understood because I wanted more too. It seemed I had purposefully left out all the things that were difficult for us. Permanence. Family. Growing old together.

Half keeping an eye on the road, I scratched around the side pocket of my car door, found the CD I was looking for, and put it into the changer.

"I Want to Know What Love Is" – Foreigner

YouTube	Spotify	Apple

I knew Gigi had already read between the lines of my choosing this song. All I wanted was her, and the thought of not having her weighed heavily on me. She had made me feel what love is, and I was desperate not to let that go. I had found love, but would time provide a way for me to keep it?

Gigi listened for a while and then, taking her lead from the song, said, "And I want to show you, my baby. Will you let me do this into the future?"

I did not answer but looked intently ahead, deep in thought, so aware how our circumstances made that such a difficult question to answer.

The more Gigi and I touched on having something more permanent, the more it made us realise how difficult and potentially unrealistic that would be. The silence that endured for the next several minutes only confirmed it.

I brought Gigi's hand up to my lips and kissed first her knuckles and then across her fingers. "You do realise that when we get home, we will be alone. I don't want us leaving each other feeling like this. I will wait until the evening and call Jamie to give him some excuse to stay the night. What do you think, Darling?" I asked Gigi.

She looked at me in a measured way and replied, "I wasn't sure which one of us was going to suggest it first. I didn't, because I don't want to impose on what is going to be an especially important new phase in your RAF career. And just for the record, even if it was an imposition, I was about to do it anyway." She squeezed my hand.

As we approached Shrewsbury, our moods lifted slightly. We arrived at what felt like home, and minutes later, were walking through the front door with no second thoughts and no need for Celine Dion to tell us to "think twice."

"Why don't you make yourself comfortable, and I'll unload the luggage?" I suggested.

Her reply was, "I love you."

I smiled and took that as a yes.

With two large suitcases in each hand, I heard Gigi call out for me to put all the luggage in her bedroom. Would this be the first time I would be sleeping in Gigi's room? Only once I was in her large boudoir—the only way to describe it—did I realise how little I knew about it. Satin cream window drapes with a light pink satin border. A lot of other whites—cushions, bedspread, headboard and bedroom furniture. It was so feminine and so serene. I liked it. Strange I knew so little about her bedroom. Then again, none of my friends had been into my parents' bedroom.

Once I had brought the bags in, I changed into a pair of shorts, a T-shirt, and sandals, and then poured us a drink, knowing she enjoyed Campari and tonic water.

Having slipped into a flowing midcalf white cotton dress, Hermès slider sandals, and, I was quite certain, nothing else, Gigi joined me in the living room. It was the type of dress that I had often seen her in before, and as before, it made her look as delectable as ever.

I instinctively walked up to her, put my arms around her waist and shoulders and rocking her from side to side said, "Welcome home, Darling."

"Welcome home, my beautiful gorgeous," was her reply.

I had long given up telling her, "Only through your eyes, my darling."

We planted our mouths firmly against each other's in a long, gentle embrace, confirming I was home, since that was where my heart was, as the cliché went.

Gigi led me by the hand into the kitchen, where she gave me instructions on making a light Mediterranean dinner we would prepare together. Each time she took something out of the fridge or pantry, she would have a taste and then let me have some as well, telling me what I was tasting and getting my approval. Sourdough bread, French butter, prosciutto, a variety of cheeses—goat milk, Stilton, and Brie—fig preserves, and then a little bowl of what looked like infant food.

"That's hummus, Darling, chickpeas that I've mixed in with garlic, lemon juice, olive oil, and a sprinkling of cayenne pepper." She put a finger into the hummus, popped it in my mouth, then licked off the little bit that I had left behind.

"Nice," I said.

"Oh yes, and olives from Kalamata. Do you see how big and succulent they are?" She bit one in half and then popped the remainder in my mouth.

I knew a little bit about cuisine, but I did not know my way around the kitchen, nor did I have the foggiest notion how to prepare anything. I was enjoying my lesson and the way Gigi sampled the different elements with me.

In no time, a delicious dinner was prepared. Gigi put on some music, and while she sipped on her Campari and tonic, we ate our tapas with our fingers, her delighting in feeding me. I thought about enjoying every little moment, knowing full well that in the coming days, I would think back on this time and wish I were here.

I brought her hand up to my mouth and gave her fingers a loving kiss.

"A penny for your thoughts, Darling," she asked.

"I love you," I replied, taking a leaf out of her book from earlier.

An unfamiliar song by Paul McCrane from the musical *Fame* started playing. I took Gigi by the hand and beckoned her to join me in the open part of her annex dining area.

Edward Charles Featherstone

"Is it Okay if I Call You Mine – Paul McCrane"

| YouTube | Spotify | Apple |

As the words "Is it okay if I call you mine," sounded, she nodded, and when he sang on with "just for a time," Gigi put her lips to my ear and whispered, "Always." We gently swayed, holding each other warmly, looking into each other's eyes, which confirmed what we were both feeling. I wanted to call Gigi mine, always.

With the song playing out, she took me by the hand and led me through to her bedroom. The gurgling sound of water jets, muffled by the overflowing bubbles of her spa bath, filtered through from the bathroom. Through the doorway I could see the scented candles and what must have been fresh rose petals. How and when had Gigi found time to do all of this? She switched off the lights, and in just the flickering candlelight, we undressed each other.

We sat together in the bath, legs interlocked, soaping each other, but in truth, mostly savouring the feel of our bodies against each other while consciously avoiding our private parts. We followed each other's lead as we progressed through this bath-time journey of exploration, enjoying the unusual feeling of the soft, soapy water lubricating our touch, and the jets bubbling and vibrating around us.

I ran my hands up and down her body, then inside of her leg, close to her vagina, but I was careful not to touch any of her most delicate areas. With the feel of her hands doing the same to me, getting close but not crossing the line, I could no longer contain myself in this little game of touch and feel we had spontaneously created.

Breaking the rules, I gently caressed Gigi's breasts, running my fingers across her nipples, sometimes softly pinching them. Loving what we were doing, our breaths became shorter as desire welled up inside us. I moved my hands down the sides of her waist, then to the crease of her hips and her thighs. Very soon I was exploring the strip of bushy growth with my fingertips. Gigi took hold of my member as we looked intently into each other's eyes. Our faces almost touching, our mouths met, hungry for our kisses. The eroticism of what we were doing had me fully captivated.

I stood up and half lifted, half beckoned her to do the same. We climbed out of the bath and dried each other off. Gigi, ever mischievous, hung a bath towel over my rigid member as if it were a bathroom hook, making us both giggle.

"That does it," I said, and I picked her up and carried her to the bedroom.

Notwithstanding our heightened lustfulness and passion, what ensued was drawn-out, loving sex that went long into the night.

I had a feeling there would be many aspects of these last few times together that I would never forget before I would be posted into the theatre of war. An example of which was something Gigi said to me after our sex that evening.

"Oh, Lieutenant, not to put too fine a point on it, I just want to say something…and that is…" Gigi very purposefully drew it out.

"I fucking love you. And…I love fucking you."

Oh, God. The things she says!

Then it struck me. My note from a couple of days earlier…

IFLY

ILFY

Her comment stirred feelings deep inside me. I loved the honest, no-nonsense expression of her feelings. Gigi saying those words then was also her doing her best to make light of our imminent separation. Any soppiness would very quickly turn our moods into sombre disquiet, which she was determined to avoid.

As I drifted off to sleep, I reflected on the changes in me. It was as if now that Gigi and Charlotte had been to Rockwell Manor, I felt more comfortable in Gigi's home. I realised I had taken a dominant role in everything this evening, except in the kitchen.

The other thing that crossed my mind was that I hadn't phoned Jamie just to let him know I wouldn't be coming to the base that night. *C'est la vie,* I thought, and I drifted off with Gigi already asleep in my arms.

Quite typically, I woke up before her, loving how she cuddled herself into me. It wouldn't be long, and we would be leaving each other. Once again, I found myself thinking how much I was going to miss her in the coming weeks—her presence, her scent, her touch, and of course, our sex. I often watched her when she slept, consuming her beauty. Whenever I was not with her, I would be lost in my thoughts of us being together. If it were not for my intense schedule, my missing her would have been intolerable.

As she stirred, I held her tighter in my arms. Her serene face of just a few moments ago, when she had been deep in sleep, now held a deep shadow of realisation, waking up knowing we would soon be saying goodbye. We hardly spoke, and when we did it was in hushed tones. The imminence of us leaving each other hung over us like a pall.

With Jamie and I starting the most demanding phase of our RAF flight training syllabus, followed by falling under the umbrella of Joint Helicopter Command and the inevitable postings into the field, there was a lot on our minds. My RAF future of what I would be doing was clear. What was not clear was where that would leave Gigi and me. It was easier not to speak about it. Deep down we both knew it, we both felt it, and we both hated it.

We made love with a heightened intensity, holding our bodies as close as we could to each other, trying to get as much of our skin to touch as we could. There was not a sound between us, yet it did not deter the same electrical energy we always had, bringing us to orgasm together.

We remained coupled, not wanting this complete closeness to end. When eventually it did, it was with audible sighs and little shudders of reluctance.

We showered together, soaping each other between snatching every moment we could to hold each other.

I got dressed in my Air Force Number Twos, with Gigi slipping into her dress from yesterday. Even though she had not bothered with either her bra or panties, there were none of the salacious feelings that normally came over me. I was sad. All I saw was my beautiful Gigi, who I was about to say goodbye to, uncertain of what the future held for us.

She made a breakfast of sourdough bread, cheese, preserves, and prosciutto, all from last night, and then a couple of soft-boiled eggs and a cappuccino for me. As nice as it was, I had difficulty mustering up an appetite. She did not eat at all and just sipped on a cup of herbal tea.

"When will we see each other?" she asked.

I paused with the weight of my next words. "I don't know, Darling. I don't know what the programme looks like or what happens after that," I said honestly, holding both her hands. "If only… If only…"

"If only what, Darling?" was Gigi's whispered response.

I didn't answer, because in truth I didn't know. We both had so much to say, but there was no way to say it.

If only we had spoken more last night.

We sat in silence for a while longer. Leaning across the table, I took her cheeks in my hands, our mouths came together, and we sat motionless, clinging to the overwhelming love we felt for each other.

Eventually I simply said, "I have to go, my darling," and with that, I slowly got up from the table and collected my bag.

As I turned to her to say my last goodbye, she flung her arms around me, her head on my chest. I felt her quiver, and I squeezed her a little tighter, careful not to let out a shudder of my own grief.

I held Gigi, clutching her close to me, and then gave her a last kiss, loving and passionate but void of anything sexual. "I love you," I whispered softly.

I turned around and went straight to my car, not daring to look back. I knew she would be shedding a tear, and I did not want that to start mine.

Once out of the gate, I searched through my Walkman and found the song I hoped would comfort me as I headed back to base.

"Don't Cry" – Guns n' Roses

YouTube   Spotify   Apple

Just the opening bars had me struggling to contain my emotions. I couldn't bear her crying, but what could I do? I knew very well what she was feeling inside. I felt it too.

Don't you cry tonight because there is a heaven above us, my darling. But please just give us a whisper or just a sigh.

I would never stop loving her and would never forget *the times we had.*

CHAPTER 26
ADVANCED TRAINING

MY DRIVE BACK to RAF Shawbury was filled with anguish. I hated not knowing how often, or even when, Gigi and I would be seeing each other again. I would just have to be content with our nightly phone call for now.

I was sure most relationships that involved servicemembers experienced complications from not seeing each other, but of course, the age difference—or more specifically, my wanting my own family—added to our difficulties. Even though it seemed impossible that we would remain in each other's lives, I wasn't nearly ready to give up and just let it happen. Regardless of my determination for us to stay together, I was already feeling the dreadful possibility of losing Gigi, knowing it was not my decision alone.

It was as if our two-week pass in Berkshire had been the most amazing fantasy honeymoon followed by a harsh jolt back to reality. On the flip side, I felt twinges of excitement as I got closer to RAF Shawbury. There were exciting times ahead.

I sped into the base and, looking at the clock in my car, I knew everyone would still be at breakfast. That's where I would find Jamie and probably face a few questions.

I walked into the officers' mess and saw him sitting at our usual table. As I went over, I half expected a barrage of questions about not getting back to base the previous night.

"I guess you stayed at home last night and had a decent dinner. Why rush back?" was Jamie's simple reconciliation.

Well, at least I didn't have to dance around that one, I thought.

"We must get back there soon," Jamie suggested. "There are a few things I need to pick up before things really heat up here. And, bud, you are still good with helping me on the flying and things?"

"No question, old chap. It helps me too," I said honestly.

"Thank you, chum. I really appreciate it," Jamie replied gratefully.

My mood lifted at the thought that I might soon be back in Shrewsbury, even if it did not change our inevitable destiny.

Over the next few weeks, I spent a lot of time with Jamie, and as I had told him, it was also good for me in equal measure. At the end of this fortnight, we had our most important ranking assessment. Now that we were at the business end of our training, the instructors made sure we knew exactly where we stood on the ladder, thereby creating a lot of competition between us. That did not hold true for Jamie, Will, and me. Our friendship and support of each other came ahead of the ladder system. This subtle change of approach was the first time the reality of the grouping system struck home. Three of the original eight Group A pilots were dropped down to Group B, and in turn, three Group B pilots moved up. Jamie and Will were unaffected, though I could see it caused Jamie quite some consternation. Once someone from Group B had been moved up, they would be determined to stay there. It was a fight to hold onto our Group A positions, creating a lot of competition. Whereas previously we had all been together, almost "against the system" so as not to be ejected, we were now firmly up against each other. Was this how the RAF made sure they were getting the best possible combat pilots?

After just a few more weeks of training and many hours of working with Jamie, we completed our first big formal evaluations and were both still in Group A. Once we had finished this appraisal, it was time to move on to more advanced training.

All sixteen of us, comprising all of Groups A and B, had been summoned to the Ops Room for a briefing. This was an unscheduled examination. And a few of the other instructors had come along to watch the morning's activities. As I scanned the faces in the room, it was obvious who was feeling confident and who was not. Jamie was looking decidedly fidgety.

"Right, chaps, less than six weeks before streaming assessments. Time to go dancing," said Captain Swales, enjoying himself.

My Rude Awakening

We looked at each other with slightly bemused expressions.

"The first move is the swirling line dance, and the next will be the pirouette."

We were lost. Dancing? I saw the bemusement turn to concern—it had to involve a helicopter, and it had to be complicated…and testing. Why else would there be a room full of instructors? Whatever Captain Swales was talking about had to be serious.

"So, this is how it goes," said Captain Swales. "For the swirling line dance, you will fly a thousand yards down the centre of the runway at twenty knots, maintaining twelve feet AGL in ground effect."

This meant the helicopter would use the ground cushion created beneath its blades and be airborne just several feet above the ground, not technically flying, per se, but doing hovering exercises.

Can't be that simple, I thought.

"In the process, you will do recurring 360-degree rotations."

Okay…not that simple!

"You will be judged on maintaining height and speed, remaining on the runway centre line, your fluidity of motion and, most importantly, the number of 360-degree rotations you complete. You will be given one practise run and then it's a go."

This was the crux of it. This "simple" exercise tested our control and fluidity because we were having to combine all three in the ever-changing parameters as we synchronised our movements in perfect, coordinated harmony and "swirled" down the runway.

Fly down the centre line of the runway whilst your helicopter is spinning. At twenty knots! How will the instructor know our speed? No sooner had I asked myself the question than I had the answer. Stopwatch.

I completely got it, and I could not wait. I had quickly worked out the best way to manage the speed element. *20 knots = 33.75 feet per second.* I needed to fly the thousand yards in one minute and thirty seconds, or ninety seconds, and that would give me my twenty knots. That was easy enough, without even trying to look at the airspeed indicator, which would be rubbish anyway, because of the perpetual change in direction of the helicopter. That alone would catch out most of this bunch. I also sensed I would have to watch the engine parameters, as I did not want to stress

297

or over temp the jet turbines. Doing so would not go down well on my assessment results.

Once I saw the exercise clearly, my excitement surged. I looked at Jamie, who was anything but excited. "Don't go first," I said out of the corner of my mouth. "You will be fine."

"Featherstone, no coaching now. This is an individual assessment," came Captain Swales's sharp rebuke. Then he asked, "Who's first?"

My hand shot up. I did not need to be so enthusiastic, because as it turned out there wasn't anyone else that wanted that dubious honour.

I got into the Bell Griffin, started up the two jet turbines without the need of the checklist, and within minutes was lifting off into a hover to position myself at the designated start point on the runway. As I leant the helicopter forward while applying power with my collective and making small adjustments on the pedals because of the change in torque effect, I got a reference for the halfway mark, which was the windsock. I would need to be there at forty-five seconds. I started the stopwatch of the digital chronometer and began my exercise.

I reached my midway marker in forty-three seconds, a tad too fast. Just then, I felt the tail begin to whip around. The fortuitously chosen windsock billowed, indicating a gusting wind. I had completed seven 360-degree rotations with perfect height and symmetry, always keeping the runway aligned with the middle of the helicopter. *Great*, I thought. I slowed the forward speed very slightly to get a few more rotations.

I got to the end of my practise run in eighty-eight seconds, with fifteen completed 360s. I was happy with that and knew I could improve on it.

Now for the one that counted. I checked my most important instrument, the chronometer, the humble watch, and began. It went perfectly. I arrived at the end of the thousand-yard mark in ninety-one seconds, with eighteen completed 360s.

Evidently one of the other instructors shared his opinion of my results. Jamie told me later that after I had completed my test, Captain Piper turned to one of the other instructors and said, "Fuck, and that's his first time. This student could embarrass us."

I knew I had flown well, and his crude remark confirmed it. More and more I was feeling that the helicopter was not something I was piloting,

My Rude Awakening

but rather that it was an extension of me. Yes, something like a dance partner, and as we got to know each other, so our ability to confound others increased.

Some of the officers could be heard using profanities every now and then. *So much for being an officer and a gentleman,* I thought. A limited vocabulary, my mother would say. None of that applied to Gigi, I thought, smiling to myself.

The next chap to fly, Terence Preston, had not worked out how to manage his speed and was just guessing. I waited for the instructors to watch the next exercise, and when they were fully focused on that effort, I took Jamie aside and gave him the important pointers.

"Jamie, listen carefully. Set up to do your 360-degree rotations in an anticlockwise direction. That way you will not run out of pedal for the tail rotor. The most important instrument is the clock."

He looked surprised.

I carried on, "Your airspeed indicator will not work because it requires a constant flow of air into the pitot tube to determine the helicopter's speed. Manage your speed by completing the exercise in ninety seconds. At the midway point, which is where the windsock is, you should be at forty-five seconds or as near as possible. That is the time to adjust for the second half, if you are behind or ahead. Do not worry too much about monitoring the engine. I found that because you are in ground effect and rotating counter-clockwise, you won't over torque or over temp the engines. Rather, use that time to check height and keep the runway centreline directly under you. The thing that is going to catch this lot out will be speed—don't make that mistake—and the wind."

I continued, "There is a gust coming from 270 degrees at around fifteen knots. It will catch you as you are facing rearward, downwind the runway, and coming around again to face forward. Be sharp on your pedals. Repeat what I said, Jamie."

We went through it one more time, and I was confident that he had the points. He just needed to bring his maximum coordination to the dance party. I finished his briefing just as Captain Swales looked at us and scowled.

Jamie's effort was absolutely fine. His speed was perfect, though he could have been a little more careful with height management and general fluidity. A bit stop-start you might say. The gust out of 270 degrees didn't catch him out; he was ready for it. Twelve rotations. I figured surely that was enough.

Once all sixteen pilots had finished the exercise, Captain Swales stood up to address us. "Since this was a preparation exercise, I am happy to give you some feedback," he said. "In terms of number of rotations in the required time, and direction and height management, Featherstone gets top spot, followed by Granger, White, Blackwood, Jameson…"

I didn't pay attention to the rest. The only thing on my mind was that Jamie and Will Granger had made it into the top eight. My two companions were doing fine. Jamie looked across at me and grinned broadly. Captain Swales saw Jamie's smile and frowned at me.

"Right, gentlemen, now for the next exercise," he said. "The pirouette is straightforward enough. You will see a clearly marked eight-foot-diameter circle on the grass apron, off the threshold of runway twenty-four. Whilst in the hover, you are to place the nose of your helicopter over the centre of this circle, then swing your tail around in a perfect 360-degree rotation. The only difference though, is that you must carry on doing this for one minute. We will count the number of rotations you complete, and if the nose of the helicopter, the pitot tube, leaves the area of the circle at any point during one of the rotations, that rotation does not count. There is an interesting twist to this exercise, gentlemen. We look forward to seeing if any of you get it. You can have one practise run of one minute, and then you must do your exercise. Featherstone, you will go last."

I gathered he didn't want me to pass on tips to Jamie. Theoretically, going lower down the pecking order was an advantage because one may pick up some tips from the pilots who go before. I guessed they didn't want the other pilots to see my effort either. A backhanded compliment if ever there was one.

I managed to give Jamie my take on it anyway. "Think of your helicopter as the second hand on a watch. The nose must be held over the centre point while you swing your tail around the dial. The trick is going to be increasing power so you can increase the rate of your rotation."

I explained to him that doing this would have a big torque effect on the helicopter, and he would need to compensate significantly with the tail-rotor pedals, keeping it all in balance with the cyclic. I understood now why I'd been instructed to go last. If I got it right, it would almost certainly give the others a good idea of how to do it, instead of them working it out for themselves.

I watched my good friend Will Granger go first. He took it slow and easy in the practise exercise, and the nose left the circle a few times, but he seemed to get it right when he did his final test. It looked as if he completed ten rotations and was in the middle of the eleventh when the clock ran out. Nothing to learn there. A few more went with nothing learnt there either. Then came Jamie's turn.

I noticed the wind had picked up, so as he walked past me, I said, "Wind, 270 degrees, gusting. It will be a factor. Don't forget, counterclockwise."

Jamie also completed ten full rotations but lost one because his nose went out of the circle. Not great, but not too bad either.

Then I watched Patrick White, the last one before me, who had come in third in the previous exercise. He did by far the best, completing thirteen rotations with one deduction.

I worked out that I could quite easily do one every four seconds for potentially fifteen total. Then I looked at the faces of the other instructors, finding them all totally unimpressed by what they had seen thus far. That spoke volumes. I had just learnt more from their expressions than from any of the candidates who had already flown. *These chaps are clearly way off the pace. Their efforts were rubbish.*

The thing I had noticed with Andrews was that his tail had been a lot higher off the ground. The aircraft had been at an angle of around 25 or even 30 degrees, nose down. I thought I would try something with my practise run and see how it went.

Then it was my turn and one of the instructors quipped, "Let's see what you've got, Featherstone."

I put my helmet on as I walked towards the helicopter, and as always, I made sure my gloves were secure and comfortable. In no time at all, I was in the hover, my nose over the eight-foot-diameter circle, and I was very aware of the excitement sitting in my gut. I was going to make my one-minute practise count.

I pulled a little bit of power on the collective while I fed in right pedal.

Edward Charles Featherstone

As my rotation began, keeping the nose over the centre point, I started pulling more power. The helicopter felt remarkably stable, so I continued, pulling even more power. My rate of rotation was considerable, and I realised that the nose was decidedly down, which meant the tail would be a long way off the ground, the helicopter was probably at an angle of more than 35 or even 40 degrees. Since it was my practise run, I carried on pulling even more power. My nose left the circle, but I didn't abort because I wanted to test how far I could carry on pulling power and feeding in right rudder, all the time accelerating my rate of rotation. I started reaching power and tail-rotor limits, with the aircraft tail spinning around a theoretically "fixed" nose, pointing down low to the ground, and the tail so elevated that the helicopter was at an angle of around 50 or even 55 degrees. I knew I had it. Now for my test.

I began my exercise with a very high-power setting, feeding in a lot of right rudder while focussing entirely on keeping my nose inside the circle. I did not even bother to count my rotations, but it felt like I was doing one every two-and-a-half or three seconds. I could hear the twin jet turbines screaming in my ear. I checked my engine parameters, finding them at the top of the green. I loved what I was doing.

I finished the exercise with twenty-two rotations completed and was certain I had worked out the "twist" to the exercise. The congratulations from all the instructors and the other chaps in Group A and Group B confirmed this.

Captain Piper walked up to me and said, "So you worked it out, Featherstone?"

"Yes, I think so, Captain," I replied.

"So…what was it then?"

"You shouldn't use finesse. I was pulling nearly full power and really attacking the exercise," was my reply.

Captain Piper just nodded his head, the faintest smile curling the corners of his mouth.

Captain Swales then stood up and said, "I don't need to tell you where you finished because you all know the number of 360-degree rotations you did. I can say though, overall, most of you did well, just a few less so." He paused, as if deciding whether he should elaborate.

Then he continued, "Pilots typically fly to the limit of their capability. Every now and then we come across a pilot who can fly to the limits of the *helicopter's* capability. I'm pleased to say that in this intake, we may just have one of those." He looked at me, as did some others in the group.

That evening after a refreshing shower, I went down to the Officers Rec Room to meet up with Jamie and Will. Jamie was typically late, and Will was sitting on his own in the corner, going over some notes. It was obvious he was not only a very competent pilot but a good gunner too. What was not obvious was what Will's aspirations were—where he would like to be posted and what he wanted out of his RAF career. It was often something that trainee pilots were cagey about, perhaps not wanting to show their hand in case they didn't get the posting of their choice. Will and I we're close enough for me to initiate the subject with him.

"Hi, Will, nicely flown today," I greeted him.

"And you…bloody hell, you were a standout," he replied.

Exactly what I didn't want to hear as it made my remark seem as if I were looking for a compliment. Shrugging it off, I carried on, "Well, you're a definite for Group A, so where would you like to be posted?"

Will did not immediately answer but gave me a measured look before saying quite simply, "Apaches, nothing else."

Speak about being a dark horse. Those three softly spoken words and the tone in which they were said shouted Will's determination of being posted to the top combat squadron.

We had been back at RAF Shawbury for over four weeks and hadn't yet been able to take a single night or weekend pass, but finally, unbeknown to me, that was about to change.

It was my university graduation ceremony and my mother had invited Gigi, Charlotte, and Jamie to attend with her and my father. I was secretly very pleased, never having been one to show how I felt about receiving any accolade, but especially because Gigi could be involved in something that had been part of my life for as long as she had known me.

I imagined the graduation ceremony was much like any other. Once the formalities were dispensed with, I rejoined our group when my mother caught me off-guard and remarked, "So you're following in my footsteps, Sunbeam."

I looked at her enquiringly before it struck me. After my mother had finished studying English Literature at university, she had studied computing and learnt to programme mainframe computers, something I had completely forgotten about when I was studying economics and computer science.

My graduation resulted in a weekend pass the following week. When I was out of earshot of everyone, I whispered to Gigi, "See you soon, Darling," with a little squeeze.

A week later, Jamie and I were heading to Shrewsbury for the weekend. As we drove down the driveway, I felt the familiar tightening in my stomach.

Gigi gave us warm, welcoming hugs and kisses, seemingly unperturbed if it appeared overly demonstrative. "It is so nice to have my boys home," she said. "I want to hear everything that has happened."

As we were taking our overnight bags out of the car, Charlotte arrived. Similarly warm greetings ensued. Now that they had all been to Rockwell Manor, more than ever I felt the closeness of our bonds. The Blackwood family was complete.

How am I going to keep it that way? I wondered. Somehow, I just had to. I didn't want to lose any of it.

We sat down early at the cosy annex dining table, already set for four. It felt so good to be home as we sipped wine and snacked on Suzie's warm homemade bread with balsamic vinegar and olive oil and two dips Gigi had prepared, one black olives and the other artichoke hearts, both having been turned into delicious, lumpy spreads.

As anxious as I was to have some time alone with Gigi, so too, I enjoyed the drawn-out evening, sitting around the table and enjoying the four of us being together again. It was perfect.

The only time I felt a little uneasy was when Jamie effused about how I had been helping him and how good it was looking for him staying in Group A.

"Charles has been brilliant. I have been cracking the assessment exercises, furiously looking at my notes he gives me just before I take my turn... brilliant, brilliant. I don't know where I would be without you, brother," he said, looking at me. "I'm going to stay in Group A, and we will be well placed to request transfer to Number 673 Squadron, Army Air Corps Apache training. Combat zone, here we come."

That is when I saw a dark cloud come over Gigi's face and knew we would speak about it later. Perhaps I could allay some of her fears.

Finally, everybody drifted off to their bedrooms, Gigi included, for the time being, anyway. And as always, she took alarm-clock duty.

As I slipped on my boxer shorts, I wondered how this evening's bedroom activities would play out. It had been over four weeks since we had last made love, and I was uncertain what mood Gigi would be in. I had seen many facets of her and wondered if tonight would be something I was familiar with or entirely different.

Amazing she can still do this to me, I marvelled.

Perhaps a little too soon after everyone had gone to bed, Gigi, still inclined to give a light tap on the door before entering, stepped into my room.

I stood up and put my arms around her. I could feel her gently but firmly pushing against me and the comforting warmth of her softness. I cupped her face in my hands, and she did likewise, in the most loving, caring embrace.

"I have been yearning for this moment…worried it wouldn't happen again," she said, her voice beginning to quiver.

There was nothing I could say as I looked intently into her eyes. I hadn't realised she was carrying *those* feelings. I kissed her first on the forehead, then her eyes, which she closed in anticipation as my lips gently brushed over her lids. I kissed her lips individually before our mouths met, opening just slightly. There was no lust. These were the kisses of two people holding and loving each other, savouring precious moments of a rare night together. It made me realise how much we cherished these occasions, not wanting to waste a moment but to just do the things that were most special to us. Tonight, there would be none of the Rockwell Manor and Throgmorton sexual madness.

Our lovemaking started in the usual way, with me lying between Gigi's legs, her face cupped in my hands as we kissed each other passionately. I intentionally tasted her mouth, taking in her natural scent, as our admiration of each other progressed. I never wanted to forget this and was relishing every sensation we were sharing.

Soon I felt a subtle increase in the intensity of her movements and her hands on my buttocks as her hips began to gyrate slightly, craving our coupling, joining us together at our most intimate parts. As if perfectly choreographed, she thrust onto me as I pushed into her, wanting to be fully consumed by her waiting womanhood.

"Aah, Darling. God, I have missed you," was all she said as we began the rhythmic pelvic dance that had become our lovemaking, a far cry from the first encounter.

We were hard and firm against each other, me reaching into Gigi's depths with a determined intensity. When we orgasmed, the climactic sensation reverberated through our united pelvises, and we remained coupled like that long after we had both crested.

I would have to endure prolonged periods of absence from her. Deep down, I knew that the coming months, if not weeks, would be defining times in the future of our relationship. With feelings of dread, I once again chased these thoughts from my mind.

I had assumed that because of how long we had been apart, this evening's lovemaking could have been more physical and lascivious. It wasn't. It was unlike anything before. I had never loved or wanted Gigi as much as I loved and wanted her then.

We lay in each other's arms long into the night, speaking in quiet tones about a myriad of different things but avoiding what the coming months in the RAF would mean for our relationship. Neither of us wanted to venture into the uncertainty and potentially heartbreaking consequences of this. But we didn't have a choice.

"My love," Gigi began in a soft, affectionate tone, "I've had a lot to think about these past weeks, and one thing I want to ask you is whether you feel Jamie is ready to join that elite RAF squadron."

I had known for some time that this was on Gigi's mind.

"The thing is, Jamie is just not like you, my darling. He doesn't have what seems to be your natural flying skill, reflexes, and the conciseness of thought you demonstrate in so many ways. I'm worried that he is just caught up in the romance of flying those machines with you. What are those helicopters, Apaches or something? I just don't think he's ready."

Gigi paused for a moment before carrying on. "Darling, he is only there because of how you have coached and pushed him," she said, now in a surprisingly brusque tone.

I could see her point but felt I should give her another perspective. "Gigi, Darling, I really believe Jamie is there because he *wants* to be there, and all I have done is help him achieve his goals. If he does get into the Apache squadron, it'll be entirely on his own merit, and his heart has been set on it," I said as gently as I could.

Gigi gave it a little thought and then replied, "Charles, my love, you would hate it if something happened to Jamie. Just imagine." She shuddered. "You are the only one who can change this."

A moment of silence followed with me absorbing what she had just said.

Gigi seemed to reluctantly accept that there was nothing she could do to stop Jamie continuing on his path. In a very sombre tone, she ended the conversation by saying, "Promise me that you will do whatever you can to protect him. Look after him as you would your own brother."

Gigi's last words on the matter not only made a very clear point but also hit home in a way that made me realise the gravity of what lay ahead. In an instant, I was feeling a weight of responsibility for Jamie.

The next morning, I woke up long before the bedside clock sounded its alarm. Almost immediately the previous night's discussion crept back into my consciousness.

Gigi's words would play on my mind for a long time into the future.

Shrugging those thoughts aside, I turned to Gigi and marvelled at how I was still so struck by her beauty, which had been the case for almost three years. As I watched her chest gently rising and falling with each breath of her peaceful slumber, I was acutely aware of my undeniable love for her. As always, I could not imagine how I would ever bring myself to leave her.

Sensing my gaze, Gigi stirred and looked at me with a face of contentment, her hand instinctively reaching over to hold my cheek. But once again her look of happiness evaporated as she gained full consciousness, realising that we would soon be parting company and not knowing how long our separation would last. Feelings that had become all too common for us lately.

Before those thoughts took hold of her mind, I leant over and placed one of my legs between hers. Taking her in my arms, I gently let her feel the weight of my body on hers and, with it the reality that here and now, we were still together.

"We have about an hour. Let's not waste it," I said suggestively, even if it exaggerated what I was really feeling.

We did not waste a moment but instead continued as we had left off the night before, with the intense passion that was an integral part of our relationship.

After a quiet breakfast and burdened by the weight of the critical stage Jamie and I next faced, all four of us decided to go for a walk around Shrewsbury. Our moods lifted with fresh air filling our lungs as we strolled down the treed lanes, into the town. Surrounded by the River Severn, Shrewsbury had lots of riverbank walks and trails that were lovely to explore. After a good coffee at the local barista, we went on to the fresh produce market to get a few things for Gigi and Suzi to prepare for our dinner.

That evening we all seemed to be making the most of a difficult situation. There was nothing like a scrumptious dinner in the Blackwood annex dining area, a few glasses of wine, a round of camembert cheese baked in pastry, and preserves for dessert, washed down with Madeira port, to make us all feel slightly better. The perfect prelude to a night of loving, lovemaking, and holding each other until the dawn, something Gigi and I relished and savoured.

The next day, our Sunday departure, was earlier than normal because of some flight training preparation that Jamie and I needed to do. We had all become so close that a level of affection between Gigi and me was not amiss, but of course within limits. We so wanted to just hold and kiss each other, share our thoughts and feelings, but we could not. Whilst I was quite sure Jamie and Charlotte had a very good idea of how close their mother and I were, neither Gigi nor I had any inclination to show them the extent of our feelings. It would have been inappropriate for us to behave with anything more than warmth and affection.

With the passage of time, the little flirtations I had been subjected to from Charlotte had first subsided and then disappeared altogether. When I reflected on this, I realised it wasn't only because we had all become much closer, but also because we had both matured and developed a mutual, loving respect. Our relationship now was almost as if I was Charlotte's "other brother," a term I detested and she used often.

We said our goodbyes, and as I kissed Gigi's cheek, I whispered in her ear, "Catch up later, Darling."

As we left, Gigi looked at me and then Jamie, and I couldn't help noticing a mixed look of love, but also worry, etched into her face. *I wish I could change that.*

We threw our bags into the boot of my car and headed back to the air base. Jamie's sombreness soon gave way to his real mood, which he'd not shown in front of his fretting mother. With Gigi feeling the loss of our leaving, it served no purpose for her to think her son was looking forward to what lay ahead.

Jamie was in particularly good spirits, feeling more confident about the upcoming streaming examinations, of which there would be a few. Captain Swales had recently reminded us that Group A pilots would be able to influence which squadron they would end up in, so I was pleased Jamie was feeling positive. I just hoped his confidence was not misplaced.

In truth though, the weight of what Gigi had said to me had persisted, and I was not entirely sure how I felt about Jamie ending up in the Apache Attack Helicopter Squadron. Even so, I realised there was no going back now, which only made me more determined to continue with our programme of me helping him. That was the best approach to ensure his safety.

The next eight weeks of our advanced training was as intense as anything we had done thus far. Testimony to that was that during this time we only managed three more trips to Shrewsbury. Coming to the end of this segment meant just one thing, an all-important final assessment.

Everyone was competing for the same thing. For this reason alone, the upcoming final examination was very intense. I would do whatever I could to ensure Jamie did not lose his place in Group A.

Am I just being selfish? played on my mind.

With the significant amount of time I'd put in with Jamie, and doing some revision with Will, our little group of three was well prepared. I was acutely aware of my benefit from coaching Jamie, because of how much more I concentrated on every aspect of my own flying and lectures, for when we went through it later.

Before we knew it, examination day had arrived!

It was a bit of an anticlimax because Jamie, Will and I had anticipated almost exactly what we would be doing. The only difference, perhaps, was that there was a significant focus on ground-proximity flying techniques, called "nap-of-the-earth." The most challenging part of this examination was how our lead instructors gave us difficult manoeuvres on the periphery of dead man's curve. I enjoyed being tested in this way, and it was crucial if we were going to be doing a lot of flying close to the ground.

An especially important aspect of helicopter flying is the dead man's curve, or more formally, the height-velocity profile. In the event of total engine failure, a helicopter either needs height or speed to land safely. Simply put, a pilot should stay out of the dead man's curve, meaning that if he is going slowly, he needs height, and vice versa. If he does not have altitude, he should have maximum practicable speed. Easier said than done when one is in a stealthy approach, flying close to the ground and searching for targets. That means potentially flying more slowly and, therefore, putting oneself and one's crew at significant risk in the event of losing an engine either through malfunction or having attracted enemy fire.

I secretly loved being put on the very edge of this dead man's curve—low and slow, one might say—knowing that I had to do a perfect autorotation to pull it off successfully.

As intense as the whole assessment was, it ended up being unusually informal. In the end, there were no changes to Group A. The overall duration of how long we had been in the top group probably weighed in favour of the instructors keeping the status quo. All three of us were thrilled but only expressing it to each other in little ways.

Jamie, Will and I formally submitted our request for transfer to No. 673 Squadron, Army Air Corps Apache training.

CHAPTER 27
FOX HUNT

FOLLOWING THIS MOST arduous stage of our training, we were given a four-day pass. I would have loved to go to Shrewsbury, but I knew Jamie would have none of it. To his mind, there was nothing going on in those parts. I put a call through to my father to see what was going on in Berkshire the coming weekend. My spirits lifted a bit when he told me that Berkshire Downs was staging a fox hunt and would I like him to book me a place.

"Make that two places please, Dad. Jamie can cut his teeth on another of our pastimes."

"Yes, I'm sure he would enjoy a little hunting," my dad replied with a little chuckle.

I knew from whence that came. Jamie was in for a surprise.

A good bit of southern England leisure, and we could have two nights at Rockwell Manor and two in Shrewsbury, I thought, feeling quite pleased with myself.

In the United Kingdom, the term *hunting* generally refers to hunting with hounds and has nothing to do with rifles or shotguns. This is rather confusing for foreigners, as in most other countries, hunting is a pastime involving the stalking and shooting of various game with the use of a firearm. There was no confusion about this for Jamie. Indeed, from playing so much polo with me in Berkshire and Surrey, he had already heard a lot about it.

Even though Gigi and I spoke every day, we missed not seeing each other and reminisced about the first couple years of our relationship, when Jamie and I would get a night or weekend pass nearly every week. I really needed to make the two nights with her materialise.

"Hey, Jamie, are you up for some hunting next weekend?" I blurted, sitting down in our usual spot in the officers' mess.

"Am I *up* for it?" he replied sarcastically. "You are damn right I'm up for it, Charles. I can't imagine anything I would rather do with our four days off."

"I thought we could go down to Rockwell Manor for the hunt and then spend a night or two in Shrewsbury," I shot back, hoping I had done a good enough job of sugar-coating our coming to his home with some time in Berkshire beforehand.

"Ah, okay, whatever," he replied, shrugging his shoulders as he looked away, acceding to my quid pro quo arrangements. Interestingly, Jamie did not press why I would want two days in Shrewsbury. Hopefully it was Charlotte he thought I was hoping to see or was that just wishful thinking? Right then I didn't want to take my mind down that complicated road.

"I will speak to Gigi and just make sure she is happy with it all," I suggested.

"Okay, and can we go past Shrewsbury on the way to your place? I need to pick up a few things," Jamie asked. Then, remembering something, he added, "Actually, I've been roped into a detail at the base. Please can you go to Mum's for me, and I will meet you there so we can then go to your home together."

I didn't voice what a good idea I thought that was.

A little while later, I phoned Gigi. "Hi, my darling. We have a four-day pass, having finished our advanced training. After a little negotiating with Jamie, I'm going to take him hunting in Berkshire for two nights and then we will head up to Shrewsbury for the remaining two nights…if you will have us," I said jokingly.

"Let me think. Not sure what I've got on. Can I call you back on that?" came Gigi's reply, almost catching me out.

Chuckling, I said, "Can't wait to see you, Darling. It's been too long. Oh yes, and we will be coming past you on our way to Berkshire, so Jamie can collect a few things first."

"I'm sure your friend needed some arm twisting to spend even a night at home," Gigi remarked, knowing Jamie would sooner have stayed at Rockwell Manor for the duration of the pass out. Then she added, "Hunting pheasant?" She had that wrong, not being familiar with the terminology. Hearing my hesitation, she remarked, "Oh, don't worry, you can tell me about it another time."

I'd been let off the hook, but for how long? I wasn't looking forward to coming clean about it. Gigi tolerated game-bird shooting on the condition that no felled bird would ever go to waste. She did not like anything gruesome, and because of that I knew she would not appreciate fox hunting with hounds. The same went for Charlotte. It suited me to not try to clear it up there and then. I would need to try and explain some of the aspects, perhaps how traditional it was, and hopefully it would soften her stance. That would take a little time, and I didn't want to do it just then. One thing I knew for certain was that my mother would not be impressed with my approach. I could almost hear her short reprimand telling me not to compromise my integrity. I immediately felt guilty for not being more honest with Gigi and for as long as I didn't say anything, it would sit uncomfortably with me.

The next day, I headed off to Shrewsbury, en route to Rockwell Manor. I had raced ahead so that Gigi and I could have a little time together before Jamie arrived. It had just gone four-thirty when I drove through the Blackwood gates. I calculated I was around thirty minutes ahead of Jamie and estimated I would get to his home at about five o'clock.

On arriving at the house, I let Gigi know that Jamie would only get to us on the top of the hour and suggested we could have a little "alone time."

She gave me a measured look, something I was becoming all too familiar with, and in an equally measured tone, she said. "Alone time, you say. What do you think we should do with our 'alone time,' Lieutenant?" It turned out to be a rhetorical question as Gigi had very quickly decided for herself how to spend the thirty minutes. Leading me by the tie, we went straight through to her bedroom where she kicked off her sandals as we entered the room. Clearly no time to waste, "I need you," was all she said. That was the extent of our foreplay. What her laconic statement didn't say, her actions did. Before I knew it, we were lying on the bed naked.

My response to her forthright approach was immediate. Still without saying a word, Gigi straddled my pelvis, sitting up with one hand on my chest while she held me vertically with the other and quite unapologetically impaled herself on my stiffness. Then with the same unapologetic expression, still sitting upright on me and watching me intently, knowing I understood her needs, she began rhythmically grinding herself against me. Just as I was wondering how she wanted me to participate, she told me, "Don't move."

Well, that answered that.

"I want to *feel* your fullness," she added, thinking that would explain her assertion. To her mind, she was selfishly fulfilling herself. Her determined expression and little moans, then rose in amplitude as she rode out her needs to their crested conclusion.

What Gigi thought was an act of selfishly satisfying herself resulted in me too being copiously fulfilled. I loved the feeling of being needed and *filling her*.

Mindful of the imminent arrival of Jamie, we quickly went through to Gigi's bathroom and wiped each other off with a warm face cloth and hurriedly got dressed.

I glanced at the clock. It was 4:52.

"That whole episode took about fourteen and a half minutes, Darling, and I have plenty of time to organise Jamie's stuff. I guess that's what you call a quickie," I said grinning broadly.

"You can do me like that anytime, Lieutenant," Gigi said mischievously.

"*Do* you?" I questioned. "And what was it you thought you were *doing*?" I asked, still grinning happily.

Another face of Gigi. *My Gigi.*

As we made our way through to the lounge area, so we heard the front door open.

"Hello, Mum. Hi, Charles darling," Charlotte called out as she breezed into the living area. Gigi and I looked at each other in mild horror.

Had Charlotte walked in just five minutes earlier, she may not have seen us but would have most certainly heard the unmistakeable sound of our actions.

In her time of need, Gigi had forgotten that Charlotte was home for the weekend. In addition, Jamie arrived just a few minutes later, way ahead of what I had calculated. Far be it I had plenty of time, it was more like in the nick of time.

My Rude Awakening

The drive to Berkshire was relaxing after having come through such a gruelling training programme and my *unexpected* surprise in Shrewsbury. We were both aware that, after the break, we would go under the wing of the Operational Conversion Unit (OCU). Converting onto the Apache was the first step to our seeing active combat service. This would almost certainly be in the Middle East, unless some other hotspot developed in some other part of the world, where UK or NATO forces were required. We were ecstatic at finally reaching this juncture of our RAF careers.

I already knew a great deal about the AH 64 Apache, the world's most advanced attack helicopter, all of which just drove my enthusiasm for flying it even more. Immediately recognisable for its tandem cockpit for a crew of two and on-display weapons and missile systems. The aircraft is powered by two jet engines with a combined output of almost 4,000 Shaft Horsepower. For the layman, *an unfathomable amount of power.* This enabled the aircraft to fly with a full weapons load at around 200 knots or 230 miles per hour, at an altitude up to 20,000 feet. It can carry 16 Hellfire missiles and 70 Hydra rockets. Other aspects were equally as advanced. Take, for example, the nose-mounted sensors for target-acquisition that also allow the Apache to perform at night and in adverse weather conditions. This helicopter also had significant systems redundancy, with its critical components duplicated. This allowed the aircraft to still fly if it lost any one of these systems, all designed to improve the Apache's combat survivability. Then there were other little niceties, such as a self-sealing fuel system. This meant if you took a bullet to a fuel cell, your helicopter wouldn't immediately start discharging fuel onto its jet engines, which could surely lead to an inferno of disastrous consequences. Yes, a very nice *little nicety.*

We arrived at my home to a warm greeting from my parents, them having become totally accustomed to Jamie and me being inseparable for such visits.

We both went up to our rooms for a quick shower before joining my parents for a wonderful Fabrizio dinner, a welcome contrast to the officer's mess at the base. We chatted for only a short while, knowing we had an early start. I did my best to keep the conversation clear of Air Force matters. The closer we got to being deployed in an operational zone, the darker the clouds over my mother became.

The polo horses were out for the offseason, being rested, and the stables were occupied by just a handful of hunter horses, four of which were for Jamie and me for the next day's hunt. Two each. I did not have the same affinity for our hunters as I did for our polo horses, so it was nothing more than a cursory glance that I gave them when I went across to the stables before going up to bed. *I should have brought Jamie,* was my idle thought.

When we arrived at the secret location the next morning, the first order of business was to check that our grooms had arrived safely and prepared our first horses for the day.

"Fucking hell," was Jamie's first response when he looked at Rambling Man, the hunter he would be using for the morning session.

Not used to Jamie swearing, I gave him a look that got a mumbled correction.

"Jeez, look at the size of that animal."

Jamie was familiar with the polo horses, typically standing over fifteen hands. Rambling Man stood a good eight inches taller at around seventeen hands, with the proportionate increase in size all round. I just chuckled, knowing that Rambling Man was not going to be his biggest challenge of the day. In fact, Jamie would come to find both his horses to be wonderfully comfortable armchair rides. It would be the crashing through hedges and going up and down embankments, through little creeks and such, that would be his real challenge. But I also knew he was going to love this.

I then helped Jamie orient himself and get used to the other hunter horse he would be riding, all the while giving him tips about hunting. Once again, I found myself behaving as his instructor.

Tapping himself on the helmet, he looked at me and asked, "How do I look, Squire?"

"Spiffy," was my honest reply.

Jamie did indeed look very smart in his beige riding breeches, black jacket, tweed tie, heavy white cotton shirt, black riding hat, polished black riding boots, and riding crop. Even though his ensemble had been assembled from probably all of our wardrobes, he definitely looked the part. Jamie looked at a bit of a loss, not unlike just before he embarked on some of his advanced helicopter training exercises, I thought with some amusement. Wide-eyed but still enjoying this new pursuit. He was especially tickled by the hunt masters in red jackets assembling all the riders in preparation for the start. Enthusiastic horsemen, excited horses, and keen hounds all milling around, blowing off steam, anxious to get going, listening for the sound of the hunt master's bugle that would signal the start of the hunt proceedings on some remote farmland, on a late autumn morning in the South West of England. That's where it would start, likely going through the woods at times. Where it would end up was anyone's guess. I had to admit, I was excited as well.

With this being Jamie's first hunt ever, I had to be sure that he understood how it worked. He was already taking a big step-up in testing his horsemanship, because fox hunting involves a significant number of jumping obstacles through the English countryside.

What makes fox hunting such an exciting sport is that when the hounds pick up the scent of a fox, they immediately give chase. Given that the fox is fleeing from the hounds, there is no telling where it will go to try to escape from its adversary. The horsemen follow the hounds on whatever merry trail the fox takes them, be it through the woods, brush, hedges, or little creeks. This procession of a fox leading a pack of hounds, with the thunder of hooves from fifty or sixty following riders, made for an adrenaline rush like few others.

I had been hunting since about the age of sixteen or seventeen, and since then, had always made sure I would do at least one hunt every season. I enjoyed many aspects of it, especially riding a big hunter, striding and galloping through the countryside on a trail determined by a fleeing fox. But in that breath and as I got older, there were aspects that I enjoyed less and less.

Foxes may have been, and still are, vermin that cause farmers endless problems, but was it necessary to be so savage in the pursuit and killing of them? Of course not. It was sport. A *blood* sport written into the annals of our family's and British history. Was that a good enough reason for it to continue? Methinks not.

A good day's hunting would involve a morning session, the occasional break for a little sloe gin, a good lunch, and then a change of steed for the afternoon's hunt session. For all intents and purposes, it would continue in a similar fashion to the morning session, just over another part of the countryside.

Our day's hunting did not deviate from this agenda. Jamie, and me, to be fair, were consuming the adrenaline rushes coming fast and furious and found ourselves trying to recover our wind as much out of exertion as from the breathlessness of our excitement. Jamie loved the pomp and ceremony. *So like his sister. So unlike his mother.* On more than one occasion, I heard him shouting "tallyho" along with some others to spur on the hounds when the fox was sighted. Something I had never done.

We finished the day's hunt in high spirits. Jamie said it was something he could happily get used to, making me promise to include him in one or two hunts every year.

I gave Jamie a history lesson on the origin of fox hunting. According to what I had been taught by the fox-hunting club, it had started in England centuries ago, when farmers were simply trying to perform pest control. Foxes were known to be nuisances, killing small livestock and chickens, so the farmers would hunt them down with hounds. Packs of hounds were first trained specifically to hunt foxes in the late seventeenth century, with many organised packs later hunting both fox and hare. What first started as a necessary duty to keep farms running smoothly soon became an admired game of the rich and noble, who added specific rules and regulations about attire and vocabulary and created the sport we have come to know.

Since fox hunting was popular with the nobility of England, who often happened to be military officers, this activity quickly became a favourite among the cavalries. Based on endurance and stamina, hunting was a wonderful way to keep cavalry horses in shape when they were not training for battle.

Hunting with hounds in the traditional manner became unlawful in Scotland in 2002 and in England and Wales in 2005, but at the time of writing, it continues in Northern Ireland. Drag hunting, during which a pack of hounds follows a scent laid by a human rather than a trail left by a fox, is an accepted alternate approach and has subsequently grown in popularity in Great Britain.

There was just one problem though. The hounds were not always clear on this new legislation and animal instinct being what it is, they quite often became sidetracked by the scent of a real fox. Unbeknownst to the following field of horsemen and women, they were unwittingly breaking the law, only discovering this when catching up to the hounds once they had already caught the fox. *Not our fault,* was the collective stance of the field, accusingly looking at the hounds.

To most, hunting laws have been changed for the better in Great Britain, which includes the method for shooting birds. In 2005 it became unlawful to shoot game birds while they are not in flight, an action which has long been considered unsporting.

Participants in the hunt that came from farther afield would stay at the nominated boutique hotel. However, even those that lived local to the event would often stay there the night after the day's activities, in anticipation of what was invariably a very festive, celebratory dinner. Revelling for no other reason, perhaps, than finishing the day in one piece—an achievement in itself after more than six hours of navigating slippery slopes, inclines and declines, ominously large hedge jumps, and generally tearing around the English countryside on horseback.

On this occasion, the private dinner had been arranged in one of the banquet rooms, but unlike the more formal dinner at the shoot, this was a casual and fun affair. A room of burgundy velvet furniture, hunt scenes adorning the walls, dimmed lighting accentuating the glow from an oversized log-burning fireplace. Typical English countryside decorating, not that anything in those parts was decorated. It was just *there*.

There was also the local brew and red wine flowing and a menu of stews and pies and desserts that could have come out of your grandmother's kitchen, like sticky toffee pudding and custard, bread-and-butter pudding, or trifle. We finished with an assortment of cheeses, sometimes baked pastry Camembert, preserves, ports, liqueurs, and cigars. Just like Shrewsbury and Rockwell Manor, except the cigars.

That made me think of Gigi. *Will she ever come on a hunt with me?* Probably not, even though she was a sufficiently competent horsewoman. Or was it just the excitement of the day and now this setting that was spurring these thoughts, imagining what would come naturally at the end of a day and a dinner like tonight's? If we didn't drink too much red wine… *"Don't dull your senses, my darling,"* she would've said. What was I feeling…

love or lust? Was there an overload of testosterone because of all the adrenaline rush?

I really did not enjoy the day after a hunt because it seemed so drawn out, and as a result, I wasted little time in leaving the next day.

It was still midmorning when we got home to Rockwell Manor, so in time for a light snack lunch, a restful afternoon, and a very welcome early night sans the rich food, the alcohol, and the stench of cigar smoke.

After a good night's rest, we had a healthy Rockwell breakfast, my mother making sure we didn't want to stay another night, and we were ready to head off to Shrewsbury. Our goodbye had to be especially brief since my mother, ever mindful of what was coming next in our RAF programme, would have difficulty holding her tears at bay. My father, as always, put his arm around her shoulders in support.

The drive up to Shrewsbury was quick and uneventful. I sped most of the way, without a word from Jamie. *Or a squeeze on the leg,* I thought, grinning to myself.

I could hardly contain my excitement at the thought of seeing Gigi again, but I made a conscious effort not to speak about her. Even though both Jamie and his sister had a good sense of how close we were, I just didn't know if they even imagined there was a romantic aspect to it all. And if they did, whether they really minded. I couldn't begin to think how I could broach the subject with either of them.

We finally drove through the Blackwood gates and were warmly greeted by Gigi. She was no longer concerned about Jamie's feelings if she did not hug him first, and quite often, she seemed to have both of us in her arms at once, as we would both kiss her on the cheek. Two similarly-aged men in her arms. One her son, the other her son's friend and her lover. I had long stopped thinking about how unconventional it all was.

Once we were indoors and had put our bags in our respective rooms, we sat down to an almost instant examination of what we had been doing. It transpired that Gigi had taken a bit of time to research hunting and did not like what she had discovered. She let me know her disdain in no uncertain terms.

"Charles, I can't believe you would take Jamie away on such a barbaric excursion," she said.

My Rude Awakening

After another few minutes of Jamie's and my trying to defend our position, the conversation finally came to an end with Gigi's last word on the matter. "And what do you do with the dead fox? Send the skin to the pelters?" she asked sarcastically.

Fortunately, it was a rhetorical question. I did not think it was a suitable time to tell her that once the hounds got hold of the fox, there would be nothing left. It would be surprising if you could find a square inch of pelt. Yes, on further reflection, fox hunting with hounds was a gruesome blood sport that did not fit well in modern society no matter how steeped it was in old English tradition and culture. I would make my apologies to Gigi and somehow make it up to her.

Later, when she came through to my room, I hoped the topic of hunting had been put to bed, but Gigi thwarted that idea. "I hope it has not been a monster I have had between my legs."

"Oh, I thought that's what you wanted," I replied, trying to lighten the conversation.

She did not seem ready to take up this banter, however. "Humph, all I know is that you have got a lot of apologising ahead of you, so you had better show me just how sorry you are."

I had been wrong, my Gigi had returned, I realised gleefully with a broad grin leaping onto my face.

That was also a cue to something slightly different in the bedroom that evening. She was feeling relaxed and content because we still had an entire day and night to go before we would be heading back to RAF Shawbury. I quickly chased that last thought out of my mind. I had started making a habit of doing that, chasing away thoughts that involved me leaving Gigi.

"Madame, what is it going to be this evening?" I asked, mimicking a French waiter taking an order, reading from the palm of my hand is if it were a menu. "I have for you an entrée *charnue* sans calories, a meaty yet calorie-free starter, as long as you don't take it too far, otherwise it will lose its calorie-free status," I said with a grin. "Or perhaps madame would prefer the '*crème des parties intimes.*' Cream of intimate parts. Something you are familiar with, Darling." I gave her a wink.

"*Non, non, je pensais à quelque chose de plus, de plus animal…. Ou tu ne sers que* ça *dans les* écuries?" was Gigi's reply.

"Oh no, Darling, you know very well my French is nonexistent except for a few carefully prepared words. Please translate."

"I just said that I was thinking something a little more, let's say, animal, but perhaps you only serve that in the stables?" Gigi said with a perfectly straight face.

Oh, God, not that again.

I didn't let that deter me. Instead, I used it as a cue and fiddled around with my Walkman until I found the track I was looking for. Making sure the volume was low, so as not to wake the rest of the house, the gyrating melody of "Physical" by Olivia Newton-John quietly drifted into the room. I started rhythmically undressing myself in time to the music.

Gigi leant back, making herself comfortable against the headboard to watch my little show.

My self-consciousness about dancing had evaporated, such was my comfort with Gigi now. As unlike me as it was, the appreciative albeit jovial looks I got from her were enough encouragement for me to continue, and quite soon I was somehow, quite expertly, removing each item of my clothing and flicking them over to her like some sort of seasoned strip pro. Her chuckle told me I had entertained her enough, but when I tried to stop, she started protesting loudly. It had me imagining Jamie knocking on the door to find out what the fuss was all about. That alone forced me to carry on, but it was really the way she seemed to be intently taking it all in that spurred me on further, with me trying to maintain my pouting expression and not break into a broad grin.

Before too long, I was down to my last item of clothing, my underpants, which I removed with a thrust and wiggle of my hips, then flicked them over to Gigi, who promptly pulled them over her head, making sure I heard her audible intake of air as she mockingly breathed in the scent of my undergarment. Ordinarily, I would have died of embarrassment, but tonight I just found myself giggling along with her.

That last little antic was too much for me, so I jumped onto the bed, my semi-erectness bouncing around with gay abandon, to recover my underwear. Gigi had other ideas.

Our sex that night wasn't exactly a repeat of what had happened in the feed room of the stables, but it was no less intense. Certainly quieter, though.

We continued like that long into the night, partly because we were free the next day, but more so because Jamie and Charlotte would probably only surface after nine or ten o'clock the next morning, such was their propensity to catch up on sleep.

The two nights and a day in Shrewsbury flew by. They were some of the most enjoyable moments I had experienced at the Blackwood residence since having first visited there with Jamie nearly three years before. Then it was once again time for us to leave. As brief as farewells were at Rockwell Manor, they were conversely drawn out at the Blackwoods'. I wasn't too sure which I disliked more.

After the customary hugs and kisses all around, I went over to Gigi for a last goodbye. As I kissed her on the cheek, she seemed to sense my anguish and then whispered into my ear, "Don't worry. We will see each other soon, Darling." This had me immediately concerned both Charlotte and Jamie overheard her. If they did, how would they read it? Romantic? Maternal? I just didn't know anymore.

I would miss these little warm-breath whispers in my ear.

We left Jamie's house hoping that we would soon be transferred to No. 673 Squadron, Army Air Corps Apache training, and shortly thereafter, be seconded to Joint Helicopter Command, with a hot posting to follow. Once we received our posting, there would be many months that Gigi and I would not see each other.

With the Blackwood residence receding behind us and my heart still in my mouth, I found myself fumbling around for a particular song on my Walkman, one that would lift my spirits and help me think about what lay ahead.

"Up Where We Belong" – Joe Cocker, Jennifer Warnes

| YouTube | Spotify | Apple |

These words had an eerie truth to them that did not give me any comfort. The road was almost certainly long, but I could not wait to begin the journey.

From the time we got into the car until we reached the end of the song, I hardly realised that Jamie was even with me. He had been sitting quietly, allowing me to deal with my feelings and not saying a word. He then gave me an affectionate pat on the shoulder, leaving his hand there for a moment. Not only was it a clear indication that he must've known the true nature of my relationship with his mother, but also that he understood and somehow accepted it.

"Thanks, Jamie. Thank you," was all I said.

The most unlikely thing was drawing Jamie and me closer and closer together. If ever I needed a friend, it was then. *Who better than my lover's flesh and blood?* I sighed openly and gave him a pat on the shoulder.

CHAPTER 28
PREPARING FOR COMBAT

THE NEXT FEW days were a whirlwind. The only thing that mattered was that Jamie, Will and I were transferred to the Operational Conversion Unit, OCU, Apache attack helicopters. We would first need to do a Conversion to Type, CTT, adapting our knowledge to the Apache AH-64. Then, because this versatile helicopter could operate in a wide range of operational war theatres, we would do a Conversion to Role, or CTR. This was a prelude to going into combat with this magnificent machine.

With just a few short months of training ahead, we were one step away from falling under Joint Helicopter Command and our first hot posting.

Our introduction to the Apache attack helicopter began with a short presentation, a lot of which I already knew, such was my interest in the helicopter. The part that stood out for me was the opening address of Lieutenant Colonel Berrycloth.

"Good morning, gentlemen. Welcome to Army Air Corps 673 Squadron," he said in a clear, crisp voice. The tone of his greeting matched his sharp facial features. "I hope none of you think you have come here to learn how to fly the Apache AH64," he said, his searching gaze scanning the room.

No one ventured a remark, taken off guard by what was contrary to all our expectations.

"You are here because you have already demonstrated that you know how to fly helicopters, and the Apache, whilst it may be the most advanced of them, is essentially no different. It's what they can do that really sets them apart." Again, he looked around the room before continuing.

"Yes, gentlemen, you're not here to learn how to fly this machine." He purposefully repeated himself in a very deliberate manner before saying, "You are here to learn how to *fight* this machine, the most formidable piece of aerial combat hardware ever developed," Lieutenant Colonel Berrycloth concluded, his steely blue eyes again taking in the faces before him.

My heart rate quickened. A moment of light-headedness. I couldn't wait.

Excited, we were led to a viewing deck to watch a flight demonstration of this extraordinary fighting machine. Studying it as it went through its paces, we couldn't help noticing the chain gun protruding ominously forward from under the nose. Rocket and missile pods on stubby winglets gave it a sinister, mechanical look that made the hair on my neck and arms stand on end. The Taliban called it the Mosquito, which was an apt description. The *coup de grâce* of the demonstration was watching the Apache flying inverted because of its rotor system that allowed it to perform loops and rolls.

When will I do that? I wanted it so badly.

This was the reason I was in the RAF, doing my own thing, on my own. Rockwell Manor and being a Featherstone was the furthest thing from my mind.

The Apache's tandem cockpits are organised so that the upper, rear position is the Pilot-in-Command station, with its array of flying controls and selectable video screens from which the pilot monitors all the helicopter systems, including weapons systems. One of the many distinguishing features of this helicopter is its Helmit Mounted Display, HMD, with an eyepiece positioned over the right eye, a bit like a small scope that shows flight and weapon systems information to help fly and fight the helicopter. This can also display imagery from the Pilot Night Vision System, allowing the helicopter to be flown at night and in all weathers. The Apache was formidable in the daytime, lethal at night. One of the other capabilities of the HMD is that the pilot or gunner can slave it to the helicopters 30mm chain gun. This meant wherever you looked, the chain gun, jutting out from under the nose of the helicopter, would point, following your gaze. *Menacing* was a good word to describe this capability.

Part of the Pilot-in-Command's duty is to back up and follow up on target assaults that the copilot-gunner has engaged.

The copilot-gunner (CPG) sits in the front cockpit, which is very

My Rude Awakening

similar to the rear Pilot-in-Command station, but with an emphasis on weapons and target acquisition. In his cockpit, he has the systems to locate targets, day and night, and fire the Apache's supremely advanced weaponry systems. The most formidable of the weapons is the Hellfire missile, each one essentially a miniature aircraft with its own guidance and propulsion system. It inflicts fearsome destruction, with a high-explosive warhead powerful enough to burn through some of the heaviest armour in existence, giving the enemy no place to hide. The CPG is also a fully qualified pilot, and he too has all the flight controls and can take over from the pilot at any time and fly the helicopter single-handedly. But his primary job is firing the helicopter weapon systems. Don't for a moment think that copilot, the first two letters of the initialism CPG, means he is any less qualified. Quite the contrary, as he is not only capable of being Pilot-in-Command but is also a very competent weapons specialist.

Ordinarily, I would share all that excited me with Gigi. But not this. It was just impossible for her to embrace it with me. I would still speak to her about it, and hopefully she would understand a little bit more. Understand what? I was not sure.

The Apache AH-64 Attack Helicopter.
Forward Copilot-Gunner and aft Pilot-in-Command cockpits, forward chain gun, side-rocket, and missile stations. A thing of beauty. There are no words.

Pilot-in-Command Cockpit.

Apache AH-64 Helmet-Mounted Display (HMD)
Instrument flying and using an eye monocle require reprogramming your brain to work in two compartments.
(Image used under licence from Shutterstock.com)

The Apache was designed and built to be effective in a wide and varied range of combat missions. All its essential systems are duplicated, which gives it great survivability, thereby giving the crew the confidence to take it into battle. The variety of weapon systems combined with the multiple choices of sights means that a crew can be inventive and tailor the way they fight the helicopter to the situation. It also has multiple radios, giving the crew the ability to monitor and talk on several separate radio nets at once. It can move around the battlespace quickly and stealthily, which gives it the advantage of being able to surprise the enemy.

Unlike jet fighters, helicopters are used in close-combat roles, near to the ground. In order to do this successfully and as safely as possible, it has a very different suite of equipment intended to keep the helicopter and crew safe in close ground proximity. This includes forward-looking infrared so that ground targets can be located at night and behind foliage during the day. It also has technology that enables the pilot to fly in the darkest locations with no external white light. Because the two systems work autonomously, the pilot can use his sensor to fly while the copilot-gunner works the target-acquisition systems to search for targets or to survey the route ahead.

Although it is primarily used as a weapons platform with a lethal array of munitions, it is also a great intelligence-finding asset. The multitude of sights and sensors allows the crew to gather a good deal of information on the battlefield and then relay this back to HQ over the secure radios. It is also used to escort more vulnerable support helicopters and prevent them from being targeted, like the big dual-rotor Chinook helicopters that carry the Medical Emergency Response Teams. This life-saving asset often picked up seriously wounded casualties from the battlefield while the firefight still went on around them, and it was our job to try to destroy attackers before our evac copters were targeted. The Chinooks were always a target for insurgents.

What the Apache does best though, is what it is designed to do. Whether it launches from a desert strip, the Arctic, or the deck of a ship, a squadron of Apaches can defeat whole brigades of armoured vehicles through selected targeting of the prized enemy assets. Its key role was to support ground forces with precision weapons when they are engaged by the enemy and pinned down. With radio communications from the ground forces, the

Apache is able to identify the enemy and single them out from the population and civilian areas before decisively engaging them.

Apaches normally work as a pair, referred to as a *flight*. During an engagement, one helicopter acts as the shooter and the other as the observer to look out wider for more targets. The observer also puts himself in a position to follow up on the first helicopter's assaults if necessary. If the squadron is fighting together, you may find two or more flights working in an engagement area to attack targets.

While the copilot-gunner is head down, looking in the sight for the enemy, the pilot is looking after the safety of the helicopter and often commanding the squadron. He is monitoring the systems and ensuring that all is in order, but more than that, he is watching for any nearby enemy trying to shoot them down.

Flying any helicopter means both hands and feet are doing different things at once. Your fingers also have to work independently as you speak on the radio on multiple channels and trim the helicopter flight inputs to create the most stable weapons launch platform, so your CPG can fire either your cannons, rockets, or missiles. Even your eyes have to learn how to work independently of each other. With the HMD monocle permanently over your right eye, your left eye is free to look outside the cockpit, saving valuable split seconds it would take you to look down at the instruments and then up again.

This small screen over your right iris can, at the flick of a button, display a dozen different instrument readings from around the cockpit. The slaving of your head position to the cannons means the CPG or pilot are only a couple of button presses away from firing the 30mm cannon or rockets. All he must do is pull the trigger to fire on a target.

In addition to everything else going on, we had to condition our bodies into doing things they had never done before. I remember explaining to a friend how, as an Apache helicopter pilot with an HMD, we had to somehow split our brains and our visual systems to be able to process two bits of information at once: aircraft controls and weapons systems. It was no wonder that we suffered daily headaches as we got used to this innovative approach to processing information.

Another of the Apache's many design features are its graphite-composite and titanium rotor-blade structure, which allows it to withstand brushes with trees and other minor obstacles when flying nap-of-the-earth at high speed. This is a mind-boggling concept for helicopter pilots, who normally do everything they can to protect their delicate rotor-blade systems. And of course, the helicopter was largely bulletproof. Very unusual.

The sensation of defying gravity and flying is one thing, but knowing you are going to war in a hugely capable machine gives you the confidence to take on anything.

The training on the Apache was extensive. It had to be. All the basic elements were the same as any other helicopter, but it is an attack helicopter designed to go and look for the fight, withdraw, and then look for the next one.

Lieutenant Colonel Berrycloth's view that the Apache was the single most lethal and effective piece of military hardware in the theatre of war was undeniable.

During my Air Force career, I flew many different helicopters, but undoubtedly Attack Helicopters were my passion. In addition to the Apache AH64, I flew the Westland Lynx AH7 and the Agusta A129 Mangusta. Although all three are amazing to fly and very manoeuvrable, nothing compares to being in an Apache. It is a battlefield helicopter in the truest sense, and the capability that it brings to a fight is quite phenomenal, unrivalled by any other combat helicopter.

I would not have given it up for the world, which wasn't something I could share with Gigi. I could not talk to her about any of this, and that fact coupled with the intensity of our training meant we missed the occasional evening telephone call, and I hated it.

I often thought back to the commitment I had made in helping Jamie. In doing my best to equip him in flying and fighting the helicopter to the limits of his ability, was the surest way for him to protect himself. He wasn't able to fly the Apache at the limits of *its* capability. Few pilots could do that. My sentiment never wavered, even though my own hands were full trying to absorb all the new information that was being imparted to us daily. This meant Jamie and I were spending a lot of time with each other, going through all we had learnt, me guiding him, and somehow I was beginning to think that Jamie would be okay. Though I couldn't forget Gigi's sage words. *"Jamie's just not like you."* The time with him gave me an even greater sense of closeness to Gigi, and I felt a level of comfort that I was doing my best at what she had hoped for—*protect him.*

There was something else. I couldn't immediately put my finger on it, but then one evening while I was trying to get to sleep, it dawned on me. Was this taught behaviour, in a way replicating what my mother had so painstakingly done with me? And something she too had learned from her governess, Mrs. Kearns, the teacher.

An element of my approach with Jamie could also be described as 'fatherly'? And was this because I was in a relationship with his mother. This weird thought stole thirty minutes of my sleep.

Over the next twelve to eighteen months, so much happened at such a frenetic pace that it is difficult to put a timeline to it. It was as if we got sucked along in one of the most advanced Air Force programmes of all, and hopefully we would come out of it as Apache combat pilots. I put this timeline against my relationship with Gigi, which by then was, unbelievably, going on five years. I checked it against my age, nearly twenty-five years old. For someone who was agile with maths, I was really struggling with this one. Where had the time gone?

We could have done so much more together, I thought remorsefully.

The one constant during this time was that Jamie and I were able to go out on night and weekend passes to Shrewsbury about every ten to fourteen days. Gigi and I were able to continue our relationship pretty much as before, though we knew it couldn't last like that forever. Each time we met, we became more aware that we would have to face an exceedingly difficult juncture that the Air Force, and indeed military life, generally put in the path of many young couples.

When we weren't at Shrewsbury, if I wasn't playing a round of golf with Will, you would often find us in the gym, making sure we were keeping fit.

During the early stages of our Air Force training, we were a lot more lighthearted about keeping fit, competing against our peers, generally having fun. Now that we were established in our squadrons, preparing for warfare, we did far more than the daily PT program. Knowing that being fit, ready, and poised could make all the difference between life and death when going into a combat zone gave an entirely different motivation for the extra hours we would spend in the gym or on the treadmill each week. We wouldn't easily admit it, but as much as we may have been looking forward to going into a combat zone, there was another element that crept into our psyche. Fear.

Along the way, Major Gifford reiterated what we had heard from time to time since beginning our RAF careers, that as Pilots and Copilot-Gunners, we would be better served by not having relationships back home. "You know, not being sure about what a girlfriend sitting at home is getting up to can be somewhat distracting and counterproductive," he sneered, as a few of the men chuckled at his insinuation.

Well, it was obvious who the single ones in the room were. For me, no amount of lightheartedness could lessen the weight that this brought on my emotions. This was the contemplation I had to face, and the effect of his words on me was undeniable.

When that briefing session was over, Jamie and I walked over to the officers' mess together. He put a hand over my shoulder and simply asked, "You okay, bud?"

I didn't say anything, giving only an unconvincing nod.

There were many things that continually brought Jamie and me closer together. Even the most unlikely of things, like this. This was confirmation that he knew his mother and I were close, but did he know in what way? Now a recurring question that I was still not yet inclined to explore with him.

Then, almost as if it had sneaked up on us, we got a night pass, our last before being posted. This time it had been more than three weeks since I had seen Gigi, both of us acutely aware that even these precious moments, now fewer and further apart, were a luxury we would soon lose altogether. I didn't even want to contemplate what that meant for our relationship. This time, I had no choice but to chase those thoughts from my mind with vehement determination before they swamped my emotions and then my actions.

Notwithstanding all the consternation about our relationship and its future, when I called Gigi to tell her I would be seeing her in three days, she was similarly elated. It seemed she also had the same ability to drive the inevitable outcome of our relationship from her mind.

Charlotte made a special effort to be there, realising it would be our farewell before our first operational tour of duty, which could mean up to a year before we would be home again. More than ever before, we were painfully aware of not knowing just how long we would be gone, which made it even more difficult for everyone. And that could well be how the next four or five years would play out, to the end of our RAF contracts.

We arrived at Shrewsbury and bundled out of the car, and the four of us stood in the driveway, warmly greeting each other.

A little while later when we sat down to supper, although it was much the same as any other delightful dinner at home, with wonderful cuisine prepared by Suzie with Gigi's oversight, it was also different. Glaringly different. When the conversation got onto our being posted in the operational area for a series of tours of duty, the change in our moods was unmistakable.

It was Gigi who first brought it up. "So do you know where you're going and for how long?" she asked, looking from me and then to Jamie.

"Not sure, Mum, and not stuff that we really talk about," was Jamie's mumbled reply.

I would, no doubt, be asked to explain in more detail later when we went to bed.

Not wanting to end the dinner on that sombre note, I cut everybody a wedge of brie cheese and gave them a good serving of port, then turned up the hi-fi system, which had just started playing the soundtracks from *Grease* and *Saturday Night Fever*. The mood immediately changed, and with the red wine, followed by the port, we all became more relaxed and indeed let our guards down, if not our hair, as everyone got up and started dancing.

"You're the One That I Want" – John Travolta, Olivia Newton-John

YouTube Spotify Apple

Having recently seen the movie *Grease*, we were all quite expert at these particular dance moves, though none more so than the Blackwoods. Gigi looked delectable as she danced to the beat of the music, not looking at me until it got to the part, "You're the one that I want," when she playfully pointed to me.

I was so enthralled by her sexy little moves and gestures that my expression was proverbially jaw-dropping. This was so obvious that Charlotte, in an animated fashion, put a hand under my chin and pretended to close my mouth, which brought loud laughter from everyone.

It was so innocent, even if Gigi and I were not guiltless. It pleased me that Jamie and Charlotte did not mind that I adored their mother. Perhaps it was not unexpected, given how much had gone under our bridge. And that I, or any younger man found Gigi very attractive was something they took for granted. They had long been exposed to their mother receiving many compliments. I had to admit, it was all quite strange, and I couldn't help smiling.

When the next track started playing, Jamie danced an amazing solo effort spurred on by the enthusiastic encouragement of his audience of three.

"Stayin' Alive" – Bee Gees

| YouTube | Spotify | Apple |

He was really enjoying himself, but it was no doubt me, who chortled the loudest each time it got to the part, "You can tell by the way I use my walk, I'm a woman's man." *Is he a woman's man, or simply a womaniser?* I thought, smiling at his comical dance moves. So uninhibited and confident.

The Blackwoods certainly knew how to dance, and it was all going splendidly well until we got to the next track.

"Hopelessly Devoted to You" – Olivia Newton-John

| YouTube | Spotify | Apple |

Gigi and I slipped into each other's arms, where we swayed and danced slowly together. I was truly, hopelessly devoted to her. I felt her holding onto me as if she were physically not going to let me go. Often in the past in situations like this, we would make light of it and just smile and chuckle, hoping that no one would realise the closeness we were feeling. At this moment though, we were oblivious of anyone else in the room.

Then when it got to the line, "I'm out of my head, hopelessly devoted to you," she drew away so we could rejoin Jamie and Charlotte at the table. I could not help seeing the wistful look on Gigi's face, a sadness about her and me, rather than the evening's mood, which had become decidedly more positive until this song.

All of us were now looking down into our glasses of port as the song played out, all feeling the gravitas of what lay ahead. It was not only the emotions of Gigi and me that were laid bare, but those of Jamie and Charlotte as well. We were going to miss these wonderfully jovial, impromptu occasions, of which there had been many. With a depressing thought, I wondered if there would ever be another evening like this one. The likelihood of it not happening again was yet another thing I would have to vehemently drive from my mind.

Soon Jamie and Charlotte went through to their bedrooms, and Gigi checked one last time to see if they needed anything. By the time she got back to the table, a cloud of melancholy had drifted over the room.

To change the mood, she took my hands, looked at me and said, "Take me to bed or lose me forever, Lieutenant."

I smiled at the words borrowed from another movie that was one of our favourites, *Top Gun*. As had become more common recently, she did not wait for Charlotte and Jamie to fall asleep like she used to in the early days of our relationship but came directly through to me instead. She did lock the door though. Personally, I thought this "rather have them think they know than know" approach had worn a little thin and our locked door was not concealing anything.

We got into bed, her in a thin nightdress and me in my boxer shorts, as always. At least, that's how we started out.

Given this would be the last night, for I shuddered to think how long, I thought she would just want a night of loving, passionate sex, something to help us endure the months ahead. Lying next to her, I reached up and lovingly held her cheek, leant forward and kissed her on the lips. With my other hand, I started gently rubbing her on the side of her neck, down her shoulders. I could have happily carried on caressing and loving her in this way for the whole night.

Gigi recognised this as a prelude to a loving evening together, as we had been doing ever since our trip to Rockwell Manor. Her earlier, more bold sexual advances did not chime with my gentle loving actions. She wanted something else, something more. An unusual expression crossed her face, which seemed to confirm it.

"What is it, Darling?" I asked.

Gigi answered me in a very soft voice that somehow emphasised what she was saying. "I love being loved by you. There is nothing better, but tonight… Tonight I want you to fuck me, Lieutenant."

Because of our closeness, I understood where these feelings were coming from. Over the past year, the uncertainty about my RAF role and its effect on our relationship, wondering where we would end up and all the emotional turmoil that had gone with it, had changed our lovemaking. Whilst it was always loving, passionate and intense, it had lost the uninhibited animal rawness we had first discovered in Berkshire. That night, she did not want to go to that place where we had recently spent so many anguished months. She needed to go back to the ferocity of unleashing our unbridled yearning for each other, when our lovemaking was unconstrained by anything as we tried to quell the raw desire we had for each other.

I was about to start taking control when Gigi said simply, "Wait, Darling, I want to play a bit."

I wasn't exactly sure what she had in mind, but was more than willing to find out.

When Gigi and I were making love, she truly felt like mine, a feeling I had never been able to fully reconcile. Right then, she was mine as I was hers, and I knew that regardless of what the future held, she and I would never forget this feeling.

We were lying next to each other when Gigi said, "Let's talk a bit, my gorgeous darling." She did not take long to get to what had been on everyone's minds the previous evening.

"My darling, I'm not sure how to say this, so let me just get it out."

I looked at her, fearing the worst.

"My baby, this is it," Gigi said

"What do you mean, *this is it*?" I shot back. "I'm not going forever, you know."

Gigi put a finger to my lips, signalling for me to stop talking. "I know, my baby—not physically anyway—but you have massive things ahead, and in that, there is no place for us."

Thrown completely off guard by Gigi's straightforwardness, I blurted, "Yes, but— What?" I was trying to deal with the onslaught of her words, only for her to again put a finger back on my lips.

"My darling, now please listen to me. I have heard what Major Gifford said in his lecture, and what others have said, and they are right, my darling. It is for your own good. For your safety. And Jamie's."

Gigi knew I would not discount Jamie's security and that I would struggle contesting that point.

"We need to move on, you and I, from what has been the most beautiful time of my life," she said, emotion welling up in her.

With me still reeling from her words, I could see she too was struggling to hold back the tears.

This wasn't her heart speaking—it was her head.

"I don't even know what dangers lie ahead for you and Jamie, but I do know that I must do this. I cannot be the distraction that could, God forbid, have far-reaching or even tragic consequences. Do you understand me, Darling?" Gigi stammered. She took hold of my hands and looked lovingly into my eyes, tears now showing on her cheeks.

As the gravitas of what she had said sank in, so a feeling of utter despair permeated through me. I could not even begin to think of not having her in my life on a day-to-day basis, even if we did not see each other as often as we liked.

"You and Jamie will soon be deployed into a combat zone, and none of us knows what lies ahead for the two of you. Right now, the only thing you should think about, my darling, is staying safe and helping Jamie to be safe," Gigi continued.

No longer able to hold back her emotions, the tears now streaming down her face, she suddenly looked fragile, and I put my arms around her shoulders and neck, drawing her close to me as she sobbed quietly. Feeling her tears on my chest, I felt exactly as she did but needed to be strong for both of us.

My mind was racing. *She'll always be in my heart. But that isn't enough! What can I do? With the* tremendous changes in our RAF careers, how could I make decisions about Gigi and me when I did not even know what would be happening in my immediate future?

Gigi realised this too, and with our safety being her most pressing issue, she had arrived at what she believed was the only solution. She was prepared to make whatever sacrifices were necessary for us not to be distracted from the job at hand, which to her mind could have fatal consequences.

Deep down I could not help feeling that we would never be able to be together. I was already feeling a dreadful void creeping into my being.

We then went through to the annex dining area and sat down to the most sombre breakfast, neither of us eating very much. When it was time for us to leave, we lethargically got our bags and headed for the door. I was desperate to put my arms around Gigi, just to feel the comfort of her embrace and kisses one last time.

Then Jamie said, "Bud, would you mind if I quickly run up to the convenience store? There are a couple of things I need to get." Not waiting for an answer, he added, "Charlotte, come with me."

"Okay," Charlotte replied without hesitation.

I looked at Jamie and then Gigi but didn't say anything, both of us realising they were thoughtfully giving us a little space so we could say goodbye.

With Jamie and Charlotte hardly out of the driveway, we threw our arms around each other. Both of us holding back the tears, and not knowing what to say, we held each other and exchanged little whispers of telling each other to be safe, take care, and that each would always have the other in their minds. Such shallow words, but what else was there. *This was the end!* Gigi had said the words, and the RAF causing a prolonged absence from each other, would do the rest. We continued holding each other until we heard Jamie's car returning, but we didn't immediately end our embrace and weren't too concerned with what Jamie and Charlotte might have seen.

Just as we were about to leave, I kissed Gigi lovingly on the cheek.

Feeling my anguish, she whispered into my ear, "We will never leave each other, Darling. You will always be in my heart." She had repeated almost verbatim what I had been thinking when lying in bed next to her just a short while ago. The words gave me little comfort, but instead only left me with feelings of emptiness.

"You will *always* be mine. I can't let you go," I said forcefully.

Had anyone heard this exchange, there would be no doubt they would have taken it for all the romantic connotations it represented. It wasn't that for me. It wasn't enough for us to be in each other's hearts. I wanted to be in her life. I wanted her in *my* life. Living only in each other's hearts would be painful, very painful. I just couldn't reconcile how this could happen. How we could leave each other now.

I drove out of the gate lost and sad, absorbed in my thoughts of Gigi and the sudden end to the most wonderful four plus years of my life. I searched through my Walkman, looking for a song that I felt echoed what I was feeling now.

"Against All Odds" – Phil Collins

YouTube   Spotify   Apple

The words could not have said it better. How could I just let her walk away?

How could I change Gigi's mind? I couldn't bear the thought of not taking every breath with her…always having something to look forward to. I was struggling to hold back the tears, knowing it was against the odds that Gigi would come back to me. I couldn't face that thought, dreading the empty space she would leave. Selfish feelings, consumed by my own grief. What about Gigi? How was *she* feeling? Not only was she saying goodbye to her lover and 'partner,' but also her son!

There was so much I wanted to say, needed to say to the person who had come to know me like no other.

The song ended, and Jamie gave me an affectionate pat on the shoulder, leaving his hand there for a moment. I didn't mind that he was aware of my sorrow. I was grateful for his understanding.

I couldn't begin to contemplate my life without Gigi even if I could not see a road ahead for us.

It just didn't make sense to me that two people who loved each other so completely could not be together. There had to be a way, or was waiting for her all I could do?

CHAPTER 29
THE MIDDLE EAST

No AMOUNT OF training in England could have fully prepared us for the baptism of fire we faced when we landed in the Middle East for our first tour of duty. One of the first adjustments was acclimatising to the temperature range. When we arrived, it was sometimes below -4°C (or 20°F). Then in the summer it was regularly 40°C (104°F), and all the discomfort that came with it. *Everything is so sandy and dusty!* Never a great sleeper, these conditions played further havoc with that endeavour.

We were warned, I thought wryly. Then with a chuckle to myself, *Another meaning to 'hot posting,' I guess.*

Just looking at the lineup of Apache helicopters had my heart racing. Any challenge was worth it, just for this. This was what I had first dreamed of, then trained for, and now I was finally here. But so too came the reality of the situation as I played with the disc hanging around my neck.

Looking at one of my two dog tags, I read again the engraving. My service number, surname and initials, religion, blood type, and my military branch. "What are these identification tags for, and why do we have two?" I remembered an air cadet having once asked.

"In case you forget who you are," had been the sarcastic reply.

The airman may have preferred the instructor to have left it there, but instead he gave the real reason.

"In case you cop it, dear boy. They will put one around your big toe so they can identify you, because by then you certainly won't know who you are."

My Rude Awakening

The chuckles around the room said it all. War discounted the value of human life to bargain basement levels.

Thank God my mother and Gigi hadn't heard about that conversation.

Just a few days into this new way of life and the myriad of different things going on all around us, I received my first two letters from home. Well, from my real home and Shrewsbury. This was something new. I guess no longer being three or four hours from home and having no easy access to telephones, it was to be expected.

I felt a little guilty that I read Gigi's letter first. A few times, in fact. I found myself trying to figure out if there was anything I could read between the lines. It seemed she had purposefully steered clear of writing anything that I might misinterpret. I hated the loss and emptiness I was feeling.

I then read the letter from my mother, with my father's contribution added onto the end. I smiled, not in the least bit surprised at this sensible approach. By the end of it I had a good idea of what was happening at home. It struck me my two letters were surprisingly similar. A catch-up with the goings-on, hoping I was doing well, taking care of myself, and thinking of you all the time.

Hang on. There was something. "Thinking of you all the time," in Gigi's letter gave me an immediate lift. I wished I could tell her I felt the same.

I couldn't help my mind drifting off to the green fields and emerald forests of Berkshire. Cool. Moist. Sometimes a fresh gentle breeze. Even the days when it drizzled incessantly seemed appealing. Then, of course, I thought about Rockwell Manor and my parents. How was my mother taking me being in a combat zone? As close as we were, it was sometimes hard to tell how she was feeling because of her stoic manner. My father's contribution to the letter had been silent on what was happening with his own polo. Was he getting more involved during my absence or withdrawing even more? And I couldn't help but think about Fabrizio. I must have been missing his cooking. I loved how he was so eager to please us with his "famous" meals, which were all of them, of course. His secret herbs and spices. Never mind Fabrizio's lavish feasts, I would give almost anything for a slice of his roasted sourdough bread with French butter and his scrambled eggs. I would happily concede that they were indeed *famous*. I smiled as I thought about my breakfast that morning. Interestingly, it had been scrambled eggs on toast. Just like Fabrizio's. Well, sort of. Just a few small differences.

Eggs in a combat zone needed no scrambling. The reason was that eggs came in a large tin container, in the form of powder, as did the milk. No need for double cream either, just add water! *How convenient is that?* I smiled at my sarcastic thoughts. And when your eggs were plated—okay, slopped into one of the compartments of your stainless-steel plate—who needed finely chopped parsley and grated parmesan cheese sprinkled over the top, with homemade tomato sauce using Roma tomatoes, secret herbs, and a little honey splashed artistically on the side? That was completely superfluous. Oh yes, and toasting the bread was just a waste of time. Instead of toast, it was far more efficient to have pre-sliced white bread with no butter, let alone French *beurre*. What did the French know about cooking anyway? At this stage, I was quite openly chuckling as I experienced the cuisine of military dining. I found it interesting how a simple dish like scrambled eggs on toast could be so vastly different.

Fabrizio's scrambled eggs were to die for. In the operational frontline, you could die from those.

And I would be sure to tell Fabrizio about the secret seasoning we *did* have in the RAF and the Middle East. Salt and pepper.

And then my mind shifted to the highlight of my daydreaming, Shrewsbury. The food, the wine, the music, and the dancing. And in the middle of it all, Gigi. The cause of my feelings of such vacuous emptiness. A woman I only ever felt was mine in those moments of our intimacy. Every part of her was engrained in my brain. From her toes to the top of her head, and *everything* in between.

Just as I was getting lost in longing thoughts about Gigi, so another oppressive wind drifted into our camp with its hot, dry, dusty character, doing nothing for my already parched skin and lips. Not to mention the tiny particles of sand that would cake in the corner of your eyes. Was this really for me? Was my mother right in questioning if I belonged in the RAF? Here? She was right about most things, but was this different? Her contention that I was not a military man may have had some validity to start with, but I certainly felt like a military man now. The greater my challenge meant just one thing—the greater my accomplishment. On my own, Serviceman M17112011. In a strange way, I was relishing every bit of it.

Born with a silver spoon in my mouth or not, no one I had come across from my basic training through to where we were now, had endured military life better. Was it because of *my* poem that I was able to shrug it off?

> *If neither foes nor loving friends can hurt [me]… [Mine] is the Earth and everything that's in it, And—which is more—[I'll] be a Man.*

My *own* man!

Everything about the military and the RAF was deliberate. Not surprising. This being our first tour of duty, we began with routine patrols. Only later did we come to realise that it was not intended for us to experience a contact in the first several missions regardless of how eager we were to engage the enemy. A naivety that in time would change.

As the tally of our routine patrols increased, so too did we settle into our new base. Whilst the temperature differences compared to home may have been the reason for us losing sleep in the early stages, very soon this became the least of our concerns. The thing that caused most of our sleepless nights were shoulder-launched Stinger missiles or, more correctly, man-portable air-defence systems (MANPADS), deadly against most aircraft but especially helicopters. The Apache cockpit may have been protected by reinforced armour and bulletproof glass, able to survive 23mm rounds, but a Stinger missile was a different proposition altogether.

Thinking about them slowly gnawed its way into every part of your brain like a cancer, and there was little you could do about it. Ironically, these lethal weapons should never have been in the hands of our foes but were supplied to the insurgents by the USA. An example of the confusion of Western politics. The problem with this weapon was that they could simply be carried on the back of a combatant and very quickly brought forward and placed onto the shoulder, ready to launch a deadly missile. An insurgent with a Stinger missile launcher could easily conceal himself in any nook or cranny and strike when one least expected it.

We were all very aware that Russian helicopter losses in the Soviet–Afghan War in the early eighties numbered more than 300 helicopter gunships and their crews. Stinger missiles from MANPADS were responsible for most of those. This constant threat was always in the back of our minds, knowing that at any moment you could be facing a lethal attack from seemingly nowhere, and this very seriously affected some flight crew members.

A case in point had been an incident just a few days earlier. I was in a flight of four Apaches, lined up and about to go on a routine patrol. We had been given start-up clearance, and as I was going through my sequence, bringing my engines and rotor system up to flight readiness, I noticed alongside me that the blades of Lieutenant Greg Andrews's helicopter were motionless. Only for a moment did I imagine he had a technical malfunction, because these machines had all been fully prepped just shortly beforehand.

The look on Greg's face and the slouch of his shoulders—with his CPG Lieutenant Harper Jameson craning his neck around, trying to work out what was going on with his Pilot-in-Command—made clear what I had begun to suspect.

As they climbed out of the Apache, Harper put an arm across Greg's shoulders, comforting him, while Greg's apologetic expression of despair confirmed the worst nightmare of every combat pilot—he'd lost his nerve. Greg couldn't do it that morning. He had surrendered to the deep-seated fear that stubbornly sat in the pits of all our bellies.

We had then sat at flight idle while the mission was reorganised to include just the three remaining helicopters. Just as well it was a low-key patrol and reconnaissance mission because we had all become distracted with what happened to Greg.

Was this also one of the RAF approaches, to do routine patrols and potentially sift out weak links? If so, then Greg's undoing was a victory for the system and probably the saving grace for a really good helicopter pilot, just not in a war zone. And that's to say nothing of his CPG. It didn't make me feel any better about Greg's departure.

We could all feel the escalating tension of the routine patrols, but it was perhaps an innocuous little notice that suggested things were about to step up a gear. The powers that be were upping the ante.

My Rude Awakening

We had by then been in the Middle East a few weeks when our intake received the unexpected instruction to attend a black ops briefing to our veteran peers. We soon discovered it had to do with an imminent operation in the southern provinces. We were to attend in a listen-only capacity.

In contrast to the bright sunlit day, the low lighting inside the presentation room gave it an eerie feel. Will and Jamie were seated on each side of me, our close-knit trio. There was an air of tension as we sat waiting in anticipation for proceedings to begin. With the aid of an overhead projector and a white board on which was written the heading SITTING DUCK, Group Captain Ralph Dogwood began his presentation.

"Today we have some of our freshman Apache crew who will be sitting in on the initial part of the briefing," the operations group captain said, explaining the nine people seated in the back row of the presentation room. The missing tenth freshman was of course Greg. Including ourselves, there must have been around forty of us in attendance.

"In summary, the mission is to flush out a group of insurgents using contrived engine failure and crash landing of a Puma HC2 helicopter as a decoy. The flight crews and SAS Operatives involved in the operation will be given preliminary details at today's briefing, with one follow-up meeting tomorrow," he said.

"This covert mission will involve two Puma gunships and two Apaches. The first Puma, designated Papa Alpha, will be fully armed, and in addition to the piloting crew, there will be twelve Special Air Service Operators. They are the main actors of this operation. The supporting roles will be the second Puma, designated Papa Bravo, and a flight of two Apaches, collectively designated Alpha Foxtrot. Papa Bravo will be unarmed and only have a pilot and copilot on board. We will need Papa Bravo's full payload capability for reasons that will become clear," Group Captain Dogwood added, before continuing.

"Papa Alpha will approach the target zone in the area of the insurgents at a height of two and a half thousand feet. It will then deploy a smoke trail to suggest an engine failure and fire. The helicopter will then enter autorotation and descend into the selected area. At the approximate point of ground contact, Papa Alpha crew will deploy a thunderflash and black smoke decoys to imply the helicopter crashed on impact. In our experience, this will bring the insurgence to the crash site out of curiosity or in the hope they can retrieve something from the wreckage. Or just to gloat," he added as an afterthought.

"Crucially, leading up to this moment, Papa Bravo and Alfa Foxtrot, the support group, must remain completely out of sight and out of earshot. This will mean being four and a half nautical miles downwind from the decoy zone. These three gunships should be on the ground, 'turning and burning' at flight idle. Anything else will compromise the mission. They will only be brought into the fray in the event of an unexpected resistance."

A wave of excitement rippled through us as we continued to listen intently. We had done a little work with thunderflashes, also known as flash grenades or sound bombs, which, as the names suggested, emitted a sound akin to an explosion.

Group Captain Dogwood continued, "Once Papa Alpha is on the ground, the two flight crew and the SAS operatives will vacate the helicopter. The SAS combatants will be placed in predetermined strategic points in relation to the helicopter. Call them the insurgent *welcoming party*, if you will."

The veteran SAS operatives in the room chuckled at the thought of this. The freshmen, of which I was one, sat there wide-eyed. *God, this is exciting.*

"When the insurgents expose themselves, it is important that our SAS friends act decisively. We don't want to lose a perfectly good Puma helicopter unnecessarily," Group Captain Dogwood said dryly. "In the unfortunate event that Papa Alpha is taken out by the insurgents and there is unexpected opposition, then the two Apaches, Alpha Foxtrot, will immediately be brought into the offensive. The Apache Flight will launch an aerial attack on the insurgents within two minutes, bearing in mind they will be some five miles away. When the threat has been eliminated, Papa Bravo will be on the ready to extract Papa Alpha flight crew and SAS operatives from the site."

That concluded the part of Group Captain Dogwood's presentation that we had been cleared for. We were then invited to leave.

I couldn't help but think of a term that I had often heard, *the theatre of war*. Well, this stage had certainly been set. And the title, SITTING DUCK. That could only have been a reference to the Puma helicopter.

Seasoned SAS could *never* be described as sitting ducks. Sitting duck my arse, as Jamie might have said.

I remember at the time being very preoccupied with the thought that this manoeuvre could very likely cost the Royal Air Force a Puma HC2 helicopter gunship. It only dawned on me years later that I had not for even a moment considered the lives being put at risk. The group captain too seemed to be making a bigger point about protecting the Puma ahead of the personnel's lives. Did discounting the value of human life simply go with the territory?

I reconciled that our invitation to this briefing was likely as premeditated as everything else. Had we been given a taste of things to come?

It seemed I got that right when just a few days later, Will and I, along with two other freshman Apache crew, were called into our own Ops meeting. The whiteboard was still blank except for the heading DEAD AHEAD.

In summary, this was a mission to launch an offensive on a convoy of enemy vehicles traversing between two of their strongholds.

Operational Command had received on the ground intelligence that this convoy would be using a route that our topographical information showed a section of road that ran for a little over a mile that would be the perfect kill zone. We were put on alert for a mission start at 0400 hours the next morning.

Will and I had already spent a lot of time flying routine patrol missions with each other, with him in the Copilot-Gunner cockpit and me as Pilot-in-Command. This would be the first time we would be flying a contact mission together. A first for both of us. I couldn't have been more pleased.

Already we were asking the question. Would MANPADS be a factor? Would the insurgence know this road section was a point of vulnerability and have shoulder-mounted stingers in place…just in case?

The following morning, the flight of two Apache with Will and me in one of them had departed the base to seek out this convoy of insurgent armoured vehicles. "AH64 fodder," as the sardonic expression went.

The planned kill zone was a length of road bordered on one side by a steep embankment and an even steeper drop off on the other side. Once on this stretch, there was only one place they could go. *Dead* ahead. *Dead* being the operative word.

The insurgent armoured vehicles had simply been no match for the Apache's weaponry systems—rockets and Hellfire missiles. The speed at which we had tracked down and then engaged the enemy was only eclipsed by the swiftness of our fiery assault as we obliterated the entire convoy. We watched what had seemed like a menacing threat being reduced to a ramshackle of vehicles trying in vain to scurry for safety, leaving behind a cloud of dust. They had no chance.

As it turned out, they did have MANPADS but not in the surrounding hills. They were on the back of two or three of the vehicles in the convoy. This didn't help them any as they scurried away at full speed to their early demise.

When Jamie, who had not been on the mission, asked me about it in a subdued tone, I went through how the mission had played out in a matter-of-fact manner. When he asked me how I felt about it, I could only describe it as "unbelievable." Jamie had been perceptive enough to leave it at that. I didn't even want to decipher those feelings. My first mission with a contact. I allowed myself to count the number of armoured vehicles that had been eliminated. Eight. When I reluctantly asked Will how many of the eight we had accounted for, he hesitantly mumbled, "Three or four." *Unsurprisingly, Will got more than his quota,* was my melancholic thought.

The thing is, for every vehicle, there was a given number of occupants—a tally of human lives. As much as I didn't want to do the simple arithmetic, I couldn't help myself.

That night I slept even worse than ever before.

More and more I was finding myself having to keep Rudyard Kipling's *IF* words top of my mind.

If you can force your heart and nerve and sinew… And so hold on when there is nothing in you, Except the Will which says to them: 'Hold on!'

CHAPTER 30
MISSION ZEERO NINER

IT WAS BECAUSE of some still classified and unique military circumstances that had us return to our Middle East posting after just a short break.

I had wanted to visit Gigi but knew it wouldn't have been the right thing to do. We had reluctantly come to terms with our circumstances, and it would have been destabilising for both of us had I interfered with this delicate balance. Instead, I spent my fortnight at home in Berkshire, savouring all of those things that I had so missed since being posted to the Middle East, and what I had previously just taken for granted.

Now in our second tour of duty in frontline operational service, we had participated in countless missions. Whilst Jamie, Will, and me were beginning to feel like veterans, technically this was not yet true. Regardless, we were decidedly seasoned, and we felt it.

Notwithstanding my transformed world, Gigi was never far from my mind and always firmly in my heart. Falling asleep at night was often delayed irrespective of how tired I was, because of the thoughts of her and the time we had shared together. I often tossed and turned until my tiredness overcame me, and I had to consciously shut down my thinking so I could finally doze off. I had occasional dreams about her and me that I loved, until I dreamt she was with another man, which was tortuous. I hated that I had no control over my dreams and far preferred my daydreaming.

For the most part, communication between us was near impossible and, at times, virtually nonexistent. Whenever I was in a location where I could make a phone call, I did. Not to my parents but to Gigi. Despite having made the painful decision to go our separate ways, the love and passion we felt for each other simmered just beneath the surface, and neither one of us dared prod it, knowing it could so easily erupt. As a result, our conversations were often bland monologues, the weather being a regular topic. Even if we had wanted to speak about what was going on in our lives, it would have been impossible from my point of view, since I was not allowed to discuss where I was or what I was doing.

As if to convince myself that we had gone our separate ways, a particular song from my playlist became a regular for me. My attempt at defiance. Unfortunately, it was not that convincing, and sometimes it seemed that I played it just to torture myself.

"Separate Ways (Worlds Apart)" – Journey

| YouTube | Spotify | Apple |

I wished everything for her, but the thought of her loving someone else was more than I could bear. How could our lives go separate ways after having just touched so beautifully? I still loved her deeply and couldn't help holding out hope for the future.

When we were in training to become pilots, we used music to pump us up and get our adrenaline going. No more. We still listened to music, but often it was to settle our nerves. Or just a bit of calm before the storm. The subtle difference now was that things were for real.

After many months passed with scant communication between us, I finally accepted that there would be no going back to what Gigi had described as "the most wonderful time of her life." She had certainly been the most extraordinary highlight of *my* life, for the most wonderful years.

My one irrefutable connection to her was Jamie, and as a result, my relationship with him flourished, as if my deprived soul fed off the connection to Gigi. I sensed Jamie felt this. He would often ask how I was, and we both knew what he was asking.

My Rude Awakening

Then, just as our time in the operational frontline seemed to become a little routine, there was a change. A dramatic change, as if to prove just how unpredictable life in the RAF and Army could be.

It was around 0650 hours on a Thursday, and I was making my way to breakfast when I received a sealed communication. It was a notice to attend a black ops meeting at 0800 hours the following day. A tingle ran down my spine.

I sat down next to Jamie, wondering if he had received the same communication. Because it was to do with a covert or secret mission, no communication of any description was permitted, even between your peers, including even our being summoned to a meeting. Then I noticed Jamie was reading something.

I thought for a moment and then said, "Jamie, any chance you can drop something off for me tomorrow at 0800 hours?"

"Negative," came his reply. "I'm tied up at that time."

We had our ways and means. Obviously, he'd been summoned to the same meeting.

The next morning, Jamie and I sat down for breakfast in the normal manner. When we were finished, we headed off in the same direction.

After three or four steps, Jamie quipped, "It looks like we are going to the same place. I could have guessed." He slowed his pace, letting me walk slightly ahead of him so we would not arrive together.

We met again in the black ops meeting room and sat together as we usually did.

The briefing was simple: A group of insurgents had established themselves in a well-protected area not far from our temporary air base, Delta-One-Fife. From this position, they had been able to launch shoulder-mounted MANPADS, which had put flight operations in and out of the temporary base at significant risk, especially for helicopters. It was to be a stealth mission, a flight of just two attack helicopters from our Apache squadron, executed by the four of us in attendance.

Watching me for a reaction, the officer briefing the meeting continued, "Your flight leader will be Lieutenant Charles Featherstone."

I didn't react. I was ready for this, and there was not anyone else in this flight of two helicopters, crew of four, who was better suited. I nodded

353

my head assuredly in acknowledgment, even if this was my first mission as flight leader.

"I will not be speaking to you collectively again before the operation. Debrief is set for 1030 hours, once the last helicopter has landed, after a successful mission. Good luck, men, and Godspeed. Lieutenant Featherstone, you can remain for further ops briefing. The rest of you are dismissed."

I was then given all the critical information, including the most up-to-date intelligence on enemy positions. I went through the tactical attack plan, alternate routes, retrace considerations, mission-abort parameters, and the always ominous mission-failure and recovery plan.

Will—*who else?*—would be my CPG, the best in the squadron. Great-Shot Granger and I had become an inseparable team. A relationship built on a foundation of a solid friendship, Will and I were more than just regular partners flying our Apache. We had seldom taken to the skies without each other. This was something the RAF nurtured, realising the value of crewmen really getting to know each other.

In life you get many types of partnerships. An example, perhaps, would be tennis partners. If they misread each other, they lose a point, maybe a set, even the match. Afterwards, they kick themselves.

When you're in a combat helicopter, in a warzone, the word *partnership* takes on a whole new meaning. There, if you misread your partner, you may lose your life. No kicking yourself afterwards. Will was my partner, and I trusted him with my life as he trusted me with his. The bond between Will and me and the trust that had developed between us based on the primal human instinct of survival was difficult to describe. As close as Jamie and I were, Will was unquestionably the one I would always choose to go to war with.

The mission log showed that the second Apache would be crewed by Lieutenant James Blackwood, Pilot-in-Command, and CPG Lieutenant Patrick White. Our flight of two helicopters had flown several missions together, but the ante had been upped with this being a black ops mission.

I left the meeting still thinking about the details but comfortable that all the particulars were clearly understood. Notwithstanding my acute focus and attention to my first briefing as a flight leader, there was something else lingering in the back of my mind.

I headed straight for the officers' mess, where I knew I would find Jamie, and saw him sitting on the far side of the saloon area, on his own and deep in thought. I went over and sat opposite him.

"How do you feel about the mission?" I asked, getting straight to the point.

"Yeah, fine, cool," he said unconvincingly.

I thought there was no point not addressing the elephant in the room. "A bit of a downer that we are both on the same stealth mission," I said. The only small consolation was that we were not in the same helicopter.

Jamie looked up for the first time. "Yeah, I know," was all he said.

I put my hand on my friend's shoulder, "Jamie, careful how you manage it—black ops, et cetera—but give your mum a call."

Jamie again looked up at me and said, "Yeah, you should speak to her too."

He made the call to Gigi as I waited for him in the officers' mess, trying to use my time to go through some of the pointers for the next day's mission.

It was impossible to concentrate and not wonder what Gigi would feel with Jamie and I going on a stealth mission the next day, but in truth, I knew exactly how she would be feeling. The idle time while I waited for Jamie to finish his call made me realise just how much I hated the fact that I would be leading a flight on a mission into a very hostile environment, with Jamie under my command. What would I do if something happened to him? But I had to chase that thought from my mind. It was exactly that kind of thinking that could get us both killed.

He seemed to be taking a long time, but eventually he came back and assumed his seat opposite me. I looked up at him expectantly.

"She is very cut up," was Jamie's short summation of his phone call. "Be sure to phone her, Charles. I said you would."

I decided to wait before calling Gigi, thinking it would be better for her to have a little time to absorb and perhaps reconcile the situation. It was a phone call I did not look forward to making. A couple of hours later, when I did finally make the call, there was not much I could say without breaching secret-mission protocols.

When she answered immediately, I realised she had been waiting by the phone. "Gigi," I said.

"Yes," came her reply.

"Hello, Darling. Jamie called you?" I remarked, not really knowing what to say.

"Yes," was her short reply. Clearly she was also at a loss for words. Then, as she inhaled slightly, I heard a quiver in her throat with her intake of breath. It told me she had spent a lot of the past two hours sobbing.

"Please don't cry, my love. Everything will be okay," I said.

"Promise me you will both be safe," she pressed.

"Darling, everything will be fine."

Gigi knew I could not make that promise.

I woke early the next morning, feeling twinges of excitement for what lay ahead. Flying these machines always brought a spring to my step, but today was a whole new ballgame.

The four of us involved in today's mission, all friends, walked amiably across to the apron of the air base, where our Apaches were standing. The weapons ground crew were already in attendance, readying the two attack helicopters with the required munitions.

Will and I began our own inspection, the engineering team having already completed a more thorough examination of the aircraft, and we circled the helicopter, going through all the preflight checks. Will's primary focus was the weapon systems, while I focused on flight controls, tail rotor, main rotor, and the like. We shared the responsibility of checking the Apache's twin jet engines, each from our opposite sides of the helicopter.

The weaponry ground crew finished prepping and checking the different armaments we would be using that day. In addition to the 30mm chain cannon, the helicopters had been armed with sixteen Hellfire missiles of around fifty kilograms each. We would also be using Hydra 70mm rockets.

Today was not an opportunity to use any fire-and-forget missiles. We would have eyes on target and be relying on the HMD and fire-control radar (FCR). Everything would be recorded by the cameras in the nose of the two Apaches. After every mission, if there was a kill, the videos would be carefully reviewed to look for culpable evidence. This had always puzzled me—kill them but follow the rules.

This mission would be close-combat fighting. No doubt the pungent smell of nitroglycerine would be more than evident after firing our weapons, even though we were sitting in our helicopters. *Hopefully keeping out of harm's way,* I thought grimly. In truth, this was the reason I was in a combat helicopter squadron, preferring to be *in the fight,* something you could not experience sitting in a jet fighter.

Preflight inspection done, Will and I came up alongside the helicopter before climbing into our respective cockpits.

"How are you feeling, Will?" I asked quietly, encouraging him to give me a truthful answer.

"Alive, excited, and as nervous as all hell."

That summed it up for me as well.

We climbed up into our respective cockpits. I pulled the safety harness and restraints over my shoulders, then around my waist and up between my legs, clipping them into the circular restraint housing. I took one last look around the cockpit, felt the free movement of my flight controls, then placed my flight helmet purposely onto my head. I did up the strap and plugged in the communications, instruments, and weapons systems.

My concentration belied the fact that I had done this hundreds of times before, because this time, it was different. I could not have been more tuned in to what had become a simple and somewhat-menial procedure.

I checked one last time that my gloves were comfortable and secure. You could call it my pet concern. In the event of an accident, and the helicopter catching fire, my hands would be better protected from the risk of burns. I pulled down my helmet visor, feeling the calm that always came over me just before I embarked on the start-up procedure. I was comfortable in this place, that old feeling of the aircraft being an extension of me.

"Base Delta WUN FIFE on TOO SEVEN AIT DECIMAL TREE, this is Mission ZEERO NINER requesting flight start-up clearance," I said into my microphone on the military-dedicated UHF-AM channel, using the strict pronunciation and procedures protocols that were standard Army and Air Force practise.

"Mission ZEERO NINER, confirm TOO helicopter flight," came the reply from the air traffic controller.

"Mission ZEERO NINER, that's affirmative," I replied.

"Flight start-up approved," said the air traffic controller.

This authorised our two Apaches to start up our jet engines, advise when we were ready, and then prepare for liftoff for our departure from Base Delta One Five. Because this was a stealth mission, I knew the air traffic controller would not wait for me to request liftoff clearance.

I began the complicated start-up procedure without hesitation. The beautiful, logical pattern was now second nature, and I went through the steps with a fluidity that came from having done the same thing many times before. I heard each of the twin Rolls-Royce jet engines as they whined and then roared to life. *Fuck, I love this.* A profanity creeping into my subconscious. The all-encompassing word conveyed my emotions perfectly.

With the rotor system at full rotational speed, I again radioed air traffic control. "Delta WUN FIFE, we are *turning and burning*." Excitement gripped my stomach.

"Mission ZEERO NINER, set mode FIFE, SQUARK SIX AIT ZEERO FIFE. Wind TOO TOO knots at WUN AIT FIFE degrees. When airborne, establish on outbound vector TOO SEVEN FOWER below TOO HUNDRED FEET AGL maintaining broad radio silence." This was air traffic control giving me our transponder setting so that we were recognisable on his radar, and he could keep track of our outbound track. This was also an instruction that there would only be communication between our helicopters.

I gave him the read-back, and once he was satisfied I had everything, he responded, "Mission ZEERO NINER, you have liftoff clearance at your own discretion."

Remaining below 200 feet AGL meant the two helicopters would engage the combat zone as close to the ground as we dared. We did this for a few reasons, not least of which was we would not easily be detected by enemy radar. Additionally, with helicopters being unavoidably noisy, if we were not close to the ground, the enemy would easily detect us if we were at say, 500 feet AGL. I knew I would lead our flight to less than half that height. We would generally be just fifty to sixty feet, or twenty yards, above the terrain. It also meant that when we came up on our target zone, they would be taken by complete surprise because it would be difficult for them to tell which direction the sound was coming from. They would likely only see us when it was too late for them to respond. By the time they did, we would have already begun our attack and deployed our missiles.

Flying missions in a combat zone was no longer cursory classroom information or training ground procedure. It was now a life-or-death situation, which gave it a vastly different complexion.

Was I ready? This was the reason Gigi and I had parted, so I would be single-minded and focused. I was ready. I prayed Jamie felt the same way too.

Our two helicopters became airborne a few moments later. We were not even through transition when the air traffic controller came back on the line. "Mission ZEERO NINER, QSY TOO NINER TREE DECIMAL FIFE. Maintain listening watch," came the curt order. This was the instruction to change our radios over to our mission frequency.

I took the command role, and the second helicopter slotted in behind me for our outbound flight into the combat zone. Mission Zero Nine was underway under my flight command. I felt confident we would successfully deliver our lethal, fiery blow, but there was one small problem.

With the insurgents in such a dangerous position, interfering with our flight operations at the base, it had been difficult to gather intelligence on this area. The screen in front of me showed a contour map that indicated the insurgents were roughly 80 nautical miles from the base, potentially behind a small hillock. We had decided that the best plan of attack was for one Apache to remain at low level and approach from around the side of the hillock, keeping close to the valley floor, while the second helicopter came over the hill at high speed and deployed its cannons and missiles from this elevated position.

A crucial element of the attack was that, even though we were coming from two different directions, we would arrive at the target at the same instant, so the insurgents had to divide their attention. I knew they would only hear us for a short while before we reached them, and with two helicopters coming from different directions, they would have even greater difficulty in discerning where we would be attacking from. As the two Apaches got closer to the target zone, they would likely be more aware of the low-flying helicopter coming up through the valley but be ill-equipped to easily attack it because of their own position relative to the flight of this helicopter. That would be enough of a distraction for the more exposed Apache approaching from over the hill to deploy its weaponry from its elevated position. As I was commanding the flight, it was appropriate that I assume this riskier situation in the attack plan.

With adrenaline pumping through my veins, causing my every sense to be heightened and on full alert, I made a very quick and informal radio call to the other three crew members. "Will, Pat, Jamie, we are sixty seconds out. Remember that our biggest threat is the MANPADS Stingers. Check that your Missile Approach Warning System (MAWS) is armed now, but don't rely on it. Keep your eyes peeled for smoke trails."

Unlike radar-guided missiles, infrared-guided missiles are difficult to detect when they are fired at a helicopter or plane. They do not emit detectable radar and are often fired from behind the helicopter, normally towards the engines. Whilst the MAWS does help, as it can automatically detect missile launches from the distinct thermal emissions of a missile's rocket motor, it is often more reliable for the flight crew to spot the missile's smoke trail and give the alert. For this to be effective, situational awareness becomes critical.

Once a Stinger infrared missile is detected, the crew of the aircraft releases flares in an attempt to decoy the projectile. The aim is to make the infrared-guided rocket seek out the heat signature from the flare rather than the aircraft's engines.

The other method of trying to avoid a missile strike is by breaking the line of sight (LOS) that the missile has of the heat emissions from the helicopter's engines and exhaust gases. This is not always possible, as you cannot simply duck behind a building or hillock without potentially endangering yourself and your crew further.

Great fun and games unless your life depended on it!

I came back onto the radio a moment later, calmly giving them the heads-up. "Thirty seconds out. Hard and sharp, chaps. Hard and sharp," a call to battle that I had adopted from Gigi.

No amount of training or preparation ever fully equipped you for what

My Rude Awakening

comes in a situation like this, for one simple and obvious reason. On the range, it was similar in many respects, except you did not have people retaliating, knowing that the only possibility of them surviving was to kill you. *There is nothing quite like that to focus the mind,* I thought dryly.

We were both flying at top speed just above the treetops, Jamie up the valley whilst I was climbing the backside of the hillock, about to break cover as I crested the ridge.

"Ten seconds out. Are you on track?" I radioed to the other helicopter.

"Affirmative," came Jamie's terse reply as we closed in on our target at around 145 knots, or 165 miles per hour.

Our timing was perfect. As I levelled out at the top of the hill, I caught a glimpse of Jamie as I scanned ahead to pick up the target. My instrument panel told me that we both had eyes on target at almost the same time.

Our 30mm chain cannons each had 1,200 rounds of ammunition and fired at a rate of over 600 rounds a minute (ten per second). Multiply that by two. In addition, we both had sixteen Hellfire missiles, deadly by any measure. The attack that these two highly sophisticated combat aircraft could deliver was brutal and lethal.

Once we were certain it was a hostile enemy position, we used the forward-looking infrared (FLIR) system to be able to see our targets through any foliage or camouflaging. It made no difference that we could not actually see the target when deploying our armaments.

"Tree, two, one, fire," was all I said.

Both helicopters immediately and simultaneously began firing the highly explosive 30mm shells and a volley of Hellfire missiles and Hydra rockets, strafing the enemy position mercilessly. We obliterated our target in less than one minute. Their post went up in a mass of explosions, fire, and thick black smoke, without the enemy firing so much as a single shot in retaliation, such was our speed and decisiveness.

Almost immediately, I radioed the controller. "DELTA HOTEL," said it all—direct hit.

The only thing left to do was survey the scene, the nose cameras of the helicopters hoovering up a photographic record of the assault and consequences, for careful review later.

As I completed my last fly past, my primary radio channel came alive. "Mission ZEERO NINER, Base Delta WUN FIFE, do you copy?"

"Mission ZEERO NINER, go ahead."

"Return to base, track route Bravo. Your route Alpha has been compromised."

This meant insurgents had positioned themselves on our return to base track, and because we did not have any intelligence on this, we could not take any chances. We certainly did not want them to spoil what had been an audacious attack and a remarkably successful mission. Route Bravo had already been planned and, once again, it required nap-of-the-earth flying, but this time it was in proximity to a nearby town.

I assumed the lead command position, and Patrick and Jamie fell in behind me a short distance back. It concerned me that our intelligence and topographical information for the region was limited. Notwithstanding this, we moved decisively so that we could exit the area as quickly as possible.

Then our radios crackled back to life. "Mission ZEERO NINER, QSY TOO FOWER TREE DECIMAL ZEERO." This was our instruction to change frequencies to the designated military emergency and guard channel. We were now being assisted by evac command, who were monitoring our activities from an Airborne Warning And Control System (AWACS) aircraft, complete with its sophisticated suite of radar technology. Flying overhead at somewhere around 35,000 feet.

We were about seven minutes into our extraction route but still deep in enemy territory. The change in tactic had us all razor sharp and alert. I was feeling extremely uncomfortable with the lack of intelligence and dependable terrestrial information, especially considering we were flying the contours of the earth.

Jamie was diagonally behind me, off to my right with about fifty yards between us, so I could still see him if I looked over my right shoulder. I was trying to calculate his best flight level, my inclination to tell him to take a little more height, but I didn't, knowing it would make him more exposed. I found myself paying as much attention to what lay in Jamie and Patrick's flight path as I did our own.

Mine and Will's cockpit activity was frenetic as we went into defence mode. He focused on interpreting flight and engine instrumentation and reviewed weapons status and our scant topographical information. At the same time, I was scanning the horizon, fervently checking the area ahead for enemy threats.

Less than ten nautical miles into our extraction plan, a gleam of reflection off metal tubing caught my attention. A feeling of dread immediately swamped me. I looked into the monocle over my right eye, set on target-acquisition mode. The infrared sight showed four red smudges indicating hotspots—probably two pairs of insurgents, each pair carrying a MANPADS. They were perfectly placed to launch their shoulder-mounted Stinger missiles at Jamie and Pat, putting my other crew members in mortal danger.

Focus, I screamed into my subconscious. Extreme urgency gripped me instantaneously. "Jamie! Johnny Jihads at your eleven o'clock low," I shouted into my microphone.

The feelings of horror were immediately set aside as my mind and body burst into action. Even though the activity in my cockpit was frenzied, a calmness came over me as I took control of the situation.

Almost instinctively, I banked hard right, and my helicopter came up alongside Jamie's. This would distract the insurgents. With them having to deal with two threatening targets halved the chances of them firing on Jamie alone. Most of all though, I could be more certain of taking evasive action. I felt better positioned to deal with this grave danger than what Jamie and Patrick were.

"Ready decoys," I shouted, making sure they were ready to deploy their missile defences. "Fire rockets, cannons, go, go, go," I shouted urgently.

I doubted we would get the insurgents before they fired their missiles, which was confirmed when almost immediately my MAWS squawked into my helmet as it detected the imminent mortal danger of the missiles. My "ready decoys" command could not have been a moment later.

I shouted my next order, "Fire decoys." As I was speaking, I saw the next volley of two Stingers heading towards me. "Jamie, break right," I barked, my headset squawking urgently back at me.

Once I felt Jamie was clear, I banked hard left, both of us moving away from the flares we had deployed. Ordinarily, we would have also reduced engine power to cool our thermal signature, but we didn't have that luxury because we were flying nap-of-the-earth.

As I watched the missiles heading towards us, I saw the result of our combined assault on the group of attackers. They had been eradicated in a flash by our Hellfire missiles and Hydra rockets.

Any comfort I got from that was short-lived, as I felt my controls begin shuddering violently. I had been hit with the glancing blow of a missile on my tail rotor, making this critical flight component inoperative. My Apache immediately yawed violently as I lost the counter torque effect my tail rotor provided against the powerful twin jet engines.

I immediately did the only thing I could do. I dropped the collective, eliminating the power completely, thereby preventing the helicopter from spinning out of control. The Apache began to drop as I initiated an autorotation. The problem was though, because we were so close to the ground, the instant we lost lift meant I was hurtling towards terra firma at an impossible rate of descent. I instinctively knew our ground impact would be way more than 10 Gs, the maximum survivable gravitational force on the body. My calm estimation was that our impact would be closer to 15 Gs and we would die instantly.

Everything had unfolded in fractions of a second, yet the whole sequence of events seemed to have played out in absolute slow motion. I was less than a hundred feet above the terrain, moments away from a fatal ground collision, and thinking, *It was worth it.*

That's when the unimaginable happened.

Instead of hitting the ground, I felt a massive deceleration of my already stricken helicopter. A split-second processing of what had happened made me realise it could only be high-tension wires. At around 75 feet AGL, I had flown into 60 KVA power lines. This unfortunately, offered no relief and statistically lowered any chances of our survival to less than 1 percent.

I remember waiting for what I imagined would be a burst of white light from the explosion, which I reckoned would be the last thing I would see before our lives ended.

It didn't happen!

The force at which we hit the power lines caused the cable to stretch and then snap, not at the point of impact but a little farther up the line.

My Rude Awakening

The next moment, the end of the cable was whipping back around us, getting caught in the main rotor mast. But still no explosion. Little comfort as we neared the collision point of the very unforgiving terrain. I was acutely conscious of somehow needing to reduce the force of the ground impact.

Somehow I managed to pitch the nose of the Apache up into a 50- to 60-degree angle so I could slam the tail boom into the ground first, reducing lethal energy before the fuselage and our cockpit crashed next.

With us angled in this way, I saw a burst of rockets as Will simultaneously fired all our remaining missiles. *Attaboy*, I thought, knowing that what he had done was crucial for us not having to contend with our own munitions exploding under us when we crashed.

As we struck the ground, we experienced the bone-jarring and organ-distorting symptoms of a high G-force impact, coupled with the deafening noise of hitting the terrain, and the screeching of tearing metal. I still had the presence of mind to think how well the cockpit shell held up, and even more, how effective my manoeuvre had been. This all went through my mind in the last split seconds of our crash.

We are still alive, I thought.

But it wasn't over yet.

In those few seconds, my next thought was the most sobering. We still faced the life-threatening danger that our highly flammable jet fuel would ignite and explode, something that was not an uncommon consequence, if not likely, when an aircraft is transformed into a mangled wreckage. It was an aftermath that airmen most feared because of it being the most painful and drawn-out demise.

I was consciously looking around in those split seconds, very fearful of seeing and then feeling the orange eruption of our jet fuel. Were the self-sealing fuel cells working?

Each second that passed had me hoping…and more hopeful. Fifteen seconds, and still nothing.

Thirty seconds…nothing.

I think we're going to be all right.

CHAPTER 31
THE EXTRACTION

THE MANIC CHAOS of just a few moments before gave way to an almost deathly silence and calm.

I pressed my transmit trigger to speak to Will in front of me in the forward cockpit, only to discover that we had no radios. I took off my helmet and immediately called out, "Will, are you okay?"

For a reply all I got was, "You are fucking amazing."

Will seemed to be okay.

I began to take further stock of our situation. Knowing we didn't have radios, I thought about activating our locator beacon and wondered if the insurgents had access to it or if it was even necessary. Jamie and Patrick would have seen where we went down and already radioed back to control.

Not necessary, I decided.

Then I thought, *Oh, damn! I didn't get permission from the controller to fire.* I thought about it for a moment and then remembered, *Oh yes, permission to fire was not necessary. We were in imminent danger.*

Then I remembered how the nose camera must have picked up the Stinger missile that got me. Now *that* was some footage I wanted to get hold of.

I smiled, realising I must have been a bit lightheaded.

While I was going through this, I became aware of excruciating pain in my legs. I looked down and saw a mess of flesh and blood, *a lot of blood,* which I just stared at for a while, wondering how bad it was. My back was also starting to ache. *Amazing what a strong anaesthetic adrenaline can be,* I thought as I felt the effects starting to wear off. Not being able to feel my feet and legs would portend spinal cord damage. I tried to move my toes and grimaced. My left leg was excruciatingly painful, but I was quite relieved that I could feel both of them. I could now smell the blood. *Not good,* I thought.

Will was very quiet, and I became more worried about him now that I had taken stock of my own injuries. Being in the lower, forward cockpit, he would have suffered a higher impact than me.

"Will, is everything okay?"

It took a while for him to say anything. Then came his uncertain reply, "I am fine," followed by another long pause. "I think my back got hammered though," he finally said.

I dared not ask him if he could move his toes, not wanting to hear the answer.

"Do you think we should try to get out of this thing?" he continued. "I wouldn't like it to pop on us after all we've been through."

He was also fearful of the possibility of an explosion, but by now I knew the risk was low and that he had sustained heavy injuries. Anyway, we would not be able to extract ourselves from the mangled wreckage on our own.

"Don't worry about that, Will. Just breathe, chum," I said calmly.

The best thing for both of us was to sit there quietly, knowing that a medical evacuation helicopter would come and get us soon. It was incredibly quiet and peaceful.

A typical injury sustained in high-impact accidents like this was to the neck and back, ranging from lower back spinal compression to something even more serious. Different levels of paralysis from spinal cord injuries were common.

My thoughts turned to Jamie. I knew he was safe because of our having killed the second lot of insurgents. *Thank God he is okay,* I thought. I also knew that he would immediately get backup, because maintaining our stealth on the mission was no longer necessary. Priority would be given to extracting Jamie and Patrick. It did strike me that they would be ordered to hold a rear-guard position while waiting for either the medevac helicopter or additional support for his extraction. What this meant was that while keeping clear of the actual crash site in order not to attract enemy attention to it, he would guard our stricken helicopter from a distance just in case there were other insurgents in the area who wanted to take a closer look.

I couldn't be certain how long we sat there, but because of the ever-increasing discomfort from my injuries and the possibility of us bleeding out, it was with some relief that I heard the unmistakable sound of the big twin-rotor Boeing Chinook helicopter with two Apaches providing aerial guard. The Chinook found a suitable landing place less than a hundred yards from our position while the two escort Apaches continued their aerial guard, now also joined by Jamie and Patrick.

The medical evac team moved with remarkable efficiency. Two jaws of life extrication tools were brought to the site, and in no time at all, they had opened the cockpit and were ready to transfer us to the Chinook. Two separate medics came to each of us, with others in attendance as well.

The medic attending to Will called out, "Oxygen. Syncope here," indicating to his colleague that Will had lost consciousness.

I had never been religious, but I said my own simple little prayer now anyway. *God, please don't take him now.*

This serious development made no difference to the medics' clearly well-versed emergency procedures. Before either of us was moved, they made sure we had not suffered cervical (neck) spinal cord injuries or head injuries. They could not be certain we did not have spinal injuries lower down the back, so our extraction from the helicopter was done in a way that indicated they assumed we may have.

We were both lifted out of the mangled helicopter and placed onto litter stretchers positioned alongside the cockpit. A minute or two later, we were in the Chinook and I could hear the two huge turbine engines spooling up from flight idle as we prepared for liftoff. That must have been just before I too lost consciousness.

We arrived at One ME Military Hospital and, with the same efficiency as before, were met by more medical staff already conversant with our conditions.

Will's injuries were far more serious than mine. His initial diagnosis was that he suffered a lower back transverse bone fracture and what was known as a burst fracture of the lower spine. This meant that one or two of his vertebrae had been crushed in all directions. Because there was a high probability that he had suffered a spinal cord injury, he was airlifted almost immediately to Defence Medical Services (DMS) back home in England.

I got off far lighter, with a spinal cord compression fracture to my lower back, which they decided not to operate on. My biggest injuries, however, were a smashed left ankle and multiple lacerations on both of my legs that would require surgery, which was scheduled and performed later that evening. It was amazing how efficient and effective medical treatment could be when medical professionals did not have to worry about bedside manner or the red tape that was typical in civilian medical practise.

Miraculously, I had not suffered any injury that a few weeks in hospital and six weeks of rest and recuperation leave (R&R) wouldn't cure. I couldn't say the same for Will. Even though what had happened was a normal consequence of war, it weighed heavily on my mind.

As I lay in my hospital bed, I couldn't help but relive the trauma of what we had been through.

There are certain light conditions that make it impossible for helicopter pilots to detect high-tension wires. This had been one of those occasions, as if I hadn't had enough to contend with at the time.

A wire strike, the term used by aviators to describe flying into power lines, nearly always results in catastrophic consequences from any one of three distinct possibilities, each almost certainly fatal. A combination of these factors decreases the likelihood of survival exponentially. The first possibility is that a 60 KVA high-tension wire acts as a lethal blade that can cut through the helicopter and its occupants much like a wire cheese cutter going through cheese. The next possibility is that the helicopter loses all or most of the flight controls as the cable rips through the control rods located on the rotor shaft, making it impossible for the helicopter to be flown at all, never mind during the critical phase of trying to land without an engine. The third, and perhaps the most dangerous likelihood, is that 60,000-volt-amps, 60 KVA, coming into contact with a helicopter carrying extremely flammable jet fuel is nothing less than an explosion waiting to happen. Any one of these possibilities, without even considering the complexity of being in a war zone, is enough to bring about one's early demise.

The extreme irony of our accident was that what should have killed Will and I had actually saved our lives. The speed at which I was approaching the ground would have resulted in an impact of about 15 Gs. Impossible to survive. Flying into the high-tension wires, which should have exacerbated our situation, had instead saved us. The powerlines had acted as arresting lines, like the type you find on aircraft carriers to arrest the forward speed of fighter jets when they land, which ultimately prevented us from the worst possible outcome. Our flight data recorder registered our impact at 10.1 Gs. The accepted survivable impact was supposedly under 10 Gs. Only because of our training, our level of fitness, and our bodies being used to experiencing elevated G-force conditions did we survive, but we had not been able to avoid serious back injuries.

While I was in the hospital, I had plenty of time to think intensely, not only about the mission, the near-fatal missile attack on Jamie and Patrick, and Will's and my near-miss, but also to ponder the experiences I'd had during the past six years of my service in the RAF. These thoughts bombarded my mind, and I was struggling to make sense of it all, eventually just shutting them out without any resolutions.

Then, on what I thought was the seventh or eighth morning, I woke up feeling decidedly better after a good night's rest. My mind was clearer, and I felt that I could start making sense of things again.

As a result of my improved health, I was able to make a phone call to my parents. My mother and father of course knew about my accident, and had been assured of my good health, even if that was not strictly true. My dad had been cheerful and upbeat, making sure I was in a good headspace, while my mother could not help but be very sombre about what had happened. My call ended with her saying, "It's enough now, Sunbeam. It's enough."

My parents couldn't reconcile me being in the RAF. Initially it had seemed fine, but since being posted into combat zones doing tours of duty, they'd felt that I'd been sucked into a system where I didn't belong.

"*Why, Sunbeam? Why? When you have so much here at home and even more to look forward to.*" I could hear my mother's words.

Deep down I agreed with her. As I lay in my hospital bed, I couldn't help but think about the alternatives to the RAF, which unquestionably became extremely attractive. I knew there were all sorts of possibilities for my future. Going into business was a strong probability, and Rockwell

My Rude Awakening

Manor Polo, with all its attractions, was also an option. These were the obvious ones.

Had I proven my point of doing something on my own? Would the RAF impact my life? And how would *Gigi* influence it? Little did I realise how much those thoughts would shape my future.

Having survived such a traumatic accident also had me consider some of life's bigger questions.

Does risking your life bring you closer to death, or does it make you more alive than ever?

I thought long and hard about the RAF. I loved it. I always had. But not all aspects. Pilots were referred to as "glamour boys." I suppose it didn't help matters that we wore T-shirts with either a jet fighter or an attack helicopter on it, depending on what squadron you were in, with inscriptions like:

> "If you are not living on the edge,
> you are taking up too much space."

After spending time in the operational zone, the last thing one felt like was a glamour boy. And once pilots had flown combat missions, they stopped wearing those T-shirts. Perhaps actually being on the edge brought with it a reality that had no place for bravado, no matter how lighthearted.

Another aspect I found myself thinking about was the overall effect the RAF and being a combat pilot was having on me. Was it ultimately going to turn me into somebody I wanted to be or something I abhorred? The one thing I knew with absolute certainty was that Mission Zero Niner and the emotional pressures it had come with would have a long-lasting impact on my life.

Since Will had been airlifted back to England, I had heard nothing more of his condition. It gnawed away at me and had me saying my own prayer for him. *An unbearable feeling.* It brought into sharp focus my role as a combat pilot.

Post-traumatic stress disorder (PTSD) was not something typically associated with pilots. The truth is, the continual pressure and stresses of risking one's life, flying attack helicopters on combat missions, would ultimately bore deep into one's psyche. The more time one spent in the operational area, the more one would think about what it was they were doing.

I loved the flying, and I knew I was good at it. Particularly good. I had chosen not to be a Copilot-Gunner, even though as Pilot-in-Command I did almost as much target acquisition and weapons deployment as the CPG. The reason was that as a CPG, it was 'in your face' acquiring targets and gunning them down. But of course, they were seldom just targets. They were people whose lives we were taking.

Military service makes young men hard and strong, but fragile too. No matter how resilient you may be, it would eventually take its toll. All that remained to be seen was how well one could handle the aftereffects and how quickly one could overcome them. Many experienced some form of PTSD in the course of their lives.

We listened to rock music and showed lots of swagger to our peers, especially about girls. But behind the scenes, we felt very differently. I imagined all our letters to our families were of a similar vein, no bravado but rather filled with many truths about our fears. As much as I had loved rock music, I began enjoying love ballads equally, still not something I would readily reveal to the chaps.

At twenty-five, men are still boys. Psychologically I don't think they handle war well, even though they would never show it. I think women would probably do a better job of that. But only psychologically, as they generally lacked the recklessness that is inherent in men. Which is why men drive too fast and take risks that result in them breaking their necks around twenty-two times more often than women do, in military and sporting roles.

Is it ultimately being polar opposites that attract men and women to each other? And the more men are men, the more women love it but dislike it at the same time. John Gray, PhD, probably understands this better than most, as it was the basis of his book, *Men Are from Mars, Women Are from Venus*.

Then, of course, I thought about Gigi. All the time. It was impossible not to. Even though I had not seen her for almost a year, I'd spent literally every day with her, through her son, who had many of her mannerisms and facial features. This made her larger than life. And it had come so close to changing.

An unfortunate reality were the many nightmares I'd been having about how close Jamie had come to being brought down by Stinger missiles. Irreversible consequences, too hideous to contemplate. Gigi would have blamed me, and I would have blamed myself.

I knew that if I left the RAF, Jamie would too, and that was how I wanted it to be. My thoughts about my future, including Gigi, were beginning to crystallise. If Jamie and I both left the RAF, the reason she—we—had ostensibly ended our relationship would be gone. Having not seen her in such a long time since we had agreed to go our separate ways, I knew I should not disturb that. As much as I loved Gigi, so too I knew the sacrifices I would have to make for the two of us to have a future, and that some of those sacrifices would be impossible for me to bear. The most glaringly obvious one was me having children of my own, even if it was the furthest thing from my mind right then.

Then, late on the afternoon of my eighth day in hospital, I received my first and only visitor, none other than Jamie, of course. He had managed to get special permission to come and see me, which I was really pleased about.

I was sitting in a chair next to my hospital bed, nursing a very tender back and legs, when he came in. Without a thought for the other patients, he leant over me and hugged me, holding me for an appreciable amount of time.

"What's up, Jamie? Are you okay?" I asked.

"God, you nearly killed us," was his reply.

I didn't understand. Surely Jamie was not blaming me for the insurgent Stinger missile attack on his helicopter.

He saw the confusion on my face and quickly gave an explanation. "God, no, not like that. You saved my life. We thought *you* had been killed. I didn't know what I was scorching. Mum has been beside herself. You have to speak to her," he rambled.

"Jamie, Jamie, slow down. What are you talking about?" I asked.

He stopped for a moment and just shook his head while he continued looking at me. Then he cupped my cheeks in his hands, just like Gigi would have. "I thought I had lost my best friend," he said, looking into my eyes again, just as his mother would have.

Conscious of others around us and to lighten the moment, I joked, "Just don't kiss me."

With that, Jamie kissed me, fortunately only on the forehead. He then put his hands on my thighs and said, "You have to phone Mum."

"Jamie!" I said, stopping him again.

"Okay, okay, I will explain, but first tell me how you are?" he asked, taking a breath.

"I am fine, just need some R&R. I am very worried about Will though. He took a heavy blow. He was airlifted straight back home," I said. I was brief because I was anxious to hear what Jamie had been going on about. "I will tell you all later. First, tell me what is going on," I demanded.

Jamie calmed down a bit and went and got another chair, which he placed right in front of me. Speaking in a hushed tone, he began, "So let me tell you from the time you said to me that you had spotted the Johnnys. I looked out but still couldn't see them and just followed your instructions. The next minute, you were alongside me in that slightly low and forward position. I wasn't too sure what you were doing until you told me to fire my decoy flares. Only when the first Stinger was coming our way did I truly realise what was going on. I was a little slow in banking right and saw the second volley of missiles heading towards you. Just when I thought the decoy flares had done their job, I saw your tail rotor being struck. I didn't think you had a chance. It is just as well we had killed our attackers because I was focused completely on you. I saw you hit the power lines, but your ground impact was concealed from me. You went down so fast, I was convinced you had copped it." Jamie took a breath.

I replied in a matter-of-fact tone, "I managed to reduce a lot of the impact by slamming the tail rotor onto the ground first. It did an excellent job of absorbing a lot of the downward force that I guess would have killed us."

Jamie shuddered.

"What happened next?" I prompted, not wanting him to lose his train of thought.

"Do you know, had you not come up alongside me to help with the decoys, those Stingers would have got me?" Jamie continued, putting his hand on my knee.

I didn't say anything, knowing he was probably right. "Carry on, Jamie," I insisted.

"Once you went down, I immediately contacted Ops Control. They told me to stay clear of the crash site and to hold a rear-guard position, staying in the area until the medevac helicopter and backup arrived. I didn't know what had happened to you, and when I radioed you frantically but got no response, I realised you must have lost all electrics.

"I just wanted to go in and see if you and Will were okay, but of course I couldn't, and I wouldn't have been able to do anything anyway." Jamie paused for a moment and collected his thoughts.

"It seemed to take forever, but eventually the Chinook medevac helicopter arrived with two Apache escorts. All three Apaches were then engaged in holding a guard position around the crash site, making sure we distracted any would-be insurgents from attacking the soft target of the Chinook and you, if you, you know, were still okay. The problem was that I still had no idea what the crash site looked like and what the medevac team was doing. To be honest, I thought they were extracting yours and Will's bodies." Jamie stopped again, tears in his eyes.

He then continued in a quivering voice, "The Chinook lifted out, and we were ordered to scorch the crash site. For a crazy moment, I wondered if they even managed to get the two of you out of there or I was about to incinerate you. Fuck, Charlie, the thought nearly killed me."[1]

I reached over and put my hand on his shoulder, truly appreciating in that moment that he had become a really special friend.

He wasn't finished yet. "We then escorted the Chinook until we were over friendlies, and they carried on to One ME Hospital with the other two escorts. I returned to base with dangerously low fuel, which was why I couldn't continue as an escort for your Chinook. I still did not know what had happened to you and Will." Jamie then took another deep breath. After

---

[1] The Scorched Earth Policy was the destruction of any assets, including military equipment, transport vehicles, communication sites, industrial resources, food and water stores, or anything that may be useful to the enemy. Until surprisingly recently, even local people themselves could be destroyed under this policy, but thankfully this law was changed. The scorching of local people, along with food and water stores for civilians, was banned under the 1977 Geneva Convention.

a while, he continued, "I got to the base, and I didn't know what to do. I knew I had to speak to Mum. She went crazy, bud. I couldn't console her, and I was in no state myself. We got no news for twenty-four hours, and it nearly killed her. When we did hear something, it could hardly have been less informative. And then the day before yesterday, I heard you had been operated on and were okay. That is when I made a plan to get here. I heard about Will. You have to speak to Mum, bud. She needs to hear from you. I think she was close to a nervous breakdown. She doesn't know that I managed to get here." Jamie had begun rambling again.

"I would like to speak to Gigi," I said. "But how can I?"

"Can you walk? On your own? I can help you," he asked, looking at the cast on my left leg.

I could tell he was busy hatching another plan. "I can. Slowly," I replied.

"Give me a moment," Jamie said, and with that, he dashed off. He left me contemplating whether I could actually walk, but then he returned before long, beaming. "All organised."

I gave him an enquiring look.

"I just sorted it out with one of the nurses," he replied to the question I didn't ask.

I guessed his disarming charm had its uses.

We went through to an admin section, and I was ushered into a small back office where the obliging Sally-Anne pointed to the phone. "Don't be long, Lieutenant. I really shouldn't be doing this," she said.

Quite surprisingly, I patched into the UK telephone network on the first attempt.

The Blackwood residence phone rang just twice, and Gigi answered in a very shaky voice, "Georgina Blackwood here."

"Darling, it's me," was all I said.

She burst into tears. "Oh, God, my darling!" And then she carried on sobbing. Eventually she said, in a very quiet voice, "Thank God. I am so happy to hear your voice. God, I thought I had lost you. I didn't know what had happened. No one could tell me where you were…or if you were…you know… Thank God you're alive."

She slowly started pulling herself together as I told her a little bit about Will's and my injuries, which I understated just a little, even if it was not strictly true.

"How have you managed to phone me?" Gigi asked.

"Jamie's here, he organised it. You know how he can organise things?" I replied.

"Thank God. What happens next, my darling? What is going to happen to you?" Gigi asked in a quiet, concerned tone.

"I'm going to be transferred to Defence Medical Services in England, Birmingham, actually in the next week or so, Darling, for about six to ten days of treatment—traction and observation. Then I should get six weeks R&R, you know, rest and recuperation," I told her reassuringly.

"Birmingham! Is that like sick leave?" Gigi shot back.

"It is, my darling," was my short reply.

"Come to me," she suggested quietly. Then, as if she had made up her mind, Gigi said more insistently, "Come to me… Do you hear me, I want you to come and have some of your R&R here with me."

I smiled on the other end of the line with Gigi showing the character of the woman I knew and loved.

"I will, Darling," I said without hesitation. All my best intentions had unravelled in an instant.

"I'm waiting," she said. "Keep me posted. I love you. I love you. Goodbye."

I couldn't wait to get back to Shrewsbury and Gigi, to that familiar, comfortable place that had become my second home. I knew the decision I had made was intrinsically wrong, but in the moment when she had said I should come to her, I had capitulated. I did not regret it though, not in any form. I did have one awkward call to make, however, and that was to my parents, to explain to them that I would be spending the first part of my R&R with Georgina. A thin excuse I would use was because Shrewsbury was close to Birmingham Hospital, where I would be receiving treatment. Then I gingerly made my way back to the ward where Jamie was waiting for me.

Eventually it was time for him to go. Just as he was getting up to leave, the senior nurse told us that Lieutenant William Granger had come out of recovery a short while earlier, following his second operation to his lower back. On all accounts, it seemed to have been a success. She told us that his prognosis was good and he was expected to make a good recovery, but it would take many months. She had sounded a little guarded, but I was focused on the positive, hoping beyond hope that he would escape what seemed like certain paraplegia.

Jamie saw the concerned look on my face and put an arm around my shoulder, giving me a tight squeeze. "He will be okay, chum."

As he was about to leave, he turned and said, "Oh, damn, I nearly forgot." He handed me my Walkman. "I had a feeling you might want this."

Jamie had such an endearing side.

Two days after seeing him, I received the devastating news that Will's injuries had resulted in him suffering paraplegia, the loss of the use of the lower part of his body, and there was almost no chance of that changing.

The emotional part of my brain questioned, *Why do I still have the use of my legs and he doesn't? Was I sitting more upright when he may have been slouched?*

The analytical parts of my brain gave me the high probability reasons.

Will had been in the more forward, lower cockpit. When I had slammed the tail structure of the helicopter into the ground to reduce our G-force impact, it had created a whiplash effect on the tandem cockpit. Because of his more vulnerable position, and his cockpit having less protection from the two landing-gear assemblies and big wheels, with their significant shock-absorbing capabilities, even Will's powerful body was no match for those forces.

Had it not been for my actions, we would've both died. I'd saved our lives, but surely ruined the rest of his. This became my biggest conundrum. I hoped that time would provide some answers. We were much the same age, and that meant a lot of ruined years lay ahead of Will. This soon began to play on my mind, subliminally at times, then at others it was an unrelenting, persisting thought. *What could I have done differently?*

In the theatre of war, William Granger would make it into the record of statistics under the column "Life-Changing Injury." I couldn't really get my mind around that. *How life-changing*? I had a sense that those words were an understatement in the extreme.

Another four days passed, and I was being prepared for my discharge from One ME Hospital. During this time, I didn't manage to speak to Gigi again. It seemed I did not have Jamie's powers of persuasion.

After losing track of time, the day finally arrived and I was on my way back to England.

My Rude Awakening

My transfer from the searing heat of the Middle East to the contrasting coolness of home, experiencing not uncommon early autumn single-digit temperatures, was an awakening I had not considered. I didn't mind. It was part of coming home, if you were English.

I was ambulanced to the advanced DMS Queen Elizabeth Hospital in Birmingham, where I was checked in by a very caring and attentive nurse, Corporal Susan Hennessey, and then settled into my new hospital bed, a far cry from whence I had just come. God, it was good to be back on home soil, if not my home in Berkshire…or Shrewsbury.

From the moment Corporal Hennessey attended to my admittance, she would always find time to come to my bedside to chat and check on my progress. As a result, I had no difficulty in arranging to make phone calls, the first of which was to Gigi.

I didn't immediately tell her I was back in England, wanting to surprise her, but when I heard the tension back in her voice, I regretted not having made more of an effort to call her sooner. It dissipated quickly enough though when I asked her if she was up for a two-hour drive to come and collect me from hospital on Friday after lunch, which was in just three days' time. Her unrestrained eagerness about seeing me elated me, and I could not wait to see hear again.

Then, with her typical mischievous chuckle, she said she would have to check her diary because she may have tea at the tennis club.

I smiled. *That's my Gigi.*

I got back to my bed, put on my headphones, and played a song that seemed particularly apt right then.

"Run to You" – Bryan Adams

| YouTube | Spotify | Apple |

I had so often dreamt of feeling Gigi's touch, and now it was going to happen. My R&R in Shrewsbury could not be described in any other way. I was running to Gigi.

"…it's so damn easy makin' love to you…"

Those words delved right into me. After so long, we would soon make love again.

During my Air Force career, I flew numerous missions in several war zones. Many people have felt I should've included more of these encounters. My young son especially has been a strong advocate of me writing more chapters, especially my own SITTING DUCK mission. I have refrained from doing so, mindful of not wanting to turn this memoir into an Air Force war story. However, as declassification occurs with the passing of time, I may well write something more on the matter in the future.

I chose to write in detail about this mission because it encapsulated so many extraordinary aspects, and of course I had been extremely lucky. Added to that, not only did it affect my near-term future, but it also had a profound effect on the rest of my life.

I have come to understand that in wartime it is seldom a single event that causes PTSD. That was certainly true for me. The one event one may have thought could have caused my condition would have been the Stinger missile attack and my subsequent accident. The one thing I am certain of is that it had no, or very little effect, on me either then or later on. No nightmares about the accident, flashbacks, or reservations about flying. Quite the country, in fact. Helicopters continued to play an important part in my life and have always been something I have enjoyed with a passion. The Middle East, and the time I spent in other war zones is a different matter. Lots of waking up in a cold sweat, shutting thoughts out of my mind, and other symptoms like hypervigilance, insomnia, and depression. One of my symptoms, which has always persisted, is not being able to see any violence, especially against women and children. Two often I saw the effects of war on those who were most vulnerable. To this day it persists. My family and friends know all too well what programs to flick past on the television, my children almost racing to get the remote. I suffered my first onset of PTSD pursuant to military service. Then there were two more events that caused PTSD later on in my life, covered in the sequel. I was finally successfully treated between 2020 and 2021, during COVID. I pointedly did not say *cured*. I don't believe it is possible for PTSD to ever be fully cured.

CHAPTER 32
A DIFFERENT R&R LEAVE

C ORPORAL HENNESSEY WAS a breath of fresh air. It was very charming the way she would put her hand on my arm, look intently at me with her big doe eyes, and ask, "Is there anything I can do for you, Lieutenant? *Anything*…" with more emphasis and a little squeeze.

I thought about asking her to cut my hair, as my last visit to the barber had been several weeks before the accident but being in hospital was not conducive to this sort of grooming. I was quite certain she would have obliged, but I wasn't inclined to open that door. I may have, were I not going to be seeing Gigi.

Counting down the hours, my hospital discharge finally arrived. With our daily phone calls having resumed, I'd told Gigi I would be cleared at around two o'clock. With excitement welling in my belly, I checked the time again. There were still forty minutes to go, enough time for me to do the last bits of paperwork.

I arrived at Corporal Susan Hennessey's desk to the warmest welcome.

"So, Lieutenant, you're leaving me today—*us* today—but we'll see each other again in two weeks. If you need anything, and I mean *anything*, before then, give me a call. Here is my direct number." She handed me a little note, which curiously had a heart drawn in the corner.

It was nice of her to be so caring, I thought, not wanting to read too much into it.

She started filling out the forms and made a little light conversation. "So, who is picking you up today? A brother, sister, your mum?"

"No, neither a brother or sister," I replied.

"Oh, your mum then. This could be her now."

Before I had a chance to correct her, Gigi bounded into the reception area and threw her arms around my neck and shoulders, pressing her body against mine, oblivious of anyone around us.

"Oh, God, my baby, my gorgeous darling, you are here! You are finally here," she blurted.

Neither of us could have cared less who was watching as we unashamedly held and kissed each other.

Almost a year of not seeing each other, after Gigi had decided we should go our separate ways, and me convincing myself not to interfere with a decision that was best for us, was forgotten in a heartbeat!

"Ooh, and this long hair, I could get used to this, Lieutenant," she said, pulling it suggestively. She clenched her teeth and let out something between a purr and a growl.

I had momentarily forgotten about Corporal Hennessey when I noticed her staring at us. Remembering my manners, I hastily introduced them. "Darling, this is Corporal Susan Hennessey who has made my stay very comfortable. Corporal, this is my…ah, this is Georgina."

Corporal Hennessey's look of shock was soon replaced by a blush, now under no illusion if it was my mother who had come to collect me.

Gigi, almost brushing Corporal Hennessey aside, took control of the last bits of my discharge paperwork, now behaving very much like my mother, save for the occasional little squeeze.

With her having dealt with all the red tape, I placed my crutches under my armpits so I could make my way towards the car.

"Oh, God, are those yours?" she asked, referring to my walking aids. Only then did she realise I was still nursing some significant injuries.

I clambered into the passenger seat of Gigi's car, and we headed off to Shrewsbury. I instinctively reached over and squeezed her thigh, and she reached down, taking hold of my hand.

Remembering that Corporal Hennessey had given me her number, I took it out of my breast pocket and held it out to Gigi.

"What's this, Baby?" Gigi asked.

"It's Corporal Hennessey's direct number in case we need anything."

"Okay, I will take care of it."

I handed her the note, and she took a quick glance at it.

Without saying a word, she opened her window and threw it out, then tendered, "You won't be needing that number, Darling. I am going to take care of you far better than she ever could."

I remembered the little heart in the corner of the note and smiled at the hint of contempt in Gigi's voice. *She clearly had read something into it. God, it is so good to be back.*

No sooner had I thought that when Gigi asked, "Are you happy to be coming home with me to Shrewsbury?"

"There's nowhere else I would rather be," I answered truthfully.

We had so much to talk about, yet for most of the journey we sat in relative silence. It was as if we were just absorbing being together again, enamoured with each other as we had ever been and comfortably slipping back into each other's lives.

We were soon confronted by the gates of the Blackwood residence, and the old familiarity swamped my feelings.

As I struggled to get out of the car, feeling the cool autumn air on my neck, Gigi shouted, "Suzie, help," which had Suzie scurrying out. "Be a honey and grab Charles's bags. Please put them in my room for now," she said, knowing full well that it was a most unusual request.

Suzie obliged without batting an eye.

Gigi slipped into her room and when she returned, I immediately noticed she had put on some sandals. *I love those feet.* Could I still think of them as mine?

She had made a special effort for my homecoming. Everything about the evening was gentle. She, and Suzie no doubt, had prepared a whole sea bass, first baked with butter, fresh flat-leaf parsley, and dill, then later put under the griller to crisp the skin. Served with lightly grilled asparagus and parmesan cheese shavings, it was accompanied by a pink La Maison French wine. This was followed by a delicate raspberry soufflé. Thoughts of Gigi's exquisite catering came flooding back with the evening's meal putting her culinary expertise on full display.

I often thought that Gigi's dishes were an expression of her mood, and this evening's mood and meal had an air of being gentle. Nothing was gentler than the way she took my cheeks in her perfectly manicured hands, put her lips against mine in an unhurried, loving, passionate kiss that had our deep feelings for each other come flooding back.

Once we finished our dinner, she filled our glasses with the last of the wine and gestured towards her bedroom. "I think it's time for a bath, my darling Lieutenant."

I could barely remember the last time I'd had one of those.

I hobbled into Gigi's room and noticed the absence of my suitcase, which suggested Suzie must've packed my clothing into Gigi's wardrobe. I smiled at this change in our routine. On reflection, sleeping in separate rooms would have been farcical. There was no question that Suzie was well aware of mine and Gigi's history. How could she not be after cleaning the guest suite following my visits all these years.

Gigi led me to the bathroom where I was met by the gentle gurgling sounds of the jets in the bubble bath. She switched off the lights, and in the gentle glow of the candles, I noticed rose petals placed around the perimeter of the hot tub. Not unlike when I'd last stayed in Gigi's room after our trip to Rockwell Manor.

"Let me help you undress, Baby," Gigi said, which once again had me smiling at the connection of "baby" and "undress."

I was still very tender, so the help was welcome. More than that though, the feel of her hands on my body immediately reminded me how much I loved her touch. Nothing had changed.

She got to my trousers and belt and began undoing the buckle.

"Can I trust you down there?" I ventured.

She replied with a flat, "No."

"Oh, goodness," I exclaimed. "And I can't even make a run for it," I said, looking down at my plaster cast. "Is there any compassion for an injured serviceman?"

"Definitely not, Lieutenant. Tonight, you are going to be punished for the anguish you have caused me," she said, feigning callousness. "Plus, it's not the bone in your left leg that I will be concerning myself with this evening, my darling."

I was not sure if this bravado would carry on into the evening, knowing Gigi's feelings were arguably more tender than my injuries.

I tottered forward and put my arms around her, quite unperturbed that the only thing I was wearing was a plaster cast. Once again, our mouths came together in a passionate kiss. Feeling her hands on my bare buttocks, I immediately became aroused.

She reached down and took hold of me, saying, "Oh, Darling, you are home…and nothing has changed down here. I'd better not start *yet*, or you won't be bathing tonight."

Another glimpse of Gigi's humour. I really was home.

With her help, I sank into her luxurious bath, dangling my injured leg over the side. I relaxed as she leant over and began soaping my body, not able to remember the last time I had experienced such comfort.

She spent a little extra time around my genitals, making expressive movements with her mouth while feeling my groin. Without saying a word, she removed her dress and revealed her glorious naked body.

My intake of breath was involuntary. Oh, God, I have missed this woman.

"May I join you, Lieutenant?" she cooed, and without waiting for my reply, she stepped into the bath.

Gigi sat down in front of me with her legs over mine on either side of my hips. She moved closer between my spread thighs and pressed her chest against mine as we once again embraced. We were more than content to just sit like that for a while, saying nothing.

Having now been in Gigi's company for several hours, I instinctively knew she had not been with anyone else whilst I had been away. Even though we had barely spoken for a year, she had not been in anywhere near the right frame of mind to have begun another relationship. Any thoughts I may have had to the contrary were just my own insecurities.

We got out of the bath and half-heartedly dried each other off on the way to the bed. We were both ready for more.

"Lie down, Baby. Do you need a pillow?" she asked.

"Yes, maybe under my left ankle, my darling."

Gigi did as I suggested, and in addition, she took another of her big pillows and instructed me to lift my buttocks as she slipped it under my bottom. This caused my body to arch so that the highest point was my pelvis. And not to put too fine a point on it, the pinnacle of this little elevation was my upstanding erection.

My bemused expression drew a response.

"I want you raised so you don't have to move," was her quick explanation.

Gigi then became more businesslike and did not waste any time in straddling my torso. We both had an urgent need to end our long abstinence.

Does Gigi also feel I'm all hers when we are making love? was the feeling that came over me as I watched her.

We then slowly began making love with just soft, gentle, little movements. Gigi was not only wary of hurting me but also wanted to prolong our first time together again after such a long time.

Needless to say, it didn't go exactly as planned.

The slow start rapidly gained momentum, and that's when things went haywire!

Not wanting to hurt me, well that went fine. But for the other, wanting to prolong our first union. Not so much.

Gigi's jovial comment of, "An early flood warning would've been nice," and my counter of, "You didn't even have time for your 'Oh, God' prayer," said it all. It had taken just a few moments for both our floodgates to open.

We made up for it though, by making love for what seemed like most of the night, taking short breaks to recover or doze a little. No one was counting how many times we orgasmed, but it was certainly a record, not that this was the intention.

My injuries caused no adverse effect given that Gigi was mostly doing me because of my limited mobility. The only pain I felt was when, during one of our close moments, Gigi had whispered, almost to herself, "Ooh, God, I have missed this cock." Perhaps I was being a bit sensitive, but I was sure that in the past she would've said "my" or "your cock."

Over the next few days, we started acting like a normal couple. We shopped at organic markets, became regulars at the local barista, lunched at various restaurants, went to the cinema, and enjoyed many activities that were commonplace within normal relationships. I especially enjoyed Gigi showing me around all the historical gems of Shrewsbury. I had always wanted to do those things but somehow never quite got around to doing so. I was aware that we drew the occasional enquiring look, sometimes a whisper, but it didn't worry us. Even when it was someone Gigi knew, she behaved in as relaxed fashion, unconcerned what they may have been thinking. *Is us being together a possibility?* I couldn't help wondering. To many, I don't think our age difference was even that noticeable. I was probably looking older and Gigi evergreen. I loved it when a maître-d' or shop owner treated us as any normal couple.

What I couldn't imagine was normal though, was our sex. We began and ended each day with enjoying each other's carnal fruits. And as each day progressed, my contribution became more evident. Eventually the biggest impediment was when I had to lift my leg over either Gigi's torso or legs, as I had to contend with the extra weight of the cast on my weakened limb.

Gigi took some delight in teasing me with passing remarks like, "Do you think if I rub your injured leg long enough, you could get the same bone reaction you produce *between* your legs?"

I discovered the joy of buying fresh produce and how expert Gigi was in the kitchen, displaying a natural artistic flair as she created one memorable healthy meal after another. It was not a surprise that Suzie's contribution when it came to the culinary department was in fact quite minimal, limited to preparation more than anything else.

I also spoke to my parents on several occasions, and quite surprisingly, they did not question why I was with Gigi in Shrewsbury. Not once did they question my thin excuse that it was more convenient being close to the hospital in Birmingham, but instead politely enquired as to when I would be coming home to Rockwell Manor. My father had arranged for my car to be transported to Shrewsbury so I could leave when I felt ready. I truthfully told my mother that it wouldn't be long and I would be coming home to Berkshire, and I would let her know. I just didn't feel like thinking about it, let alone speaking about it.

Gigi and my mother also spoke to each other whenever I phoned home, and on each occasion, I thought how normal it was. Except for one thing: they didn't know that we had been, or were, in a relationship. Or did they? I knew my father would just brush it under the carpet, but my mother was different. She was uncannily perceptive, and there had been over four or even five years for her to work it out. For whatever reason, it didn't really worry me.

During this R&R, my injuries healed surprisingly fast, and I was able to quickly dispense with dressings on my lacerations. Instead, every morning and evening after sex, Gigi would apply a topical cream to aid the healing. Every time she did this, I wondered whether I was enjoying the sensuality of a lover or the care of a mother.

After two weeks of enjoying each other, shopping, cooking, and healthy eating, listening to music, dancing, and being out and about in Shrewsbury, it was time for me to go back to the hospital to have my cast removed.

When we got there, we were met by the same nurse, Corporal Susan Hennessey. Very cheekily, she said, "Goodness me, Lieutenant, you look a picture of health. Do tell what brings you here in such fine fettle?" With a smile creeping onto her face, she winked at Gigi.

Gigi smiled back, happy with Corporal Hennessey's graceful acknowledgment of our relationship and her indirect compliment.

We got back from Birmingham, having again gone via the fresh produce market and fishmonger, both of us in high spirits and looking forward to another evening together. I loved hanging around the kitchen as Gigi prepared our meals. This evening would be king crab, a favourite, and an array of dips, which she would then invariably feed to me. There was always something so sensual in the way she did this that it often ended up with us in the bedroom. In fairness though, during this time, many things led to us having sex regardless of whether Gigi fed me or not. Making up for lost time, perhaps.

I was helping her carry the food to the annex dining table, still limping slightly because of the tenderness, when she asked, "I just want to know just one thing, Darling. Do you think my lieutenant is ready to fuck me now? I need one of those."

I felt the excitement come up from my belly, Gigi once again taking pleasure in trying to shock me and extract me from the clutches of my "sheltered upbringing," as she put it.

I had to try hard not to get swallowed up in my love for this astounding woman, as had been the case all through our relationship.

In the two weeks that had passed, we had not spoken about us. I knew it was coming, but neither of us was quite ready for it. As much as I loved Gigi, I knew a future for us would be difficult. Very difficult. The possibility of Jamie and me leaving the Air Force had me contemplating my future with earnest, and I found it impossible to reconcile how she and I could fit into this life together, even before considering children.

Two days later, we went to a nearby woods, Attingham Park, so I could get a little exercise on my healing leg. After a lovely walk, we found a nice spot to lay out a picnic blanket and enjoy a glass of wine and some cheese and crackers.

Gigi sat between my legs, facing me, with her legs over mine. She quite unexpectedly said, "Charles, I want to speak to you about your accident in the Middle East."

This was not the conversation I had expected or wanted. Ever since that fateful day I had been struggling with what transpired. I preferred just shutting it out of my mind.

"You nearly lost your life, my darling. It happened because Jamie nearly lost his life too, and he certainly would have, had it not been for you."

I began to protest, but she would have none of it, putting her index finger on my mouth.

"Jamie has told me everything. I know the danger he was in. How he had to destroy your crashed helicopter, scorching or something." Then she said very quietly, "It has had a huge effect on him, my love. I can't even imagine the effect it has had on you."

It was not the time for me to interject. Gigi needed to get things off her chest.

"You once told me something your mother had said about intrinsically knowing someone in a short space of time. It was like that for me, from the time I first met you. When we spent those wonderful days at Rockwell Manor, it only confirmed what I already knew. I have seen your life and your future, my darling. You are not a military man. Yes, you are an amazing pilot, which I now understand more than ever, but you're *not* a military man."

I knew what Gigi was saying was true. It was never my intention to become a permanent Air Force officer, aware there was always the possibility of getting sucked in and your being becoming so moulded by your military life that it coloured your future, sometimes impregnating it with irreversible consequences.

Gigi carried on, impressing upon me, "You have such a bright future.

You have your degree and a family steeped in business tradition and polo." Then to lighten the conversation she added, "Just stay away from those polo groupies. They would love to get their hands on you. And yes, you love your flying. You don't need to be in the Air Force to fly. Who was the Patrón you beat in the Barrett Cup?"

"Jerry Kapper," I answered.

"Yes, him. He doesn't need to be the only person who commutes between polo matches in his own helicopter. The only difference is that you'll be flying it yourself," Gigi concluded.

That thought certainly resonated with me, yet somehow I dared not admit it.

"And, Darling, that brings me to us," Gigi said.

So she was finally getting to the topic that had been bombarding my mind for the past two weeks.

"Your future that I have seen, it doesn't include me, my darling. How can it?"

We were both quiet for a long while, Gigi watching my downturned face as these words sank in. Unlike the last time we had decided to go our separate ways, borne out of concerns for my safety and the uncertainty of our futures, this was for an even deeper reason.

Gigi broke the silence first. "It won't be much longer now before you will be thinking about a family. Your *own* family, my darling. Your own *children*."

She did not have to say more than that, even though it was the one irrefutable fact that confirmed our having a future together was an impossibility.

"So, Darling, it is time for you to leave the Air Force." This was more an instruction than a suggestion, her sounding more like my mother than my lover. "And you must take Jamie with you. I don't want you there, regardless of our future, and I don't want Jamie there either. I certainly don't want him there without you. You said you would be there to support him, and you were. But you must realise, it is a miracle that you survived. Statistically, you had no chance." Then in a more emphatic tone, she simply stated, "Jamie isn't a military man either, my darling. It is in your hands, you know that. It is time for you to both leave." The expression on her face told me it was the end of the discussion.

What was top of Gigi's mind was Jamie and me leaving the Air Force. This is what had driven her emphatic view. Not her and I, and that we could not be in each other's future. I knew that the complications of our relationship caused us both tremendous anguish. But was I ready to give it up? Was Gigi? And if it were to end, what was not clear was when she thought this should happen. Would we stay together until things changed, perhaps me meeting someone else or because of me developing a yearning to start a family. Would leaving the RAF mean we could be together for another year, possibly two years?

Already I was feeling more in love with Gigi than ever before. Was I subconsciously conniving how we could stay together?

There was nothing for me to say right then. I leant forward, taking her in my arms as she wrapped her legs around my body and her arms around my neck. I felt her little quiver as the tears rolled down her face, her emotions spilling over, her logical mind having given way to her aching heart.

How can I ever leave her?

Once her sobs had subsided, I took her moist cheeks in my hands and we kissed a long, loving, caring kiss. We finished our wine, packed up our picnic, and holding hands, slowly made our way back to Gigi's car.

That night our lovemaking was quiet and tender. It was only when we climaxed that the intensity of our passion became evident. She held my buttocks firmly, pulling me as hard and deep inside her as she could, our chests pressed firmly against each other's as I concentrated all my energy on our coupling. As our orgasms began, the pulsating waves of our release played out to a quiet but fervent, "Ah…ah…ah…ah," from Gigi. She put her hands behind my head and kissed me firmly, again with hardly any movement, just wanting to feel the closeness between all the sensual parts of our bodies.

A day or two later, whilst we were sitting in the drawing room after dinner, sipping a glass of wine and chatting quietly, Gigi said, "Darling, my very good friend is coming to spend a few nights with us from tomorrow. In fact, she is my best friend, Jacqui. I know you have never met her, but I'm sure you have often heard us speaking."

The only thing I remembered about Jacqui was the phone call I had overheard on one of my earlier trips to Shrewsbury. "Oh, okay," I replied, without volunteering that I knew anything of her.

"Be warned, my love. She's quite a handful. I was going to just keep you to myself, but she insisted."

Then, as if she had stumbled onto a good idea, Gigi turned to me and said, "Hold on for a moment. I'm just going to get something." With that she got up and went upstairs. A short while later she returned with her manicure and pedicure set.

"Ooh, Jackie must be very special for you to be doing your nails tonight," I said with a twinkle in my eye.

All I got in reply was a smile and a cheeky little wink as she took up her seat next to me on the sofa. "Feet," she instructed, patting her lap.

Without giving me an explanation, she spent the next thirty minutes giving *me* a pedicure and a manicure.

CHAPTER 33
AND THEN THERE WAS JACQUI

I DIDN'T NEED TO ask Gigi why we had not met before, since our relationship had always been under wraps and, in truth, still was. I had a feeling that she had arranged this to finally share with her best friend the relationship she had been hiding for the past five years.

Interestingly, we did not have sex that night, nor the following morning.

I could not figure it out, so as we were finishing breakfast, I asked in my most polite tone, "My gorgeous darling, has my sexual rationing got anything to do with Jacqui's arrival this afternoon?"

"Of course it does," came Gigi's candid reply. "You will soon discover that Jacqui is demonstrative, hot, and naughty as all hell. I just want to make sure you are focussed on me tonight," she said with a smile.

"And these clothes you put out for me, has that got something to do with Jacqui as well?"

"Another 'of course'," again without hesitation.

I wasn't sure how that squared with what I was wearing, which was nothing more than a white T-shirt, loose-fitting navy-blue track pants, and Havaianas flip-flops. I would definitely explore that with her at some stage. Perhaps I was not the only one who had a foot fetish.

The gorgeous, curvaceous, and bubbly Jacqui arrived like a whirlwind, bounding up the pathway, and in a most spontaneous and affectionate way, she scooped Gigi into her arms and planted a smooch on her lips.

She could have been wearing clothes out of Gigi's closet except a size or two bigger—a sand-coloured, loose and flowing midcalf-length dress, and a thin tan leather belt; a plunging V-neck showing her very ample cleavage of her large, bouncy breasts; open leather sandals with beautifully pedicured feet; and lovely manicured hands with a bare wedding-ring finger. A MILF if ever I saw one!

Jacqui gave me similar treatment, holding me close with no qualms that we were strangers. She was brimming with personality, and I took an instant liking to her.

"So where am I sleeping, darling?" Jacqui asked her friend, walking into the house with me in tow, carrying her bags.

"You are in the guest suite, my love," was Gigi's reply.

"Ooh, you're letting me sleep with Charles and it's only the first night?" Jacqui quipped.

"Go to hell," was Gigi's rapid-fire response.

"Come on, Gigi, turn the music on, open the wine. We have got some catching up to do now that you have finally let Charles out of his cage, or is that out of your toy cupboard? Not that I blame you," Jacqui joked, looking me up and down whilst teasing her friend.

Jacqui was right at home in Gigi's house, breezing through to the kitchen, interfering with the cooking—which Gigi didn't mind—gesturing for me to pour her more wine and taking control of the music. It was wonderful, really, and I enjoyed the easy, close interaction between these two best friends.

We sat in the kitchen, chatting while we sipped our wine and, fortunately for Gigi, not interfering too badly with her meal preparation.

"So, I would just like to say, darling, this is very nice." Jacqui put a hand on my arm, speaking about me as if I weren't there. "I think I am up for an RAF pilot. Should I ask Charles to organise something, or perhaps Jamie could be my matchmaker? He is a ladies' man, after all," she continued, really enjoying herself.

Gigi was surprisingly quiet, seemingly not sure what she should say, until Jacqui said, "Or even better, why don't I just hook up with Jamie, darling? You wouldn't mind, would you?" Jacqui nudged me so that I wouldn't miss Gigi's reaction as she carried on her mischievousness at her friend's expense.

"Go to hell! Don't you dare. He is like a son to you," Gigi replied, quickly finding a plausible reason why her friend should not do with Jamie what she was doing with me.

We were all chuckling now at Gigi's double standards and how it was dealt with in such a lighthearted and humorous way.

Having given Suzie the night off, Gigi handed Jacqui and me a platter of oysters and a salad bowl and ushered us through to the annex dining area.

With the music playing far too loudly and the wine flowing too freely, Jacqui convinced Gigi and me to eat our oysters by taking them between our lips and passing them from one to the other. Needless to say, this resulted in the occasional oyster falling to the floor.

Jacqui remarked that the resultant creamy splattering looked surprisingly similar to something she had not been getting enough of recently.

"A good balanced meal as well, I am told," she said. "I imagine you've had some catching up to do in that department, my darling." She looked at Gigi and winked. "Oh, I get it, you can feed Charles oysters now and he'll feed you his later," she said with a straight face.

God, she is incorrigible, I thought, smiling.

We went on to have our main course of grilled lobster and plain white rice, both of which tasted wonderful with the sauces they had prepared.

"Just dip the meat from the tail and claws into either the creamy butter, lemon and dill sauce, or the Portuguese *peri-peri*, alternating the subtle and soft with the vibrant and hot," Gigi explained.

"Isn't that how sex should be, darling?" Jacqui asked. "Because I've forgotten. Right now, I would settle for the shell," she confessed wistfully, confiding in us about her unwelcome abstinence.

"Well, stop looking for perfection," Gigi shot back.

Even so, both Gigi and I looked at her genuinely sorry she did not have a partner.

"Darlings, after such a sexual demonstration of how to eat oysters, can I show you a nice way to eat meaty lobster?" Jacqui suggested.

Gigi nodded hesitantly, knowing this would be another mischievous antic. I probably said yes a bit too quickly and enthusiastically, judging by the look she shot my way while wiggling her index finger at me. Her friend did not need any encouragement.

Jacqui chose a piece of meaty lobster, the length of a finger. "Charles, darling, what sauce would you like?"

"Oh, the creamy lemon dill," I said.

"Okay, then I will go for spicy and hot. Almost my preferred diet, which is actually *hard*, hot, and spicy," she volunteered, just having to bring sex into the conversation.

She dipped one end of the lobster into the lemon dill sauce and the other into the *peri-peri*. As she moved towards me, she put her hot and spicy half of the lobster into her mouth and brought her lips towards mine with the obvious requirement that I bite off my half.

I realised that the consequence of this would be our lips brushing against each other's. Even though I did not want to be a prude, I hesitated slightly before taking my half of the lobster into my own mouth to bite it off.

An onlooker may have thought Jacqui's behaviour was overly flirtatious or even untoward, but in truth it was all just jovial bravado, her simply having fun. And Gigi knew her best friend did not have any ulterior motives and would never do anything to hurt her. No doubt, there would be more to come.

Gigi then brought out a substantial red velvet cake covered in a glistening crimson cherry glacé and placed it on the sideboard, "To have with our coffee a little later," she explained. It looked big enough to feed a dozen people.

"God's truth, darling, is the rest of Charles's squadron coming over as well? I hope so," Jacqui said mischievously.

We were about to get into a conversation about the Air Force, and more specifically, my accident, which I was not at all inclined to speak about, so I was relieved when a popular song started playing that immediately had Gigi and Jacqui up and enjoying the rhythm of the tune.

It took me back to when Jamie, Charlotte, Gigi, and I had been sitting around the same table, listening to the *Grease* soundtrack. Those were happy times, tinged with sadness about knowing we would be deployed to a combat zone, and those days were now firmly set in the past. So much had happened since then, including Jamie and me very nearly meeting an early demise.

"The Best" – Tina Turner

YouTube　　　　　　Spotify　　　　　　Apple

This was a song shared between Gigi and Jacqui, two best friends, describing their feelings for each other. As I watched them, I was sure they had been each other's sounding boards on many aspects of their lives. Listening to the opening chorus, I loved that they felt they were "simply each other's best." I could well believe they would call each other when their hearts were on fire and hang on every word the other would say when they shared advice.

As if they had had enough of dancing with just each other, they both put out a hand and insisted I join them. I did not have a choice, and before long, I too was dancing with them.

Jacqui and Gigi played a little game where I was passed from one to the other, each taking turns dancing with me. Jacqui was especially tactile and demonstrative with me, behaviour that Gigi was evidently familiar with as it did not seem to worry her one iota.

Just as I was thinking that, Gigi said to me in a devilish tone, "Carry on like that, my darling, and you will be begging for mercy later when I get my own back."

Jacqui responded immediately, "Ooh yes, can I come and watch? Please can I come and watch?"

The look on Gigi's face showed she would not be entertaining any of that as she scowled, no matter how idle the threat may have been.

This only spurred on Jacqui's teasing further. "Ooh, darling, if you were really a good friend, you would share all your toys with me," she said, still taking the mickey out of Gigi.

Clearly having had quite a bit to drink herself, Gigi leant forward to make sure Jacqui had a clear view of her kissing me. She brought her lips against mine and very visibly and suggestively put her tongue in my mouth whilst making little sexual noises and thrusting her pelvis against my thigh. "Is that what you want to come and watch, darling?" she asked naughtily.

Another first for me, I loved this roguish side of her.

"Stop it, stop it," Jacqui insisted. "I can't take it, unless Charles would like to stick his tongue in my mouth."

With that, I whipped around and took Jacqui in my arms, one of my hands behind her head, and leant towards her, opening my mouth and sticking my tongue out looking as if I were about to pounce.

As expected, she got a big fright, not sure whether I was going to carry out the deed, which caused Gigi and me to break into raucous laughter. Gigi knew full well that I would never do anything like that.

"Oh, God, the two of you are impossible. I am going to have to carry on dancing, because if I sit down now, I will surely slide off my chair," Jacqui retorted, which had us all laughing again.

Gigi and I sat down while Jacqui attended to the sound system. She scratched around until she found what she was looking for. This familiarity with Gigi's music collection was further proof that the two of them had spent a lot of time together. I felt a wave of gratitude knowing she had such a good friend who would always be there to support her. It made sense to me now that Gigi would want Jacqui and me to meet.

I was also seeing another side of Gigi, which I enjoyed. She was clearly less of a lady when she was with Jacqui. It made me wonder how many women shared things with their best female friends, more than they did with their partners. Probably a lot more than I realised, was my conclusion.

As a Barbra Streisand song filled the room, Jacqs came back to the table. "Come along, Charles Featherstone, Esquire. I warned you I could not risk sitting down. Come and dance with me. Let me feel a little of what my friend has been hiding from me all this time."

"A Woman in Love" – Barbra Streisand

YouTube   Spotify   Apple

I instinctively glanced at Gigi, wondering how she felt about it. Her expression showed she was quite unperturbed, perhaps even quite happy to watch her best friend and her lover dancing.

So I leant in, and Jacqui put her arms around me, feeling no qualms about being close to me as we started gently swaying to the music. Then she started feeling me all over while saying to Gigi, "Ooh, he really is nice, darling. I can't believe you didn't give me a little taste."

Jacqui and Gigi were giggling again, as we got into the rhythm of the song. I felt a wonderful warmth towards this woman who played such an important role in my first love's life. A role I had until then been oblivious to. *And bloody hell,* I thought, *these people in Shrewsbury sure know how to dance.*

For all her bravado though, I could tell she was a woman of integrity and the only reason she may not have been having sex recently was due to her discerning standards, as Gigi had suggested.

As I listened to the lyrics, I had a feeling that the three of us were all listening quite carefully to the words. It seemed Jacqui had made her selection quite intentionally.

Was this a little subtle warning to both Gigi and me? I knew there would be times of loneliness for me. Jacqui being in Gigi's life made me feel better about her future. We both had dreams about us, and it was painful that our circumstances did not facilitate our love and passion.

It was difficult to imagine our relationship being just a moment in space, and that the dream may soon be gone. Being back again after so long, and after so much, had matured me. Gigi and I had become even closer, the age difference even less noticeable, but our future was no more certain.

As the chorus played out, Jacqui drew herself a bit closer to me and said very quietly, "Gigi has never been so in love. Thank you for that, Charles."

I liked what Jacqui had said, but was she not aware of Gigi's discussion with me in the woods?

Then Gigi chimed in, "You two look like lovebirds. I will take this stuff through to the kitchen before I get jealous."

Whilst we had quickly become comfortable with each other, there was neither a romantic nor an impious spark to it. The cohesion was that we both cared deeply about Gigi, and Gigi knew that. We were all smiling, knowing that our closeness was sincere affection, mixed in with the joviality that had been part of the entire evening.

As Gigi left the room, that joviality evaporated when Jacqui looked intently into my eyes. "While Gigi is out of the room, I want you to know that I don't think there is anything I am not aware of when it comes to your relationship with her. I hope you don't mind that, Charles," she said in a lowered voice.

I shook my head. I did not mind in the least.

"I know your relationship cannot last forever. Thank you for coming here for your R&R. I am really pleased you did that, and I know that you have covered a lot of ground in these last days," Jacqui said, showing me again how much she really cared about her friend. "Now that I have met you, I want to thank you for what you did for Jamie. He *is* like a son to me, and I would have died had something happened to him."

She was quiet for a moment and then carried on. "Don't underestimate how much she loves you. Look after Jamie. There is one more thing you have to do with him, and you know what it is."

"I will, and thank you," I said, understanding perfectly what Jacqui was insisting I do.

"Oh, God, oh, God, get a room," we heard Gigi say as she came back from the kitchen and joined our embrace.

I realised she must have had an inkling of the essence of what Jacqui had said to me. The three of us, all with moist eyes, held each other, listening and swaying to Barbra Streisand singing out the remainder of the song. We were all barefoot as we carried on drinking and dancing, enjoying the closeness of each other.

I loved it when Gigi stood on my feet. Seeing what her friend was doing, Jacqui started doing the same thing to me when we danced.

"The only reason I'm standing on your feet is to keep them clean for when you nibble and suck them later," Jacqui said, chuckling.

"Like fucking hell!" Gigi replied.

I couldn't believe what I had just heard. Not the profanity, but that Gigi had clearly told her friend about the occasion on the Throgmorton shoot when her feet had been very much a part of our sex.

Jacqui noticed my expression and smiled, enjoying my reaction.

Without me saying anything, shrugging her shoulders, Gigi defended herself. "She's my best friend, and besides, I had to tell someone."

Well, Jacqui had warned me that Gigi shared everything about our relationship with her. Now I really understood. Gigi shared *everything*.

Oh, well. If anyone is going to know about this, then why not Jacqui? I thought.

Right then, I knew this mature openness was something I would almost certainly never find in a more age-appropriate girlfriend. How could I even begin to compare a girl in her early twenties to either Gigi or Jacqui? Goodness, was I destined to be beholden to more mature women for my entire life?

Then, needing a bit of a rest and rehydration, we sat down and had some water. Jacqui once again walked over to the music system and made another selection. For the second time that evening I heard Tina Turner's voice filling the room. I imagined she was one of Jacqui's favourites—plus half the planet's at that time, mind you.

The moment the intro started, Gigi took my hand and said, "Dance with me, my darling."

It appeared she also knew this song well. As Tina Turner started singing, she put her arms around me, her head on my shoulder, and nestled into my neck as we started swaying very gently and slowly to the rhythm of this well-known song.

"I Don't Wanna Lose You" – Tina Turner

| YouTube | Spotify | Apple |

I realised that Jacqui had put this song on specifically for Gigi and me. The words seemed to describe Gigi's position entirely. Despite having gone almost a year without seeing each other, and after we had supposedly gone our separate ways, nothing had quelled the love we felt. I understood that she did not want to lose me, and neither did I want to lose her. I didn't *have* to lose her, but I also knew what I'd be sacrificing if I didn't.

Perhaps she had made a mistake with her first marriage, but was *I* going to be another mistake? And would the mistake be me leaving, or would it be staying? Even though we had agreed to go our separate ways prior to my deployment, I now realised Gigi had been waiting for me. The past three weeks had confirmed it. Before Jamie and me being deployed to the Middle East, she had done what she believed she needed to. I had often seen that strength and selflessness. I wondered how many advances she had attracted and turned away in the last year.

We both wanted to hold on to our love, but how could we? That was what made our situation so painful.

As the song played out, I felt Gigi holding me tighter, unable to hide her emotions as a quiver rippled through her body. When the song stopped, we continued holding each other. I found her lips and kissed her mouth warmly and passionately, oblivious of Jacqui.

We knew we could not stay together because of the one irrefutable fact that I should have a chance for a family, to have my own children. But when, was the question I was asking myself.

Gigi looked up at me, tears in her eyes. I kissed them, feeling the moisture on my lips. Regardless of where our relationship was destined to go, I would never stop loving this woman.

The sombreness of the thought of us at some point ending our relationship hung over the room with a heavy presence. We were so good together. Leaving someone who you fall out of love with is one thing, but leaving someone you are deeply *in love with* is entirely another. We were two people deeply in love, a love unblemished by neither time nor turmoil, just wanting to be with each other.

How could we accept that nights like this could not go on into the future? The three of us having such honest fun with each other? We were all feeling this and questioning it, acutely aware of how unfair life could be.

"Why don't you get a surrogate?" Jacqui said out of nowhere. "Get a surrogate," she repeated, in case we didn't hear. "Will either of you ever find love like this again?" She was blurting out thoughts that we had not ever contemplated, and tonight was no time to try and get our minds around it.

Shaking her head, Gigi turned to Jacqui, purposely changing the subject and the mood as she said, "On that note, I think it is time for bed. And, darling, don't worry about washing your feet. Charles won't be coming anywhere near them. He's got other responsibilities tonight."

Jacqui gave me a warm hug and a full kiss on the mouth. "I would kiss you with tongue if I could, darling, but my friend would probably cut it out," she said with a chuckle.

"Ooh no, I would never do that," Gigi said. "Once Charles is gone, I may need it."

What did I just hear?

Both Jacqui and I burst out laughing. Gigi certainly knew how to lighten the mood, but in so doing, I had seen a little more of her licentious side. More than I realised existed, even if it was in a jovial mischievousness.

I recognised then, with great regret, that there were many folds to this extraordinary woman I had yet to explore. Another thought to chase from my mind.

Jacqui came across, gave us each a peck on our cheeks before turning on her heel and saying over her shoulder, "Goodnight, you two gorgeous humans. I hope you have a *fucking* good night or, should I say, a good *fucking* night. Don't worry if I should come in. I'll just be scratching around in your toy box, darling."

"Oh, I keep my toys in the refrigerator. Bottom drawer. I think you will find a cucumber there," Gigi said, giggling.

"Ah, nice one, Gigi!" And with that, she disappeared down the passage to her room.

I would have been very mistaken if I had read her waywardness and demonstrative nature as being untoward. For all her mischief, Jacqui was a very loyal friend, making sure she was keeping Gigi's spirits up. I couldn't help wondering though, if there was more to her having been invited to Gigi's home.

CHAPTER 34
RED VELVET CAKE

GIGI AND I were still chuckling when we left the living room and made our way to her bedroom. When she turned back, I asked, confused, "What's wrong?"

To my amazement, she returned having retrieved the red velvet and soft cherry glacé cake from the sideboard.

"We may need some sustenance later," she volunteered, a little too mischievously for me to take her reason at face value.

"Sustenance, Darling? You're not serious? I won't be having any cake tonight, Baby. I have a different dessert in mind," I said as I patted her bottom.

Gigi gave me a wicked little smile as we entered the bedroom and dimmed the lighting, then she placed the cake on the bedside table.

Red velvet cake with soft cherry glacé

Our recent abstinence had me yearning, so I couldn't wait. With Jacqui in the house, I assumed our sex would be the quiet, loving variety, something we were expert at.

"So, what do you think of Jacqui, Darling?" Gigi asked with a smile, as we began undressing.

"Delightful. I'm so pleased you have such a wonderful friend," I said sincerely.

"Yes, you liked her, didn't you? She is a very special friend, and I'm pleased I have her, especially now."

I realised what Gigi was *not* saying but didn't go there. "And what I like most about her," I added, still wanting to make a point, "is the happy, mischievous side she brings out in you."

She neither commented nor denied it.

There was a palpable sexual energy between us as we watched each other undress. I exchanged my T-shirt and underwear for a fresh top and boxer shorts, my normal bedtime attire.

"Ooh, Darling, you're in trouble tonight. You shouldn't have starved me the way you did," I warned.

"Mmm, that goes double for you, Darling. The way I spruced you up for Jacqui's arrival hasn't quite gone to plan."

Not sure what she meant, I gave her an enquiring frown.

She continued, "Oh, she loved you all right, but there has been an unintended consequence."

As she removed her underwear, my eyes absorbing her nakedness, I asked, "What do you mean, Darling?"

"Never mind, but be warned, I am crazy for you right now."

That doesn't scare me, I thought smiling, still drinking in the sight of her glorious nudity.

The thought of us ravishing each other was already having an effect. She held my gaze as she brushed her hands over her areolae, the usual strumming of her nipples between her open fingers quickly bringing the little pinnacles to their most protrusive erectness.

"It kills two birds with one stone," Gigi had once remarked.

When I asked her what she meant by that, she'd replied simply, "It gets us both hard."

With a fullness flowing into my genitals, my hand went down to my crotch.

Gigi followed suit, copying me while with her other hand she continued stroking her breasts.

Theatre or not, I was ready to pounce on her. She made her way to the bed, which she had prepared to her liking, the pillows positioned up against the padded headboard as always. Once settled, she seemed ready for whatever it was she had planned.

"Baby, I would like you to kneel between my legs. I want to show you something."

Even though I was sure I'd seen it all before, I obliged without hesitation.

As she leant back on her carefully prepared throne, I eagerly took up my position. Her legs were bent, perfectly placed for me to push her knees farther apart. I had a clear, close-up view of her, as she did of me.

Gigi then proceeded to entice me in the most erotic way imaginable, and soon I couldn't bear it any longer, wanting more than the continuation of our private show. But even if I'd had an imagination for what would happen next, which I didn't, I could never have contemplated what was about to happen.

Just as Gigi sensed I was about to seize her, she leant over to the bedside table. I watched her wipe her fingers across the top of the cake, meticulously removing the syrupy cherry glacé. Then with a menacing expression, she reached over and clawed out a handful of cake.

That was the start of the most extraordinary night of passion, played out in vivid technicolour…okay, mostly in red…cherry red.

Our lovemaking first involved Gigi using the red velvet sponge cake and soft cream layers, handful after handful, before I joined in, and we continued to cover each other's most intimate parts, and then 'play and eat it' in the most unmentionable, lascivious ways.

I was mesmerised. "Oh, God, you have no idea how that feels," I effused.

Gigi's little intakes of breath and the look of sensual enjoyment etched on her face made me realise she was experiencing a similar sensation to me as she continued these antics with the velvety cream and sponge cake.

Once things had calmed down a bit, and with a naughty smile, Gigi said sarcastically, "I thought you didn't feel like eating cake tonight, Babe."

Never had I enjoyed eating cake more, and never had cake tasted more delicious.

We were both engrossed in the sensation of this cake-and-cream mixture on our most sensitive parts, our lust amplified by the mess and debauchery of what we were doing.

When we finally made love, we quickly reached the point of no return and our orgasms mercilessly surged through our bodies.

"So beautiful, Baby…so beautiful. Aaah…I love you. I will always love you," Gigi said, pulling me down onto her, wanting to feel the weight of my body on hers.

Without speaking, we lay there, just breathing into each other's necks.

After a while, I got up and went through to the bathroom to get damp facecloths as Gigi began organising the pillows against the padded headboard, ready to resume her position on her throne. I smiled as I watched her, in complete nakedness, making sure she would be perfectly comfortable.

I couldn't help teasing her. "Now that my matriarch is comfy, would you like some refreshment, madam, but I do apologise, we seem to have run out of cake!" I said, chuckling as we began wiping each other down.

"Oh no, no more cake for me, Baby. But I would hate to waste what's left!" she shot back.

Looking at the platter, I saw there was nothing more than a piece the size of two fists in a pool of thick red cherry glacé syrup. Conversely though, the bed was covered in cake, cream, and a sludgy pink mess of the combined mixture strewn all over the bottom sheet.

"But yes, please, Baby," Gigi replied. "I will have some Diet Coke."

As I turned to leave in my stark nakedness, since that is how it had been during the past two weeks, Gigi remarked, giggling, "Oh, if you bump into Jacqui, tell her there is a little bit of cake left for her."

"Oh, fuck," I said. "Sorry, I completely forgot about her, and bloody hell, what about the noise we were making?"

"Oh, don't worry about her," came Gigi's reply. "She would have been fast asleep, and no doubt still is."

Regardless, I slipped on my sleeping shorts and turned to get our Cokes.

"Oh, and Baby, no need to apologise for using the f-word," Gigi teased. "Especially after demonstrating it so admirably." She chuckled.

As I made my way through to the kitchen, my head was in turmoil. The glimpse that Gigi had given me only hours earlier of her provocative, most licentious side yet, had now played itself out in vivid technicolour, with an extra smattering of red! I had a myriad of thoughts bombarding my mind, the overriding one though, being how I loved this woman and how I wanted more of her…always. Mingled among these thoughts was one of me trying to fathom how, after all these years, I was still discovering more about her, loving all of it.

Returning from the kitchen, I was about to lie down next to Gigi when she said, "Uh-uh, get those shorts off. The way you were looking at Jacqui's boobs today cannot go unpunished," in her most schoolmistress tone.

I smiled. No point in protesting that.

"Have a little Coke, then come and take your punishment," Gigi admonished.

If I had thought our night of passion was over, I was wrong. The cake may have been all that finished, but the soft cherry glacé lay thick on the bottom of the cake platter.

What ensued was akin *to* a repeat performance, just this time it was with the gooey cherry red glacé.

Gigi was a woman of so many contrasts and surprises. So many facets. A woman of style, charm, grace, and impeccable good taste. A lady in every sense of the word. And as much as she was all of these and more, she was also a woman of abundant sexuality, mischievousness, and the most desirable, wilful behaviour, all in the sanctuary of our relationship.

Thinking this, I wondered which side of her I would get if I asked how she was feeling right then. Would it be something like, "Happy, content and wonderfully satisfied…and tired," or would I get her other side, with a reply along the lines of, "Properly fucked"? I smiled as this crossed my mind, knowing it was unlikely I would ever find anybody like her again.

Gigi gave me a quick but passionate kiss and said, "Let's clean up the bed and get some sleep. It's after one o'clock in the morning, and there are things to do tomorrow."

Before settling in for the night, I began our customary little after-sex chat. "You have been different, my darling. Very sexual. Tell me, please, what are you feeling? Not that I didn't like it," I added hastily.

She had a distant look in her eyes as she summed it up in a short sentence. "I would rather be lost in the fantasy of our visceral sex than think about the reality of the coming days."

This caused me to shudder, knowing that I would need to leave in the next week or so to spend some time with my parents. I needed to change the subject, so I asked, "And why did you want all of me in you, when you had first said just the tip?"

"For just that reason, Baby. I wanted all of you to plunge yourself into me," she replied without hesitation. Before I knew it, she had drifted off to sleep.

I thought a little more about everything that had happened this evening. I was now firmly of the opinion that it was because of our closeness and the absolute trust between us, that she felt free and safe to be so extraordinarily adventurous in our sex. Thinking back to some of our earlier sexual interludes, I realised she had often said many of her experiences with me had been a first for her. Gigi had an adventurous sexuality that I loved, but it had definitely been more primeval and shameless these past three weeks, and this evening had been a *glacé cherry on top*.

I smiled when I thought of the part the red velvet cake and soft cherry glacé had played in the whole evening.

Were Harrods aware that they were the purveyors of the most extraordinary sex toy?

Surrendering to my absolute contentment, I fell asleep.

CHAPTER 35
THE NEXT DAY

WE UNCHARACTERISTICALLY HAD a late start the next morning. Gigi seemed solemn, which I took as a result of an evening spent in something of a sex marathon.

After a relaxed shower—during which we soaped and fondled each other in our usual way, kissing and holding each other very passionately, if not sombrely—we finally got dressed.

Looking at the bundle of red-velvet-and-glacé-soiled sheets, Gigi remarked, "I think I will put this in the washer. I don't want Suzie thinking there was a murder in the house." She never failed to have a sense of humour, no matter how tired she might be.

We emerged to find Jacqui sitting happily, reading her book in the sunny bay window.

"Good morning, you gorgeous, awful creatures. Have you finally come—aah, sorry—arrived? I'm sure you did enough of the former last night." Jacqui chuckled as Gigi and I went puce. "So, I don't suppose you'll be having any red velvet cake for breakfast then?"

Gigi and I could only laugh along. Somehow, she had found out, or perhaps worked it out.

"Well, I hope you two slept well and at least got a better night's rest than I did. I believe exercise before going to bed works marvels for your sleep," Jacqui teased, which had Gigi throwing a napkin at her.

"Charles, Darling, regardless of Gigi's protestations, I *am* going to find out what you did with the red velvet cake."

Putting the blame on me for its disappearance, Gigi surreptitiously put a finger on her mouth, imploring me not to say anything.

We sat down in the sunny dining room and drank cappuccinos while chatting happily about nothing much. I was sorry I had not met Jacqui sooner.

A little while later, Jacqui took it upon herself to make a light lunch and went off to the kitchen to begin her preparations. As she walked through to the kitchen, she chided mischievously, "I don't want to hear any facetious remarks about there being no cucumber in the salad. Unless of course you want to tell me about the red velvet cake, Charles. I will be more than happy to swap stories."

The moment she was gone, Gigi moved her chair closer to mine and, facing me, took both my hands in hers. "Baby, it is time for us to talk."

Her expression immediately gave her away. Right then I knew she was putting on a brave face and this would be about our future.

"Darling, a few days ago in the woods, we spoke about us, and last year we had a similar discussion. My love, we both know what is right, and now is the time for us to finally say goodbye."

Seeing the tears welling up in her eyes, I cupped her face in my hands and gently pressed my lips onto her forehead.

As a feeling of dread permeated through me, Gigi continued, "It is not going to be easy for me. It is going to be excruciating. You are home now, and you are going to bring Jamie home. You know this is what I want, and I know you want it too. I will never stop loving you, and I know I will never find love like the love I have for you." Tears now rolled down her cheeks.

I leant forward to hold her in my arms, but instead of wrapping her arms around me as she normally did, she kept them bent protectively up against her chest. As I cocooned her in my embrace, I could feel her body quivering as she tried to contain her sobs.

She settled a little before carrying on. "I have had the most wonderful five years with you, and a sixth year of anguish, but still, in all that time you have been the biggest part of my life."

There was more that Gigi wanted to say, so I let her carry on.

"I know you didn't like this the last time I said it, but I'm going to say it again anyway. You will always be in my heart, and I will never feel anything like this again. I think I'm okay with that." Trying to chuckle through her tears, she said, "What is the cliché? Something like, it is better to have loved and lost than never to have loved it all." The look on her face said she didn't really believe that. She gently held both my hands and looked intently into my eyes as she continued softly, "Go and phone your mum, and tell her you are coming home…this evening."

The suddenness of what she had just said had me reeling.

She paused for a moment. "And, my love, your mother knows about us. It wasn't right not to tell her. And I didn't want the most beautiful thing in my life to be part of a lie."

I stood there dumbstruck as I absorbed what Gigi had just said. After it sank in, I understood perfectly, and deep down I knew she was right. In many ways, I felt the same. In hindsight, I am quite certain my mother and father would have understood, and I wished then that I had taken them into my confidence when all the Blackwoods had come to stay. It shouldn't have taken a war and Jamie and me coming within inches of losing our lives for our relationship to have been shared with the ones we loved.

Gigi went on to tell me that she had visited Rockwell Manor immediately after my accident. She had initially gone for only the Friday night, wanting to speak to my mother face to face, but she ended up spending the entire weekend with my parents. No longer concealing any secrets, the two women, both mothers of sons in military service, united in convincing us to leave the RAF, gravitated towards each other in the sympathy of their circumstances.

I once again held her safely inside my cocoon as she sobbed gently. Once she'd regained some composure, she looked up at me and gave me a tender kiss. Then, as a tear rolled down my cheek, she said, "Phone your mum now, my darling."

As I got up to make my call, Jacqui came through with a chicken-and-mandarin salad she had managed to draw out making for over forty-five minutes. I wasn't surprised to discover that there was indeed cucumber in the salad.

She came up to us, put an arm around each of our shoulders and said, "You are both the most wonderful people. You should just let today pass and then only think about all the good times you have had."

It was sound, sage advice from someone who was wonderful herself.

Such a special woman. Thank God she was going to be staying with Gigi for as long as she was needed.

My mother answered the phone in an unusually short amount of time. I got the impression she had been waiting for my call. I told her we were going to have a little lunch, and I would then set off on the three-hour journey home.

My mother could hear the immense sadness in my voice, and wanting to make me feel better, she spoke to me very personally in the most loving tone about Gigi and me. "Don't be so sad, Sunbeam. I know it hurts and that you must move on, but you have to take all the good out of what you and Gigi had."

This complete understanding and sensitivity from my mother did not surprise me.

"You have been so lucky to have been with a woman who has loved you, cared about you, and taught you some of life's most complicated lessons in a most selfless way. Things you can only learn from a loving, trusting partnership. Just imagine how it could have been with say, one of the young girls at the polo club."

My mother having this insight though, *did* surprise me.

"Yours and Gigi's relationship has been very different for her than it has you, Sunbeam. In your youthful naivety, you have been able to enjoy every moment of your time with Gigi, not thinking about the future. From her more mature and experienced position, she has always known this day would come, which has made her time with you much more difficult. It is now time for you to let her go and allow her to try to find her way in what will be a far more complicated world for her."

I got off the phone as Jacqui was finishing serving lunch, with Gigi absentmindedly watching her friend. I walked over and sat down in front of her, holding her hands much as she had done with me a little earlier, and I simply said, "Thank you for doing that. I think we should have probably told my mother a lot sooner."

Gigi nodded her head in agreement.

We were about to start having lunch when the phone rang.

Gigi got up to answer it, and I half expected her to beckon me over, thinking that it was probably my mother having forgotten to tell me something. All I heard was a few muffled bits and pieces.

"…fine…okay. We are just about to have a quick salad." There was a pause as she listened to what the caller was saying. "I will be fine, Darling. I love you. Hold on a sec." With that, Gigi looked across at me and held out the receiver.

I went over to her and took the handset and put it up to my ear.

"Hello, Charles."

I was taken aback, not having expected to hear from Charlotte.

In a very soft voice, she said, "I just wanted to say goodbye, that's all. I would've liked to have been there, but Mum needed time alone with you."

That one short sentence spoke a thousand words. Charlotte knew about her mum and me, which meant Jamie knew as well. In fairness, I had pretty much thought that for a long time. They clearly didn't mind, or perhaps they even understood. Understood what, as was often the case, I wasn't too sure.

"Thank you for…for…" Charlotte searched for the words. "Thank you for being there for her…for loving her. I don't think you realise how much you gave her. And, Charles, thank you for looking after my brother. You said you would take care of Jamie, and you did. I will always love you for that."

I had spent the past hour trying to be brave, but once again, Charlotte's words had me failing in that endeavour.

We sat quietly through lunch, with not even Jacqui saying anything.

I could sense we should not draw out our farewell, so I turned to Gigi. "Well, I guess I'll go and pack my bags."

"I already have, Baby. Your bags are packed."

I would probably normally take this as a sign that my host couldn't wait for me to leave, but I knew exactly what Gigi was feeling. Only once I left could her healing begin. There was really nothing left for me to do but leave.

I said a quick and warm goodbye to Jacqui, and she too kept it brief. I would have liked to have told her how nice it was meeting her, but it would have only highlighted that I would almost certainly never see her again.

As much as I wanted to keep my goodbye to Gigi brief, I couldn't help but just stand there and hold her in my arms, inside my cocoon. I found it especially painful not being able to say that I would see her soon, or anytime, for that matter.

When I did turn to go to my car, I did not look back. I knew the slightest thing would bring us both to tears, and I wanted to spare us both that emotional torment. This was a typical Featherstone goodbye. For the first time, I fully understood the merits of our family's approach to goodbyes.

As I drove out of the Blackwood gates for the last time, I put my destination into my navigation system, not because I didn't know the directions but more because it gave me something to do.

"You have one-hundred and eighty-four miles to go. You are on the fastest route, three hours and twenty-eight minutes," my GPS advised.

I made my way to the M40 south, feeling the world's weight on my shoulders.

When I was on a quieter road, leading up to the main road, I looked down and noticed an envelope on the passenger seat. I immediately recognised the handwriting on the envelope and knew it was a note from Gigi. *My Love Always* was written on the front. I picked it up, thinking it must be a card.

Other than what Gigi had written on the envelope, there was nothing inside the envelope except a CD in its plastic cover, containing just one track.

"I Will Always Love You" – Whitney Houston

| YouTube | Spotify | Apple |

As I listened to the opening lyrics, while it might not have been Gigi's voice, they were her words and could not have conveyed her painful message more clearly. She couldn't stay. She would only be in my way.

The song had barely begun, but my thoughts of leaving Gigi and of how she would always love me made it impossible for me to hold back the tears. Alone in my car, there was no longer a reason for me to put on a brave face, so I let my tears flow.

How could so much become so little?

"Goodbye, please don't cry," was impossible.

Gigi would have known that I would be crying now. She knew *me*, not just what I showed to the world.

I pulled my car over into a small lay-by and listened to the rest of the song, almost to the end, before I pressed the Back to Start function, still making no effort to dry my tears.

Gigi meant the words, "I hope life treats you kind," and her sentiments that she hoped I would have all I dreamt of were completely sincere. She knew I had many dreams. What I wished I could tell her then was that, more than anything, I wished all of these things for her. Oh, God, I wished all of this for her.

How am I going to live without her? was my only selfish thought then.

It took a long while before I started making sense of my jumbled thoughts again. All I knew was how difficult it is to leave someone you truly love. I sat there awhile longer before eventually resuming my journey, my thoughts still deeply immersed in Gigi.

My father had often said to me that, in life, there are typically just two types of decisions: easy ones and correct ones. Too often, he warned, we make the easy decisions because that's what they are, easy. It is the correct decisions that are the toughest.

Accepting Gigi bringing our relationship to an end was the most difficult decision I had ever been part of, regardless of who ultimately made the decision. I was certain it was no different for Gigi.

I was so caught up in my thinking that it surprised me when the GPS blurted, "You are now halfway. You have ninety-two miles to go."

That had seemed quick. I was on the downhill leg now, heading home to my future.

I had missed those old, familiar surroundings and my parents, not have I seen them for many months now. I couldn't help feeling a glowing warmth towards my mother and remembering her reassuring voice over the phone earlier made me feel better. Rockwell Manor was indeed my *rock,* not least because of my ever dependable parents.

My thoughts around the RAF were quite straightforward. I had made the decision to leave. My mother would be thrilled but not too quick to show it.

Jamie was due back at RAF Shawbury any day now, and I would find out when he got there and then invite him for the weekend. Between his mother and me, there would be no difficulty in convincing him to do what I had already decided for my RAF career, which was to convert the remainder of his service to a reservist role.

Would this be my last deed for Gigi? The one that even Jacqui had now insisted on.

I turned on my Walkman connected to my car's stereo and solemnly listened to a recently added song. It had a special significance now.

"Here I Go Again" – Whitesnake

| YouTube | Spotify | Apple |

The very first line of the song said it all, because right then, I did not know where I was going, but I sure knew where I'd been—in the bosom of the most astounding woman who had so starkly contrasted with my military life.

Getting on with it was how I'd managed being without Gigi before. With little choice, I'd made up my mind and couldn't waste any more time. I would do that again.

Will it be that easy?

As the words played out, they resonated more and more with me.

Here I was again. Would I keep searching for an answer, and would I find what I was looking for?

Ooh, Lord, I pray you give me strength to carry on.

CHAPTER 36
THE REALITIES OF LIFE

AS I DROVE into Rockwell Manor, I couldn't help noticing the trees had shed their autumn leaves. *Depressing!* Not a thought I'd ever had about my home. None of the elation I normally felt. Not surprising, given all I had gone through, I surmised, trying to rationalise my feelings. The warm greeting from my parents made me feel a little better, even though it was somewhat subdued.

As is often the case, things did not play out as anticipated. I had hoped to invite Jamie back to Rockwell Manor, at least to speak about his RAF future, but as it turned out, we discussed all that we needed to over the phone. With my decision to leave the Air Force and the ending of my relationship with Gigi, he had already started making his own plans for his future.

When I quipped that I liked his independence, he replied, "When you went to Shrewsbury for your R&R, I knew you wouldn't be coming back. There was no point in me hanging around, and I wasn't going to stay here without you."

I got two things out of that: Jamie was not *that* independent when it came to the RAF, and he probably knew me better than I knew myself.

Our circumstances had made it impossible for our relationship to endure and as a result I had lost a very special friend in Jamie. I would miss him terribly, and already I was feeling the loss of not having him and his roguish sense of humour around me. It seemed strange that he, Gigi, and Charlotte would likely never come back to Rockwell Manor.

I would soon learn that when I lost Gigi, I lost far more than just my first love and lover. With no Jamie to entertain, the first few days after arriving back at Rockwell Manor were strange. Not being much of a sleeper, I would get up at dawn without being sure what I should do next. It was a little like an Olympic athlete looking for his kit, then realising he didn't even know what event he was competing in.

There should have been so much to look forward to now that I was back home. Shooting still had a few weeks left of the season. Polo would be starting soon, and arranging a mini tournament for the kick-off on our home field, should have really excited me, but I barely gave it a thought. Going into business should've been top of my agenda. Technology was what I had studied, along with economics, and that was what I should do.

Let me focus on those things! I thought, but it made no difference. I couldn't.

This carried on for over two months. Something that could only be described as a "lethargic approach to life." Something that was totally out of character for me—the person who could not walk up stairs but had to bound up them four or five steps at a time.

What is wrong with me?

And then there was the void of no more Gigi. How was I going to stop my mind from drifting back to her?

The stables were empty with the horses having been turned out after the season, so there was no reason to go over there. Guy wasn't around either, still being away on his offseason break. No doubt he would be somewhere in the Southern Hemisphere. Argentina was my guess, where he not only had the summer but also some good polo. It was also my guess that Grace would be with him. I found myself feeling envious of them.

Leafless trees and animals in hibernation. Nature shrinking away from the onset of a cold, depressing winter. Had winter taken me down with her?

Christmas at Rockwell Manor was always a highlight, and this year was no different. Lots of guests, dinners, which now I mostly missed, preferring to just be in my own space in my North Wing suite. Fabrizio was also trying to play his part in lifting me out of my doldrums with food. Not even that was working.

The one thing that did get me out of my room was the rowdy kitchen pizza evenings. I had a feeling my dad had arranged them with that purpose in mind. It worked to an extent but nothing like the old days. Even so, I mostly kept to myself, lost in thoughts of the past, like my handprints on Gigi's top or her little dance on the centre of the field as we made our way over to the stables. That's when I would take myself up to my room.

It struck me that there was no small talk about the RAF or what had happened there. Had everyone been briefed about steering clear of that topic? It suited me.

In the grip of a cold, gloomy winter, looking out of my bedroom window, staring at Osric's memorial, wondering why there wasn't one for Granddad, I was feeling decidedly miserable.

It was all getting too much. Then one evening in the family dining room while we were having dinner, I decided to speak to my parents. After explaining to them what I was feeling, my dad let my mother do the talking. It would have surprised me if he hadn't.

"Sunbeam, you have Yuppie Flu."

"What?" I replied, and then a little bit disrespectfully, "I don't have flu! I don't think I have ever had flu."

"No, Yuppie Flu is not flu," was my mother's curt response. "Its formal name is chronic fatigue syndrome."

Once we had got past that little hurdle, we carried on chatting quietly about my condition and how it was quite normal for returning servicemen. Uncle Alexander had also given my parents some insight. After all, he was an ex-RAF airman. He had explained to them that almost every serviceman, after several years in the armed forces, invariably struggled with this.

"Fran, just remember, for the last six or seven years, Charles has been in a system where every minute of every day, every activity, even meals, has been set out for him. Then suddenly he comes back into civilian life. How could he not be anything but affected?" he had told them.

Then, as if it were a delicate subject, my mother voiced my parents' belief that I was also suffering with the early onset of PTSD.

"You should see someone, a doctor," my mother suggested in her most appealing voice.

"I don't need a doctor," again my reply too abrupt and impolite. "Sorry, Mum, I know you are just trying to help, but I really don't need to see a shrink."

All my father could do was look on helplessly.

"Think about it, Sunbeam. It makes perfect sense after all you have been through," my mother impressed reassuringly, holding my hand.

We had carried on speaking for a good while thereafter, enjoying an after-dinner port together. As we all began to relax more, I thought about all I had heard, and it began to make more sense to me.

What wasn't mentioned during the conversation was my relationship with Gigi, but there was no question my mum was acutely aware that this was a big factor as well. Her remark at the end of the evening confirmed it.

"It's time to get out there, Sunbeam. Just don't go breaking too many hearts."

I guessed every mother thought this of their sons.

Five months since I'd left the Middle East and subsequently the Royal Air Force, I was slowly getting on top of my chronic fatigue syndrome. I had gingerly begun with aspects of my new life but was still beset with slow starts and unrelenting lethargy.

Then late one Friday afternoon, I received a letter from Eleanor Granger, CPG William Granger's mother.

I had occasionally called Will to find out how he was getting on and how he was coping with his paraplegia. Whenever we spoke, he sounded upbeat and positive. On more than one occasion though, I put the phone down wondering if that was really the case. He was English, after all, and being honest about his feelings was more than likely something he'd never be too comfortable with. I was regularly plagued by the nagging concerns I had about him.

> Dear Charles,
>
> I hope this finds you well.
>
> I am writing to you in confidence and to ask if you could make your way to Norfolk to see William sometime soon.
>
> You're probably unaware, but from the outset he has been struggling with pressure sores that he got shortly after his accident,

brought about because of his immobility and not being able to feel anything below his midriff.

It seemed so innocuous at first, but without getting into the details, it led to him getting septicaemia. This in turn very nearly brought an end to his life in a most devastating way, as, in the final throes, the major organs begin shutting down. Let me hasten to say that thankfully he is finally over it. However, it has left him very weak both physically and emotionally, which is why I am contacting you.

I am hoping a visit from you will improve his spirits.

He used to love telling stories of what an incredible pilot you were and how you saved his and your own life, something that I will always be grateful for. Unfortunately, that spark is absent now.

Please let me know when it'll be convenient for you.

William Sr. sends his best wishes.

My very fond regards,

Eleanor

Feeling sick with guilt that I had had no idea what my friend was going through, I immediately rang Eleanor and arranged to visit the following day. It was around a three- to three-and-a-half-hour drive to Norwich, and I said I would be there before lunch, which Eleanor said they would have at around one o'clock.

I ended the phone call with, "Let Will know I'm coming. Before noon."
"I will, Charles."

The next morning at 8:23, I was driving out of Rockwell Manor gates, my navigation system telling me I would arrive at 11:41 a.m. I would have plenty of time with Will before lunch. In fairness, I didn't know how I felt about this trip except that I didn't want to delay seeing him for another moment.

It also had me pondering some of the questions that had been playing over and over in my mind for many months. I just knew that losing the use of his legs didn't tell half the story. What Will had gone through in the past five months was a case in point. When they referred to "life-changing injuries," were they even remotely aware of just how much of an understatement that was?

According to my GPS, I arrived thirty-seven minutes ahead of time, a testament to my speeding. This time, I didn't give it a second thought.

I didn't need to knock as William Sr. opened the door, having heard me arrive. I walked into the warm and sunny conservatory and gave two quick kisses on Eleanor's cheeks, paving the way for my more protracted greeting with Will. I bent down and hugged my friend, feeling my throat closing as a lump formed and tears welled in my eyes. I simultaneously drew up a stool so I could be at the same level he was in his wheelchair. Almost immediately, his parents left the room so we could be alone.

Will had suffered pressure sores almost immediately after arriving at the rudimentary One ME Hospital. In the rush to get him back to England, infection of this serious injury was unnoticed. Within days, he'd contracted septicaemia, which he eventually overcame by being bedridden for a prolonged period. As a result, muscular atrophy had quickly depleted his statuesque body of around 60 percent of his muscle tissue. It was still in this state that I found my dear friend.

I was shocked at his condition, seeing firsthand how muscular atrophy had ravaged his once powerful, athletic legs. His belly distended into pot-like disfigurement, replacing the corrugations of what used to be "the best six-pack in the squadron," and his once broad, open shoulders were slumped into surrendered submission. As alarming as this was, it did not compare to where he showed the consequences of his injury the most. The wounded expression on his sullen face and the vacant look in his eyes told of the excruciating suffering of these past five months.

We chatted for a long time, so long that Eleanor moved what was meant to be an early lunch out to a late lunch.

Given that my parents felt I may have suffered PTSD, then Will certainly would have. By now I knew enough about post-traumatic stress disorder to know the best thing for Will to do was to speak about the circumstances, which are referred to as a PTSD event.

Eventually, we got onto speaking about what he had lost. This was, after all, the crux of the matter. Had Will *only* lost the use of his legs, it might have been tolerable. I knew he had lost so much more—his pride, his confidence, his self-esteem, and his stature in every sense of the word. Once his mind told him he was less, he was less.

We spoke about these losses, and he said they weren't his biggest loss.

Holding his hand, I pressed him. "What, Will? What is the biggest thing you've lost?"

"I've lost the chance of having children," was his terse reply.

"Doesn't it work?" I asked, alarmed.

"It works, not that I could be bothered," was his solemn reply.

I didn't want to push him further, but I needed to hear the rest and felt he needed to get it out. As I took his hands in mine, he continued speaking.

"If I am able to get a wife in my state, I could never offer her a family. I could never bring a son into this world and not be able to kick a ball with him. Or a daughter, and never swing her around or help her practise ballet dance steps."

The tears welled up in my eyes again. I had just heard Will, who had been thought of as the squadron catch, a man who "could get any girl," questioning, *Can I get any girl?* And was he going to miss out on one of the greatest gifts of all, having children?

I didn't care that his parents saw me holding his hands. I didn't care that we were two grown men sitting there with tears streaming down our faces.

When we had consoled ourselves, we went through and had our very late lunch. The conversation was light—just small talk, like the health of my parents, the weather.

"And you play polo, don't you? How is that going?" William Sr. questioned.

Anything outside of the pleasantries, I understated, not wanting Will to feel as if he was missing out on anything. How tired he must have been of these types of conversations with people trying to protect his feelings around all the things he couldn't do. *But what else could one do?*

It was after five o'clock and already dark outside when we got up from the dining-room table. Correction: William Sr., Eleanor, and I got up from the dining-room table. Will wheeled himself away, and all of us wished there was some way we could help him so he didn't have to do that.

"Thank you for the visit, Charlie." I didn't mind what he called me then. "You don't know what this means to me. You are still the best combat helicopter pilot I have ever known." But he stopped short of thanking me for saving his life.

"Great to see you, Will. I won't leave it so long till next time."

Whatever time I had saved driving from Rockwell Manor up to Norwich, I gave back with interest as I slowly went back home. No rush. No radio. Just my own solitude as I absorbed the six-odd hours I'd just spent with my old friend and CPG.

Unbeknownst to anyone, after having seen me, he had given himself a very specific amount of time to see if things would change or if he could find the will.

Very sadly, things didn't change during that time, neither could he find the will.

We lost William Granger on his own terms, exactly forty days after I had seen him in Norwich.

My conundrum of whether I had helped or harmed Will when I had saved our lives was answered in the most upsetting way imaginable.

I was aware that forty days had biblical relevance, so I went to the study and did a little research.

Matthew 4:1-11 portrays Jesus being tempted by the devil after fasting for forty days and forty nights.

Acts chapter 1 talks about there having been forty days between Jesus's resurrection and ascension to Heaven.

Lent (Ash Wednesday until Easter) is a forty-day period of reflection, repentance, and spiritual growth observed by Christians as a solemn reminder of human mortality and the need for reconciliation with God.

And I didn't even know he was religious.

The obvious emotional response, *if only we had known*, was almost certainly the most overused sentiment in circumstances like this.

His mother had reached out to me, hoping I could help her son. She knew he needed saving. Had our accident given him the most painfully slow death?

My melancholy turned to anger. Anger directed at myself for not having realised. Not having paid attention. Not being there when my friend needed me the most. I dwelt further on these thoughts before slowly bringing myself back to equilibrium.

I managed to get my hands on a single blade from an Apache helicopter tail rotor and had the connection point fixed onto a base. A four-foot-tall metallic tombstone. I placed it a short distance from where Osric was buried, under his brace of flushed pheasant.

I then said goodbye to my dearest friend, my golfing partner, my combat flying partner, my CPG. My loss was nothing compared to what his family had lost that day. More than they could ever possibly list. I shuddered.

I went up to my room and looked down from my north-wing bedroom window at these two unusual memorials now standing in our garden. This was the second very special person I had lost in my life, Granddad and now Will. And I had no Osric to comfort me. And as before, the tears rolled down my cheeks and I made no effort to dry them. But as before, I eventually did.

In Memoriam

Osric
Twelve years of childhood bliss.

William
A CPG like no other.

My mother's words echoed in my head, *"Chin up, Sunbeam. Chin up."*

I later learnt more about the place Will had found himself in. Those men and women who "put themselves out there" and suffered a spinal cord injury are sometimes referred to as the "Hero to Zero" spinal cord injury group.

Will was the first of my friends to become a victim of a Hero to Zero spinal cord injury. Once all powerful, more than just capable, at the top of his game, until in the blink of an eye, he found himself fighting death… and winning, only to be rewarded with a life sentence of dependency on others, in a prison of immobility.

Veteran or other, statistically there is a high probability that a person in this group is an alpha male with around a 90/10 male to female split, I am told. An obvious reason for this is that alpha males show a propensity for joining the military, playing physical sports, or generally engaging themselves in more risky behaviour compared to their female counterparts. You may know, or at least understand, that the highest incidence of suicides is in this group.

To all those veterans and others who have suffered a hero to zero spinal cord or neurological injury resulting in them becoming imprisoned by their immobility and risen above it, I salute you.

For those who are understandably still under the debilitating psychological oppression of it, find something you can succeed in, no matter how small, and build on it.

My grandfather was right. Success, no matter how small, is the foundation for more success.

Will's death pursuant to his injury had a profound effect on me, and writing about it as part of my therapy was one of my most difficult tasks. Even though I had dealt with it then, with the loving help of my psychotherapist, when it came to my memoirs, I was simply not prepared to share it with the world. Right to the end I kept it buried deep inside. But as with other things, there was someone who instinctively knew I was holding something back, and in her own gentle way, she gently prodded me. (see Dear Reader) Then just as the first book of my memoir was supposedly complete and ready for proofreading, after a night of intermittent tears, I wrote the true story of my dear friend Will. You see, in the first version of the book he made a full recovery—the easiest way for me to deal with it. Cowardly of me, and disrespectful to his family and his memory. There's no prize for guessing who was not in the least bit surprised to find this about turn on her desk the next morning in America. What was her reaction? A little note in her editing comment box. "Well done for adding this. You will feel better about it soon."

My grandfather's death showed me life was not everlasting. Will's death showed me how fragile the mind and life can often be. I still struggle to read it.

You will never be forgotten my friend.

CHAPTER 37
A NEW LIFE

I NEVER FULLY UNDERSTOOD what Yuppie Flu was, but if I needed a catalyst to free me from the restraints of chronic fatigue syndrome, then what happened to Will was it.

After having visited him in Norwich, and perhaps because of the guilt I felt for having been so lucky, I went through a period of mourning, then soul-searching and introspection. As a result, my situation began to improve. But it was his death and then pallbearing at his funeral opposite his father as we led the way that ratcheted up my determination.

How dare I be so lethargic, I berated myself.

After several days of trying to come to terms with what had happened to my dear friend, my approach to life changed dramatically.

I had everything, and I wasn't speaking about Rockwell Manor and its trappings. I was speaking about my health, my vitality, and a myriad of other things that should have fuelled my enthusiasm for life in no uncertain manner. *How dare I waste that?* was my brutally honest condemnation of myself.

And then, as if it were unusual, winter was drawing to a close. A sure telltale sign were the polo horses having come in to begin their preparation for the season that lay ahead. I loved the muffled sound of their hooves on the silica sand track. The slower tempo signalled a gentle introduction to their training program.

It was Monday morning, the first days of spring, clear and crisp, and with my mind in overdrive, I sprang out of bed. *I remember that feeling.* And it was good.

As I arrived at the breakfast table, my seat between my parents having mostly been vacant these past six months, I blurted, "Right, Dad, time to get my head around my future. What are your thoughts?"

My parents had already seen that I had been moving in the right direction as far as getting on with my new life was concerned, but neither of them commented on this obvious new clarity and determination. Perhaps they feared jinxing it.

My father had plenty of suggestions. "Give Hugh Mackintosh a call," he said without hesitation.

Hugh was an old school friend of mine who had ended up studying economics and business science at university, not unlike my majors.

"And let me set up for you to meet one of the partners at Deloitte's, our auditors, to see what business-acquisition possibilities are out there. There are often good businesses that are just short of working capital that we could potentially buy," he continued.

As I shifted my thoughts to the future, for the first time in months I felt a twinge of excitement welling up inside me. Apart from business, playing polo and shooting, there were other things that excited me. Developing Rockwell Manor Polo Team was one. Would I get another dog? Yes, there was a lot to be excited about. And what about building a heliport at Rockwell Manor and, in time, buying my own helicopter as Gigi had suggested? That thought took me straight back to her. But now it was somehow okay.

Whilst I had been mulling over the prospect of going into business, I knew my approach would be different. This was something I wanted to do myself, not an endeavour that would be thanks to my family.

I did not have much time to think about it as my dad then caught me off guard when he announced to his audience of two, "It's time for you to take over Rockwell Manor Polo Team, son." His tone made it clear it was not up for debate. "I have spoken to Guy, and he is ready to discuss any management ideas you may have."

There was no surprise in this decision. I had just not expected it quite so soon. I finished my breakfast in high spirits, my parents noticeably more relaxed than I'd seen for a while.

"Excuse me, Mum, Dad, I think I will go for a stick and ball."

Smiles lit up their faces.

My Rude Awakening

As I walked across to the stables, I smiled to myself. Yes, they were feeling better about me. Ordinarily, telling them I was going to ride a horse would not have earned a smile.

It was the perfect day to start the new chapter of my polo career. Guy was not around, which suited me fine, and I had one of the grooms prepare a horse for me for my quiet stick and ball session.

I was particularly enjoying cantering around our beautifully manicured polo field that morning, watching how my polo ball left long, straight lines on the dewy emerald-green surface. I was so absorbed in what I was doing that I only noticed Guy when he cantered up alongside me a short while later.

"Good morning, Patrón," he said, chuckling, knowing full well that I disliked that title.

"Fuck off, Watkins," I replied with an element of seriousness.

"No, seriously, it is wonderful that your dad has handed over the reins to you. It's the right time," Guy said with sincerity. "What are your thoughts for *your* team now?" he said as we began a gentle canter up and down the field, passing the ball between each other.

"Well, we can't be too far off from being able to field a Queen's Cup team," I replied, knowing the Rockwell Manor horses and players had become a very competitive unit.

"Yes, I quite like that plan," Guy responded a little unconvincingly.

"You have a different idea?" I challenged.

"I like the thought of the Argentine Gold Cup. It's at the same level as the Queen's Cup and our own Cowdray Gold Cup, but a far more difficult competition for an English team to win. It would present a whole new dimension to a world we are so familiar with."

I kept a deadpan face as the thought caused an excitement in my belly that threatened to tangle my intestines. Guy had made a suggestion I hadn't previously considered, but no sooner had the words left his lips than they resonated with me.

I could not help remembering a recent comical incident though and decided to tease him, thereby disguising my enthusiasm. As nonchalantly as possible, I asked, "Guy, is this all because of that lost-in-translation incident with those visiting Argentinian polo groupies?" My smiling eyes betrayed my efforts to keep a straight face.

Guy's spontaneous laughter meant he knew exactly what I was speaking about.

We had just finished playing a match at Guards Polo Club when three attractive, slender, brown-eyed, olive-skinned, pert-breasted Argentinian girls came over to us. Two of them looked to be in their early twenties and ostensibly quite shy, while the third was a lot more confident and probably a few years older. Finding courage in their numbers, backing each other up, they'd attempted to strike up a conversation.

"*Nosotras queremos lamer tus cuerpos*!" said the eldest and naughtiest of the trio, biting her bottom lip.

Guy and I looked at each other blankly as the cute, younger ones giggled mischievously.

"*No entiendo español*," Guy volunteered, shrugging his shoulders.

All three of them now giggling happily, it was Pert and Proud who attempted to say something in English. "Vee vant ta leek your, how you say, *cuerpos sucios*."

Guy and I were still lost.

"Ve vant ta leek your dirrty baadies," blurted the one who had seemed the quietest. She clearly had the most urgent intent.

The eroticism was certainly lost in translation, especially when I still had to spell it out to Guy that what they wanted was to *lick our dirty bodies.*

Playing in the Argentine Gold Cup would need serious planning. No time for any romantic or other thoughts.

Over the next months, I began reviewing and sifting through different business opportunities as Guy and I secretly worked towards taking Rockwell Manor Polo to the next level, which primarily involved replacing the bottom end of our string with horses that would come in at the very top. At £40,000 to £80,000 a horse (some people even paid over £100,000 for true champions), they were not cheap. We had a few of those. I had to remind myself I should be grateful that I didn't have to worry too much about the budget. Even as a twenty-six-year-old, whilst I understood economics, I had

432

very little direct awareness of the cost or value of things. This may seem surprising. Consider for a moment that up until the age of eighteen, I was just a scholar. Then I went to the Air Force. No chance of learning about the value of things there, when you routinely jump into a £50 million helicopter. And that was just the beginning. The cost per hour to operate this rotorcraft—over £4,000. Then throw in a few missiles—a Brimstone fire-and-forget—£160,000. A Stinger Missile—£30,000, and that's each, of course. I have used present-day cost estimates, because back then this was the furthest thing from our minds. Had they told us, assuming they knew themselves, it would have drawn nothing but blank looks. It just wasn't relevant.

I soon had a busy schedule researching different business opportunities and advancing my polo aspirations, yet I still couldn't put Gigi behind me. Was that about to change?

Guy and I had been having a polo meeting and had just finished having lunch on the upstairs patio with my dad when Hamilton arrived, portable phone in hand. Turning to me, he disdainfully looked down his nose and announced, "Miss Sandra Rawling on the line for you, *sir*."

I couldn't help noticing the wry tone of his voice. Was he trying to remind me how I should behave? I had a sense that Miss Rawling's reputation was not lost on our butler.

As if subconsciously giving myself space for some privacy, and more than just a quick conversation, I took the handset from Hamilton and made my way through to the north wing and my bedroom.

As I lay down on my bed, taking the phone off mute, I greeted my caller. "Hello, Sandra."

"Hello, Charles," Sandra's sultry voice sounded down the phone line.

"To what do I owe this pleasure?" I asked, in a flirtatious tone.

"Ooh, well, that depends on what *pleasure* tickles your fancy," she said provocatively.

I smiled, knowing the game was on, and I was feeling more than willing to play along.

"Sandra, you called me, don't forget." I teasingly reminded her.

Her little giggle was a sure sign she was enjoying herself.

"Well, before we get into what pleasures you, I was just wondering if you were ready to come out of your shell and play a bit?" she said with more than just a little suggestive mischievousness.

"What do you have in mind?" I asked as coolly as I could, doing my best to hide my sudden excitement.

"Well, *to start with,* there's a dinner dance at Royal Berks on Saturday night, and I have two tickets," she said, referring to the Royal Berkshire Polo Club.

I smiled again. This had been well planned. "Oh, okay," I said without even giving it much thought.

"I could come to you early evening, and since I know what a gentleman you are, we could then go together from there."

I smiled again and said nothing, even though I liked her plan. Definitely no spontaneity here.

Just as I thought our conversation was coming to an end, Sandra added in a most seductive tone, "And, Charles, darling, when we go back to Rockwell Manor to collect my car, *to end* the evening you may want to show me Winston Cottage…and some of your tricks. Perhaps play some of your games." I couldn't help the quickening of my pulse as she paused before continuing. "I know you *must've* learned lots of tricks," she purred softly.

It is fair to say that by the age of twenty most young women and men would have had several sexual partners. Of course I hadn't, but in Gigi it was as if I had had multiple partners. Our sex was often different, sometimes adventurous, always exciting. Had Gigi consciously done that? Would it be very different with Sandra? I secretly wanted to find out. And the bit about me having learnt lots of tricks. This could only be what she imagined I would have been taught by Gigi.

I quickly reconciled that my mother wouldn't have had any reason not to speak more openly to one or two of her closest friends about Gigi and me. And no doubt, in the strictest of confidence, it had been passed on from one to another. By now, what I may have wanted kept secret was well known to all who knew me.

Aah well, was the extent of my concern.

Could anything ever become of Sandra Rawling and me? My parents would certainly approve, Hamilton wouldn't, I thought as a smile crept

My Rude Awakening

onto my face. Maybe she would teach *me* some tricks. Unlikely. She may have had more sexual partners than me, but my solitary one had experience, and I dare say 'sexual adventurism.' if there was even such a thing. Was Sandra Rawling a younger Gigi, not having yet learnt to be more refined? Was she sexually adventurous? I found myself thinking a lot about Sandra.

My heart skipping a beat, I replied with a simple, "See you Saturday evening, Sandy." I was not sure where the more affectionate "Sandy" had come from, nor why during our conversation I had been lying on the bed with my hand in my white polo jeans? But I was sure that Winston Cottage was way too special a place for me to tarnish it because of my carnal needs. If it were my animal instinct that was busy coming back to the fore, then what better place than our stable block for that exploration? Not the feed room though. That seemed almost sacred too. The lounge area was a good idea.

Not wanting to forget something I had been thinking about, I went downstairs to the key cupboard and found a bunch with Stable Lounge engraved on the brass tag. It was also an opportunity to get some fresh air and think about what lay ahead.

As I strolled across the polo field, the clear, crisp, starlit spring sky made the hair on my arms stand on end. Was it the coolness or the anticipation? I took my sandals off, feeling the dewy grass on my feet as I made my way to the stables. As I got closer, I could hear the occasional snort of a horse, the calming sound of them munching away, their heads in the manger. That old feeling of being very much alive had come back again. I thought about Sandra and the exchange with her friends in the Beauford polo barn. Would she be the one getting her "hands around that derrière?" as they had lamented. Giving her something to hold onto when I was "working it." And would she really "let her friends know when she had had some of that?" I imagined my pelvis nestled into Sandy Rawling's, her shapely legs wrapped around my torso, me pressing hard against her, me reaching into her depths. Then the thought, *I wonder what she smells like, tastes like?* had my hand in the top of my jeans again. This was not the first time I had found myself in hand, thinking about Sandra Rawling.

Once inside the expansive horse barn, I took the spiral staircase up to the seating area. I unlocked the door and stepped inside for a quick look around. When I was done, I left it unlocked, knowing it would remain so through the following night. I walked back to the main house and returned the key to the cupboard.

I couldn't help contemplating what Saturday night would bring. The last time I had been with a woman, Gigi, had clearly been a lot longer than I realised.

I had always been silently judgemental of Sandra Rawling's behaviour, but was this because I was secretly jealous of what I imagined? A thought banished because of my relationship with Gigi. And now that Gigi was behind me, could I admit Sandra's physical attractiveness, her intelligence, and that she was a very sexy young woman, brimming with personality, whose sexuality captivated me? Was it not wrong then that I judged her for having enjoyed her sexuality with other men? And on that point, was this a repellent or an attraction on some animal, carnal level? And did I just want a taste of her or was I looking for something more? In shrugging off the shackles of my recent past, was I looking for overt sexuality because of my experience with Gigi? I quivered with excitement at the thought of finding out.

Something had been stirred in me that night because I slept well. Very well.

"Gigi, Baby, I need you." She held my gaze, knelt over me, and brought her mouth down to between my legs and began playing with me in that old familiar way. "Fingers, fingers," I almost pleaded. She responded by sitting up, her hand reaching down to her womanhood. She then obliged me by putting both fingers into my mouth. I instinctively drew them in as she leant down to resume her consumption of my manhood. She then attempted to reclaim her fingers by pulling against my forceful sucking. I was having none of it and drew them into the back of my throat, as my manhood lodged in the back of hers.

With my alarm clock ringing, I woke up to the vacuous emptiness of Gigi no longer being in my life, let alone in my bed.

Would dreams like this help me or haunt me? Time would tell.

I knew I had to move on. Would Sandra be the one to put me on that road? Was this the first step in moving on with my new life?

INTERLUDE

I NEVER SAW ANY of the Blackwoods again. Under normal circumstances that would not have been altogether unusual. Many, if not most servicemen try and put their military careers behind them once they go back into civilian life, especially if they have been beset by traumatic events. But my relationship with the Blackwoods, especially Gigi, was nothing close to being a *normal circumstance.* My closeness to Gigi made me consciously try and put it behind me, as I looked at forging my way into what lay ahead.

My mother's words of, "It is now time for you to let Georgina go and allow her to try to find her way in what will be a far more complicated world for her," was another reason. I didn't want to cause Gigi any more upset and maintaining my friendship with Jamie would have further complicated her already challenging future.

And of course, there is always a selfish reason. Not seeing Gigi was a defence mechanism for me. Any contact with her would have had my mind rushing back into the past and imagining what could have been in the future.

That doesn't mean I did not think about them—especially Gigi, who I never stopped thinking about. Over the years, every time I heard a Whitney Houston song I immediately thought of her. And of course, in writing this first book, I was with her constantly.

I changed my mind about thinking my relationship with her was "rude." In many ways, I feel it was nearer the opposite. Was it not what happens between two people in a deeply loving and trusting relationship? And didn't even being licentiously "rude" have its place in that loving couple's lives, through the course of fulfilling each other's needs when those needs arise?

But did I need to write about it? Well, in both this book and the next, it was the therapeutic balance that allowed me to write honestly in telling all of my truths and experiences—far more serious things in my life.

There is nothing unique in that I, like everyone else, am the product of my background, upbringing, and individual experiences. There is also nothing unique in that it was the first quarter century of my life that moulded me the most. Some of what shaped me remains a mystery, even though I have delved so deeply into my past. What is unique for all of us though, is that background, upbringing, and our experiences. I realise mine were more privileged than most, which included more opportunities for a wider range of experiences. I now appreciate those differences and have done my best in my life to make the most of it. I am also acutely aware that what happened to Will and the circumstances of his death, are what helped me recognise other aspects of my good fortune.

The sequel will shed light on the man I became as a result of my first quarter century. And was it a blessing or a curse that my life continued to be filled with many triumphs and tragedies? You can be the judge.

Gigi, if you read this, I want you to know that all through my life there have been many reminders of how you lovingly guided me into the adult world and taught me so much about some of life's most crucial aspects. What you gave me was immeasurable, and I know it came at a huge cost to you. It is against you that I have measured all others. Neither fair on them nor me, as you set the bar such that it has not easily been eclipsed.

I have used the thinnest of veils to disguise your identity, but I know you won't mind, even though I have shared some of our most intimate moments together. I know it deserves a better author than one as novice as me to convey the beauty that was our relationship, my first love. I have done my best. Please forgive what needs forgiveness.

When I left you for the last time in my twenties, it felt as if I had already lived a full life, but of course, it really was just the beginning. I hope you will read the next book and discover how my life continued to unfold.

As you turn the pages of the sequel, you will almost certainly laugh, you will cry, and you may enjoy, or at least marvel at, some of the excitement, the triumphs, and the disasters. I know you won't be jealous when you read how I carried out the lessons I learnt from you into my future liaisons and relationships, with an immense understanding and appreciation for the glorious female form.

Even if it was the right decision, had I truly understood what I would be losing when you sent me home, I would never have acceded so benignly. As it turned out, it affected me all through my life. The bar of my expectations having been set so high, and the pain I suffered from losing you, the most honest love of my life, cut so deeply that falling in love again became very difficult.

I will always love you, Gigi.

TO BE CONTINUED…

ABOUT THE AUTHOR

Edward Charles Featherstone is a pseudonym for a hugely successful international entrepreneur. Having grown up amongst immense privilege in the bucolic English countryside, he went on to enjoy an unrivalled education, both academically and socially. The lessons he learnt from these teachers would guide him throughout the rest of his life as he triumphed on the polo field, as a combat helicopter pilot, and in business, with interesting romantic liaisons along the way. He lives between London and Berkshire, still enjoys polo, and is occasionally a guest in the Royal Box at Guards Polo Club. Most of all he loves being in the English countryside shooting clay pigeons, but also game birds in the shooting season. There is a difference now though. He gets immense pleasure enjoying these traditional English pastimes with his young son, who is already one of the leading young Colt clay-pigeon marksmen in the United Kingdom.

Visit the website:
www.anenglishmansjourney.com

Connect on social media:
Instagram – @ecfeatherstone_author
Facebook – ecfeatherstone
X – @ECFeatherstone
YouTube – @ecfeatherstone

Bestselling Author

The candid and extraordinary memoir of Edward Charles Featherstone—Englishman, Businessman, Polo Player and Combat Pilot—*My Rude Awakening* reveals an astonishing account of life lived with passion and intensity.

From the lush green Berkshire's polo fields, through the ardours of military helicopter training, to the white heat of flying combat missions in the Middle East, Charles's journey is a riveting tale of privilege, peril and profound personal transformation.

Raised amidst the traditions of English upper-class society, Charles's life takes an unexpected turn when he embarks on a forbidden, intoxicating affair. This passionate relationship not only challenges societal norms but also ignites a deeply personal awakening that defines his transition into manhood.

Then as a combat helicopter pilot in the Royal Air Force, Charles faces the brutal realities of war and harrowing experiences that still live with him to this day.

Prepare to be shocked, captivated and inspired by this shy boy's unforgettable journey of love, loss, and survival into adulthood.

This is only part one of Charles's incredible memoir—An Englishman's Journey—as the story of his life continues in part two, coming soon.

Discover more at
www.anenglishmansjourney.com

Trigger warning:
This book contains game bird shooting and fox hunting content, references to suicide and PTSD.

ISBN 978-1-917111-07-2